ON THE ROAD
WITH WELLINGTON

NAPOLEONIC LIBRARY

August Ludolf Friedrich Schaumann

ON THE ROAD WITH WELLINGTON

The Diary of a War Commissary

New Introduction by Bernard Cornwell

Greenhill Books, London
Stackpole Books, Pennsylvania

This edition of *On the Road with Wellington* first published 1999 by
Greenhill Books, Lionel Leventhal Limited, Park House,
1 Russell Gardens, London NW11 9NN
and
Stackpole Books, 5067 Ritter Road, Mechanicsburg, PA 17055, USA

British Library Cataloguing in Publication Data
Schaumann, A. L. F.
On the road with Wellington: the diary of a war commissary. –
(Napoleonic Library; 34)
1. Peninsular War, 1807–1814 - Personal narratives, German
I. Title
940.2'7

ISBN 1-85367-353-6

Library of Congress Cataloging-in-Publication Data
Schaumann, August Ludolf Friedrich, 1778–1840.
On the road with Wellington: the diary of a war commissary/by
A. L. F. Schaumann; introduction by Bernard Cornwell.
p.   cm.
ISBN 1-85367-353-6
1. Schaumann, August Ludolf Friedrich, 1778–1840—Diaries.
2. Peninsular War, 1807–1814—Personal narratives, German. 3. Great
Britain, Army. King's German Legion—Diaries.   I. Title.
DC232.S43 1999
940. 2'7—dc21   98-49193
                                                CIP

Publishing History
*On the Road with Wellington: The Diary of a War Commissary in the
Peninsular Campaigns* was translated and edited from the German by
Anthony M. Ludovici and first published in 1924 (William Heinemann Ltd.,
London). The text is now reproduced complete and unabridged, with the
addition of a new Introduction by Bernard Cornwell. The original water-
colours have been omitted for reasons of reproduction quality.

Printed and bound in Great Britain by
Creative Print and Design (Wales), Ebbw Vale.

INTRODUCTION

WELCOME to the diaries of Lieutenant Augustus Ludolph Friedrich Schaumann, a deputy assistant commissary-general in the service of the King's German Legion. Or, alternatively, a footloose Hanoverian who marched through Portugal and Spain with Wellington.

Strictly speaking this is not a diary at all, but rather a memoir based on diaries that Schaumann compiled in later life for the benefit of his children and grandchildren. The first quarter of his book told the story of his childhood and youth, and Anthony Ludovici, who translated the memoirs into English in the early 1920s, sensibly decided to leave out those formative years and plunge the reader straight into the Peninsular War. This explains the book's abrupt beginning: 'At about ten o'clock on Sunday morning the 28th August, 1808, we were given the signal to land.'

Schaumann was thirty years old on that fateful Sunday, and he was about to experience the six most adventurous and rewarding years of his life. He had been born and raised in Hanover, the son of an impoverished lawyer who was determined that his son should establish himself in a respectable career, but as Anthony Ludovici's Preface reveals, the young Augustus Schaumann consistently disappointed his demanding father. He failed as a soldier, then as an official of the Hanoverian Post Office, and was finally trained as a clerk. He endured four years of ledgers and double book-keeping and then, to escape his father's disapproval, left Hanover to seek his fortune abroad. He found work as a clerk in Holland, then in England and afterwards in Gothenburg, Sweden, where he was stranded during a vain attempt to reach Russia. He was nearly thirty years old and his life had been aimless, unrewarding and frustrating.

Then, in 1808, war broke out between Denmark and Sweden. France joined this war on Denmark's side, seeing in the conflict a chance to seal one of the biggest loopholes in Napoleon's Continental System which attempted to bar British goods from the continent of Europe and so break Britain's economy. Sweden was one of the biggest importers of British goods, and no port was more active in the trade than Gothenburg, and so Napoleon despatched an expeditionary force to Denmark with orders to find ships with which to invade and capture the Swedish city. The British, naturally enough, saw it was in their interest to protect Gothenburg and so they, in turn, sent a fleet and an army to protect the city. The army never disembarked, which hardly mattered because the French never invaded either, and eventually the British fleet and army sailed away. Napier called it an 'eminently foolish expedition', and so it probably was, but when the Royal Navy left Gothenburg it carried a civilian passenger – Augustus Schaumann. The rolling stone was moving on, but this time to a career which proved as satisfying as it was useful. Augustus Schaumann would join the King's German Legion.

The Legion, like Schaumann himself, was from Hanover, and Hanover was the German state which had given Britain its ruling family. George III was monarch of both the United Kingdom and of Hanover and so when, in 1803, the French overran Hanover, many patriots fled to Britain where they formed a King's German Regiment, which consisted of two battalions of light infantry. Soon, however, there were so many recruits that the regiment was expanded into the Legion; a small army consisting of five cavalry regiments, ten infantry battalions, six artillery batteries and a small corps of engineers. They proved superb troops. Their cavalry, in particular, was reckoned the best in the Peninsula, and it is no surprise that it was KGL heavy cavalry that broke the French squares at Garcia Hernandez, a famous and unrepeated feat. Wellington, who was not swift to offer praise, said of the KGL, 'It is impossible to have better soldiers than the real Hanoverians'. Even the French conscripted a Hanoverian Legion, but their experience was less happy, for the best of the French Hanoverians invariably deserted to join the KGL as soon as they could. The King's German Legion was, in brief, a famous and formidable unit that did Britain real service during the Napoleonic Wars.

It was this unit which Augustus Schaumann joined in 1808, though not, officially, as a soldier. He wore a uniform and carried the courtesy rank of lieutenant, enabling him to mess with the officers, but his job, deputy assistant commissar, was a civilian appointment carrying a salary of seven shillings and sixpence a day. It was also, and I suspect the first Duke of Wellington would not have disagreed with this judgement, one of the most important jobs in the whole army, a war-winning job indeed, for the commissary had, among other things, to provide the army with all its daily rations. An assistant commissary-general (one rank above Schaumann) was responsible for providing a division's rations, a daily total of ten-and-a-half thousand pounds of bread, seven thousand pounds of beef and seven thousand pints of wine. Every day. It was an unglamorous job compared, say, to leading a company of riflemen or riding at the head of a troop of dragoons, but without men like Schaumann the British army could never have thrown the French out of Portugal and Spain.

Wellington understood the commissary. He prized it. He knew, better than any other contemporary general, that an army which was properly supplied was an army that would fight better than a force that was left to forage for its own food (as the French frequently were). As a consequence Wellington demanded high standards from his commissary officers. They had to buy food from peasants (never steal it, for an aggrieved peasant became a fearsome guerrilla enemy); they had to find mills to grind the corn, ovens to bake the bread and women to do the baking; they had to supervise the enormous train of pack animals that followed the troops and ride herd on the beef cattle that trudged in the army's wake ready to be slaughtered for the evening pot. All this while their unit might be marching in unexpected directions. Not only that, but the British Treasury, which, rather than the War Office, had authority over the commissary officers, held them and their heirs responsible for every penny of public money that passed through their hands, so each night was spent in writing up receipts and copying accounts. It cannot have been an easy life, yet Augustus Schaumann took to it with ingenuity and delight.

It is that delight in a difficult, dangerous and picaresque life that infuses Schaumann's diaries, for they are among the very best memoirs ever to have come from the Peninsular War. Schaumann had a roguish eye, a good pen, and an appetite for life. His description of the retreat to Corunna is the best that we have, and he manages to infuse that melancholy episode with excitement and verve. Schaumann enjoyed his war, and he communicates that enjoyment. This is no dull account of troop movements and supply difficulties, but a lively account of a young man unleashed to the pleasures of a foreign campaign. When I was writing the novels of Richard Sharpe's exploits in the Peninsular War, and had much recourse to diaries and memoirs, I used Schaumann twice as much as any other source. He had an eye for detail and an enthusiasm for campaign life that makes him the most immediate of all the war's chroniclers.

Schaumann survived the war and returned to Hanover as Napoleon was banished to Elba. The following year, when Napoleon escaped back to France, Schaumann again volunteered for the KGL, but he never reached Waterloo and so missed that battle. He lived on in Hanover, surviving on his half-pay pension and investments, and died in 1840, aged sixty-two, leaving eight children. It was for those children that he re-worked his diaries and the manuscript stayed in the family until 1922 when a grandson, Lieutenant Colonel Conrad von Holleufer, published a shortened version. Ludovici, when he translated the German edition into English, edited the memoirs still further, but more than enough remains. Anyone who is interested in the Peninsular War must be delighted that Schaumann's book is being republished, for it is truly the most entertaining and keen-eyed account of the wild and triumphant years when Wellington led his men from the coast of Portugal, across Spain, and into the heartland of France itself. Schaumann marched every step of the way, and this, now, is his splendid story.

Bernard Cornwell, 1999

TRANSLATOR'S PREFACE

THE following pages consist of the diary kept by a member of the famous King's German Legion throughout the duration of the Peninsular War, and constitute one of the strangest and most interesting documents that we possess, connected with that dramatic period. The original, which is in German, was written by August Ludolph Friedrich Schaumann, a Deputy Assistant Commissary-General in the British Service in Spain, Portugal and France. It was contained in nine thick quarto volumes of manuscript, adorned with illustrations by the author's own hand ; but the first German printed edition of the work, published in 1922, from which this translation has been made, is a slightly abridged version of the original work, and fills only two large volumes of some 400 pages apiece. The special merit of the work seems to lie in the singularly graphic and vivid account which it gives of campaigning life in Spain, Portugal and France during the years 1808–1812 from the point of view of an eye-witness who was a junior officer in the British Army ; and as it gives an enormous amount of detail that could not possibly be included in any official work on the subject,* and throws much light upon the men and methods of the British Army in those far-off days, as also upon many matters not unusually overlooked or suppressed in military histories, it cannot fail to be of interest to English readers in general, and in

---

* To what extent this work overlaps, or has been anticipated by the scores of diaries and reminiscences of the Peninsular War already published, I fear I am unable to say, as I do not pretend to have read more than one or two of these private records. As, however, among the hundred and more volumes of Peninsular autobiographies, journals, letters, etc., referred to by Sir Charles Oman in his " Wellington's Army," only five deal with transport and the commissariat, it will be seen that a new diary by a commissary would not seem to need the same apologies as would an additional contribution to the purely military memoirs of this great war, more particularly as this work appears to be unique in the sense that it deals with the commissariat from the standpoint of a member of the German Legion.—TR.

particular to all students of the memorable campaigns which it describes.

The author, a German, was born in Hanover on the 19th May, 1778. He was the son of a poor, but hard-working lawyer established in the city of Hanover, and received but the scantiest education. His life at home was hard and very often wretched. His father evidently treated him and his brothers and sisters with great severity ; and after Mrs. Schaumann's death in 1791, when our author was thirteen years of age, his life was far from happy. Against his will he was compelled in his sixteenth year to join the Army, and he became a cadet in the 13th Infantry Regiment. He rose by slow degrees to the rank of lance-corporal, corporal, and ultimately junior subaltern ; and then his father, thinking that his son's military career offered but doubtful prospects, removed him from the Army in December, 1799, and procured a position for him in the postal service. Wretched as his military career had been, owing to the exiguous allowance given him by his father, his life in the post office was even more intolerable, and in a very short time he left the work in order to enter business. Early in 1803 he was studying business methods in a commercial school run by a certain merchant called Bischoff in Hanover, and in April he left home in order to proceed *via* Holland to England, where he had found employment as a clerk. For four years he was engaged in this capacity by a firm in Newcastle ; and then, in response to a friend's invitation he decided to go to Russia. While on his journey thither, however, heavy storms forced him and his fellow passengers to take refuge in Gothenburg, where for some time he again found employment as a clerk ; but growing dissatisfied with his work, he soon became restless once more, and in 1808, when the English fleet, as Napier says, returned from " that well-known and eminently foolish expedition to Sweden," he went aboard one of the ships in order to be taken to England to join the King's German Legion as a war commissary.

As Major Ludlow Beamish, the author of the excellent

"History of the King's German Legion " * declares,
" the claims of the King's German Legion to the notice
of the historian are founded upon the distinguished
services of that corps in the British Army during the
whole extent of a period marked by the greatest exertions
which England has ever made and the most brilliant
victories which her arms have ever achieved ; " † and the
fact that these journals are from the pen of one of the
members of this gallant force lends a peculiar interest to
the narrative they unfold.   As is well known, the German
Legion was recruited almost entirely in Hanover, and
consisted of those men who, deprived of redressing their
country's wrongs in the ranks of her national armies,
sought that object in those of Britain ; and, as Beamish
says, " sacrificing the ties of home and kindred to the
more exalted feeling of national honour, became voluntary
exiles in another land, and fought for the recovery of their
own under the banners of England."

" Throughout the whole of the Peninsular campaigns,"
the same author continues, " they bore an active part,
and few of those memorable engagements, whose
names now stand commemorative of British valour,
have not been honourably shared in by some part of
the corps."

When Schaumann's journals were first placed in my
hands, I immediately referred to Major Beamish's
classical work in order to discover whether all the claims
of our German author were strictly true, and had been
officially recorded ; and although the German's diary
itself bore the stamp of genuineness and accuracy, I was
not unpleased to find the following brief record of
Schaumann's services on page 663 of the second volume
of the English history of the Legion : " 1258, 7th line
battalion—Lieut. Augustus Schaumann, N.C.O. 5th–
18th April, 1809 (p. 1808–9–10–11–12), resigned 21st
July, 1812 . . . deputy assistant commissary-general on
half-pay . . . in Hanover."

Schaumann was not an author by profession. He

---

* Published by Thomas and William Boone, London, 1832 (2 vols).
† See Preface, Vol. I.

wrote the history of his life for the entertainment and edification of his family. For almost 100 years these journals have lain in the private possession of his relatives, and unknown to the general public, and it was only in October, 1922, that one of his grandsons, Lieut.-Colonel Conrad von Holleuffer, published them to the world. The hero of all the adventures they contain lived to rear a family of eight children, and in the later years of his quiet life as a retired officer on half-pay in his native country filled the post of auditor to a kind of Ecclesiastical Commission. He died on October 19th, 1840, and was buried in the cemetery at Hanover, in that part of it which forms the corner of the Marien-Warmbüchen Strasse.

He was a garrulous and sometimes coarse diarist, and it has been found necessary to proceed to certain abbreviations of the original in the process of translation. As, however, I have adhered strictly to the substance of the work, and have given the whole of those parts of it which throw any light upon the life and operations of our army in the Peninsula and France, it has seemed much better not to indicate places where paragraphs or pages have been omitted as superfluous. At all events, for the purposes of the English translation, it did not appear necessary to give the long account, entertaining though certain parts of it are, of Augustus's childhood and youth ; and starting off on page 181 of the first volume of the German edition, where the author ends his career as a clerk and joins the King's German Legion, I open the Schaumann journals at the point where he describes his first landing in Portugal on August 28th, 1808, with the British army.

In addition to the two volumes of the German work, I have also seen the records of the Waterloo campaign which formed part of Schaumann's diary, and which were not included in the German edition of 1922. As, however, Schaumann himself was not present at the battle, and the account he gives of it lacks the personal touch which lends so much interest and attraction to the memoirs, I decided not to include it in the present translation, and I was the more inclined to adopt this course seeing that my space was limited and that I should have had to sacrifice much of the Peninsular narrative in order to find room for it.

I have endeavoured as far as possible to test the accuracy of Schaumann's statements of fact and his descriptions of battles, but apart from a few slight discrepancies, which I have noted in the text, I have found him singularly reliable. Naturally, the very nature of his narrative renders it somewhat difficult to check him with the help of official records ; for his personal adventures and his own point of view present a picture too narrow and too detailed to be compared at all points with the broader, more sketchy, and more general record of facts to be found in any of the well-known histories of the Peninsular campaign. Nevertheless, it is the very quality of the personal standpoint that lends Schaumann's narrative so much interest, while his outspoken and frequently very unflattering references to the British army and its commanders, from Wellington downwards, and still more so to the Spanish and Portuguese armies and peoples, often reveal facts that will probably be new even to the most learned student of the period.

In coming to a decision concerning those passages which it was necessary to curtail or to omit altogether, I was always guided—apart from considerations of propriety—by the principle that historical matter, or details concerning campaigning life in the Peninsula, must take precedence of mere descriptions of scenery and of personal adventures having only a purely human interest. The result is a version in which I have played the part rather of an editor than that of a strict translator. It is, however, I trust, an accurate version, and one which gives all that is most valuable to the historian and to the lay public in Schaumann's journals. Much of the material is probably more or less new, and it is this, in addition to their humorous and entertaining side, which constitutes the following pages at once an instructive and diverting contribution to British military history.

Schumann's spelling of the names of places is not at all consistent, and in some instances I have corrected it, but in many have left it as in the original.   With regard to the quotations in Spanish and Portuguese, I have endeavoured to reproduce these exactly as they are given in the German edition.

My heartiest thanks are due to Mr. F. J. Hudleston, C.B.E., Librarian of the War Office, London, for having kindly undertaken to read the proofs of this work, and also for many valuable hints and suggestions.   He has helped to remove many blemishes and errors from its pages ; if, however, some remain, I alone must be held responsible.

THE TRANSLATOR.

AUTHOR'S PREFACE

J'etais jeune et superbe

SURELY nothing is more affecting to a man than to recall all he experienced as a youth, and to think in later years of the pleasures he once enjoyed amid the dangers and upheavals of an adventurous life ! Such thoughts lure him back to the spring and summer of his life ; and, transfigured like fairy scenes, the years of his early manhood shine through the mists of the past. He imagines he has recovered a valuable treasure, which he buried long years before— a restored picture of all that he hoped, performed and felt. May we not pardon him for wishing his family to have a share in his discovery ? True, many a line of thought, and many an incident, have been suppressed and curtailed, but the backbone of the history itself remains unchanged. The reader who seeks in this work after accurate information concerning political events, romantic adventures *à la* Casanova, or heaven knows what else, will certainly be disappointed. Like their author, the following pages bear the impress of truth, and are yet free from any touch of rhetoric or graceful and well-rounded phrases ; they have many faults of style, and are sometimes dry, and yet are simple and unassuming. Nature alone, and my own heart, find expression in these chapters.

Driven from the paternal hearth when I was still very young, my life resembles a magic lantern, in which bright and gloomy pictures follow each other in quick succession. I did not always lie on a bed of roses. Amid trials, privations and vicissitudes of all sorts, as a pilgrim tramping the high road alone, as a sailor upon the

treacherous sea, and ultimately as a soldier, I defied
every kind of danger.   But

> I thrust life's worries all aside,
> And had nor fears nor sorrow ;
> I rode towards my Fate with pride,
> And trusted in the morrow.

Or I acted like a reed in the wind—I bowed my head
until the violence of the commotion was over ; and, swept
hither and thither by the broom of war, I often had to do
without the most pressing necessaries of life, quite apart
from my wretched and frequently desperate condition
and prospects.   Bread and water were often all I had to
sustain me, and a stone was my pillow, the earth my bed,
and the star-bespangled sky my awning.   The bulk of
these memoirs were dotted down at odd moments, while
I was on the march, in bivouac, or on the foaming
sea, for

> The city's life, the village green,
> I've had to pass them by.
> The harvest too, I've often seen
> With longing distant eye.

A good deal of my diaries has been obliterated and
rendered illegible by the hand of time, and large portions
of them have been destroyed by Spanish and Portuguese
rats and other vermin ; but, with the help of my memory
and by reference to my commissariat records, I have
endeavoured to fill in the gaps as far as possible, and
contrived to make a complete whole out of the innumerable
fragments.   The drawings, which are my own handi-
work, and were elaborated from sketches made on the
spot, together with the preparation of the memoirs as
they now stand, helped me to spend many a dark
evening very pleasantly, as well as to dispel many
an anxious hour ; for, after all, the bitterness of my
experiences lay in the past and too far behind me to be
felt.
     Should the reader discover in this true narrative of my
life certain events which might well have assumed a

more creditable aspect, and where it may seem to him that I might have acted with more circumspection, more caution, and more honesty, let him not judge me too severely. Let him in the goodness of his heart, and with a charitable hand, conceal those defects, or rather weaknesses, that could not always be avoided.

As a commissary, and therefore as a non-combatant,* I received neither honours nor orders of any kind, despite the fact that often enough I risked both my life and my health in the discharge of my duties ; nevertheless, I maintain that I deserved them much more than many a combatant who strutted proudly about with his medals on his breast ; for the zeal which we of the war commissariat showed was always multiplied in accordance with the difficulties we encountered. Every kind of system was attempted, from that in which the supplies were organised long beforehand to that in which armed marauders and foraging parties were sent out, accompanied by a commissary, and sanctioned and admitted to be necessary, both by the local authorities of the nation as well as by the general in command. But on this very account the life of a war commissary was constantly in danger. At any moment he might be assassinated by the natives whom he had despoiled, or otherwise fall a victim to the peculiar vindictiveness of southern peoples. True, nothing was ever taken except in exchange for cash or receipt notes payable by the Commissary-General ; but, as the Spaniards and Portuguese ingenuously declared, in the event of a total lack of supplies, and in the face of the quantities absorbed by the armies, they could not eat our money or our receipt notes, neither could they purchase anything with them for miles around. How were they to live ? The war commissaries showed the most extreme devotion to duty. Nothing was too much for them—no trial of

---

* It should be borne in mind that at the time when Schaumann was employed in the British army, a war commissary was a civil officer appointed to inspect the musters, stores and provisions for the army. Schaumann happened, as we have seen, to have had some military experience. But this was not an essential qualification.—Tr.

their spirit, no physical hardship, no sacrifice of self-esteem, no amount of contempt on the part of combatants for their position as non-combatants—provided they could make themselves useful. The end of a tiring march, when the troops were allowed to bivouac and officers and men were able to rest, sleep, or enjoy some leisure, was precisely the time when a commissary's hardest work began. It was then that he had to mount a fresh horse, scour the country in order to discover some concealed hoard of corn, accompany foraging parties, proceed to organise the baking of bread and the slaughtering of cattle, and find his way to headquarters to boot. Finally, when he returned, wet to the skin and thoroughly exhausted, to his bivouac hut, he had to take up his pen to write, prepare statements, make out orders for the morrow, and at the end of it all snatch, perhaps, only, two or three hours' rest on a hard bed before again jumping into the saddle at the break of dawn. Very seldom supported, and frequently even obstructed by those in authority, the commissary's efforts were particularly useful whenever there was any difference between the army and the natives, and at all times when the generating powers of order had to be made to spring as it were spontaneously from prevailing chaos. During the war in the Peninsula it was not unusual to see a commissary displaying more administrative skill, and more intelligence, in establishing a stores depôt, in organising transport, in supplying the needs of a cavalry or infantry regiment, and in provisioning a fortress, than in peace time would have been necessary to rule a whole State. Feats of this kind are usually buried in oblivion ; but when the magnitude of the difficulties overcome, and the importance of the results achieved, give them the stamp of grandeur, history is bound to preserve them, if only for the encouragement of those who may find themselves in similar circumstances.

Orders and honours were showered upon the combatants. An officer of the line was thought very highly of for exposing his life, and he was given regular promotion, the privilege of choosing his own billets, orders, medals, and heaven knows how many other advantages. The commissaries, on the other hand, who accompanied foraging parties, or who were on the divisional or brigade staffs, and who were exposed to the dangers of skirmishes or battles, received none of these things. Their lot was to sacrifice their health through bodily and mental strain, to expose themselves on their various raids to the danger of meeting enemy forces, to shoulder the greatest responsibilities, to keep the most complicated accounts, to be constantly threatened with assassination at the hands of the outraged natives, and to be treated shabbily by the generals, who either made the most preposterous demands upon them, or else were only too ready to ascribe to them the blame for any unsuccessful or bungled undertaking. We did not even get permission to wear the Waterloo medal,* and this in spite of the fact that we were placed on the same footing with combatant officers as regards all compensation for wounds, which proves that the authorities must have known our duties exposed us to similar dangers. The combatant in his pride insisted on a war commissary being an intelligent, energetic, brave and thoroughly indispensable officer, but at the same time an inferior assistant in so far as his alleged privileges as a combatant were concerned. And, all the while, our commissions and our uniforms were not only identical with those of the combatant officers, but we belonged to the staff, which made us really superior to the ordinary line officer. What contradictions ! The fact, however, remains that I received no official recognition, nor was I disposed to solicit any. Nevertheless, I am comforted by the thought that the duty I performed for my king under the strain of all manner of exertions and privations, forms a star which now glows indelibly on my naked breast, whereas the official orders and medals only hang on the combatant's tunic.

Therefore, my beloved relatives, when once I shall have departed to that land whence no wanderer returns, and you take up these remains in remembrance of me,

---

* Officers of the Medical Department also did not get the Waterloo medal, though it was granted to the regimental surgeons.—TR.

may my memory seem dearer to you than ever, through these lifeless letters, and I shall look down on you and bless you.

Written in Hanover in our small house at number 363 Georgen-Platz, in December, 1827.

AUGUST SCHAUMANN,

Deputy Assistant Commissary-General in the British Service.

LIST OF CONTENTS

xxi

LIST OF CONTENTS

ON THE ROAD
WITH WELLINGTON

A. L. F. Schaumann.

Chapter 1

Perilous Disembarkation in Maceira Bay—How Mr. Augustus starts His Career as a Commissary.

AT about ten o'clock on Sunday morning the 28th August, 1808, we were given the signal to land. In five minutes all the troops were under arms. Parties were told off, and at the command, "March!" with my portmanteau under my arm, I climbed with a portion of my cousin Plate's company into one of the flat-bottomed boats supplied by the men-o'-war. Preceded by two sloops, we rowed rapidly towards the rocky, sandy shore of the bay, which the huge breakers had converted into a sheet of raging foam. The men sat four by four on the thwarts, all pressed closely together, with their packs and muskets between their legs. None of the officers was allowed to take more than a valise with him.

Right and left the coast formed two lofty headlands of rock, on one of which stood the ruins of an old Moorish castle. On both of these headlands English signalling flags were flying and directing the landing—that is to say, informing the fleet of the ebb and flow of the tide, and of the state of the breakers, so that the debarkation of the troops might be properly timed. Between these two headlands, which were about 1,000 yards apart, lay about 300 yards of sandy beach enclosed by a lofty chain of rocks. Upon this stretch of sand the raging breakers, raising their heads houses high when they were still some considerable distance from the land, rolled in from the Atlantic and the Bay of Biscay, and, hemmed in on either side by the two headlands, pressed forward in lofty walls of water, that swept in a roaring storm of foam far over the beach.

With beating hearts we approached the first line of surf, and were lifted high up into the air. We clung frantically to our seats, and all of us had to crouch quite low. Not a few closed their eyes and prayed, but I did not close mine before we were actually in the foam of the roaring breakers on the beach.   There were twenty to thirty British sailors on the shore, all quite naked, who, the moment the foremost breakers withdrew, dashed like lightning into the surf, and after many vain efforts, during which they were often caught up and thrown back by the waves, at last succeeded in casting a long rope to us, which we were able to seize.   Then with a loud hurrah, they ran at top speed through the advancing breakers up the beach, dragging us with them, until the boat stuck fast, and there was only a little spray from the surf to wet us. Finally, seizing a favourable opportunity, when a retreating wave had withdrawn sufficiently far, each of them took a soldier on his back and carried him thus on to the dry shore.   At last it was my turn to be carried, and thus it came about that at eleven o'clock on the morning of the 28th August, 1808, with all my earthly belongings in my portmanteau under my arm, I stood with wide-open eyes on Portuguese soil, on the sandy shore of the Bay of Maceira, hale and hearty, and muttered to myself : "Here I am, now what next ?   God help me !   Amen ! "

What a teeming multitude there was on the beach ! I sat down on my portmanteau in the shade of the cliff, and watched the troops landing.   It was funny to see a boat coming in through the breakers with its load of horses, which, by the bye, were unsaddled.   They would all dash helter-skelter out of the reeling vessel into the surf, and then swim to shore, while the hussars, who had released their bridles, had to thank their lucky stars that they were not pulled overboard with them.   Think of the feelings of the poor brutes !   After having been confined for four months in the stuffy hold of a ship, to be suddenly thrust into the light of day and into the middle of foaming breakers into the bargain !   As soon as they reached the shore they galloped wildly along it, to and fro, snorting, panting, neighing, and biting and kicking one another, to the great danger of all those gathered on the beach ;   and then they would roll over on the sand.

The sun was hot.   I undressed and dried myself. The tumult on the shore was interesting.   There were soldiers, horses, sailors ;   officers, both military and naval, shouting and directing the landing ; guns, wagons, some of which were being fitted together, mountains of ship's biscuits, haversacks, trusses of hay, barrels of meat and rum, tents, some of which were already put up, and dragoons busy catching and saddling their horses. But the latter could not be mounted, for, owing to their long sojourn in the ship, during which they had been standing, they had lost the use of their legs, and the moment a trooper mounted one of them, the horse folded up his back legs like a dog, or rather dropped his hind quarters to the ground. Orders were therefore issued that the horses should be led about for a day or two, to get rid of the weakness. The animals looked as if they had been fattened, and were in terribly bad condition. But it was wonderful to see the zeal of the British naval and military officers who, stripped to the skin like ordinary gunners and sailors, helped with the landing of the troops, munitions, equipment and guns, ran into the breakers and pulled at the ropes, and with their own hands put the guns and the gun carriages together. Everywhere you could see soldiers who were undressing and drying their clothes. As soon as they had done this they would receive their rations, and then march through a defile in the rocks into bivouacs. The rocks and the sand were so burning with the heat of the sun that everybody went about barefooted, and paddled in the surf from time to time to cool themselves. Fresh or spring water was not to be had, and we suffered terribly from thirst. Lieutenant Otto, who landed with me, ultimately sent one of his men for water, and we allayed our hunger with ship's biscuit. Sadly we contemplated the fleet, which lay on the horizon, encircling the bay in one mighty arc, and regretted the little luxuries we had been forced to leave behind us, which would now become the spoil of the ships' captains.

As soon as the tide began to rise the landing operations ceased, because the breakers then became too powerful for anything. At last the day drew to an end, the air grew heavy, dark clouds began to gather in the sky, and lightning could be seen in the distance. It grew dark very quickly when the sun went down, and everyone tried

to find a corner to rest in.   The fragments of a broken
boat were gathered together, and here and there a fire
flared.   Lieutenant Otto and I managed to steal a little
hay, and with the help of our coats and valises, made
ourselves a litter in the hollow of a rock.   Here we
discovered the padre of the 3rd Hussars, Herr Pohse,
with his batman, and he also wanted to do the same as we
did.   When once we were settled, however, we could not
sleep, for the moment we covered ourselves with our
cloaks the heat became insufferable, and if we threw
them off we were maddened by mosquito bites.   At last,
when from sheer exhaustion we no longer heeded our
discomforts and were beginning to fall off to sleep, it
began to rain and thunder, and before long we were in
the midst of a most appalling storm.   It grew worse and
worse, flashes of lightning followed each other quickly,
and the rattle and roar of the thunder was accompanied
by a drenching downpour of rain.   It was dreadful to
listen to it, particularly as the breakers on the beach
raged more wildly than ever.   We were just congratu-
lating ourselves on our ingenuity in having found such an
excellent refuge in our dry hollow under the cliffs, and were
beginning to pity the poor fellows who were lying about
outside, when suddenly a tiny trickling stream of water,
which soon, however, swelled into an impetuous torrent,
mixed with sand and stones, burst over us with such fury
that there was nothing left for us to do but to jump out
of our lair, seize our valises and cloaks, and flee into the
open.   The water had poured down our necks and out at
our breeches, washed away the hay from under our feet,
and covered our belongings with wet sand and mud.
We had evidently been lying in the dry bed of a torrent.
And so there we stood on the edge of the raging sea, with
a deluge and thunder and lightning overhead, and with
nothing but our cloaks to protect us, wondering what to
do.   At last we decided to walk up and down the beach
until daybreak ; there were no tents, for the few that had
been landed had been erected for the use of commanding
officers.
    At last, as the dawn approached and it ceased raining,

a number of German bakers belonging to the Commissariat, attempted to make a fire out of one of the flat-bottomed boats which had been smashed, and in which eight sailors had lost their lives. The antics of these men amused me during this tiring and terrible night, and it was odd to hear people on the coast of Portugal greeting each other with, " *Pruder Wirzpurger, Pruder Anklamer,* and *Pruder Schweinfurter.*" Soon a number of fires flared, and various groups formed round them, all pressing towards the flames to warm themselves. There were soldiers, sailors and women among them, and, in their midst, the Portuguese bullock-drivers, with their tawny faces, their long black hair, their big old three-cornered hats, their naked brown and hairy legs, cut picturesque figures. They wore a sort of blanket over their shoulders with a hole in it for their heads, and carried poles six feet long. All of them with jaded eyes and pale faces stared silently into the fire ; and at last the dawn began to break. The storm had entirely subsided, the sky was clear, and the sun rose in all its glory above the horizon.

On Tuesday, the 30th August, it was already quite hot at eight in the morning, and everybody made haste to dry their things. I went behind a bend in the cliff, opened my valise, spread my wardrobe in the sun, and began to shave and wash myself. At ten o'clock everything was dry, and I was summoned before the Commissary-General, where, without further ado, I was made a clerk in the British Commissariat, with pay at 7s. 6d. a day, and rations and forage for my horse, and was immediately dispatched with a writing tablet in my hand, on to the hot sand at the edge of the surf, in order to record and keep count of the sacks and barrels of foodstuffs as they were landed. Nobody troubled to ask whether I had had any breakfast ; so, contriving to escape for a moment, I was lucky enough to be able to beg a cup of tea and a piece of ship's biscuit for myself ; and then my splendid life began ! The whole of the day I had to stand in the boiling heat ; the sand was like a furnace, and what with the waves reflecting the rays of the sun, I almost suffocated. Commissaries-General, officers of high rank, generals and other important people, were running about barefooted and in shirt sleeves, and everybody was perspiring furiously.

The whole of the day we continued to land the 3rd Hussars and the Artillery. Commissary-General Rawlings, a puffed up and very uncivil fellow,—who, by the bye, was cashiered two years later,—had set up a large marquee on the beach, and provided himself with all his London camp equipment, consisting of camp chairs of red morocco, small mahogany tables, a silk camp bed with steel springs, a canteen of silver knives, forks and spoons, and a costly apparatus for his personal ablutions. Three or four fat monks, who about mid-day came down to the scene of debarkation from a neighbouring monastery, and whom Rawlings invited into his marquee, could not take their eyes off his beautiful tackle. Several clerks, including a certain man called St. Rémy, an *emigré*, belonging to the family of the Count of Toulouse, were appointed at the same time as myself. In the afternoon we, too, were given a tent. But in the evening the brute Rawlings would not hear of our making up our beds with a little of the hay that had been landed, although two of his own goats were standing up to their bellies in it. As soon as he had fallen asleep, however, we robbed the said goats of their hay and laid ourselves upon it. Meanwhile a number of our bakers, and some men of Plate's company had wandered inland, and had returned with a quantity of melons, grapes and peaches ; while the peasants also began to appear, offering foodstuffs for sale, and we were at last able to cool and refresh ourselves to our hearts' content in the appalling heat. It was my duty to provide the disembarked men and horses with rations and forage before they marched off. This lasted the whole of the night. Scarcely had I lain down, however, utterly exhausted, and begun to close my eyes, before a voice called " Mr. Schaumann ! " and I was again obliged to get up. This made me desperate at times.

August 31st (*Wednesday*). My cousin Plate is now also on shore, and has put up his tent. Thank God he has brought as much of the lovely provisions we left on board as he possibly could, and has proceeded immediately to establish a kitchen under the rocks ; for, no matter where he is, his first care is always to start cooking and roasting—like me exactly—so that now I am feeling quite comfortable. Landing operations are still proceeding briskly, and it is now the infantry's turn. It is a thrilling sight to see the boats packed with men plunging violently through the breakers. The heat is insufferable, and we are almost baked through. Everybody is thirsty, and there is scarcely any fresh water. Plate had a turkey brought in from the country, and had it cooked in a soup and invited me to dine with him, but owing to my duties I could not go. I was constantly being called for, not a moment's peace or rest ! Only at ten o'clock in the evening was I able to escape and to hasten to my cousin Plate. He had put my portion of the turkey aside, and famished and parched as I was, I thoroughly enjoyed it. At eleven o'clock that night, just as a cool sea breeze began to blow up, we bathed in the breakers, and I thought of the line in Haydn's " Four Seasons " :

" How the cool of the evening delighteth our hearts ! "

Yes, by Jove ! It did, indeed, delight us after a day like that one !

September 1*st* (*Thursday*). The landing of the troops which is still continuing, looks as if it would be so dangerous to-day, the wind having grown violent and blowing towards the land, that I shall not be able to close an eyelid. The breakers come on fifty deep, with a terrible roaring and thundering, and sweep so high up the shore that the spray almost reaches our tents. It is only by the most careful steering, rapid rowing, and the most skilful manipulation of the tug-ropes through the surf that the boats can be saved. The bravery of the sailors in all this is really admirable. In the sweat of our brows did we have to eat our bread !

September 2*nd*. The wind to-day is even worse than it was yesterday. Nevertheless, at eleven o'clock the landing operations were continued. At twelve o'clock, just as I was standing by the hay store, I heard some distressing cries and voices calling. I ran on to the beach, and there witnessed a sad sight indeed.   A boat full of soldiers belonging to the Legion, which was to be landed to-day, had turned turtle in the breakers, and the poor devils were struggling in the water.   All available boats were rowed with genuine British seaman's pluck into the raging foam. They didn't seem to care how they got along, but bravely pressed forward to the rescue.   One of these rescue boats also turned turtle.   I saw many of the men sink, and others clutching at their comrades in their death agony, and drawing them under with them.   In a few moments the whole lot had vanished, and the boats were smashed to atoms.   We stood on the shore dazed and silent, and filled with anguish at not being able to offer any help. Three dead bodies were washed ashore almost imme-diately, and in another moment an English gunner was borne along, who, being a good swimmer, had ventured into the heavy breakers in the hope of saving someone, but had received a fatal wound in the chest while trying to climb on to one of the overturned boats.   As fast as the bodies were washed up they were stripped and laid on the beach face downwards, while a hole was dug under their heads.   But, although they were covered with hot sand and rubbed with it, it was impossible to resuscitate them.   This is the fourth or fifth boat that has come to grief in this way.

When we got up on the morning of the 3rd September, we found a dead trumpeter of the 3rd Hussars not very far away from our tent.   He lay near the edge of the rocks with his body on the sand and his head in a pool of water left behind by the tide.   How this man met with his death here was a puzzle to us.   He must have been staggering back to his bivouac dead drunk on the previous night, and fallen with his head in the pool, and thus been ignominiously drowned.

To-day fifty Portuguese bullock-carts came down on to the beach to fetch victuals for the army, and with great interest we contemplated these vehicles, which in their primitiveness seemed to be exactly like those which had been found by the ancient conquerors of Lusitania. They consisted of rough planks nailed on to a massive pole or shaft. At right angles to the shaft, and under the planks, two blocks of semi-rounded wood were fixed, having a hole in the centre, and through these holes the axle was fitted. It was a live axle fixed firmly to the wheels. As these axles are never greased they make such a terrible squeaking and creaking that the scratching of a knife on a pewter plate is like the sweet sound of a flute beside them. And when a number of these carts are moving together, it is enough to drive one quite mad. Be this as it may, the infernal noise is the most heavenly music to the bullocks ; for, as all bullock drivers have unanimously assured me, the animals would stand stock still and refuse to move another inch if the poles were greased and the noise abated. The draught bullocks are very large animals in this part of the world ; they are also docile and fine to look upon. They are harnessed by means of a wooden yoke, which is fastened behind their horns and attached to the axle by leather straps, there being a peg in the front of the axle for that purpose. Moreover, they are shod with a kind of iron shoe, and in this way manage to drag a load of about half a ton up hill and down dale along the roughest mountain roads with the greatest ease. The wheels are solid, massive, and have no spokes, and are most skilfully designed for resisting the terrible shocks and jerks they get, as the wagons go over the stones and rocks. The driver walks alongside with a long pole at the end of which is a spike, with which he goads the bullocks on by striking them over their shoulders.

Towards evening, when I was tired and hungry, and just getting ready to go to Plate's for a meal, I was summoned before Commissary-General Kennedy, and was told that I must hold myself in readiness to convoy 100 loaded carts forthwith to Torres Vedras. I hardly had time to take any food before I was again called up, and just as it was getting dark the way-bill was placed before me to sign. An infantry officer and sixteen men, together with one of the 3rd Hussars, who was carrying orders, were allotted to me as escort. We started off inland to a bivouac behind the rocks where we were supposed to find the wagons. But when we came to the appointed place we found that the whole convoy had marched off without waiting to receive orders, although we could hear their appalling squeaking and creaking away in the hills. As we did not know the way we were compelled, in order to reach them, to crawl on foot at top speed over the rocks which here encircled a small lake. The sun had already set and the sky was overcast. It began to rain and was very dark. The rain made the loamy soil on the steep slopes so slippery that I fell again and again, and what with my cloak, my bag of provisions, a melon and a bottle of rum that I carried, I found the journey extremely tiring. At last we reached a valley where some artillery details were bivouacked, and dis-covered the direction in which the carts had gone. As, however, they had to follow a very devious route round the hills, the officer of my escort, a young coxcomb, asked me whether it would not be better for us to make a straight cut across the hills. I surveyed these hills in the dark, and thinking they were very high, regarded the adventure with the greatest suspicion ; as, however, I wished to prove to the officer that even I did not lack the courage for such an adventure, I replied : " Why not ? Between two given points, the straightest road is the shortest road in Germany as in England." And we therefore started off. The hill was very steep and slippery, and at every step one or the other of us stretched his length upon the ground. The bushes, the thorns, and the thistles tore our hands and faces unmercifully, and stuck to our cloaks, which, dripping with the rain, were a heavy load to drag along. At last, when we were quite out of breath, and wet through with rain and sweat, we reached the summit, and at the same time recovered our train of carts.

It was so dark that you couldn't see your hand before your face, and the rain was falling in torrents. Our instructions were to be careful that none of the wagons gave us the slip in the dark ; for these Portuguese peasants had already been so much overworked and badly treated by the French, and were so thoroughly sick of the war, that they took advantage of every accident in the ground in order to fall away from the column, conceal themselves, and then escape. As soon as we had reached the train my fine young officer and his men calmly took possession of some of the carts, settled themselves comfortably upon them, covered themselves with straw, and. left things to take their course. Our convoy was at least two miles long, and I was now supposed to keep it in order, to run on foot hither and thither, and be everywhere at once, to make sure that none of the peasants got away in the dark ! The hussar of the 3rd Regiment of the Legion certainly helped me as much as he could, and flew up and down the column, making good use of the flat of his· sword whenever it was necessary ; while I, armed with a stick, ran behind him through thick and thin, shouting incessantly the only Portuguese word I had as yet picked up, which was " *Arrivo, arrivo !* " (Go on !)

Thus the column moved slowly on through mud and darkness and under pelting rain along the most impossible defiles, accompanied by the heartrending uproar of gratings, squeaks, creaks and screechings of the ungreased axles. Every ten minutes one of the carts would stick fast in the mud, or in a hole, or run against a stone ; whereupon all the carts in its rear would naturally come to a standstill, and their drivers, finding themselves unoccupied, would mount the vehicles, lay themselves down and fall asleep. If I went forward for a moment to set the column in motion again after it had been held up in this way, when I returned, to my surprise I would find a huge gap in the train and all the drivers deep in slumber. With the help of the hussar the cart that had stuck would be released and moved on ; but the others would not follow, for the drivers would be fast asleep. Then we would shout the most horrible of German curses and use our sticks both on the men and their beasts ; and at last they would waken and the column move forward again. Hardly ten minutes had elapsed, however, before there was another stoppage ahead. This time, owing to the fact that the column had got into a very narrow gorge, it was impossible either for the hussar or myself to get by in order to discover what was wrong. At last, after

climbing over the tops of the intervening carts, I found
the head of the column standing stock still, with all the
drivers fast asleep.   Once more we used our sticks, and
the train moved forward again.   In short, it came to this,
when the head of the column moved on, either the centre
or the tail of it stuck fast, or *vice versâ*.

At last I went in search of the officer of my escort, and
reproving him most severely, threatened to report all his
irregularities, and assured him very angrily that he would
be held responsible if any of the carts were lost.   I told
him how the hussar and I had sacrificed ourselves in the
performance of our duty, while he, far from helping us,
had lain calmly on one of the wagons; and that I was
becoming ever more and more convinced that when it
was a matter of making the best of a job and of doing one's
duty with perseverance and steadfastness, neither Englishmen nor Frenchmen were any good, and only Germans
could be trusted.   Growling and yawning, he at last got
down from the cart : " But, sir, what can I do ? " he
cried.   " How can I help it ? "   Then, calling his men,
he gave one or two orders ; but it was not long before he
vanished again.   In one village, I believe it was Maceira,
five of the wagons managed to sneak away into the yard
of a chapel, and the drivers unyoked their bullocks there.
But the hussar found them out, and despite the torrential
rain they had to rejoin the column.   We reached the
village of Vimiera, the place which on the 21st of the
previous month had seen the defeat of the French by the
British Army under Sir Arthur Wellesley, and we went
straight across the battlefield, where the stench created
by the half-buried corpses of men and horses was appalling.
At midnight the rain had penetrated my great cloak, and
everything I wore, right through to my skin, and my
nankin breeches hung wet and loose round my thighs.
I was almost dead with fatigue and thirst, for I had
thrown away the melon—my only means of refreshment.
My tongue stuck to my palate, and what with all the
shouting, cursing and yelling I had done—and in the
whole of my life I have never cursed so much as I did that
night—my throat was quite sore and dry.   Anxious to

do my duty, for it was the first time that I had served the English, I actually wept again and again out of sheer rage and despair ; for I fancied that if any carts were missing on the morrow I should be cashiered.

At last we emerged from the defiles and hill tracks, and entered a piece of country covered with cork and pine trees. But I could go no further, for my strength was utterly exhausted. I thought, let everything go to the devil, and mounted one of the bullock carts. Hardly had I settled myself, however, before my cart stopped dead, and the bullocks of the following one, which I could not stop, pressing forward, drove their large horns so fiercely against my legs that, overcome with fear and pain, I had to jump down again immediately. At this the driver of the cart began to laugh maliciously, which made me give him a most telling blow, and forced him to cry out, " Oh, Jesus ! " I then proceeded on foot again. In about an hour we emerged from the wooded country on to a heath with abominable roads, and in about another hour on to a paved highway, which, left and right, as far as the eye could see, was lined with the fires of a huge bivouac. I then learned that this was our army which, under Sir Arthur Wellesley, had been victorious at Vimiera. A picket on a bridge made me and my whole convoy come to a halt. I called the officer of my escort to explain matters to the picket so that we might be allowed to pass ; and here, to my great regret and sorrow, the hussar, whose name I should very much like to know, for he was an able and reliable fellow, left us in order to join his regiment. " Go ahead ! " cried the picket, and the horrible axle music started afresh. I begged the officer most fervently to give me better assistance than he had done hitherto. " Look ! " I said, " your party are all asleep. This night, what with getting no sleep, running about, cursing, belabouring the drivers, and counting the carts, the hussar and I have almost done ourselves to death. We are only eighteen against 100 Portuguese armed with staves and knives, so we have no business to sleep. I am completely exhausted and cannot move another step ; I shall therefore lie down for a bit on this hay cart, and it's your turn to keep awake and to look after things." He promised he would, and although the cool morning air, my wet clothes, and the damp hay on which I was lying made my teeth chatter with cold, I soon fell fast asleep.

How long I was asleep I cannot tell, but when I was but half awake it seemed to me as if one of the carts had ceased to move, and the excruciating screeches of the ungreased wheels had died away. I roused myself, and looking about me, immediately beheld the most delightful confusion. All the peasants had unyoked and were fast asleep.

I jumped down from my cart and ran to the end of the column. Another convoy, which was on its way to the army had met our train. Both columns of carts had become mixed up, and all the drivers had unyoked and were sleeping soundly. In despair I sat down on a stone and contemplated the glorious muddle for a while. At length I could stand it no longer. Not one of the escort was to be seen, and I therefore went in search of the officer. When I found him I showed him all the disorder that had arisen, and reprimanding him severely for having no apparent authority over his men, I explained to him and bade him consider that it was we who would have to answer for it if a dozen carts with their load were found to be missing. With a deep yawn he intoned his old plaint : " But, sir, how can I help it ? " " I will show you," I replied. " In the first place, make the whole of your detachment fall in on this spot." At last he succeeded in doing this, but only after great trouble, as his men were hiding themselves. " Now," I cried, " order them to draw their ram-rods ! And you take your stick while I take mine. There are eighteen of us. One of us will climb on each of the eighteen leading carts and will proceed to beat both bullocks and drivers indiscriminately. As soon as this proves effective we'll move on to the following eighteen carts and continue beating until the whole column is in motion again, whereupon you will distribute the men of your detachment in such a way as to keep the whole column moving. I'll go in front, you behind." The English soldiers appeared to be listening to me with complete approval. " I'll warrant you," said

one, swinging his ram-rod about. " We'll make them
go," said another; "besides, we shall have some fun."
And the row began ! We beat them right and left without
ceremony, and at the first blows the peasants sprang in
terror to their feet, then, falling on their knees—for in
their sleepy condition they imagined we wished to attack
them suddenly and murder them,—they cried : " *Oh
Jesus, senhores, misericordia ! misericordia !* " " *Arrivo !
Arrivo !* " I rejoined. The officer also cried " *Arrivo !* "
and his men soon followed suit. If the weary bullocks
would not get up under the blows, the soldiers drew their
bayonets and pricked the beasts' ribs with them.

After much beating, swearing and spurring with the
bayonets, we at last succeeded in getting the whole
column into motion again. With a good deal of rattling,
accompanied by the music of the ungreased axles, we
proceeded along a most horrible paved highway, beside
which a number of infantry and cavalry pickets were
posted ; and just as the morning sun was beginning to
gild the tops of the pines, the cypresses and the chestnut
trees on our way, we perceived the town of Torres Vedras
surrounded by its old ruined walls and ramparts. Another
ten minutes and we had halted at the gate. To the right
we could see an old tower and a conical hill, on the summit
of which there stood the ruins of a Moorish castle. I took
up a position under the archway, and making the carts
drive past me, proceeded to count them. The streets
seemed to me narrow and dirty. The houses, with their
shutters and their iron lattices and balconies, were like
prisons. This was the first Portuguese town I had ever
seen. Nobody was up ; the whole of the place was
deserted and quiet. The silence was broken only by the
ungreased axles of our carts, and in the narrow streets the
abominable uproar was increased a thousandfold.

At last we reached a large square filled with bullocks,
carts and mules. The whole lot were lying pell-mell on
the hard flags fast asleep. The drivers were on their
carts, the bullocks lay close by, the muleteers were resting
on their pack-saddles between the mules, while a detachment of soldiers were stretched on the steps in front of the

church, with their heads on their knapsacks and their muskets clasped in their arms.   With great pains we drove our convoy into the midst of the crowd of men and beasts, and I entered the church where the stores depot was situated.   I found Commissary Baxter sitting at a long table right in front of the high altar, with his two assistants, Wakinger and St. Rémy, and they were writing by the light of four huge wax candles stuck in richly chased gilt altar candlesticks.   It was a beautiful church, all draped and decorated with crimson cloth fringed with gold.   They gave me a friendly welcome.

I then complained to Mr. Baxter about the trouble to which I had been put during the night through the carelessness of the officer in charge of the escort, and assured him that it was only thanks to my own and the German hussar's efforts that half the carts had not gone to the deuce.   Mr. Baxter set my mind at rest about the things that might be missing, promised to make my strenuous efforts known in a higher quarter, and summoning the officer of the escort, called him to account and threatened to report him.   The latter, probably relying on the fact that I was not a commissioned officer, and that I would not dare to denounce him for giving me the lie to my face, denied everything ; whereupon, citing the hussar as a witness, I demanded to be heard before a court martial. At this the young man, beginning to see that matters might take a serious turn, muttered a few unintelligible words of apology into his moustache, and hurried away as if he were not in the least inclined to wait for the worst. " Let the miserable hound go ! " said Mr. Baxter.

The carts were now made to drive up to deliver their load.   The goods were counted and noted, and to my great joy, but for a few trifles, everything was found in order and we were not a cart short.   At nine o'clock, Mr. Baxter, who was a good friend of my cousin Plate, took me to his quarters in the town hall for breakfast. The basement consisted of the prison, and a crowd of dark yellow ragamuffins were looking through the iron bars of its windows, and with clanging chains greeted us with piteous cries for alms, or otherwise entertained themselves with other ragamuffins in the street. In the entrance hall there was a dense throng of soldiers with their camp kettles and canteens, who were all pressing round a huge cask from which a storekeeper was dispensing wine. We went upstairs. Mr. Baxter's quarters were in the court room, and upon the judge's table lay his writing desk and our breakfast. The mayor's and the magistrates' seats were at once covered and desecrated by heaps of blacking brushes, uniforms, boots, saddlery and cooking utensils. Otherwise this hall, with its walls mellowed by smoke, cobwebs, dust and filth, looked imposing enough. In one corner lay a sack of dried beans. Baxter, with great solemnity, settled himself in the judge's somewhat elevated seat, while I, as a mere mayor or magistrate, took the place opposite him. Amid much laughter and chaff over our ludicrous situation we breakfasted on tea, eggs, beefsteaks and ship's biscuit. After breakfast Baxter returned to his church, while I, seizing his shaving materials, installed myself proudly in the place he had just vacated, and began to strop the razor. While I was lathering my chin I thought to myself : " How wonderfully the broom of war sweeps mankind about in the world! For who would ever have dreamt that thou, Monsieur Augustus Schaumann, who in July wast still in Sweden, wouldst on the 3rd of September be in the town hall of the good old town of Torres Vedras in Portugal ; and, if you please, installed in the judge's seat and actually shaving yourself there ! "

The town itself is ugly. The streets are narrow. Here and there a fine house can be seen, and the churches are magnificent. One sees nothing but gloomy little shops and market stalls selling onions, fresh pork, smoked ham and bacon, codfish and rice. There are also countless barbers' shops, in which the barber, in order to while away his time, strums on an old guitar. In spite of the heat the inhabitants are all swathed in large brown cloaks, and in their huge three-cornered hats they loaf about the corners of the streets staring at the British soldiers. I therefore made preparations for my return journey. As, however, I had no intention of walking back on foot, and all carts and mules were required for the further transport of victuals, I resorted to cunning, and boldly ordering two carts in a remote side street, placed them in charge of a detachment of Plate's company, which also intended returning to the Bay.   The Headquarters of the British Army were in this place, and as I left the church, after taking my leave of Baxter, I saw one of the French Emperor's aide-de-camps followed by half a dozen *chasseurs*, pass by, on his way to General Junot in Lisbon, bearing the preliminaries of the Convention.*   I also saw several deserters from the French Hanoverian Legion, who wore red uniforms.   At four o'clock in the afternoon I left Torres Vedras, and in spite of the screeching of the wheels and the many jars on the road, had a most delightful snooze in my cart.

On my way back I went through the village of Vimiera again and made a sketch of the battlefield.   In the foreground Colonel Taylor appears with the 20th Dragoons, marching out to fall on the left flank of the retreating enemy, which he succeeded in doing, and the French were cut to pieces.   Colonel Taylor, however, was left on the field of battle.   Vimiera lies in the middle of the battlefield, and to the south of it, beyond the two windmills, stood the two brigades of Generals Fane and Anstruther, which forced the enemy to retreat into the wood, while a French corps, advancing on the village from the left of the valley was attacked by General Acland's brigade.   This brigade marched across the valley in order to gain the heights held by Sir Arthur Wellesley, and the English artillery, which was bombarding the centre of the French troops attacking the village.   The whole of the French Army under Junot was defeated on August 21st.   They lost thirteen guns, twenty-three ammunition wagons, General Berncire,† and suffered

---

* This was to be the famous Convention improperly called " of Cintra," which caused so much indignation in England, and which Napier, in his " History of the War in the Peninsula," defends with such vehemence.   By it the defeated French Army under Junot was allowed to retreat, lock, stock and barrel, from Portugal, and was shipped back to France.   (See Napier, Book II., Chap. VI.).—Tr.

† General Brennier is meant.   Schaumann who obtained most of his particulars about French and English commanding officers and names of places from hearsay, frequently makes mistakes of this sort.—Tr.

heavy casualties. At seven o'clock in the morning the French, debouching from the Lourinhão road, attacked our outposts, and then under the cover of the pine woods, advanced boldly in three columns to the attack. The English artillery are said to have done much better than the French on this occasion. When the two armies came to grips the French were thrown back all along the line at the point of the bayonet, and then they were pursued and ignominiously slaughtered. Up on the hills to the left there is a small village called Toledo, in front of which General Junot took up his position and issued his orders. To the right, as far as the eye can see, lie the heights of Torres Vedras. A pestilential stink still hangs over the whole battlefield, and numbers of vultures are busy scratching up the corpses. The famous hollow shell, called shrapnel, which has just been invented,* and each of which contains 100 grape shot, are said to have worked untold havoc among the French.

Vimiera is completely deserted, and there is no one there except English doctors and the wounded. In the previous action on the 17th August at Roleja,† the French had attacked in echelon ; on the 21st, however, they attacked in column. But neither formation helped them in any way.

At dusk we reached a small village at which we halted in order to get a little food. All the peasants' gardens were surrounded by hedges of aloe. One hedge in one of these small gardens had an aloe plant in full bloom. A stem as thick as my arm had shot out from the centre of the plant to a height of six or seven feet, and like a candelabrum bore clusters of bloom on its branches. The stem looked as if it had been made of leaves rolled together, and was so hard that the staff-sergeant of the detachment had some difficulty in cutting it off with his sword. As hitherto I had seen the aloe plant only in green-houses, it was extremely interesting and novel—I might even say surprising—to see it used as hedging for a garden. In

---

* The shrapnel shell was actually invented in 1785 by Henry Shrapnel ; but did not receive official recognition until the Peninsula War (*Journal of the Royal Artillery*, Vol. XLVI., p. 453).—Tr.

† Schaumann means Roliça. Napier speaks of Rorica.—Tr.

the middle of the village there was a flat open space, common to all, where the corn was thrashed by means of bullocks or mules trampling on it. The peasants came out of their hovels, surrounded us, and shouted incessantly " *Viva, viva, Ingleses !* " To which we replied every time : " *Viva, viva, Portugueses !* " Then they asked : " *Vamos matar os Franceses ?* " * " Yes," we replied, " *Vamos matar os !* " † Having tested our patriotic spirit in this way, they brought us bread and wine.

It was almost dark when we started off again, and after we had rattled on for about two hours we came to a large wood through which the road ran up and down like a switchback. Meanwhile it had grown pitch dark. Suddenly we halted, and the carters confessed that they had lost their way. Fortunately the moon rose soon afterwards, and after a long confabulation it was decided that we should go on. After wandering about aimlessly for an hour, we reached a more open piece of country and descried on a hill a small white castle, surrounded by a wall and slender cypresses. We drove up to it, and found the door open. There was no light to be seen, no dog barked, and no watchman blew his horn in the tower. All was still. One of my carters, whom I had sent in to enquire about the road, suddenly shot out of the place like an arrow, and crossing himself, exclaimed : " Oh, senhor, no men live there but *demonios o Ladroes !* " (demons and thieves). " *Vamos fugii* " (Let us fly), he cried. I summoned the men of the detachment, bade them take their muskets, which they had loaded ready at Torres Vedras, and follow me into the castle. We yelled and shouted in the entrance hall, but no one answered us except a gruesome echo and the hoot of an owl. We went into the courtyard, which was built in the form of a square, and was almost completely covered by the branches of two huge chestnut trees. Here we found a side door which led us into the castle, and we descended some steps. The doors were open, and all the rooms and apartments

* " Were we going to kill the French ? "
† " We are going to kill them."

completely deserted. Furniture and domestic utensils lay broken all about, the moon shone through a shattered window, and bats were flying in and out. We concluded that it was a castle that had been plundered by the French, and returned to our carts.

Feeling very much annoyed, we drove back, and tried to find another road, and at last came upon a few houses, where we managed to summon a peasant. He told us that he would direct us to a distinguished gentleman who knew the way to Maceira—for these peasants are so stupid that they often do not know either the way to, or the name of, the next place on the road—and who was a chief of the district and commander of the national militia. Having reached a small mean-looking house with a balcony we knocked at the door, and an old woman poking her head out of a hole in the roof, cried, " *Quien es ?* " My drivers replied that we were friends and that among us there was an " *excellentissimo Senhor Commissario das Tropas Ingleses* who wished to speak to the *excellentissimo Senhor Generalissimo das Tropas Portuguesas.* At the same moment a door on the balcony was thrown open, and there appeared a little man in a dressing-gown, who addressed us in broken French. I explained our trouble to him, and he described the road through the forest to Maceira to my carters ; but all in vain, for they immediately forgot every word the moment he had uttered it. At last he advised us to take the road through the village, and this would lead us very soon to another little village that lay quite close, at the entrance to which we would see a pump, and close to the pump a garden hedge. Here we were to clap our hands and cry, " Lopez," and then a man would rise from behind the hedge, who would take us to the *Alcaide,* or chief of the district, and from him we should have to obtain a guide. We begged the *Generalissimo* for a little water, whereupon he let the old woman hand us a large wooden scoop full through the half-closed door, which was secured by a chain on the inside. We thanked him and went our way.

We soon reached the village and the pump, and when

we clapped our hands in the approved Moorish style, and cried " Lopez ! " to our great amusement a man did spring up from behind the hedge, who, when he heard what we wanted, led us to the *Alcaide*, who gave us a guide. After a most vexatious march we at last reached Maceira Bay at three o'clock, and feeling as tired as a dog I crept into the first tent I could find and lay myself to sleep on the bare sand.

September 4th. I had not been asleep two hours, however, before I was called. Commissary-General Kennedy was just about to jump into the saddle and leave the bay. I handed him a letter from Commissary Dunmore, whom I had fortunately met in Torres Vedras, in which the latter begged that I might be appointed his assistant in the place of Mr. Nissen, his present clerk, who was a dirty beast and always drunk. Mr. Kennedy agreed with pleasure, for this Dunmore was a friend of his, and being a Scot, a fellow-countrymen to boot. Immediately afterwards I met Mr. Murray, the new commissary in command at the bay, who told me that on that same evening I was to convoy another train of fifty carts and fifty mules to Torres Vedras, and then, in pursuance of Mr. Kennedy's order, I was to place myself at the disposal of Mr. Dunmore. I accordingly went off to Plate and slept, ate and drank in his tent the whole day long. Towards evening I got ready for my journey, packed my valise, put it on a cart, counted the convoy, checked the loads with the way-bill, signed the latter, was given a small detachment of cavalry and infantry as an escort under my own orders, and at length, placing myself at their head, moved off at dusk to the accompaniment of the famous axle music, and entered the defile leading to the valley and over the rough road up to the hills. As the mules went faster than the carts, I sent them with the cavalry ahead. I and the infantry, consisting of a sergeant and twelve men of the Irish Armed Train,* remained with the carts. The sergeant was an excellent, lively

---

* This appears to be the Irish Wagon Train referred to by Sir Charles Oman, in his " History of the Peninsular War," Vol. I., p. 231. The author there informs us that Sir Arthur Wellesley insisted on bringing two troops of the Irish Wagon Train with him to Portugal.—Tr.

fellow, who told me all sorts of stories to while away the time.

It was a warm heavenly night.   At last we came to the woods which I knew so well, and the moon gleamed brightly through the bushes, the lofty pines and other trees, and shaped them into all kinds of figures.   If by chance we happened to take the side paths over green fields, which in this country seem to be full of rosemary, sage, mint and thyme, a most beautiful fragrance was emitted, owing to the bruising of the grasses by the bullocks and the cart wheels, which scented the air all along our way.   Meanwhile, to the *obligato* of the ungreased axles, my carters would now and again intone a most melancholy song.   It was a sort of improvisation glorifying the Virgin, in which they lingered an almost unconscionable time over the last syllable in each line—probably in order to gain time to think of the next—and then made a long pause before they began again.   For instance, "*munto Santa-a-a munto bonita nossa Senhora Maria-a-a-a-a !* " *   While we were thus travelling through the woods, we passed a small peasant's cot, and I saw one of the Irishmen hang behind.   Then, in less than ten minutes, I gathered from the piteous bleats of a goat and the loud cackling of poultry what had happened. The goat's throat had been cut in a twinkling as we passed by, and it had been hung on to one of the carts in order to be skinned on the march.   The turkeys did not fare any better, and were plucked as we went along.   I attempted to point out to the fellows how disgraceful their behaviour had been, but as the Irish are a notoriously bloodthirsty and predatory crowd, my remarks made not the slightest impression on them, more particularly as I was not a commissioned officer.

At midnight I made a halt under a group of cork trees. Someone was sent for water, a light was struck, and very soon a thick larch bush with long needles was ablaze, the flare of which we kept up by feeding it with rosemary stalks, rock-rose plants, and pine cones, which burned like pitch.   The bullocks were driven among the bushes to

* " Supremely holy and supremely good is our Lady Mary."—Tr.

graze, and we stretched our limbs. The group formed by the carters, with their wild faces, their shaggy hair, naked legs, and long poles, all magically illuminated by the fire into which they stared silently, was most picturesque. I pitied these poor devils with all my heart. In the midst of the harvest they had been torn away from their homes, or pressed into our service, and were forced with their beasts of burden to follow the army night and day along highways and byways, without knowing when they would behold their families again. We gave them a piastre a day ; from the French they had got nothing. When, therefore, the goat and the turkey had been roasted at the fire, or on ram-rods, I begged the soldiers not to forget the poor carters. And now the Irishmen showed the good side of their nature, for they cheerfully surrendered half the goat, together with the offal, while I added thereto my water-bottle filled with wine, after I had taken a good draught from it. The poor carters blessed me for it, and everybody was now happy. When we had had our meal we managed, after a good deal of trouble, to catch the bullocks and harness them, and off we marched again. At last we reached Torres Vedras, without anything special having occurred, at four in the morning. The whole town was buried in the deepest slumber, and I therefore made the carts line up in the market place ; then, assuming a semi-recumbent position on one of them, with my back against some sacks of ship's biscuit and my legs propped up against the side-posts of the cart to prevent me from slipping off, I soon fell asleep.

How long I slumbered in this picturesque attitude I do not know, but I was suddenly awakened by the command, " Order arms ! Stand at ease ! " and the thundering crash of muskets upon the paving stones. It was an English infantry battalion which, while I slept, had taken up its position just in front of me. The regimental colours were standing quite close to me, and were fluttering about my nose. Very much startled, I sprang up, and the whole of the battalion laughed, for I must have cut a funny figure confronting them with

outspread legs.   The sun was already high, so I hastened
to the church in order to report the arrival of my convoy
and deliver the goods.

When this was done, I had tea with Baxter at his billet,
and then went with St. Rémy, who offered to lend me his
bed, so that I might rest myself a little, for I had spent
three successive nights on the high road and was very
tired.   Unfortunately his house stood near a church in
which a grand mass or some other festival was about to be
celebrated ; for the moment I had lain down there burst
forth at short intervals such an ear-splitting peal of all the
bells that I could not sleep a wink.   It sounded to me as
if one of the bell-ringers first tapped lightly with a small
hammer on one of the bells, and left it for a while to ring
or vibrate with a kind of trill ; then he started again with
gentle taps, until gradually he included all the other bells,
which he struck with hammers, first *piano*, then *tutte*,
and then *unisono*, with ever-increasing strength up to
forte fortissimo, all in time, as if he were threshing corn;
and the blows fell with such force that they caused the
house itself and my very bed to shake.   The rhythm of
this peal, which was certainly more hellish than holy, was
like this : " Timboom, timboom, timboomeldiboom."
At the end of ten minutes the ringing gradually ceased,
drawing to an end with single blows of the clappers which
died away in a sort of soft tremolo ; but, oh God ! it was
only to begin again at the end of five minutes' profound
silence, and to be even worse than before ! At every
repetition of the uproar I said to myself : " Now, this is
the end ! This is the last time ! " ; but just as I turned
round in bed and closed my weary eyes, it would start
afresh.

The bed in which I was supposed to be sleeping, stood,
moreover, in a room through which the landlady's
numerous family had a right of way.   Several full-grown
daughters and young children dashed into it every
minute, and would stand inquisitively at the side of the
bed staring at me, until the slightest movement on my
part would send them hurrying away again with much
laughter and trampling of feet.   I got up and found that

St. Rémy had come home meanwhile to luncheon. I
begged to be allowed to contribute to his *déjeuner à la
fourchette*, a wonderfully fine piece of cold roast beef with
which Captain Plate had honoured me on the day of my
departure, and had specially roasted for me and packed
in my haversack. The table was laid, the knives were
sharpened, and we sat down ; then, taking my haversack
and opening it, to my horror and surprise, I drew out, not
the roast beef, but two boot brushes and Johnson's
English dictionary. " *Peste !* " cried St. Rémy. " What
the devil does this mean ? " I said. On the title page of
the dictionary I read the name of my tent companion
of the bay, Mr. Pattison. Then it became clear that in
my hurry I had seized his haversack instead of my own !
What was to be done ? Nothing, except to laugh heartily
over this *quid pro quo*.

I lunched with Baxter, and while we were at table, our
eyes were constantly directed towards the balcony of the
house opposite, on which some Portuguese soldiers were
picking the lice from their breeches. When I reached
home I found that the sergeant of my escort had brought
me one of the turkeys that had been stolen the night
before. I would not have accepted it, but as the sergeant
had already gone, I made a virtue of necessity, and
thinking that, after all, it was war time, I gave it to
St. Rémy's landlady and begged her to roast it for me.
Meanwhile I wandered out into the streets and beyond
the gate of the town, in order to inspect the place a
little.

On returning home after my excursion, I met Captain
von Voss of the 2nd Light Battalion of the Legion, who
had remained behind owing to a slight wound. He took
me with him to his billet, and as he had ordered his dinner
late, I was obliged to eat a second meal, this time with
him, which pleased him very much. Headquarters had
been moved from here, and no one knew where Mr.
Dunmore had taken up his new abode. With the view
of finding this out people advised me to go to Lisbon,
and as Captain Voss also wanted to travel thither, we
decided to set off together. I told him that I was having

a turkey roasted, which we would take on our journey, and this pleased him very much indeed. After dinner we drank a good deal of wine, and entertained ourselves with his host, a pleasant, well-informed man, who told us a good deal about the tyranny and the robberies of which the French had been guilty ; also that on the night of the battle of Vimiera, as they were retreating through this place, they spread the rumour that we had been beaten, and then forced the inhabitants to make elaborate illuminations.

I slept at Voss's billet that night, and was given a good bed by his obliging host. Early on the morning of the 6th of September, I ran hastily over to the old lodgings I had shared with St. Rémy, in order to get my roast turkey from his landlady. But nobody was about ; the whole place was asleep, and as time was pressing I walked without further ado into a large room in which the landlord's whole family slept in various beds. In the middle of this room there stood a huge vessel which, full to overflowing, exhaled such a nauseating odour that, still fasting as I was, it made me feel quite faint. " *Senhora da Casa !* " I cried in a loud voice ; and she, putting her head through the curtains, replied, " *Jesus ! Quien es ?* " I demanded my turkey. " Oh, your turkey, sir ! " (*O Perun de v. Senhoria*), the woman exclaimed with astonishment. " Yes," I replied. " But we ate it up last night," she said. " Woman," I cried, " who gave you the order to devour my turkey ? Get me another ! " " There isn't another turkey in the whole town ! " (*No ha otra Perun in toda a villa*), she rejoined. " As you did not return home, we thought you had marched off, so we ate the turkey ! " Meanwhile the children and other members of the household sleeping here had woken up, and were accompanying our conversation with loud laughter. Feeling very angry, I turned away.

We left Torres Vedras with a cart for our luggage, and a detachment of convalescent Highlanders under the command of their physician, Dr. Gordon. About an hour's distance from the town Captain Voss showed me the place where his battalion had been camped opposite the French, and the remains of a hut in which my brother William * had lived. At about ten o'clock we came to a small village where we decided to have breakfast. It was Sunday, and we stretched ourselves upon a grass plot in the shadow of the church. While our servants were getting eggs and making tea in the village, we entered the church, the floor of which was covered with straw. We only saw three old women inside, who were squatting down in a corner. A lamp was burning in front of the altar, and upon the latter there was a seated figure of the Virgin Mary, with her hair curled, and wearing a bright silk dress, which made her look not unlike a doll from Nuremburg. Two very fine diamond bracelets had been fastened to her arm by someone as a pious legacy, and in order to discover whether they were genuine we were turning them about, when suddenly one of the old women shot out from her corner like a ferocious dragon, and with her face all distorted, and making the most angry gestures, she cried : " *Santo ! Santo !* " It was quite impossible to appease her, and so we left the church. Immediately afterwards we saw a young, genial, and portly Franciscan monk coming towards us across the fields, bearing a parasol. He was evidently about to say mass in this chapel, and we greeted him respectfully. The bells began to ring, and he walked genially up to the altar. Immediately one of the old women sprang up, knelt before him, and pointing angrily at us, told him about the desecration of the altar. The monk first glanced smilingly at the Virgin Mary's bracelets, and then angrily at the woman ; whereupon after he had said a few sharp words to her, which we did not understand, she went grumbling away. Our lives were in his hands. One word from him, and the throng of peasants coming in for mass would have killed us.

After mass all the villagers came round us to watch us have our morning meal, and they admired Voss's canteen and his corkscrew, shouting from time to time : " *Viva Ingleses !* " We begged the priest, who seemed a very friendly, communicative and enlightened man, to

---

* This was the brother who was killed at the battle of Waterloo.—Tr.

have luncheon with us.   The French had plundered his
monastery and reduced it entirely to ruins.   A peasant
brought a mule for him, and as we were going the same
way we travelled together.   With the most flattering
words he pressed Voss to ride his beast, saying that
Portugal owed us both her freedom and her existence ;
that the Portuguese would always remain under an
obligation to us, and that although we belonged to a
different religion, the enlightened sections of the nation, of
which he was a member, did not like us the less for it.
Thereupon he embraced us, pressed us to his bosom, and
kissed us farewell in a most pleasing manner, and went
off along a side track to another village, where also he
had to say mass.   As we were tired from walking, we
requisitioned the first bullock cart we came across in the
fields, and willy nilly made it come with us.

At about mid-day it grew very hot, and as our way took
us through villages surrounded by vineyards and gardens
full of melons, we ate an enormous quantity of exquisite
grapes and melons.   At one house on the road we bought
a turkey from an old peasant woman.   She had a charmingly pretty and well-brought-up daughter, a real beauty
in face and build, with whom we had great fun ; for,
among other things, we made her kiss us each in turn
before taking our leave, and as the last to be kissed always
ran round to the tail of the line in order to be kissed again,
the poor girl never came to an end with her kissing.   As
at length the mid-day heat became intolerable, we soon
entered an inviting-looking peasant house which stood on
a height close to the road, and begged its owner kindly
to allow us to cook our food in his kitchen and to rest
there awhile.   The peasant family, all in their clean
Sunday clothes, were both friendly and willing.   We
plucked the turkey, Voss was the cook, and Dr. Gordon's
servant was sent to a small town in the valley for bread,
vegetables, wine and condiments.   Meanwhile we made
lemonade, and with much laughter and banter assisted in
the kitchen.   When the food was ready we settled ourselves in the shade of a fig tree and banqueted like kings.

The view over the valley from this elevation was

heavenly ; our host was friendly, the turkey was tender, and the wine delightful.   Never in my life have I been in a happier, more cheerful or more genial mood than I was on this occasion ; for the future lay before me like the beautiful valley below, romantically encircled by distant blue hills.   The Highlanders, too, lay about in picturesque groups, cooking their rations.   When it grew cool we set off again, and soon reached the beginning of a massive white wall, which we were told belonged to the great park of the huge castle of Mafra.

It was already dark when at last we came to the end of the long wall and to Mafra, and we made our way through a small gate on to the square in front of the castle. A gigantic building confronted us, which, magically lighted up as it was by the last rays of the sinking sun, seemed to us almost unlimited in extent, and for a moment we could not move for astonishment.   We heard that the whole of the General Staff was here.

We were billeted in a rather attractive house, and presented ourselves before our landlady and her son, who was a cavalry officer.   They were very polite, asked a number of questions about a thousand and one things— chiefly political—and examined us *ad nauseam* about England.   As we were very hungry we waited every minute for them to offer us something to eat ; but when they had no more questions to ask they gave us a glass of liqueur, and informed us that our beds were ready.   We therefore withdrew.   On the table near our bed there was a bottle of red wine and water, but nothing else.   So we comforted ourselves with thoughts of breakfast on the morrow.   In the night Dr. Gordon got up and cursed furiously about the bugs, and on the following morning we put on our best things, hoping that we should be asked to have breakfast.   But the time went by and no one appeared.   Growing angry, we sent one of the servants of the house upstairs to enquire how much we owed for food and drink.   " Nothing ! " was the reply.   But we had hardly got to the end of the street before the servant ran after us and presenting us with the lady's compliments, asked whether we did not wish to have breakfast.   " No," we replied haughtily, " they should have asked us before ; we must march off now."

In the market place we bought bread and milk, and saw the English generals ride away in the direction of Lisbon. Then we went to the castle in order to have a hasty look at it. This immense building is a castle and monastery combined, and like the Escurial in Spain, was built by John V. in the years 1717–1731. Everything is on a massive, regal, gigantic scale, but it has already been much damaged by the French, and is badly decayed through want of repair. Some of the best furniture and pictures went to Brazil with the Royal Family, the remainder was carried away by the French. The monastery was in one of the wings of the castle, and, if I remember rightly, it had room for 103 monks. They spoke with great indignation about the bigotry of John of Portugal, then Prince Regent. When he resided in this castle the monks were his principal companions, and he is said to have risen at four in the morning, and while still in his nightshirt, to have rung with his own hand a silver bell that summoned the monks to matins. This bell was stolen by the French. In the courtyards of the castle the horse dung left by the French stood houses high, while the walls were blackened with the fire from the bivouacs.

As Captain Voss happened on the market place to meet a hussar of the Legion leading a horse which did not mind being mounted, he took his leave of us and rode away, while we followed slowly in our cart along a road that wound from left to right up the hill. As the heat was oppressive, we retired to an ordinary public house to have something to eat and to rest ourselves. We had chocolate and a dozen eggs with us, which we cooked ourselves, and we also bought bread, wine and a few cucumbers from our host and made ourselves a salad. After a trying march we at last reached the foot of the hill and admired its romantic shape. Up on its crest we noticed a tower, a church and a monastery belonging to the Heironymites, 3,000 feet above the sea, which at that great height looked like a swallow's nest hanging in the air. Close to the town of Cintra, which lies as it were in the lap of these jagged volcanic hills, there stood on a plateau the remains of some British Army bivouac-huts, which looked rather like a deserted Red Indian village.   At length we reached Cintra, that paradise of Portugal, with its pleasant white houses, clean streets, orange, lemon, fig and bay trees, and its gardens, the bushes of which, laden with fruit, hang over into the street.

Here we parted from the Highlanders with their excellent Dr. Gordon ; and the other doctor, Voss's servant and ourselves with the bullock cart continued our journey to Fort St. Julien, which we reached at sundown. We obtained billets at the neighbouring village of St. Pedro, in the house of a widow, who seemed to be quite pleased to receive us.   This was really the doctor's billet—my own was in another house ; as, however, we wished to be together, I stayed there as well.   But the doctor soon regretted this arrangement, for what pleased, or rather struck us most forcibly about this cottage apart from its cleanliness, was a beautiful girl of sixteen, dressed in town fashion, who gave us a very charming welcome.   In ten minutes we were quite at home in the house, and the girl, seating herself between us, asked us all kinds of questions, told us her name was Anna Joaquina, of St. Pedro, that she was chambermaid to a Lisbon countess, and that she had come here to help her mother with the vintage. Ten more minutes had scarcely elapsed before my own heart and the doctor's burned so fiercely with love for this maiden, that we scowled jealously at each other, and wished each other at the devil.   Both of us tried hard to please her and to win her heart ; and as ingenuously as a child the fair Joaquina sat between us, so that at one moment it seemed that it was I, and the next that it was the doctor, to whom she was the more partial ; then suddenly she would play the prude towards us both.   I had hold of one of her hands, the doctor held the other ; it was touching to behold !   Her mother, probably with the object of diverting our attention, and thus raising our siege, opened a window, and pulling in a branch of the vine laden with the most gorgeous grapes, proceeded to fill a small basket with them, which she then laid before us and invited us to partake of its contents. At last we plucked up heart to do so, and as we found that love in no way stilled the pangs of hunger, we dispatched our servants into the village, to get us whatever food was to be had. And then the good mother went into the kitchen to prepare our supper. Meanwhile Joaquina sang us a few Lisbon opera airs, not at all badly. When everything was ready, we sat down with the ladies to table, and ate, drank and sang until twelve o'clock at night, whereupon we retired to the bed—I mean the doctor and myself—which the mother had prepared for us on the floor. The ladies withdrew into a small room, the door of which, to our great distress was securely locked and bolted ; and I dreamt the whole night of Joaquina.

At six o'clock in the morning we had to part. As our bullocks were tired, we hired a donkey, which we loaded with our valises ; and after Joaquina had given each of us a kiss instead of breakfast, we left St. Pedro, and passing the walls of Fort St. Julien, in less than an hour we reached the town of Oeyras, where Headquarters were installed. The doctor declared that he wished to remain here. " *A la bonheur !* " I cried, taking his valise from the donkey's back ; and, throwing it down in front of the public house door, we jealously turned out backs on each other and parted *dos-à-dos*, without saying good-bye, he to find a billet for himself, I to look up the resident commissary, a Mr. Rawlings. From him I heard that Mr. Dunmore was in Porto Salvo, and was with the division. As the 2nd Light Battalion formed part of this division, I would be able to see my brother William every day.

Was there anybody happier than I ? For sheer joy I administered a sound blow across my donkey's haunches, and strode gleefully along the road to Porto Salvo. But woe to me ! When I was only half way, I came to a village where an officer of the 2nd Battalion told me that Mr. Dunmore had been transferred from this division to General Moore's, and had just passed through with bag and baggage on his way to Paço d'Arcos. This news distressed me greatly. From sheer bad temper now I gave my donkey another sound blow, and turning round, took the road to Paço d'Arcos. Mr. Dunmore welcomed me with open arms, and assured me that he was delighted to see me, as he was badly in need of me, and there was a great deal to do. We went to his quarters, and after we had had a meal, I was given my instructions, and repaired to my station, in the village of Toroge, which lies on a height far from the town.

Chapter 2

How Mr. Augustus goes into camp ; suffers many hardships there, and ultimately marches towards Spain.

THERE were two divisions encamped between Paço d'Arcos and Toroge, and I was placed in charge of the stores depot, where I was to receive supplies, distribute rations and fodder to the troops, keep account of everything, and repair to the town every evening to report. I was billeted in a fairly salubrious peasant farm ; but my room was only so-so. In addition to a million fleas, two peasants also slept in it. Otherwise, however, the people of the house did all they could to please me, and I started my arduous duties. Supplies had arrived so plentifully from the provision ships lying in the harbour, that a veritable mountain of salt fish, oats, hay, straw, ship's biscuit, rum and wine had accumulated in one of the large barns of the farm ; and on the following morning at four o'clock the quartermasters of seven regiments were already standing at the door, together with the servants from Sir John Moore's, Lord Bentinck's* and General Hill's staffs, and many others, in order to fetch their rations and fodder.

The whole day long I had to bake in the sun, reckon up and calculate, weigh and measure, keep accounts and order fresh supplies. I had no assistant and no servant. As a rule our butchers prepared my food for me. In the evening I had to take all my records and a long report to Commissiary Dunmore at Paço d'Arcos, and give details about the state of the stores. This often kept me busy until ten or eleven o'clock ; and then only was I free to grope my way back amid the faintly gleaming bivouac fires, to my little village on the hill, while at every turn I was challenged by the English sentries : "Who's there ?" Tired, jaded, hungry, and thirsty, I then supped on a soup of marrow bones, and some roast beef—for every day it was the same—drank a glass of grog, and finally, sitting in my shirt sleeves in front of

* Schaumann means Lord William Bentinck.—Tr.

my door to cool myself, I would smoke a cigar before creeping into my flea nest. Very often, however, I had hardly been asleep an hour, before some god-forsaken detachment would come along, which had to march off early, and I was obliged to turn out to distribute provisions. I also had a number of carts and mules under my charge, which I had to lend to regiments drawing rations, or having sick men, or regimental baggage to transport ; and this was an additional anxiety and trouble. In short, I found that the duties of a store keeper or a war commissary are the most laborious in the field, and the most poorly remunerated ; for when the war is over one is given the sack.

My village was small, decayed and deserted, but from it there was a beautiful view over Paço d'Arcos and the sea. Mr. Dunmore's landlord, a rich wine merchant, was a foolish lout, who took a great fancy to me. He possessed a large vineyard, in which he grew grapes the great size of which always astonished me. Every time that I had any business to transact at his house he loaded me with melons, grapes and peaches. I had no friends ; the officers in the bivouacs were strange to me; and I did not even have a love affair ! My company consisted of peasants, ill-bred quartermasters, blaspheming soldiers, bullocks, donkeys and mules. My wild bullocks, which we killed for meat, also caused me great anxiety ; for although they were shut up in a garden surrounded by a wall five feet high, they nevertheless used sometimes to jump this height like stags, and charging into the bivouacs, would send the tents, the huts, the sentry boxes and camp kettles all flying ; or they would escape into the open country, or, after being surrounded by me and my men, supported by the military, would be shot at and killed at the end of a regular hunt. A couple of them once overthrew an English sentry, although he was standing with bayonet fixed.

I remained in this pleasant position until the 15th September, when the division suddenly received the order to break up the camp and march to the royal castle of Queluz, near Lisbon. Now I had a tremendous deal to do. I was on my legs the whole of the night. Towards the evening I received another herd of wild bullocks, which gave us a great deal of trouble, and four of which jumped the five-foot wall of the enclosure and escaped. At six o'clock in the morning we marched off. I was very anxious about the escaped bullocks, as I held myself responsible for everything that was lost. When, therefore, we passed a field on our way, in which there were about twenty bullocks grazing, I said to myself, wait a minute! Here is an opportunity of making good your loss! I then gave my butchers and bullock drivers the order to drive our forty bullocks as if by accident among the strange herd, and be careful in the end to collect forty-four. There was no herdsman anywhere near, and the trick succeeded. Towards two o'clock in the afternoon we halted with our whole train of carts before the royal castle of Queluz, which struck me as being a very beautiful and imposing place. Close by, in the fields, there was a large camp. We were not quartered in the castle but given billets in a small group of houses at the end of the white wall encircling the castle grounds, where the road bifurcates to Lisbon and Belem. As soon as we had reached this point the four fresh recruits among the bullocks were immediately slaughtered, and the marks on their hides obliterated, for in a very little while a fellow came running up to us in search of the missing animals, but was obliged to go away disappointed.

There was a lot of work to be done. We got up at four in the morning. Seven quartermasters were standing at my door, with the usual numerous following, and there was the usual outcry for bread, oats, hay, rum and rice. Every day at ten o'clcok I had twenty bullocks killed— that is to say, 600 in all, during our two months' stay at this place—and their blood and entrails, which soon became putrid in the great heat, created the most appalling stench, not to mention clouds of blow-flies, which were so thick that every surface was black with them. In the end I had pits dug, in which I buried this offal. The Portuguese butchers had a good way of slaughtering bullocks ; they used a small instrument, which was half concealed by the hand, and had a blade not larger than a penknife fixed into a wooden knob.   With this they approached the bullock in a coaxing manner, stroking him the while, and feeling for a slight depression in the back of the neck behind the torus and between the horns ; then they would plunge their small spike into this depression, and the bullock would drop to the ground as if struck with apoplexy ; and in most cases would hardly stir a limb again.   Our German slaughterers ought to take a lesson from this.

We hardly had time to eat anything or to make a meal ready at mid-day.   As a rule we simply put a camp kettle on the fire, filled it with the finest marrow bones and meat we could find, added rice and ship's biscuit to it, and whenever one of us had a moment to spare, he would have a look at the kettle and skim its surface—a duty which ultimately devolved entirely upon me.   Naturally, I often used to steal into the royal kitchen garden close by and rob it of its best vegetables and herbs.   It is strange but true, that Englishmen would rather starve than trouble themselves about cooking ; that is why it is so hard to be an English war commissary ; for the men, together with their officers, are like young ravens—they only know how to open their mouths to be fed.   Not so the German.   In the end, everybody, Mr. Dunmore *à la tête*, depended entirely upon me.   The latter was so childish that when at five o'clock he jumped down from his horse, feeling as tired as a dog, and his batman, Peter, who was as childish as himself, handed him a glass of rum and water with a little ship's biscuit, he regarded that as his dinner, and thought there was nothing more to be had ! *O sancta simplicitas !*   No one could understand where I got all my things from, for not one of the Englishmen had either a pot or a spoon, nor the genius to procure this or that *brevi manu*.   Gentlemen, I declared, if a commissary is expected to starve in the midst of all his stores, then the devil take the whole business.   As soon, however, as I took command, we had tea, milk, butter, eggs and beefsteaks in the morning, and marrow soup, roast beef, cauliflower and salad for luncheon.   We also had glasses and spoons, and I collected a dinner service by borrowing in the neighbourhood. The milk we obtained from our neighbours' goats ; our butter was preserved, for fresh butter was not to be had ; we obtained our tea and sugar from Lisbon, and the fruit and vegetables were taken from the royal garden. And this was the whole of the secret. My chief, Mr. Dunmore, could never cease singing my praises. " If you were not here," he used to say, ".we should all perish." His servant Peter, who looked on me as a magician, and was just as eloquent in his praise as his master, had orders to pay all my expenses. In the afternoon the supplies used to arrive, and the business of weighing up, which lasted until eleven at night, often continued till the early hours of the morning. The vehicles on which the provisions were brought to our stores presented a comic spectacle. The Portuguese Government had requisitioned all hackney carriages, and had ordered their owners to remove all the superstructure, and to load the provisions on the naked framework. Just think of the framework of an old-fashioned chaise, on the main braces of which, instead of a box, half a dozen barrels of salt fish and bundles of hay and wood were rocking about, the whole drawn by two large pack mules ridden by a fellow wearing a collar, a gallooned hat, and a powdered pigtail. Towards evening hundreds of such vehicles would arrive. It was here that I first got an idea of southern vehemence. Two of these coachmen who had quarrelled were springing at each other with drawn knives, their lips foaming with rage, when the rest of them rushed towards them, seized them from behind, and held their arms, while their knives were wrenched by force from their clenched fists. Whereupon the two quarrellers fell first of all into a fit of epileptic convulsions, and then into the soundest of sleeps. They were laid on the ground, and at the end of ten minutes they awoke and returned to their mules as quietly as if nothing had happened.

A few months passed by in this way, and then what with the great heat, the cold nights, the eating of fruit and the drinking of young wine, the health of the army

became so much impaired that typhus and dysentery
broke out and spread rapidly, affecting even the inhabitants of villages lying close to the camp. The pestilential
stench of our slaughter-house refuse also contributed
somewhat to the trouble ; while, in addition, a huge
hospital was installed in one of the wings of the castle,
not far behind and below our stores depot, and separated
from it only by a long ditch which was used as a latrine
by the dysentery patients, and was not 500 yards away.
Infection was bound to occur, and it was not long before
I, too, got dysentery ; but great as was my pain and
unspeakable as was my exhaustion, I stuck to my duty,
and was soon cured by an English doctor by means of
opium pills and thick rice water.

On September 25th I was granted leave to go to
Lisbon. Meanwhile the French army had embarked
at that city, and in accordance with the Convention of
Cintra (August 20th, 1808) had been shipped in English
vessels in fine style, with all their belongings, back to
France. This convention could not help arousing indignation in the heart of every Portuguese and every Englishman ; for after the battle of Vimiera, the French were as
good as trapped in Lisbon, and we ought to have met
their threats of setting fire to Lisbon and of withdrawing
beyond the Tagus through Alemteyo into Spain with
more unconcern, and after encircling them, made the
counter-threat of putting the whole garrison to the sword.
Our general, Sir Hugh Dalrymple, who concluded this
treaty with Junot and Kellerman, and Sir Harry Burrard
and Sir Arthur Wellesley, who added their signatures
to it, behaved, as most English generals have hitherto
always behaved in like circumstances,—that is to say,
proudly, arbitrarily, foolishly, and in a manner revealing
their total ignorance of military diplomacy. Moreover,
the way in which this committee cavalierly rejected the
wiser counsels and the urgent prayers of the Portuguese
Government and their generals, who, after all, ought to
have been allowed to have some small say in their own
country concerning an affair which was their own business
—for we were only auxiliary troops and not masters—

was truly an indignity. In pursuance of this convention
the French, with drums beating and flags flying, with all
their guns, arms, thirty rounds of ammunition per gun,*
loot and plunder, bag and baggage, were decently
embarked at Lisbon in English ships, and then gently
deposited on French soil.

The Portuguese foamed with rage, and rightly too.
The stupidest owl in the army saw how badly Sir Hugh
Dalrymple had allowed himself to be diddled by the
French generals. Nor were the consequences slow to
make themselves felt ; for scarcely was the news of the
convention published in England than the Opposition
in the Commons and the whole of the English Press
poured out their wrath upon Sir Hugh Dalrymple.
Even the Government was compelled shamefacedly to
acknowledge that the Opposition was right. The
General was recalled to England to answer for his actions,
and shortly afterwards was placed on half pay. Sir
Harry Burrard, an obtuse pig, and Sir Arthur Wellesley,
were reprimanded, but were given the supreme command
until they were relieved by Sir John Moore, who retained
it.†

While we had been lying so inactive here, there had
been a good deal of talk about our being destined for
Spain ; as, however, the fine season had been allowed to
go by, we thought that the idea had been abandoned at
least for this year. Meantime I heard that this was not
the case, and that for months we had already been discussing with the Spanish the ways and means, as also the
conditions and the nature of the force, with which we
should advance into Spain. Our general, Sir John
Moore, who had had some experience of war in Brabant
and the East Indies,‡ was certainly said to be a very brave

---

* Napier says the number of rounds per gun was sixty. This is also the number
given in the text of the Convention.—TR.

† See p. 18, *ante*. Napoleon, who thought that Junot ought to have resisted and
beaten the English, made the following comment on the convention : " I was going to
send Junot before a council of war, but, fortunately, the English tried their generals,
and saved me the pain of punishing an old friend ! "—TR.

‡ Sir John Moore had seen service in Holland, but it was in the north in the region
of the Helder. Also Schaumann must have meant the West Indies here. Sir John
Moore never saw active service in India.—TR.

man, but too much concerned about detail, and, moreover, hypochondriacal. From all accounts it appeared that when he took over the command he did not find the army in the state of order that he desired ; he was also displeased with the fact that the command of two corps had been given to Sir Arthur Wellesley and Sir Harry Burrard respectively, and that he was not made Commander-in-Chief. Apparently he had written to the Government in England to say that his army was too weak to be used with any effect against the whole of the French forces in Spain ; and furthermore, that he mistrusted the Spanish character and promises, and that, whatever might be said to the contrary by Mr. Frere, the English Minister attached to the Spanish Junta in Cadiz, whom the Spaniards had completely taken in with their grandilo- quent fanfaronades, he had nothing good to say of the campaign. Besides, he pointed out that the season was too far advanced, and in short, that the undertaking was inopportune, foolhardy and ill-considered. Later on, when Lord Castlereagh wished to send him reinforcements, General Moore is said to have declined them on the ground that it was impossible in this country to provision a larger army than that which had already assembled. He also refused the supreme command of the Spanish armies because he saw no prospect of gaining any honour with such a conglomeration of ruffians without either training or discipline, and vain, boastful, and cowardly into the bargain. Much of this may have been very true ; for all the Portuguese declared with one voice : " Do not trust the Spaniards and their promises ; for all they tell you about ample stores and large armies are sheer lies ; all they wish to do is to lure you into their country, claim your victories as their own, hardly mention the help you have given them, and not even thank you. If things should go wrong, they will vanish in a twinkling, and return to their homes, and leave you to your fate in the heart of Spain, surrounded by your enemies, and exposed to every possible privation. Furthermore, the year is too far advanced, and the rainy season will hurry you on too much and do you a lot of damage." The

Portuguese themselves also admitted that even in their own country they would be at a loss to indicate any road that was practicable for artillery.   Be this as it may, all this delay and hesitation, together with our general's refusal to assume the supreme command of the Spanish armies, was very detrimental to our cause, and gave the French time to see through our plans, and arm themselves accordingly, while it also disheartened everyone and placed the English Ministers in the unpleasant position of not knowing what policy to adopt.   Over and above all this, we heard that the 20,000 French troops, which had been so kindly shipped off and landed upon French soil with the promise that they were not to take up arms against us again for I do not know how many years,* had marched across France and had already arrived in Spain. This was only to be expected.   That is how matters stood.

Our army was constantly being reviewed,† and it was a fine spectacle, for everybody was in the best possible condition, particularly the Hussars and the Highlander Brigades.   What horses, what men, what gun teams, and what order, uniforms and arms ! Everything was in the highest degree perfect.   The army then consisted of about 19,000 men, to which were to be added the 11,000 coming from England under General Sir David Baird. Unfortunately the Commissariat of this army was not so brilliant.   Most of its *personnel* had never yet served with such a large force, and had neither sufficient skill nor sufficient experience to overcome all the difficulties which were very shortly to be encountered.

Meanwhile, the Spaniards, supported by Mr. Frere, the credulous English Minister, never ceased to promise us substantial support, huge stores and vast armies. In addition we received the good news that Marshal de la Romana, who, with a Spanish army had been held prisoner by the French in Funen, Laaland and

---

* Here Schaumann appears to be mistaken.   Article 2 of the convention stipulated that : " The French troops . . . shall not be considered as prisoners of war, and on their arrival in France they shall be at liberty to serve."—TR.

† *Cp*. Robert Blakeney, " A Boy in the Peninsular War " (London, 1899), p. 20 : " The new commander of the forces . . . appeared to be continually riding through our ranks, or inspecting the different regiments."—TR.

Jutland,* had, through the help of the English fleet, succeeded in escaping with 10,000 men, and had landed at Corunna † with guns and all.   On the other hand, from a letter addressed by the Governor of Bayonne to Marshal Jourdan, which was intercepted by the Spaniards, we also had the distressing news that between October 16th and November 16th 66,000 infantry and 7,000 cavalry to reinforce the French Army would march across the Pyrenees and enter Spain.   The Spanish Junta published a long, bragging, theatrical and inflaming manifesto, which, however, was well written, and was dated " Aranjuez, October 16th, 1808."

We had heard from Madrid that the French were preparing a formidable armament with the view of annihilating the Spanish armies before they could unite with us, and then driving the English, as the French said at the time, into the place to which they were best suited—the sea !   According to all accounts the Spanish army under Don Josef Palafox in eastern Spain numbered 20,000, while there were 55,000 under Blake in the west, and 65,000 under Castaños in the centre.   Judging, however, from the reports made by British officers specially despatched to the three armies, these were not in very brilliant condition, for they were found lacking in training and discipline, badly organised and defectively armed.   The Spanish generals were stupid, proud, headstrong, and deaf and ill-disposed towards every reasonable and intelligent measure which the English advised.   They preferred to follow their own counsels ; hence the fact that hitherto they had always been beaten.   King Joseph Bonaparte had left Madrid, and had come to a stand with his right on the sea, his left covered by the River Aragon, and his centre on the Ebro ; while Napoleon had ordered a conscription of 100,000 men at home, and intended coming to Spain in person, in order to drive us out.

Meanwhile the lamentable news reached us that Sir David Baird, who had landed at Corunna, was suffering

---

* They were, as a matter of fact, quartered in Holstein, Sleswig, Jutland, and the islands of Funen, Zealand and Langeland.—TR.

† Napier says the troops numbered 9,500, also that they did not disembark at Corunna, but at St. Andero.—TR.

from lack of food supplies, and that the Spaniards were not behaving as they should.   This contrasted strangely with the bombastic promises of the Junta and the Spanish commissaries.   The Portuguese informed me that, in order to cross Portugal our army would, owing to the matter of provisions, have to divide up, and that our guns would not only have to go another way, but owing to the great mountain ranges, they would be obliged to take a circuitous route.   Finally it would be our misfortune, if we had to march in winter, to fall in with the rainy season. " A fine prospect ! " thought I.   As, however, all the above only consisted of army rumours, and there was no mention of marching, I comforted myself for the time being with the thought that nothing would come of it all.

On the 9th October, 1808, however, an order suddenly appeared that we were to hold ourselves in readiness. This brightened the spirits of the army, and roused its fighting ardour, for the long spell of idleness in camp had made everybody rather ill-tempered.   It was said that we would be embarked again, sail to Corunna and land there.   Shortly after that, however, another general order appeared : " Headquarters, Lisbon, 15th October, 1808. The Commander-in-Chief hopes that when the troops under his command enter Spain, they will feel it necessary both to their credit and to their own interests to deserve the high opinion which the good and courageous Spanish nation holds of the English people.   As a compliment to the Spanish nation, when the army enters Spain, it will wear the red cockade next to the English one."

On the 19th of October the army began to move, and at the rate of a division a day slowly marched off.   In our stores depot things now began to look lively.   Dunmore, our chief, suddenly departed in the night, in order to accompany a division, and he thanked me again for my efforts in housekeeping.   Peter also wished a touching farewell to me and my fleshpots.   The next senior Commissary was Mr. Boys, who lived in the castle, and he now became our commanding officer.   He fancied that incivility constituted zealous service.   His unpleasant natural failing was that he could not sleep at night.   After we had retired to bed at eleven o'clock throughly tired and jaded, he would come to the depot as early as three in the morning, and kicking the door so hard that it was almost unhinged, would roughly order us out of bed. But harsh taskmasters have a short reign. Very soon he had to depart, and we came under Mr. Dillon, who also lived in the castle of Queluz. He was a gentle, good-natured and genial person. The largest bivouacs were now gradually emptying ; after a while all one could see was empty tents and huts, around which the Portuguese peasants crawled in search of plunder. Then at last even the tents were pulled down and despatched to Lisbon.

I and one of my colleagues now moved into the Castle of Queluz, and were given a room at the top of the building with round windows—called *Oeuils de bœuf*— which the royal chambermaids had once occupied. It had no table, no chairs, and no bed, and so we installed ourselves as usual upon the bare floor. We had spent a few days in this way, when suddenly there arrived an order from Mr. Erskine, Chief Commissary-General, to the effect that I was to repair to Lisbon immediately, and report myself to him. "Now I'm in for it," thought I. All tense with expectation I entered Lisbon *per pedes apostolorum*, and presented myself before Mr. Erskine. He received me very kindly, and informed me that he had appointed me commissary to the 32nd Infantry Regiment. They were marching early on the morrow, and escorting a convoy of carts, laden with ammunition, to Salamanca. " Go into my office and receive your instructions. You will get a mule from the Prince of Portugal's stables. I wish you a pleasant journey."

I went to the office. They kept me waiting two hours. At last, losing patience I exclaimed : " Gentlemen ! If you had any idea of all I have to do, with my regiment marching in the morning, and it is now already four o'clock, you would surely try to settle particulars with me as quickly as possible. It is hard enough to have been given such short notice, in order to make adequate pre-parations for such a duty and such a march. I have no

office, no assistant, no map, no statistical and topo-
graphical description of the country through which I am
to lead these troops ; I haven't even got a book of rules
relating to my duties and accounts as a commissary."
This pathetic speech was met by loud laughter on the
part of the office staff. They seemed to gloat over my
discomfiture. At last they pacified me with the assurance that I was a foreigner, and that foreigners were
famous for helping themselves out of difficulties. " Yes,"
I replied, plucking up courage, " I hail from Hanover,
and will certainly be able to look after myself, you can
take my word for it ! " Again there was loud laughter !
At last, when I had been given my instructions, I went
off to the Royal Stables at Belem in order to get my
mule. After a long walk, which took me half an hour, I
reached the stables and presented my order. But what
was my horror when they coolly informed me that my
order must first be countersigned by the Master of the
Horse, who lived outside the town, near the aqueduct!
They also told me where to find the house. With furious
curses I walked off, and when I reached the Rocio it was
already dark. But by dint of questioning, and thanks
to the help of a *Gallego*, or water carrier, whose services
I hired, I at last found my way out of the town to the
house of the Master of the Horse. At first they wouldn't
let us into the house, which was shut up ; and then it
appeared that the gentleman in question was at the opera
at St. Carlos, and would not be back until midnight. A
coarse German curse was my reply. What was to be
done ? Very much enraged, I trotted back to the city,
and down to the Tagus. I was so tired that I could not
put one foot before the other, and I was so much covered
with sweat and dust and so thirsty that my tongue stuck
to the roof of my mouth. Almost in desperation I cried
out at last, " God help . . . ! " But I got no further.
" Let them all go to hell ! " I exclaimed. Whereupon
making my way in sullen despair to the Quai de Soudré
and into an hotel, I ordered some roast meat, a salad,
and a bottle of Cacavelos, and regaled myself. It was
very late when I went to bed, and having consigned the

32nd Regiment, Mr. Erskine, his impertinent staff, the mule and the Master of the Horse, to the lowest depths of hell, I fell asleep still burning with rage. The next morning, as might well be expected, I first had a jolly good breakfast in perfect peace ; and then only did I attempt to go in search of the Master of the Horse, beyond the city walls. He was at home and counter-signed my order ; and then I started on my long journey again, in the boiling sun and through foul-smelling streets, to Belem. At the stable I was shown a dozen mules to choose from—one lame, another almost lifeless, another blind, another seedy, and so on—and I stared in astonishment at the stable hands. Well, it appeared that the whole army had already drawn their mules here, and that these were the rejected ones which nobody wanted. I had come so late that they could not help it. " But," I replied, " Mr. Erskine, who sent me here, can help it." The Portuguese grooms shrugged their shoulders.

At last I was shown a huge mule stallion, which had been used for carrying the royal litter, and though other-wise sound, had a broken hoof. As, however, they assured me that this did not matter, for in the first place, the hoof had been clamped together, and the mule was only slightly lame, and secondly, I should easily be able to exchange it in Spain, and with the help of a little cobbler's wax on my brush, cheat a Spaniard into the bargain, it suddenly dawned upon me that they might be right. As time was pressing, therefore, I accepted the mule, and hiring the services of one of the men to lead the creature back to Queluz with me, I departed. When I reached Queluz, I was bathed in dust and perspiration, and proceeding to prepare for my journey, I saw Mr. Dillon, who gave me some money. Then, as there were no saddles in the place, I proclaimed to a large throng of people assembled in the great square, that whoever had a saddle and bridle for sale would find in me a willing and generous purchaser ; whereupon I jingled my Spanish dollars in my pocket. Ten minutes had hardly elapsed before I was offered a good saddle and bridle, a large leather valise, a blanket, and everything else I needed, and I bought the lot. After which I dined with Mr. Dillon, obtained a courier, and towards evening—not without some trepidation, for at that time I was a bad rider—I mounted my mule and amid the cheers of the local inhabitants, who shouted : "*Viva Senhor Commissario, viva viva feliz, viva munitos annos ! bom viagum, passe muite bem Senhor Commissario,*"* and waved their hats and handkerchiefs after me, I rose hastily away.

* " A long and happy life to the Senhor Commissary, may he live many long years, a pleasant journey to him. Fare you well, Senhor Commissary."—Tr.

(N.B.—For an excellent account of all the circumstances connected with the Convention of Cintra, mentioned in this chapter, together with the subsequent proceedings of the Court of Enquiry, see "*A History of the British Army*" (pp. 235–8, 249–54), by the Hon. J. W. Fortescue.)

Chapter 3

AFTER a while my guide who was striding smartly ahead of me, cried out : " *Eren boa gente* " (They were good people), and then proceeded to sing his " *A nossa sanctissima Senhora Maria-a-a-a-a-a-a* ! " The moon rose magnificently, and only half awake I rode dreamily at a good pace up hill and down dale, and the whole time across country in the direction of Sacavem, which I reached at last at eleven o'clock, feeling very tired and feeble. We knocked up the Juiz de Fora,* and I was delighted to hear that the regiment had already been provided with everything. I was billeted with the baker who made the bread for the troops that were marching through, and as we sat talking together in broken Portuguese, he suddenly looked at me somewhat intently, and then exclaimed, " *V. Senhor no e Allemno ?* " (Are you not a German ?). " Yes." " God ! " he cried, " then why did we give ourselves all this trouble ? " He then told me that he was a Swiss, and that he had married a Portuguese woman. At first he had suffered many hardships owing to the bad state of justice and the priests ; but now he lived happily. After talking until midnight, I went to bed.

I was called at three o'clock, and had to water and saddle and bridle my mule myself—unwonted task!—then, having breakfasted, I left the place with my host's good wishes. The 32nd Regiment was just starting off, and riding up to Colonel Hinde, I presented myself before him as his commissary, and gave him my credentials. I was welcomed in a friendly manner, and after having been introduced to the major of the regiment, the quartermaster, Mr. Smith, and all the officers, I took my leave, and availing myself of the services of a guide, hurried ahead, in order to discharge the duties of

* A kind of town magistrate.—Tr.

my new office at the next halting place. The road to and from Sacavem is paved with large stones, which makes marching very difficult, and driving in a carriage intolerable. The district is exceedingly beautiful, and adorned with country houses, farms and gardens. Beyond Sacavem, I was obliged to avail myself of a sort of floating bridge in order to cross a lake* which empties itself into the Tagus here. I admired the rustic surroundings of this place, as also the church. The latter stands on the banks of a piece of water, consisting of five small streams, which flow into the Tagus. Sacavem forms the right wing of a strong position covering Lisbon. The village of Lumiar in the centre guards the road to Oporto, while the left wing would be defended from the heights of Bellas and the Lake of Sacavem.* The River Sacavem was constantly to my right. At the time of the floods it is still briny here, for I saw large tracts of level land— one of which had an area of about twelve acres, I should think—which after being flooded are dried up by the sun, the salt alone remaining behind. It is accumulated in large heaps, after which it is covered with straw, and then left standing there until ships come to take it away. From a distance these heaps of salt look like the round tents of a large camp. I also observed enormous stacks of unthreshed corn, which were made out in the open and without shelters, after the English style. They were built along the banks of the Tagus and from a distance they almost had the appearance of villages.

After we had wound our way round a hill we came to a vast plain, into which the hemmed-in river flows, and behind which there stood a lofty chain of mountains, the beauty of whose bold and romantic shapes was enhanced by the masses of dark pines and pale green olive trees that grew upon them. The violet grey colouring of these mountains and hills, and their wildly fantastic shapes, reminded me of Cervantes, and on every precipitous height one half-expected to see a Cardenio

* Schaumann appears to mean the Rio de Sacavem.—There also appears to be a mistake in the German text here. The right wing, and not the left wing, would be protected by the Rio de Sacavem.—Tr.

emerge from the bushes in order to intone his lover's plaint. How exquisite such country is! What vegetation, what air, what brightness and serenity everywhere! As happy as a king I rode along, concocting schemes for the future, smoking one cigar after another in the balmy blue air, and partaking freely of the *boraxa*—a leathern bottle—which hung from the pommel of my saddle. With every one we met I tested the progress I had made in speaking Portuguese, and rejoiced when they understood me.

Thus at last I reached Villa Franca on October 21st. It is an unsightly town of narrow streets ; but it has a fine quay and much shipping. It enjoys a big trade with Lisbon, and is famous for its wine. Unfortunately the grapes had already been pressed, and I was therefore unable to see the method by which this operation is performed in these parts. The vintage takes place at the beginning of October, and while it lasts the town is said to present a very attractive and lively picture. I went at once to the Town Hall to see the Juiz de Fora (*judex forum*), announced the arrival of the 32nd Regiment, and found all such things as meat, bread, wine, oats and hay already prepared. At last the regiment marched in, and drew their rations. Then I dined and went early to bed, and on the following morning started off once more.

[TRANSLATOR'S NOTE.—Reaching Azambuja on the 23rd October, Schaumann went *via* Cartaxo, Santarem, Gollega and Tancos to Abrantes, which he reached on the 24th.]

I careered solemnly through several narrow streets to the billeting office and was given quarters at the house of Senhor Raphael Reposa. Then I went to the Juiz de Fora, a refined and cultured man, who informed me that a proper commissariat had been installed in this town, where I could obtain my supplies for the regiment regularly every day. The regiment marched in and I heard to my joy that we were to have a few days rest here. It was high time ; for, what with heavy rains and the difficult roads, many of the troops were completely exhausted. At all events, there were signs enough

indicating the approach of winter.   The more sensitive
trees and shrubs were shedding their leaves, and the
woods and meadows were looking brown—a colour which
changes to bright green after the rainy season.   This long,
much-dreaded and melancholy rainy season is now at
hand.   It is said that the waters pour down from the hills
with a force of which we have no conception, destroying
bridges, flooding roads, and converting brooks and
streams into raging torrents.   The atmosphere becomes
damp and unhealthy, and our marches are likely to be
terrible, while the condition of the men will be much
deteriorated.   Had we only begun our march a few weeks
earlier, we should have escaped a calamity which was to
prove much more harmful to us than the enemy's fire.

My quarters were good, except that my room, as in all
parts of Portugal outside the palace, had no windows, but
only wooden shutters.   My mule, which was installed in
a stable beneath my room, stamped and made such a
dreadful noise, that it drove me almost mad.   Opposite
my room there was a garden concealed by a lofty wall,
which belonged to an imposing-looking house.   Three
startlingly pretty girls lived there, the daughters of a
gentleman, and they used to make their appearance in the
vine-clad verandah which was built against the wall.
It seemed to amuse them to look into my room and
examine my little home à l'anglaise.   I greeted them, and
they returned my greetings, and very soon we started a
sort of pantomimic correspondence in which our hands,
eyes and mouths did heavy work.   What a pity that a
lofty wall and a street separated us !   In the morning one
of them always made an effort to appear on the balcony
first, so that I might waft her kisses and other lover's
tokens before the others arrived.   Then the others would
come, and there would be one or two little jealous quarrels.
How beautiful and interesting those three girls were !
What figures !   What expressive black eyes !   How
exquisitely animation, innocence, and coquetry were
combined in them !   They seemed to have been born for
no other purpose than to promote and bestow love.   Was
it to be wondered at that my poor heart soon became very

much distressed ? Meanwhile, my landlady, or the *Senhora da Casa*, as she is called in this country, was also far from unattractive, more particularly as she had the most beautiful pair of arms that I have ever seen in my life. Naturally, as was only proper, as soon as her husband's back was turned, I used to kiss those arms a good deal—an attention which she seemed to accept with very good grace. Both she and her husband were extremely inquisitive. Quite early in the morning, sometimes when I was still in bed, they would come in to admire my English dressing-case and shaving tackle, and to look on while I shaved and cleaned my teeth. Then my breakfast, consisting of tea, eggs, butter, and a huge beefsteak was also something entirely new to them. In Portugal in those days tea was known in the chemist's shops only as a drug. I gave my rations, which, as a commissary's portion, were certainly far from exiguous, to my landlady, and begged her to prepare them for me according to the custom of the country ; and a soldier whom I employed as a batman was instructed to help her whenever a beefsteak or any other English dish was required in addition. The principal Portuguese dish consisted of a tureen full of strong meat broth, together with rice and all kinds of herbs and vegetables, such as sage, thyme, parsley, onions, leeks, tomatoes (*pommes d'amour*), cabbage, haricot beans, and quantities of white bread : hence its name, " *sopa secca*." The cabbage, the haricot beans (*feiaon*) and the rice were frequently taken out of the soup before it was brought to table, and served as a vegetable on a separate plate, with butcher's meat, chicken, and pork sausages. The latter, with the meat, were frequently cooked in the soup. Pork and mutton are also frequently cooked with the beef in the soup. My table was always very neatly laid for luncheon ; but hardly had I been seated five minutes before my host and his wife, their son and the maidservant would appear, and taking chairs and crying " *Con licença !* " (By your leave), would seat themselves in a semi-circle round me in order to watch me eat. The way in which I plied my knife and fork seemed to amuse them ; but the quantity of meat

I ate and of wine I drank completely baffled them, for in these parts the people live most temperately. These visits on the part of my landlord and his wife in the morning before I was up, and at breakfast and dinner, seemed to constitute a part of the national good manners, of the *politica portuguesa*, but they were most embarrassing.

The Commander-in-Chief, Sir John Moore, arrived, and summoned me to appear before him. He was a refined, somewhat pallid and interesting-looking man, with a *je ne sais quoi* of melancholy in his expression. He was grave but courteous, and asked me how everything was going, what I had thought of the provisioning and the spirit of the Portuguese on the way, and what were the methods of victualling the regiment in these parts. He also told me that we should leave here immediately ; and indeed marching orders appeared on the following day. After we had loaded a convoy of 200 bullock carts with ammunition, therefore, and taken charge of it, we marched on November 2nd, 1808. I bade a sad farewell to a number of girls, with whom I had fallen in love, and also took leave of my host, and once more kissed·his wife's beautiful arms, blew a few tender kisses towards the lofty wall, behind which the young ladies were weeping, and off I went.

We belonged to the column of the army which, on its march to Spain, was to pass through Abrantes, across the Tagus, and keep to the left bank of that river. This route was chosen because, owing to the enormous number of troops that had already marched backwards and forwards on the right bank, provisions were short on that side. The road led downhill in the direction of the Tagus, where we were taken across in a ferry. A few ships from Lisbon, bearing victuals and munitions of war, were at anchor there. On leaving the Tagus the road ran to the left through pine woods and moors, and, from this spot, Abrantes with its convents, churches and old Moorish castle which, overhung with heavy rain clouds, frowned menacingly into the valley, presented a truly magnificent spectacle. I passed through small woods of beautiful cork trees, from which, here and there, a bit of bark had been torn away. The valleys, full of aromatic shrubs, such as strawberries, rock-rose, thyme, myrtle, sage, rosemary, lavender, woodbine, dog-rose, and lovely blossoming brambles of all kinds, together with poppies and buttercups, are said to be a perfect paradise in spring, when the whole heath is in bloom. Then it is nothing but a sheet of flowers as far as the eye can see, as if Flora had emptied her cornucopeia into it. At this time of year, however, after the heat and the drought, all one could see was brown heath.

Our route lay through Casa Franca to Gaviao—a place consisting of only a few houses, which lies on a high hill four leguas * from Niza. We were to bivouac here for the first time. As the task of getting the bullock carts across the river took a long time, the regiment arrived late. The surrounding country consisted of a heath, the granite subsoil of which occasionally projected above the surface in great gray blocks. The wind had risen and it was raining ; so we encamped in the shelter of these innumerable lofty granite blocks, and lighting a big fire, kept it alive with dry rosemary and rock-rose shrubs, together with some branches from the cork trees which we found here and there. Our bivouac, with its numerous grotesque fires lighting up the granite boulders, presented a strange but picturesque scene. The carts were formed into a circle, in the centre of which we herded the bullocks, and then sentries were posted all round. While the camp kettles were warming on the fires, and tea and soup were being prepared, many of the soldiers, who had discovered numbers of beehives on the heath, went out with the object of robbing them. I despatched my servant Pat, an Irishman, to join the robbers, and he brought back a wrap full of the most beautiful honeycombs. With eager haste we grabbed at them and bit off large chunks. But a moment later many of us were heard to utter the most piteous yells ; for the honey was full of live bees, one of which stung my lower lip so badly that it swelled up at once to a tremendous size, and caused me the most excruciating pain. Feeling

* A *legua* is five English miles.—Tr.

very angry I repaired to my lair ; but here a fresh misfortune awaited me ; for my servant in the dark had
imprudently laid the wrap full of honeycombs on my
bed, and the honey, warmed by the heat of the fire which
had been lighted meanwhile, had run out of the cells,
and having filtered through the wrap, had already soaked
my great coat and blankets before it was removed.
Unaware of the sweetness that saturated my bedclothes,
I crept into my bed fully dressed, wrapped the clothes
round me, and moved about in them. Very soon, however, I became aware of the disaster, for which, alas!
there was no help. Cursing savagely, I resigned myself
to my fate. Shaking with the cold, I lay there, with my
swollen under lip, in the rain and the wind, covered from
head to foot with honey. At last, thank God ! the day
dawned, and mounting my mule, I rode away at top
speed through the mist. But our trouble did not end
here, for the confounded honey had given me and the
rest of the 32nd Regiment the most violent diarrhœa,
which lasted throughout the whole of the following day.

On November 3rd we again pushed forward, but as
our guides had run away, and the mist remained thick
the whole of the morning, we found ourselves astray
among impassable mountain paths, in which the carts
could move only with difficulty ; and at last, after an
extremely fatiguing march of nine leguas, or forty-five
English miles, we reached Niza at nightfall.

Chapter 4

A March in very bad weather over the San Miguel Range—The Passage of the Tagus—Arrival at Castel Branco—Sojourn in Castel Branco— Partridges.

THE square tower of an old Moorish castle which we saw from the distance, told us we were nearing Niza. To judge from the remains of the walls, the town must once have been quite important. I was given a fairly good billet. The regiment marched in, and when once I had discharged my most pressing official duties, my first thought was to get my clothes, my cloak and my blankets washed clean of honey. I also bought a mule here for fifty Spanish dollars and let my servant, Pat, who carried my baggage, ride the large mule with the cloven hoof. The town is small and insignificant, and as it lies off the high road, has been more or less spared by the French. Owing to the bullocks, which were worn out, we halted here a whole day. The paymaster and the adjutant were quartered at the presbytery, where they were very comfortable ; for among other things their wash-basins and water-cans were of massive silver. At the approach of the French such things are, of course, concealed. I, on the other hand, was quartered with a priest who was a skinflint, and gave me very frugal fare. I, therefore, escaped from his house and spent the evening very happily at the presbytery, where I met a Dr. Francisco Assisi, a very pleasant, cultivated man, who had been the Juiz de Fora at Beira, but had fled from his post and crept to this place for refuge. The horrors perpetrated by the French in Beira had been so ghastly that the recollection of them had made him quite hypochondriacal.

Before daybreak on the 4th of November, the bugles sounded the march, and as a number of carts which were supposed to take the place of others whose bullocks were exhausted had not yet arrived, the Juiz de Fora was fished out, and so fiercely upbraided that in a moment the two of us were as mad with each other as a couple of fighting

cocks.   When once this had been settled I left the place
in a downpour of rain.

The road across the San Miguel range is very bad, and
often quite perpendicular.   Many of the carts containing
the ammunition were smashed to pieces, despite the fact
that they are built expressly for that kind of road.   It
often happened, too, that when they were drawn by weak
or exhausted bullocks, the weight of the carts would prove
too much for the beasts, who could not hold them, and
then the whole equipage would start running backwards,
and with much scraping, scratching, rumbling and
bellowing, plunge headlong into the abyss.   This was in
itself sad enough, in all conscience, and yet it looked so
comic that often we could not help laughing.   The sun
sank in the west, and threw dark shadows across the
mountain depths.   This mountain chain is a branch of
the Serra, or principal range, and it consists of a kind of
red marble, whereas the other is of weather-worn granite.
Meanwhile the rain came down with ever greater violence,
and I was wet to the skin.   When at last I reached the
famous Pass of Villa Vilha, it was pouring so hard—for
the rainy season was now in full swing—that the track
which I was following was like a forest stream, which sped
roaring beneath my mule's feet.   There was a ferry here,
a sort of flat-bottomed boat, which took me across the
river, and then the road went up hill again, until, very
soon, we reached Villa Vilha.

I found everybody in the house of the Juiz de Fora,
busy baking bread, and there was also some slaughtering
going on ; but I was much distressed to hear that no
brandy could be given to the troops as there was none to
be had.   Colonel Hinde was also very much grieved at
this news, for, as the men were wet through to the skin,
a ration of brandy would have been very good for them.
The Juiz de Fora was very severely rebuked about this
both by the colonel and myself ; but like all the Portuguese, when they are apologizing, he shrugged his
shoulders until his ears rested on them, and assured us
that the French had plundered and consumed all the
brandy, and that consequently there was none to be had

in the whole of the neighbourhood. " *Senhores !* " he exclaimed, " *os Francesces rumperon toda ! A qui no ha aguardiente mingun ; no, nada, ni nada !* " * Then he pressed his thumbnail just behind his top front teeth and let it spring past them, which is a Portuguese method of conveying the fact that there's not a drop to be had. What was to be done ? The soldiers grumbled ; I grew angry, and the poor bullock drivers who, soaked to the skin, had to bivouac with their bullocks in the open, and who had been obliged to leave many a bullock cart behind on the road, complained bitterly. Meanwhile everybody crawled as far as possible into shelter, and dried and tidied himself. Rations were then distributed, columns of smoke began to rise up everywhere, and cooking began. The fuel consisted of rock-rose, rose-mary, myrtle, and other shrubs, and it filled the air with fragrance.

Villa Vilha, once a large town, now consists only of a few mean-looking houses, and lies under the brow of an overhanging hill which, while it attracts the passing clouds causes a continuous fall of drizzling rain. In the evening I went to Colonel Hinde in order to join him, the major, the adjutant, Thornton, and the paymaster in drinking a glass of mulled wine. While, however, we were sitting quite calmly, smoking our cigars and talking politics, the sergeant-major suddenly walked in, saluted, and exclaimed : " Colonel, I come to inform you, sir, that the whole regiment, including the guard and picket, is dead drunk ; many of the men are lying like dead, and the most urgent measures will have to be taken if we are not all to go to the dogs." Never shall I forget the expression on our faces as we looked round at each other. Our cigars fell from our lips. Dumb with horror, the colonel turned to me, and I turned to the colonel ; then the adjutant stared at the sergeant-major, as if he wished to discover whether he were still sane or completely daft. At last we were able to speak. " But, God in·heaven ! " we all cried out at once, " how can it be possible ? There

---

* " Gentlemen, the French have destroyed everything. No one has any brandy, or anything else for that matter."—Tʀ.

is no brandy to be had here ! " " The Juiz de Fora lied, and, please your honour," ejaculated the sergeant-major indignantly, " down in a coach-house by the river there are ten casks full of strong brandy. The men who wanted to get water for cooking saw the casks through the chinks in the door. They then climbed on to the roof, and after having removed a few stones they entered the place, opened a cask, quietly filled their camp kettles with the stuff, and secretly told the others about it. And just now, when I inspected the guard, I found the corporal with all his men stretched out on the floor dead drunk." * We all sprang to our feet, and the adjutant, with all of us close on his heels, dashed off in the direction of the coach-house. The moment we arrived a number of fellows who had been busy pumping, ran away as fast as they could with their camp kettles, which they emptied of brandy as they ran. A few poor devils who were sitting up on the roof and handing up the brandy from inside, were placed under arrest, and one of them was found quite unconscious. An order was then issued for all houses to be visited and all the brandy found to be poured away and the owners notified ; but, unfortunately, the disaster had occurred. From that day forward the regiment became lifeless and insubordinate. But that is the fate of all English regiments, particularly when there are many Irishmen in their ranks, as there were in the 32nd.

The colonel was furious and solemnly swore that he would have the fellows whipped from here to Salamanca. On the following morning a short and summary court martial was held, and for a start ten men were flogged so severely with the cat o' nine tails by the drummers that the blood poured from them. Every morning the others will take their turn until the whole regiment has been flogged. Even the poor Juiz de Fora was summoned before the colonel, and after having been received with a volley of abuse, was placed under arrest. But he managed to escape a penalty by proving and piously swearing by all the angels and archangels that the casks did not belong

* A similar incident is described by Robert Blakeney. (See " A Boy in the Peninsular War," pp. 41, 42.)

to him, but to merchants in Lisbon, and had only been deposited with him in transit, and furthermore, that he believed they contained oil. " Fine oil ! " cried the colonel, " and be damned to you ! "

On November 6th in Castel Branco I was given quarters in a large house ; but the people made so many difficulties about opening the door to me and taking me in that at last an apothecary, who was standing at his door on the opposite side of the road, irritated by the way I was treated, asked me whether I would not prefer to go to him. Wet and weary as I was, I gratefully accepted ; but hardly had I settled myself under his roof before the distinguished people opposite, having heard meanwhile that I was the commissary of the troops which were expected on the morrow, and concluding that it would have been wiser to have me rather than two or three officers or half a dozen men, sent over to fetch me.   But I thanked them kindly, and remained with my hospitable apothecary.   The latter, after taking my mule to a warm stable, led me before a large fire, handed me slippers and a dressing-gown, and finally gavè me a wonderful supper, in which a dish of partridges—which being a keen sportsman he had brought down himself—and a basket of delicious grapes, gave me particular pleasure.   He also provided me with some mulled wine, which we drank together, sitting up talking till late in the night.   Then I was shown a clean bed in the good old Portuguese style—that is to say, without a frame and made up on the floor—and there I enjoyed a long and well-earned sleep until nine o'clock on the following morning.   Half the regiment marched in ; the other half was apparently still lying with the bullock carts somewhere between this place and the San Miguel range.   I gathered that we should stay here until the ammunition had arrived, been collected together and inspected, and the damaged portions replaced ; also until all the bullock carts had been exchanged for fresh ones— all of which could not possibly be done very quickly.

Meanwhile we had the most magnificent and enjoyable existence.   I had a good billet, an amiable host, very little to do, and rode out every day for pleasure or else wandered round the town with the officers, visiting churches, flirting with the local beauties, or lounging about. After spending the day thus, partly occupied with business and partly with tomfoolery, we would foregather somewhere and spend the evening merrily round a *brasero*—a sort of copper brazier filled with charcoal—drinking mulled wine, eating roast chestnuts, and smoking cigars. I spent most of my evenings at the house of a *Capitao-Mor* (a sort of district military officer) on whom our quarter-master, Smith, and his pretty wife were billeted. This *Capitao-Mor* had a very beautiful daughter, who was more-over—a rare occurrence in these parts—highly cultivated, and played the pianoforte and sang most divinely. Our adjutant, Thornton, and many other officers also visited at this house. The former was madly in love with her. Never shall I forget the evening when this girl sang a soft plaintive Portuguese ditty, in which a maiden swears fidelity and constancy to her doubting lover, and each verse ended with the words " *ou morere* " (or die) which were wafted from her lovely lips in tones scarcely audible, like the last sigh of a dying angel.

The weather continues rainy, one heavy shower following the other. The people here pity us, and rightly, too ; for a march in the rainy season, God knows whither, over impassable roads, is regarded here as no joke. The air, moreover, is thick, heavy and damp, the houses are full of draughts, and the floors are either of bricks or cement. The consequence is we can hardly ever leave the dear old *brasero*.

By the bye, the patron saint of Castel Branco occupies a dangerous position ; for when the people here had con-cluded a solemn pact and contract with St. Anthony, and chosen him as their patron saint, and he allowed the town to be plundered by the Spaniards notwithstanding, the infuriated populace smashed his image to atoms. One of the finest statues of him actually had its head knocked off, and the head of St. Francis was placed on it instead. In fact, the statue now bears the name of St. Francis.

The country around is very desolate, though in the distance the blue hills, the cultivated valleys, and the olive trees provide a romantic view. There are also quantities of partridge and quail, and these are very cheap. My host had a peculiar method of preserving partridges. He would first roast them quite brown, then lay a dozen of them at a time in a great earthenware pot, with vinegar, pepper and spices, as for a pickle, and between each layer he would have a bed consisting of slices of the very large and beautiful onions which grow in these parts. Every morning at breakfast, one of these partridges would be taken out of the pot and eaten. I can thoroughly recommend this method of preserving partridges, for it provides a most exquisite dish.

Meanwhile many regiments had come and gone, among them the 88th ; our ammunition carts had also been brought up to their full quota, and placed in the charge of gunners and a commissary of stores ; and marching orders having been issued, amid the farewell greetings of my host and all my other acquaintances, I left on November 15th for Escella de Sima and San Miguel d'Acha, and reached Pena Macor on November 17th.

Chapter 5

How Mr. Augustus reaches the Spanish Frontier—Entrance into Spain—
The National Character and Costume—Wretched Prospects.

[TRANSLATOR'S NOTE.—Schaumann left Pena Macor on the
19th November, and travelling *viâ* Sabugal, and Aldea da Ponte in the
most appalling weather, reached the Spanish frontier on November 22nd.]

ON the 22nd we pushed on again through mountain gorges and forests, *viâ* Povoa, where Portuguese territory ends, to Fuente Guinaldo, the
first Spanish village. The moment we crossed the
Spanish frontier, we noticed to our surprise that in the
very first hamlet a sudden change had occurred in the
language and garb of the inhabitants. On the Spanish
side the houses are kept extremely clean, and reveal a
state of comfort which is frequently missing in England.
The inhabitants wear a national dress which is at once
dramatic and picturesque, albeit it is worn only from the
frontier as far as Salamanca, and in a part of the kingdom
of Leon.

As I entered Guinaldo I admired the church, which is
so big that it would be a credit to many a town. The
churchyard was full of men, who, owing to the fact that
it was a holiday, were wearing their best clothes, and
amusing themselves with all kinds of games. One of
these games consisted in the throwing of a very heavy
iron bar, three feet long, which the men seized in the
middle and, after swaying their body from left to right
in order to increase the momentum as much as possible,
flung at a target. Is it not possible that this is a relic
of an old Roman or Saracenic warrior's game, which
was played with the javelin? My sudden appearance
attracted a large crowd. They surrounded me and asked
questions and shouted, until at last, in answer to my own
question, " *Adonde sta el Alcalde ?* " (Where is the
mayor?) the Alcalde himself stepped forward, and taking
me to his house, gave me a billet. I was lodged at a
widow's—a rotund, rosy-cheeked woman, with a reso-
lutely gloomy countenance—who showed me a pleasant

little room, and then, if you please, paid no further heed to me whatsoever. What a difference between the friendly, hospitable Portuguese and these disobliging Spaniards ! Everybody here is grave, monosyllabic, and gloomy ; not a soul inquired whether I wanted anything to eat or drink. At last, by dint of great pains, I succeeded in getting them to procure something for me at my own expense. Everything in the house was extremely clean and tidy and all the brassware was glittering. There were chairs and benches with backs to them round the fire, and on the fire itself were a number of small pots. My little room was very comfortably arranged, and covered with straw matting. On its white walls there hung a small mirror, a few pictures of the saints, an oxtail in which were stuck a few combs, and at the side of the extremely clean bed, a crucifix with a small china bowl under it full of holy water. Thus the devil could not get at me while I slept. In the evening a few of the village notabilities gathered round the kitchen fire, among whom there was an old fellow wearing gaiters, a blue coat with copper buttons as large as plates, and with a long Spanish rattan and black silk hair net, whose parrot-like face struck me particularly. There was also a German who came to see me. He had lived here for some time, was married and had a beautiful daughter ; but he behaved exactly like a Spanish peasant. He rejoiced in finding a fellow countryman in me. All the neighbours sat round the fire, solemn and grave, and now and again one of them would open his lips to discuss politics. The whole time they smoked cigarettes, which they rolled and lighted with a remarkable swagger ; and the man who rolled them handed them round after he had taken one or two puffs from them. All this made me feel very uncomfortable ; for of me and my needs no one took the smallest notice. At last I went to bed.

The regiment marched in on the following morning. On the 23rd I again moved forward across a wooded height, then over a large plain to a few sand hills, from the summit of which I saw the white towers of Ciudad Rodrigo, standing on the threshold of another large plain. Late in the afternoon I reached the beautiful bridge of seven arches that spans the Agueda River, on the banks of which, built upon solid sandstone, stands the proud and imposing city. A lofty tower, built of solid stone, with embrasures and Gothic buttresses, stands on the far side of the bridge, forming an abutment to the city wall. The road winds a short distance round this wall, and then leads through a large tower-crowned gate into the city. The streets seemed cleaner than those in Portuguese towns ; but the houses and churches bore a massive and gloomy aspect, and the heavy iron bars across their windows contributed not a little towards this effect. In short, the whole place bore the stamp of a certain Oriental or barbaric and heavy splendour, and made me feel quite uneasy.

I went to the town major and was billeted upon a well-to-do, or rather wealthy tailor, for he lived in a large house and kept a well-fed private chaplain. My room was a sort of dark alcove, lying off a corridor, so that I had to leave my door open if I wanted to see to write. The first evening I sat with the family round the brasero, and complained about my room. But they assured me there was no other to be had. This was a Spanish lie, for I had observed that the chaplain had several rooms, covered with good straw matting and filled with beautiful furniture, for himself alone. They asked me all kinds of questions, to which, owing to my unfamiliarity with the language, I was only able to reply in Portuguese. They left me in peace, therefore, and turned to the priest, who in this country is always an oracle. When they heard that I was a German from Hanover, they asked me where that country was, and whether it had any towns, and was inhabited by Christians. To this, with much affected importance, the chaplain replied for me as follows : ." Hanover is a country that lies between Denmark and Sweden. Like those two countries it is inhabited chiefly by heathens and heretics who worship Luther; that is why God has given them long winters and a barren soil—a miserable land ! For it has neither wine, oil, chestnuts, nor melons. The inhabitants do a little cattle-rearing and agriculture, but they are half wild.   Spain is a paradise in comparison ! "

The worthy tailor's family all made the sign of the cross and regarded me with horror.   Feeling angry, I wished to show the priest his mistake, but as I did not know the language I was obliged to content myself with violently shaking my head at him and laughing in his face.   My servant Pat had a much better billet, where my mule was also quartered.   I had to get him to cook my food, and bring it to my dark room, where with the help of a light, I ate it alone beside my brasero.

The regiment marched in and were equally bitter in their complaints about the unfriendliness of the inhabi-tants.*   My duties now gave me enough running about to do, and also the opportunity of seeing the town.   The streets are mostly narrow and have no foot-paths ; but they are clean and well-paved.   The costume of the ordinary citizen is a waistcoat with split sleeves, laced in front, pantaloons also laced down to the ankle, or pro-vided with small buttons from top to bottom, and their coats are like a short mantle, turned back to front, and thrown over their shoulders.   They also wear hats with low crowns, but enormous rims, and all their clothes, even their stockings, are of the same dark brown colour. Round their waists they wear a red sash.   How ludicrous the fellows look when they roam about in the dark in this garb !   They are like monstrous horned owls.   The meat market is disgusting, and shows how much bar-barism still requires rooting up in this country before it can lay claim to being fully civilised.   The butcher stands on a sort of scaffold six feet high, and when he has sawn off the raw and roughly handled meat, by pounds and half pounds, from the dead beast, he throws it down into the basket of the purchaser, who, though

---

* This contrasts strangely with Sir John Moore's own view. See his Diary, edited by Major-General Sir J. F. Maurice, K.C.B., Vol. II., p. 279, where, speaking of the advance into Spain, Moore writes on November 14th, 1808 : " No change, whether in the face of the country, in men and manners, can be greater than that immediately perceptible upon entering Spain from Portugal. The advantage is entirely on the side of the Spaniards." For a similar view to Moore's, see Robert Blakeney (*op cit.*), p. 27, and Oman (*op cit.*), Vol. I., p. 505, footnote.—Tr.

frequently skilful enough to catch it, as frequently allows it to fall and roll into the gutter. All the meat looks as if it came from animals who had died a natural death, and the butchers look exactly like the Scythian, who, at Apollo's order, flayed poor Marsyas alive ; or like the executioner depicted in the masterpieces of Spageoletti and Murillo, who performed the same operation on poor Bartholomew.

Colonels Roche and Lopez are here, in order to direct the march of the troops ; and to this end Mr. Ogilvie, an assistant war commissary, has been placed at their disposal. Thanks to my host, I have seen the latest newspapers from Madrid. According to them and the various rumours that are being circulated here, the French general, Dupont, was forced to surrender to the Spanish general, Castanos, and Reding at Andujar in Andalusia on the 19th July.* On the 25th and 28th July, King Joseph left Madrid and withdrew to Segovia, and at Saragossa the French had been forced to raise the siege after losing 49,000 men, and had been obliged to withdraw to a concentrated position on the Ebro, where they were awaiting reinforcements from the Pyrenees. It was said that their total force then consisted of only 40,000 men, but ever since October it had looked as if they intended to take the offensive. They first succeeded in surprising and taking prisoner a column consisting of 1,200 Spanish troops. The Spaniards had three armies. The one in Aragon, commanded by Palafox and Castanos, constituted the right wing ; the one in Estramadura under Cuesta formed the centre ; and the left, together with the troops from the island of Rügen, consisting of 8,671 men of the Marquis of Romana's corps, manœuvring towards Bilbao, combined with the armies of Galicia and Asturias, was commanded by General Blake. The French began their operations by advancing against General Blake, and after several sharp encounters, finally swept. him completely from the field of Somorosa on

---

* Although the two armies were engaged from about July 17th to the 22nd round Andujar and Baylen, it was at Baylen on the 22nd that the French laid down their arms.—Tr.

October 31st.* He retreated through Almaseda † on Espinosa, and on the 5th November he did indeed make a stand at Almaseda † ; but on the 10th and 11th he was again heavily attacked at Espinosa, and through his left wing giving way, the French seized the heights which covered his retreat, with the result that the Spanish army was wholly defeated and scattered. In his dispatches to the Junta, Blake praised the courage and endurance of his troops to the skies ! Eye-witnesses also declare that it was impossible for the poor devils, half naked, badly armed, starving and incompetently led as they were, to offer a steady resistance to an enemy like the French and their allies.

From this short sketch, the reader will be able to gather more or less how things stood at this time in Spain. The Spaniards rely entirely upon us, and after leading us into a most dreadful mess through their deceitful and mendacious promises, they run away and say : " Now try to get out of it as best you can ! " This is the general feeling, and it is shared even by cultivated and enlightened Spaniards. The people here have the cool effrontery to look upon the English troops as exotic animals, who have come to engage in a private fight with the French, and now that they are here all that the fine Spanish gentlemen have to do is to look on with their hands in their pockets. They do not regard us in the least as allies who are prepared to shed their blood for Spain ; they simply look upon us as heretics. In our billets it is as much as we can do to get a glass of water, and even that is given to us with a growling " *Ande usted en el coral al fuente !* " (Go and get it yourself). Why, only the other day there was an uproar in the town, because a few English soldiers had asked their landlords for a little salt. This is a fact ; but, truth to tell, the whole attitude of the people has made an extremely disagreeable impression upon us, and we think of the future with horror. On the 12th November General Moore

---

* Schaumann must mean Zornosa where Blake suffered a bad defeat on October 31st, 1808.—Tr.

† Does Schaumann mean Valmaceda ?—Tr.

passed through here, and he is said to have looked very much displeased.*

At last, after having spent three very tiresome days here, marching orders arrived, thank God ! On the 26th November we had to exchange the bullock carts we had brought with us for new ones. The Spanish bullock drivers, however, were not so loyal as the Portuguese ; for many of the former deserted at once and left their bullocks in the lurch. Quartermaster Smith and I were very angry about this, for we had to run our legs off almost to pester the Spanish authorities before we could get others. Out of revenge we sold the bullocks and the carts to a butcher, who had a daughter who was so beautiful that, as Smith laughingly assured me afterwards, I stood before her quite a long time utterly speechless. We divided the spoil, and my share was all the more welcome to me, as I hadn't a penny to bless myself with. " *C'est la fortune de guerre,*" we cried. The detachment which was despatched ahead for billeting purposes was commanded to accompany us as a protecting escort.

At about midday on a cold, misty and frosty morning, I left Ciudad Rodrigo. Once again I passed through the ancient, strongly built and tower-crowned gate. The fortifications of this town have the appearance of being very strong, and were manned at that time by a militia consisting of a corps of young men armed with English muskets and good Toledo swords. Their behaviour on sentry-go was very theatrical, or rather romantic. The country round the town appears to be rich in corn and pasture land, and the river on which the town stands flows into the Duro. Half a legua from the town we got into a sloping, rugged ravine, where the road ran alongside of a mountain stream, and then across the top of a lofty chalk hill through San Spirito, San Minor, to Martin del Rio. On the way a young Spaniard attached himself to our party, and was most communicative and confiding. He showed me a paper, from which it appeared that he was

* *Cp.* p. 68, *ante.*

on his way to join a certain Spanish corps—which I cannot now remember—as a volunteer.   He was full of praise for the English, and extolled the fine workmanship of the light infantry musket, which the corporal of my escort, who belonged to the light flank company, had slung over his shoulder by the strap.   When we got into billets— for safety's sake we all remained indoors—this Spaniard walked in with us, sat down beside the kitchen fire, and let the landlady plait and comb his hair, and behaved in the most gentle and affable manner.   As we were all freezing, we also sat round the fire.   After a while, the Spaniard stood up, and, going out, did not return. Shortly afterwards one of the men happened to go out into the hall, and the first thing he saw was that the corporal's cartridge box was lying on the floor empty, and that his musket had vanished !   We immediately gave the fellow chase, but in vain !   The poor corporal, a young and very decent fellow, with great ambitions, was mad with fury ; but what good did that do ?   From that moment we regarded all Spaniards as born thieves and false to the core ;   and subsequent experience never made me repent this hasty judgment.

On the morning of the 28th the bullock carts filed past their pay commissary, and as each one went by he threw it a Spanish dollar.   This performance took place every morning, and looked very funny.   We came to a village and halted.   My hosts were a family of genuine Spanish peasants, well-to-do, and rather pompous.   The kitchen was the principal living-room, and was consequently very clean and well kept.   On one side of the fire sat the land-lord, with his large round hat on his head, smoking cigarettes with a good deal of swagger.   He was thought-ful, gloomy, and as dumb as a fish.   On the other side the landlady ditto.   Only when the dog approached the fire did they open their lips to say " Ssh ! "   An ugly girl was cooking, and allowed a lad, who was sitting behind her, to flirt with her the while.   The son, a lout of a fellow about twenty-four years old, lay on a bench asleep.   Round the fire there stood all kinds of small, elongated pots, and one larger one, all secured against falling by means of iron supports which were placed behind them. As the number of pots is the measure of prosperity, my landlord looked proudly down upon the array of vessels.

While they were eating they paid not the slightest heed either to me or to their son. A German peasant would at least have said, "Would you like a bite as well?" Suddenly there was a most alarming noise outside. The son sprang up and went out, but soon returned rather downcast, and implored my help against some highlanders who had broken into the fowl-house. Very coldly I replied to him, "How can you expect me to stand by you, when you treat us English, who are your allies, so badly? You don't even give us a glass of water when we are thirsty. What do I care about your fowls, therefore? Let them go to the devil? *Demonio Caraxo !* " (dirty dogs). Looking very much ashamed, the lout stood there, not daring to contradict me. Proudly the old man now lifted up his voice and said : " *Hijo mio ! Que levan los gallinas, que levan ! No es por nosotros cosa de gran importancia, que las levan, hijo mio !* "* Then the old woman crossed herself and added : " *Valganos Dios !* " † When they had finished their meal both of them belched most violently, and ordering water, a huge glass was brought to them, which must have contained at least a quart. Each of them emptied this vessel at one draught, and then returning to the fire, they smoked cigarettes. Then the son had his meal, and was followed by the maidservant, the farm labourer and the dog. My servant Pat watched all this with his eyes starting out of his head. At last he lost all patience. I had given him some money with which to buy food. When, therefore, he asked my hosts to sell him a little ham and a few eggs, and they replied that he could go into the village to fetch them, he swore by St. Patrick that he would make a change in my affairs ; for the fellow was so fond of me that he quickly grew indignant if he thought that I was not being sufficiently honoured. Slap bang ! went his fists against the son,

* " Son of mine, they have taken away the fowls ! But it doesn't matter very much to us."—Tʀ.
† " God help us ! "—Tʀ.

the farmhand and the maidservant, who were still eating, and in a moment the small table was overturned and they and their stools and all were rolling on the floor.   Then he stood the table up again in front of me, took a plate from the dresser, and demanded a clean table-cloth, knife and fork.   He asked for these articles first in English ; then, as they did not seem to understand, he repeated his demands in Irish and Gaelic—which made me die to laugh—and then, finally, in his rage he drew his bayonet, at which stage I was bound to interfere.   Amid much grumbling they now gave us what we wanted in exchange for cash, and we set to, and began roasting and baking, while the Spaniards, for their part, did not fail to gape with astonishment, not only at our methods of cooking and eating, but also at the quantities of wine we drank.   On the following morning the peasant and his wife were drinking chocolate and eating toast by their fireside, when probably remembering my speech of the day before, the fellow was polite enough to offer me a cup, and we parted friends.

On the 29th of November we pushed on towards Siete Carreros, and went through a number of woods of evergreen oak, in which I encountered large herds of swine. The way in which the acorn crop is collected here is very strange.   The swineherd walks in front, armed with a long stick, at the end of which another stick is fixed, rather like a threshing flail.   He strikes this instrument right and left against the oak trees, in rhythmic fashion, and thus causes the sweet and ripe acorns, which make excellent fattening, to fall in hundreds.   The black troops instinctively follow this fellow, as the sucking pig follows the sow, and they show their delight by sonorous grunts and by rapidly wagging their little corkscrew tails.   And thus it goes on from tree to tree, the whole crowd veiled by a cloud of dust.   We also went by a lovely peasant farm, behind which there were a few turkeys running free. Pat, for whom I had hired a mule, and who sat thereon, wedged in between my valise and his knapsack, with his musket slung over his shoulder, dismounted like a flash, and killed one of the birds and stuffed it into his bag before I could upbraid him for his conduct.

I reached Siete Carreros early, and found the provisions all ready and in order. My own quarters, however, which were in a huge house with enormous stables and mule sheds, was not in order, for when I walked into the kitchen with my escort, I found that the fire that burned in the middle of the room was surrounded by muleteers, the hostess, an old grandmother who was lousing the children, and the servantmaids. Nobody made way for me. Nobody uttered a friendly word. The paymaster of our regiment who had arrived before me, and who wanted to cook some chocolate, had not succeeded in getting them to give him the chocolate saucepan, or to let him come near the fire. I said I wanted to buy a little ham or sausage, both of which in this pig-fattening district are extremely plentiful and of excellent quality, while specimens of both hung over the mantelpiece. "*No se vende*" (We sell nothing here), was the reply. I therefore asked one of the servantmaids to go into the village to buy some for me. "Go and fetch it yourself!" was the insolent reply.

Meanwhile a small detachment of the 60th Jägers marched through, escorting a convoy of baggage, women and children. My billet was the last house in the village, and the yard was full of chickens. In a moment there was a wild outcry. The 60th, all Germans, had killed some of the fowls and taken them away with them. My hosts and some of the muleteers wanted to attack one of the soldiers. With cold-blooded phlegm, however, this man dropped on one knee and raised his musket to his shoulder, whereupon at least twenty of the Spaniards fled for their lives. My hostess came to us for help. "*No se vende*," was my reply, and she understood me. We now lost patience, and with many harsh words and various digs in the ribs, we made room for ourselves, while the Spaniards set up loud cries for help. The chocolate saucepans, which are to be found in every well-to-do peasant farmhouse, were placed on the fire; some ham and eggs were obtained with the assistance of the mayor, and breakfast was got ready. This mayor was a decent fellow, and was most indignant at the behaviour of my landlady. The landlord and his farm hands were not at home, but busy building a bridge on the high road. Meanwhile I gave my landlady to understand that I would have my revenge, and that as I did not intend to stay, I proposed to hand my billet over to a grenadier company. She seemed to be very much startled at this, and after offering me a very fine room with a clean bed, which the paymaster subsequently appropriated, she declared herself ready to do anything I wanted. " It is too late now ! " I replied defiantly, and went to meet my regiment.

My friend, Captain Makilla, just happened to be stand- ing in front of his company of grenadiers, when, with a loud voice I deliberately described the way I had been treated at my billet, and begged him to quarter his men there. My request was granted, my billet was given to the sergeant, and the whole company was marched into the house, and a portion into the kitchen. Hardly had the men laid down their muskets, however, than there was the most appalling uproar, and when I pushed my way in to see what had happened, several sausages had already been removed from the chimney. " The cure is begin- ning to work," I thought, and forthwith ordered my men to pack and saddle up. Having finished all my prepara- tions, I was just about to mount my mule, when the land- lady, with her hair all falling about her face and neck, came out shrieking, while the impertinent servantmaid of whom I have spoken, seized my stirrup in a familiar manner and assured me that from that moment she would go out into the village for me and get me as many eggs and as much ham as I wanted—at my expense, of course —if only I would stay and turn the grenadiers out. I laughed in her face. " *Ande usted a ciento mil Diabos malditos !* "* was my reply, as I dug my spurs into my mule and rode away.

<hr />

" Be damned to you. Go to the devil ! "

Chapter 6

Quarters in Salamanca—Mr. Augustus gives up the 32nd Regiment and is sent to Ledesma—Duties in Ledesma—Spanish Patriotism—General Beresford—Bound for Zamora.

ON the 30th November, after we had almost overslept ourselves, we continued our journey. As the Colonel wished me to reach Salamanca a day before the regiment, I left my escort behind, took a guide, and riding on ahead, at last reached the bridge at Salamanca in the moonlight, after a very long march. It was ten o'clock at night. I watered my mule in the river, and rode through the gate of the town, where, after exhaustive inquiries, I at length found a man who showed me the house of the assistant quartermaster-general, who allotted billets. This officer was most comfortably installed beside a brasero in a magnificent room, and was reading a book, while at his side there stood a bottle of wine and a dish of roast chestnuts. I asked him for a good billet. "You must take your chance, sir," was his reply, and dipping his hand into a bag of billets as if we were at a lottery, drew mine forth in a perfectly haphazard manner. It turned out to be a bad draw, for the house, from basement to attics, was full of soldiers. There was only one smoky attic kitchen free, and this was on the fourth story and occupied by an old woman not unlike the witch of Endor. I took possession of this place. At first the old dragon who lived in this inferno spat fire and flames ; when, however, she saw my money, she grew more tame ; and by the time I had put some wine and a cigar between her jaws, she became quite friendly and talkative. My usual food in these parts, consisting of chocolate, ham, roast pork—the loin—and onions, was procured and prepared for me at the cost of great pains— for it was midnight—by the witch herself ; whereupon wrapping myself in my cloak, I laid myself down on the bare floor close to the fire, and in spite of the fleas and bugs, and the cries of the old woman, who was singing a litany to the Virgin Mary, I was so tired that I was soon asleep.

On the following morning I reported myself to the Commissary-General, Kennedy, and then proceeded to wander about the town, partly in order to despatch my duties for the regiment, and partly in order to see the sights. Almost the whole of the English army was here, and in a beautiful square, surrounded by magnificent buildings, I witnessed a grand parade. One sees nothing but red coats in all the streets. Our regiment will be the last to march in.

The inhabitants do not inspire us with much enthusiasm. They seem cold and parched, like the environs of their town. The national costume is scarcely worn, and among the upper classes the cut of the clothes is more or less what used to be the fashion in France about twenty years ago.

The army here numbers only about 13,000 men, and is quartered in monasteries and other religious institutions in and around the town. Twice daily it is marched out regiment by regiment on to the esplanade outside the town, and now that the men have recovered from their hardships and fatigue they look most formidable. The strictest discipline is maintained, and cases of drunkenness are rare. Although the country for miles around is occupied by our pickets, no French soldier has been seen anywhere near ; and it is therefore supposed that Bonaparte is pretending not to have noticed our movements, in order to clear the Spaniards out of the way first, and then take possession of the capital. After that it will certainly be our turn !

Not being able to stand it any longer with the old witch, a commissary who was in charge of the meat stores, put me up at his quarters, and also found a place for my mule in his stables. On the following morning, the 2nd December, I presented myself before the Commissary-General, and was informed that my work with the 32nd Regiment having come to an end, I was to get ready to take up other duties, and go to Ledesma immediately, and also that in the office of Mr. Commissary Bell I should be given an interpreter. I therefore went thither. As they were unable to let me have Mr. Nesbit, who was the interpreter intended for me, I was given another one, a Portuguese called Senhor Antonio Falludo. But he spoke neither English nor German. " A fine interpreter this ! " I thought, but all the same, I had picked up enough Portuguese to make myself understood by him. Truth to tell, he was not in the least necessary to me ; but as he struck me as being a cheerful sort of customer, I gladly took him at John Bull's expense as a sort of companion. The following day, after I had taken leave of the 32nd Regiment, I left the famous town of Salamanca and not without deep regret, for there was still a good deal to be seen there. But a soldier has no permanent billet— the city's life, he has to pass it by—so quick march !

At midday on the morrow we reached Ledesma, a town standing upon the rocky banks of the River Tormes surrounded by an old wall, and with a massive bridge leading to a fortified gate built in the form of an arch ; and I was billeted at the house of a young married couple who were very friendly to me.

The bad news which I had heard in Ciudad Rodrigo was confirmed. The French having received considerable reinforcements across the Pyrenees, had completely defeated General Cuesta's army of 14,000 men at Burgos on the 10th November.* A rumour is already current that we shall have to retreat on Portugal. General Baird, who is marching from Corunna, is said to have turned round and halted with the heavy guns and army stores at Almeida and Ciudad Rodrigo. The French are said to be very strong in cavalry. A fortnight ago they carried out a reconnaissance with 1,200 men in Valladolid, and raised a contribution from that town. We have not much cavalry with us, only the 3rd Hussars of the Legion and the English 10th and 18th Hussars ; and of these, all except two squadrons have marched to Badajos with General Hope. Poor General Moore is, therefore, in a parlous plight, and the more one sees of the Spaniards the more discouraged one gets. Everything that has been so blatantly trumpeted in the papers about their

* This would appear to be the battle of Gamonal, at which the Spanish troops were commanded by the Conde de Belvedere.—TR.

enthusiasm, their great armies and the stampede to join them, and their spirit of self-sacrifice, is simply lies. It often looks as if Spain were not even willing to defend herself.   In all the hamlets, villages and towns the inhabitants, wrapped in their brown cloaks, lounge about in their hundreds, completely apathetic, indifferent and gloomy, and sunk in utter idleness.   Is this the daring patriotic and impetuous race about which the Press has raved so bombastically ?   It seems to me as if the people here loathe us as much as they do the French, and would gladly be free of us both.   Sunk into inactivity, they wish we would mutually break each other's necks.

According to the latest news, the Spaniards under Castanos and Palafox appear to have suffered a bloody defeat at Tudela.   The officers of Beresford's Brigade entertain grave doubts regarding our success.   Owing to our lack of cavalry we cannot even reconnoitre properly. General Hope, with his infantry division, cavalry and artillery, will have reached the Escurial by this time, but it is feared that he will be cut off ;   then woe to us ! Many are blaming General Moore very much for having allowed all his cavalry and artillery under General Hope to go ; but they forget that it would have been impossible, particularly for the latter, to march along the roads which we took under General Moore's command.*   As we had reckoned upon the Spanish armies holding together and covering the concentration of Hope's and Moore's troops, the fact that the Spaniards have already been annihilated has so upset our plans that no one now knows what will happen.   It is clear that we are in a very critical position.   It would appear that orders have been sent to General Baird to retreat on Corunna, and that we are to return to Portugal.   This, however, would simply make the Spaniards desperate ;   the more enlightened among them have this good point, that they do not try to conceal

* It will be remembered that General Moore divided his army and sent General Hope with one column by the Tagus, while the other marched under his own personal command by Almeida and Ciudad Rodrigo.   The artillery and cavalry were thus separated from the rest of the Army and went by the southern road, because the roads north of the Tagus were considered impracticable for these arms.   This Moore discovered to be an error only when it was too late.—TR.

their disasters, but discuss them coldly and thoughtfully, and stake all their hopes for the future upon us. According to the Madrid newspapers, the worthy old Count of Florida-Blanca has been made the head of the Central Junta. In our general orders we are commanded to respect and not to scoff at the religious and other peculiarities of the Spaniards. All of us have also had to stick the Spanish national cockade in our hats. It is scarlet, and the words " *Viva Fernando settimo* " are stamped in gold upon it. This cockade is also worn by the Spanish, rich and poor alike ; but apart from this patriotic sign everything is as quiet as in the palmiest days of peace. There is no energy, activity, military organisation, or effort towards a general armament to be seen. As Shakespeare says, " Everything dead, flat and unprofitable ! " *

I am worried to death here by the workmen I employ, for although they are well paid for unloading, weighing, storing and again loading up the biscuits, they nevertheless throw everything down and run away—no matter how urgent the work may be—the moment the bell rings for morning mass, whenever there is a Church festival, a procession, or when the Blessed Sacrament is being taken to the sick, when their luncheon hour comes round, or when they want to rest. And there is no genuine piety beneath all this, but only habit and indolence. No kind of appeal or threat will induce them to return before they think they will.

I was summoned before Brigadier-General Beresford to-day. He was leaning over a table covered with maps, and seemed to be in a very bad temper. He wanted to have a list of my supplies. I gave it to him and seized the opportunity in order to ask him whether he would appoint two officers to form a Board of Survey for the inspection of my lame mule with its cloven hoof, and to give me a certificate for it. For the mule was not my own, but public property, and by this means I hoped to be able to buy another one. He answered me very roughly that he

---

* Schaumann is thinking of the lines in " Hamlet " (Act I. Sc. 2) :

   " How weary, stale, flat, and unprofitable,
   Seem to me all the uses of this world ! "—Tr.

could convene no Board for that purpose. Then, in order to put him in a good temper I took the liberty of pointing to his maps, and of remarking that if he took a number of pins and dipped their heads in red, black, green or blue sealing wax, or used any other means for distinguishing them, and then stuck them into the maps, he would find that a very clear and pleasant way of indicating the position of the enemy's army and our own, as also of showing the different corps, the headquarters and the marches and flank movements, while it would also enable him to effect all the changes that occurred, and thus facilitate the task of forming a general view. He looked me up and down : " I don't want your advice, sir ; mind your own business, and take yourself off this instant ! " he snorted angrily, showing his enormous face and his squint-eyed glance ; and I quickly rushed from the room.*

Thanks to good food and plenty of rest, my large mule had completely recovered, and was fat and glossy. And the miller outside the town, who saw it in this condition when it was ridden out to be watered, was very much taken with it. He could not see that it had a cloven hoof for after a long rest it never showed any signs of lameness. He wanted to buy. I told him to come to see me. The cleft in the hoof was now hastily stopped up with cobbler's wax and smeared over with blacking, while the other hoof was made very glossy and clean. He rode it to and fro for a little while, and we settled the bargain for 100 Spanish dollars. It was so unusually large and strong that if it had not had that cloven hoof it would have been worth 300 dollars. The man looked as if he thought he had gulled an Englishman. How he will open his eyes, however, when one day at the smithy the cloven hoof is disclosed ! *Mundus vult decipi, ergo decipiatur !*

General Hope appears to have come to Salamanca on the 4th December, *viâ* Alba de Tormes, and to have succeeded in joining up with General Moore's advanced guard. He was obliged to go through Avila, and Villa

---

* Beresford, of whom Wellington said that " he alone [of the Peninsular generals] could feed an army," could hardly be expected to welcome advice from a commissary.—Tr.

Castrini in order to avoid the French cavalry. Thereupon the enemy occupied Segovia, and under cover of a heavy mist stormed the Somosierra Pass, took it, and drove General Don St. Juan from the position on the 29th November.* Then the French left the Escurial and entered Madrid. After a French courier, who had been seized by General Hope's troops in the Escurial, had been sent to General Moore, a grand council of war was held at Salamanca. According to all accounts, other plans have been adopted, and the retreat on Portugal has been abandoned. The French private letters and newspapers which the captured courier carried are, however, said to have been full of the most extravagant and ludicrous nonsense. According to them we are lost, and a number of French officers in Bayonne are said to be bewailing the fact that they cannot be present when we are crushed, overthrown, and all our baggage is plundered. In one letter the writer requests his friend to secure him a couple of fine English officers' chargers. Things seem to have gone pretty badly in Madrid when the French entered the city. To-day, the 9th December, Mr. Mackenzie, the commissary, passed through here and ordered me to go to Zamora to assist Mr. Kearney, who is the commissary there. I therefore made all my arrangements, handed over, and left on the 10th. I stayed the night in Zamayon and reached Zamora at about 12 a.m. on the following day.

* The actual passage of the Somosierra, which was effected by the troops under Napoleon's own command, took place on the 30th November.—Tr.

Chapter 7

MR. MACKENZIE had already reached Zamora, and seemed very much annoyed that I should arrive so late. I replied rather warmly that I did not possess such excellent English horses as he did, and could not therefore travel so quickly ; also that I had a good deal to hand over in Ledesma, and otherwise was quite well aware of my duties. This answer vexed him so much that when I had gone it appears he said to Kennedy that I seemed to be an impertinent fellow, on whom he would have to keep a tight hand. For a long time after that I could not understand Kearney's strange behaviour towards me, until at last, overwhelmed by my strict attention to duty, my industry and my careful observance of his orders, he had to admit that he himself, as well as Mr. Mackenzie, had been mistaken in me after all. I was billeted upon a well-to-do and friendly old gentleman, who lived alone with his wife and two pretty daughters.

Our business here consisted in baking biscuits, for which purpose an enormous number of women were employed and many of the bakers' ovens in the town requisitioned. The biscuits when baked, were stored in an empty monastery, which towards the end, we filled up completely. A number of detachments also passed through the town, and we had to give them supplies of victuals. All this gave us plenty to do. Never have I seen such beautiful biscuits as we made here with bolted wheat flour. I may mention that the Spaniards only eat bread that has been made with fine bolted wheat flour. The biscuits were as large as pancakes, and their outsides of a glossy golden colour, while inside they were as white as snow. They were really delicious.

Owing to the capitulation prepared by the Prince of Castelfranco and Don Thomas Morla, Madrid was surrendered to the French on the 12th December, 1808.* Some said that this happened through the treachery of the two gentlemen concerned, for the captain-general, together with a number of officers of high rank, refused to sign the capitulation, but left Madrid.   Everybody pities General Moore and the critical position in which he has been placed by the stubborn attitude of the British Ministry, which continues to give a wholly sympathetic hearing to the lies and insinuations of the Spanish Junta, and Mr. Frere, the British Government's representative on that body.   As the result, in the first place, of his fatally compromising mission to Sweden, whence, owing to the mad demands of the Swedish King, he was obliged to withdraw ; secondly, of the difficult command which has been given to him here, and thirdly, of the fact that the despatches from the Spaniards receive more credence than our own, General Moore is said to be very much at loggerheads with Lord Castlereagh.   Sir John Moore is respected everywhere because of his high sense of honour, his jealousy of his country's fame, his great knowledge, and the warmth of his feelings.   In addition he is a brave and experienced soldier and a perfect gentleman.   But what can he do with his small army against the French ?   It appears that the army is to march to Valladolid, for no further purpose can be served by lying inactive at Salamanca any longer.   Several detachments pass through here daily, and we get to know a great deal from them.   Our cavalry, under Lord Paget, passed through here the other day, and seems to have opened the war, as far as our side is concerned, by causing a French cavalry foraging party to be attacked at Rueda by the 18th Hussars under Brigadier-General Stewart.   They made thirty-five prisoners, and left sixteen dead on the field, including a major.†

On the 15th December the headquarters of our army moved from Salamanca *via* Calizal and Abejoz‡ to Toro. As the result of an intercepted dispatch, the plan to

---

* On the 4th to be more accurate.—Tʀ.
† Napier speaks of fifty French infantry and thirty dragoons in the engagement, almost all of whom were either killed or taken prisoner.—Tʀ.
‡ Does Schaumann mean Canizal and Alaejos ?—Tʀ.

march to Valladolid has been abandoned, and we are now marching to Sahagun to attack the Duke of Dalmatia.

The army will march westwards and headquarters are to be in Castronueva.   Every moment we receive letters from the Commissary-General, Kennedy, who asks us to go on quietly baking, and assures us he will let us know in good time if there is any danger.   It is beginning to be very cold, and ice is forming on the water in the gutters. In the monastery where the biscuits are stored my fingers and feet often get quite frozen when I have to stand for hours on the cold stones with my notebook in my hand, receiving ship's biscuits and having them weighed (about 25,000 lbs. a day).   But then I console myself with the pleasant prospect of a comfortable evening beside a warm brasero.   I also pity very much indeed the unfortunate detachments of troops who have to bivouac at night among carts and other vehicles in the open streets or on public squares.   Several infantry regiments have marched through here towards Toro.

I was standing at the corner of a large building watching one of them pass by, when I saw a clumsy old coach, of the kind that was used in the year 1701, drawn by four mules in bright harness, with footmen in large hats and blue jackets hanging on behind, roll heavily up to the door of the building and pull up.   The footmen sprang to the ground, opened the coach door, and with the help of two *famuli* who were sitting inside, drew out a short, round, little body of fat wrapped entirely in violet silk, with a cloak on, and a hat opened on both sides and lined with silk, and dragged it, amid much croaking and groaning, up the steps of the palace, and sat it down in a vast upholstered chair standing on a large balcony built at the corner of the house.   As I found it difficult to decide whether the lump of fat in violet silk was a pig or an old woman, I made inquiries and was told it was the bishop, who, tormented by pangs of curiosity, wished to have a look at some English soldiers.   Up on the balcony he was received by a crowd of priests and young seminarists, whom he had probably ordered to be there, so that when the English troops went by, they might do the honours, and shout " *Viva, viva los Ingleses !* " And, indeed, they discharged this duty faithfully ; for they yelled as if they were being roasted on the spit. But John Bull, displeased by the reception he had been given in Spain, looked angrily up at the bishop, and passed sullenly, silently, mutely, and with warlike majesty on his way, which greatly surprised the old boy.

Meanwhile, I have not failed to see to my own personal welfare. I have bought myself a couple of pistols curiously wrought with inlaid silver in the Saracen style ; I have decked out my harness, had a strong and warm pair of riding breeches made, and have also got my mule into the most excellent fettle. He won't leave me in the lurch when we start marching. And we are certain to march now, and possibly under the most dreadful conditions. Otherwise I amuse myself as best I can. In a café here the landlord's son plays the violin so extraordinarily well —a rare occurrence in Spain—that I often go there and get him to play. I have also had a little adventure with a very beautiful Spanish lady who lives with a maid-servant in a small house on the market-place. Thither I go every evening at dusk. But the beginning, the middle and the end of this adventure remain locked up in my heart.

On the 17th December an officer came from Ciudad Rodrigo and wanted to go on to headquarters. He announced the arrival of a large convoy of carts bearing money and clothes for our army. We told him that he would have been wise to remain where he was, for probably his convoy would no longer be able to join up with the army, which was already in motion. Fat General Hamilton of the wagon train has also turned up here with his useless wagon corps. Everybody is beginning to move. The people in the town have grown uneasy and have formed a Junta to which we have been invited. The defence of the town is being considered. General Hamilton, who was offered the command, exclaimed in a great rage that they were to leave him alone, and that he was not going to let himself be besieged here with his wagon train.

To-day, the 19th December, Captain Waters arrived from headquarters, to see whether, and by what means, the place could be defended in case of need. He conferred with the Junta and inspected the walls and ramparts. According to the latest news our cavalry have carried out two brilliant skirmishes. Before the advanced guard reached Sahagun, Lord Paget, who was on his way thither from Mayorga, had ascertained that six or seven hundred of the French cavalry were there.* At four o'clock in the morning he broke cover in order to fall upon them. Unfortunately a patrol of the enemy caught sight of the English beforehand, and galloping into the town, gave the alarm to the French, who sallied forth and took up their position behind some vineyards, in order that the English horses might fall over the vine branches and roots. After a few pistol shots had been exchanged, however, Lord Paget charged at them with the 10th and 15th Hussars,† and the English horses and troopers were so far superior to the French that the greater part of the latter were literally rolled over, so that both men and riders were left lying with their legs in the air. Another brilliant affair was the taking of the fifty large carts laden with fine merino wool for France, by the 18th Hussars. The wool was brought into Salamanca in order to be despatched thence as booty to Portugal, where it will be in safety. A Spanish officer has also arrived here as a spy, but as he is ill he cannot go on to our headquarters. The Junta has accordingly had several sittings, and to-day I was obliged to sit up until one o'clock in the morning in order to transcribe a long report made by this officer, which Kearney translated into English, as it had to be sent that same night by special messenger. Things look bad. Bonaparte is forming three armies : one to amuse and then to crush us, another in order to cut our way off across the mountains from Leon through Spain to Corunna, and

---

* Napier says that the number was 600.—TR.

† Napier says that only 400 of the 15th were engaged (*op. cit.*, Book IV., Chap. IV.). As a matter of fact, the 10th under General Slade were scouring the town. The result, according to Napier, was a loss to the enemy of 20 killed, and 2 lieutenant-colonels, 11 other officers, and 154 men taken prisoner. Oman (*op. cit.*, Vol. I., p. 536) gives 157 men prisoner, otherwise his figures agree with Napier's.—TR.

another to stop our retreat into Portugal through Avila.
A charming plan !

On December 26th, at three o'clock, Kearney had me
called up, and I had to go to see him.   Delightful news !
General Moore has sent messenger after messenger to
General Romana, to tell him to send along the great
Spanish armies that have been promised, so that they may
join up with the English forces.   But Romana only
replies that the great Spanish armies have all been beaten
and scattered ; of the supposed 80,000 men he has only
10,000, chiefly recruits, and he therefore advises a speedy
retreat.   Commissary-General Kennedy has written to
say that we should hold ourselves in readiness to depart,
cease baking, and try to save as much of the stores as
possible.   Accordingly all vehicles were requisitioned
this morning, laden with biscuit, and despatched to
Benevente.   We were also summoned by the Junta, and
the walls, the towers, the ramparts, and all the guns—
most of them useless, were inspected *in corpore*.   The
result is that as soon as the English have evacuated the
district, the town will not attempt to hold out against a
proper siege, but will keep the bridge gate barricaded
until the English stores have been transported to Benevente.   I am on my legs night and day, and am utterly sick
and tired of this constant state of commotion.   The English
army has begun its retreat.   Everybody is leaving us.
We alone are forced to remain behind, for our instructions
are that so long as there are stores in the place we are not
to move until the French are within a mile of the town.

General Hamilton took his departure to-day.   When
he left his horse for a moment tied up with the other
officers' horses outside our office to-day, in order to settle
something with us, some Spanish loafers, who were idling
and staring about the place, stole the beautiful pistols
from his wallets.   Captain Inglis, paymaster, I believe,
of the 1st or 2nd Battalion of the King's German Legion,
also rode up here early this morning and reported that
the French were in Salamanca, twelve leguas from here.
This officer had been ordered to transport the fine spoil,
consisting of fifty cartloads of wool, to Portugal.   On

reaching Salamanca, however, the muleteers assured him that their beasts were tired, and that he had better exchange them for others there. He was stupid enough to agree to this, and allowed the wool to be unloaded. But while other carts were being procured, the advanced guard of the French army suddenly appeared outside the town ; they took the wool, and Mr. Inglis, being obliged to flee, came to us.

I was invited by Mr. Kearney's landlord to spend the evening of Christmas Day with his family. I was in a rather sorrowful and solemn mood, for my thoughts were with the dear homeland. I was full of pleasant recollections of my youth, when this was the most joyful day of the whole year. No other day binds the family together with closer ties of affection. And here I now stand, far away from all those I love, and the Spaniards have no idea how these hours, with all their sacred evening colouring, gild the glowing clouds for me with tender memories. There were many ladies present. We joked and laughed round the brasero, and then a very simple supper was served. But the essentially Spanish part of the feast, or Christmas dessert, consisted of a huge platter of roast chestnuts, wine, and a large cake of sugar and almonds. This was baked as hard as a rock, and pieces had to be broken from it with a knife and hammer. That was all ! How different from the Christmas evenings and the Christmas trees in Germany ! But we were all very happy, and it was very late when we separated.

A messenger arrived on the 28th December : we are to leave this place the moment we hear that we are no longer safe. Meanwhile we are to despatch all the biscuits we can to Benevente. Our steeds are therefore standing, day and night, saddled and packed. Early in the morning Mr. Kearney summoned all those people who had helped in the baking to congregate in the street in front of his window, in order that he might pay and dismiss them. He placed a large bag full of piastres on the table, spread out a list which I had compiled, took two Spaniards of the Junta as witnesses, and then proceeded to call out the names. And every time one of the crowd cried, " *Son io !* " or " *A qui sta !* " in answer to his name, his money was thrown through the lattice into the street.   There were so many people to be paid that we could not wait to be ceremonious about it.

At four in the afternoon the Junta informed us that they had news that a large French patrol of chasseurs were on their way from Salamanca to Zamora.   Then the *Corregidor* (the chief magistrate) was called, and the remaining stores of biscuits still lying in the monastery (about 200,000 lbs., all of which ultimately fell into enemy hands) were solemnly handed over to his keeping ; he even had to give a receipt for the key of the monastery door.· A good deal remained to be done.   Several carts full of biscuits were ordered to march ahead, with our valises strapped upon them.   And thus the time flew by like lightning, when a cry arose in the town : " The French are on the bridge ! "   At the same time the Junta informed us that it was now really high time for us to be off.   In great haste we bestrode our steeds, and amid a general cry of " *Viva, viva los Ingleses !* "—for we had many friends here—we dashed forward at a gallop, amid a cloud of dust and sparks, and much snorting, both of horse and rider.   At the corner of a street, however, there stood a confounded barrow, which made my horse plunge so violently that I was knocked insensible.   I was helped on again, and apart from a few bruises was not hurt, only my watch-glass and the water-bottle on my saddle being broken.   Then, hardly had we reached the gate of the town, than Kearney remembered having left a bag full of gold in the drawer of his table.   We therefore halted, and with much wailing and gnashing of teeth, his poor servant, Juan, a Spaniard, was obliged to go back. However, he soon returned safely with the bag, and we went on.   Night came on, and it began to rain.   It was late when we halted at Pedreita* three or four leguas from Zamora, and we were so tired after the exertions of the day that we resolved to have something to eat here, and rest awhile.   We assumed that they would not have let the French into Zamora before nightfall, and that by then

* Piedrahita ?—Tr.

the latter would have been too tired to pursue us at once. We therefore had a cold meal, and laying ourselves in the straw, slept peacefully. We had decided to start off again at midnight, but the exertions of the previous day had so much fatigued us that we overslept ourselves, and the dawn was already breaking when we awoke. While the horses were being saddled we quietly drank our chocolate, and then mounted.

When we reached Ariego, two miles from our night quarters, we overtook twenty-five of the carts which we had sent off on the previous day laden with biscuit and other impedimenta, or with the sick, or English soldiers' wives, and we urged the drivers to hurry up. When we reached Lagranja, a mile further on, we were just riding up a hill when we heard some shots in the rear. We quickly turned our horses, and looked back into the plain, and there, with the help of Mr. Kearney's telescope, we distinctly saw the French chasseurs, with shining sabres, rounding up and capturing the whole convoy. These devils could only have been a few minutes too late, otherwise they would have set about us as well in our night quarters. We therefore spurred our horses, and off we went through St. Antonio, to La Barca, a mile further on, where we crossed some water, and warning the ferryman who took us across of the proximity of the French, advised him to sink his ferry and take to his heels. We were then only a mile from Benevente.

The first view we got of Benevente was extremely picturesque, and the moment we entered the town, we saw that it was full of the most wonderful things. By dint of much effort and noise we at last got our billets from the Junta, which was crammed full of soldiers of all ranks. My host, an amiable *bourgeois*, was a nice, pleasant man. The town is almost as big as Toro, and lies on an eminence one mile north of the bridge over the Esla.

I looked into the castle of Benevente, and contemplated the life and doings of its present inhabitants somewhat sadly. There were two regiments of infantry, together with three batteries of artillery, quartered in the apartments of this magnificent ancient building, where, in the old

days, none but proud knights, barons and bannerets aired
their armour, and quaffed golden goblets to the accompaniment of songs and string music ; and the soldiers
were carrying on their noisy life, vouchsafing the relics
and artistic treasures that surrounded them neither
attention nor admiration. What the English soldier
cannot see any purpose in does not interest him.   Everywhere bayonets and nails were stuck into the crevices of
precious columns, or into the beautifully decorated walls,
and knapsacks and cartridge boxes were hung upon them.
In the large fireplaces, decorated with marble, there
burned huge fires, kept alive with broken pieces of
antique furniture, either gilt or artistically carved ; and
the same thing was going on in the courtyard, where the
walls were all black with smoke.   On these fires stood
a number of camp kettles. The soldiers' wives were
washing their things and hanging them just where they
chose.   A good deal was wantonly destroyed, and every
corner was scoured for hidden treasure.   The English
soldier, who was now quite well aware that he had been
lured into this country and into a parlous position by the
Spaniards under false pretences, and had then been left
in the lurch ; also that he only had the choice of flying in
ignominious retreat before an enemy thrice as strong as
his own army in numbers and in whose defeat he had come
to assist, or else of being uselessly sacrificed through
treachery, set about burning everything out of revenge.
It was a good thing, though, that he wreaked his vengeance
only on inanimate objects, and not on the inhabitants of
the country.   The officers, who were residing in various
parts of the castle, enraged by their men's lust of destruction and desecration, seemed crushed with grief, and did
all in their power to limit the damage as far as possible ;
but the numbers were too much for them, and the hidden
corners too numerous. They could not be everywhere.
Besides, insubordination was already apparent among the
men, and in spite of all the discipline, it was impossible to
stop it in an army which already felt that it was retreating
from a country it hated.   Poor castle of Benevente !
How quickly thy splendour vanished !

When the rearguard marched in, the alarm was raised, for the French could already be seen upon the opposite heights.   Accordingly, all the troops were got under arms and marched to the points of rendezvous, and the cavalry galloped through the narrow streets and through the gates of the town.   The town was in an uproar, and the plain in front of it teemed with monks and other fugitives, who, with their belongings were endeavouring to reach a place of safety away from the advancing enemy.   Meanwhile, the women and children remaining in the town filled the streets with their wailing and tore their hair with fright. When, however, the French on the heights had reconnoitred our position, and had seen our army ready to meet them, they withdrew again.   Then the corps of artificers under the command of an engineer, were ordered to go to the bridge which leads across the Esla not far from the town, in order to blow it up.   First of all the houses lying on the opposite side of it were burnt down, then a few arches flew up into the air, and thus the road was obstructed for the French at least at this point.   A portion of the army then marched out to bivouac, and the remaining portion was also commanded to hold itself in readiness to march.

General Moore, who had mustered his army at Toro, and found it to be 29,000 strong, had intended to take the offensive at once, and with the assistance of the Marquis de la Romana, to attack the French right wing ; but when he suddenly learnt that Bonaparte had altered his plans and had ordered the corps which was marching to Talavera, with the view of entering Lisbon, to proceed as quickly as possible to Salamanca, and that Bonaparte himself, with 35,000 men was marching on Benevente, and Soult with substantial reinforcements was advancing towards Astorga, he realised that the plan was to envelop us, and that now it was only a question of who would be the first to reach the great defile at Villafranca.   If we reach there too late we shall be lost.   A retreat, no matter whither, is now inevitable.

The retreat really began as far back as Salamanca.   At the very beginning of the retrograde movement disorder, a lack of discipline and subordination must have set in, and this was brought about in the first place through the rapid marches, secondly through deficient victuals, appalling weather and bad roads, and finally through the dejection and sense of ignominy caused by a continuous retreat and the inability to measure oneself with the enemy, complicated by the fact that General Moore maintained throughout the most absolute secrecy and silence regarding the movement.   He was very much blamed for this, for it was the wrong time for secrecy, and he ought to have acquainted all officers and men with the necessity for the retreat long before.   Even the officers became careless ; and no one knew the why or the whither of all that was happening.   The only thing that everybody believed was that all must now be lost.

Meanwhile Salamanca * was full of tumult.   All the streets were full of men, horses and wagons.   On the morning of December 29th I was ordered to assist in a large store depot.   The work consisted partly in helping to distribute rations, and partly in opening cases, boxes and barrels, and laying out their contents—salted meat, biscuits, boots, shirts, collars, stockings, or the most magnificent English woollen blankets.   Scarcely had we done this than almost the whole army came along, regiment by regiment, and each man was allowed to take what he liked and as much as he could carry.   The destruction of the bridge over the Esla occurred on the same day ; but on the following morning at daybreak, the French cavalry appeared on the heights again notwithstanding ; and, thinking that in Benevente they would only have to deal with the 3rd Hussars, who were our rearguard, and whom they imagined they were going to surprise, they marched quickly across the river not a hundred yards away from the demolished bridge.   All our infantry and heavy artillery had just been marched off, but Sir John Moore and Generals Lord Paget and Stewart were still in the town.   All the English piquets, some of whom had not yet saddled up, were ordered to advance. The brave 3rd Hussars of the German Legion were the

* Schaumann must mean Benevente.—Tr.

first to get into formation and to charge the enemy just as they had reached the bank on the Benevente side and fallen into position, while the English cavalry piquets, which had been ordered to advance, were able by degrees to support the attack.   The long-pent-up fighting spirit of our brave men, together with the strength of the English horses, soon decided the issue.   A number of Frenchmen—they consisted of squadrons of hussars of the Imperial Guard with huge bearskin helmets and green uniforms with white facings *—were rolled over or sabred ; and when the field artillery posted two guns close to the bridge and opened fire, the enemy gave way and tried to withdraw.   And now a terrible, though picturesque, scene was enacted.   The wounded men and horses sank down into the river, while here and there on the bank, groups formed to protect them, and a bitter hand-to-hand struggle ensued.   Nevertheless, one after the other fell or retreated across the river, on the other side of which they formed again with remarkable speed, and were then badly caught in the flank by our gun fire, and were obliged to make for the open country and vanish. Verily a picture worthy of being handed down to posterity by the brush of a battle-scene painter such as Louther-bourg or Bourgoin.   We took about 100 prisoners, including General Lefebvre.   The French are said to have left 200 men dead on the field.†   We had only thirty men wounded, among whom there was only one officer, Major Burgwedel, and no men killed.‡   The sword work during this cavalry *mêlée* is said to have been terrible, and our Germans are believed to have been mad with rage.   Most of the enemy's wounded had their arms cut off, and in many cases their upper limbs hung from their shoulders merely by a shred of their uniforms.   Lieutenant, now Major, Heise, told me about many of the heavier blows that had brought men down.   He saw one Frenchman

---

* Napier gives their number as 600.—Tr.

† It is probably true that the total loss to the French amounted to 200 excellent soldiers ; but these were not all killed ; many were wounded and many others taken prisoner.—Tr.

‡ As a matter of fact, the total number of men killed and wounded on the British side amounted to fifty.—Tr.

lying on the ground who had had the whole of his head cut off horizontally above the eyes at one blow, and many others with heads split in two.   He also noticed one man who rode by with outspread arms who had received a diagonal blow across his face which had cut his mouth right open so that his jaw, as far back as the tongue, hung down over his chest, and you could see his gullet.   One of our hussars had had his head cut off, and many of our fellows pursued the enemy right into the middle of the stream and brought back prisoners.   Small and insignificant as this encounter was, it will teach the enemy to leave our rearguard, consisting as it does of such soldiers, unmolested in future, and to keep at a respectful distance.

One of the 18th Hussars, of the name of Grimsdale, is said to have captured General Lefebvre.*   The officers of the 3rd Hussar Regiment deny this and say that he was caught by one of the men of their regiment.   But on board the transport which took me from Corunna to England, I spoke to an officer who said he had been assured by a good-looking young lad in the 3rd Hussars of the Legion, who was on board the same ship, that it was he who had taken Lefebvre prisoner, and as a proof of what he alleged, he exhibited as his spoil the French general's cartridge case and bandolier, heavily mounted in silver.   His story was as follows : During the action he saw a French officer dashing across the plain towards the river, and he followed him.   Thereupon the officer turned round, coolly laid a pistol across his left arm, and taking aim, fired.   But the shot missed, and fearing his pursuer's sword, he rode up and surrendered himself.   At this moment General Stewart himself came up, comforted the general, and complimenting the hussar in very flattering terms, assured him that his bravery would not go unrewarded.†

* Oman says Grimsdale belonged to the 10th Hussars (*op. cit.*, Vol. I., p. 550).   In any case Schaumann must mean the 18th Light Dragoons and not the 18th Hussars.

† Major Beamish's account of this incident not only clears up the matter satisfactorily, but also proves the accuracy of Schaumann's story in most of its details.   It is as follows (Vol. I., *op. cit.*, pp. 165–166) : " A young private of the German hussars named Bergmann, who had already cut down a French officer, and possessed himself of his sword and pouch, having mounted on a fast English horse . . . came up with a person dressed

The prisoners, chiefly Poles, Italians, and Swiss, also a few Germans, are all collected together in one house. They wear large bear-skin busbies, dark-green uniforms with white facings, and are powerful-looking fellows. A crowd of Spaniards are standing before the door, and bitterly regret that they are prevented by the English sentries from murdering the prisoners on the spot. Many of them are Germans only just come across the Pyrenees from Germany, and they remarked jokingly that the Emperor was waging a war on their legs. They say that the corps to which they belong had on the previous night already reached a village sixteen miles from here, and that it was on its way to Villafranca to cut us off, if we lingered too long. All the stores which could not be distributed to the troops in the way described above, were burned in large fires in the garden of the monastery ; for the stores depot was a monastery. Then we had to break open the majority of the casks of rum and pour their contents down the gutters. All the inhabitants of the town rushed to the spot, and were regularly invited to snatch what they could. And what an orgy it was for the Spaniards, who are so good at snatching ! I, too, was not idle, and laying a number of the finest blankets and a quantity of biscuits and rum aside, fetched my landlord and made him take the whole lot to his house. At midnight the tumult in the stores depot reached its zenith, and no one any longer felt safe. The bulk of the army, headquarters and everybody had gone, and the French, who were at the gates of the town were, according to all accounts, expected to enter at any moment, or at the very latest, early the following morning. While, therefore, the whole crowd were amusing themselves, eating, drinking, raving, shouting, quarrelling and destroying, I

in a green frock, and cocked hat, who rode in the rear of the flying squadrons. The fugitive made a thrust at his pursuer with his sword, which being parried, he demanded ' pardon.' At this moment one of the English hussars, who was close at hand, seized the bridle of the prisoner's horse, and led him away. Bergmann, then only a lad of eighteen, and little knowing the value of his prize, suffered the shrewder Englishman to bear it off, and giving himself no further concern about the matter, rejoined the pursuit ; meantime the person in the green frock was taken to General Stewart, as the prisoner of the English hussar ; nor was it until Bergmann's comrades reproached him for not retaining his prize, that the unsophisticated Hanoverian learned it was the General Lefebvre."—Tᴿ.

took a last piece of salt meat, a handkerchief full of barley, some biscuits, a pair of boots, and three woollen blankets, and creeping out softly like a fox from a dovecot, reached home at 1 a.m. I then fed my horse, made my amiable host a present of everything I had taken from the stores, and lay down to rest a bit, but scarcely had the dawn broken when I galloped out of Benevente and away.

It was high time, for I had hardly covered a mile or so when I heard from many officers travelling my way that even the road we were taking was scarcely safe any longer, for the French were surrounding Benevente with their cavalry, and might outflank us. Lieutenant Heise, of the 3rd Hussars, had remained behind alone in Bene-vente with twenty-five men to observe the French. The road led through Villa Brazero to La Baneza (five leguas) where I halted for the night. It was raining heavily, and I was wet to the skin. I found the last-named place full of troops, but I was able to find shelter in a house where the officers of the 1st and 2nd Light Battalions of the Legion took me under their protection. And here I started a method which kept me fit throughout the retreat. It was as follows : I kept my great coat tightly rolled up the whole day on my saddle, and let the rain soak me through as much as it liked. Then when I came under shelter, I opened my valise, put on my only dry suit of clothes, some woollen socks—for I had thrown all superfluous things away in order to lighten my poor horse's load—and a pair of slippers, and rolling myself in my cloak which had kept dry, I got close up to the fire, and was able to laugh at the others, whose cloaks had got quite wet with repeated changing, and were no longer any use for a dry outfit. Finally, I would hang my wet clothes before the fire, produce some chocolate, and cook it with wine and a little pimento and sugar—which ingredients I had brought with me from Zamora and carefully preserved—eat a few ship's biscuits, and lay myself in my horse blankets on the bare ground and sleep splendidly. On the following morning I would take my dry clothes off, and would often put my other clothes on when they were still either wet or damp, for if one moves about in them it does not hurt one. If I should happen to freeze on the way, I was soon comforted when I said to myself : " Augustus, just you be quiet, to-night you will have dry clothes to put on, and will be able to make yourself nice and snug, whereas the others will have chattering teeth."

On the morning of the 30th December I woke and wanted to start off, when I was caught by the Commissary-General, Kennedy, who showed me an enormous number of bullocks just outside the town, and ordered me to take them under my charge, together with their drivers, among whom there were numbers of students from Salamanca. These young men, fearing they might be badly treated by the French, were marching with us. They had implored General Moore to employ them in some capacity in the army, and many of them were consequently turned over to the commissariat, and among other things, set to driving bullocks. Although I saw that, owing to the slow progress of the bullocks, I should be certain to fall in with the French advanced guard, I had to obey, together with two other unfortunate clerks, who had been selected for this duty.

It was absurd to see the students running behind the bullocks, with their black gowns flying in the air. But off we marched, and soon reached a stone highway which ran across a marsh. The latter, however, was covered over with tall grass, and looked like a beautiful green meadow. This deceptive appearance misled the poor bullocks, which, having been confined the whole night in empty wooden enclosures, called " Corrals " here, were mad with hunger, and longed to graze. The whole lot, therefore, left the stone highway for the marsh, and before many of them had got very far, and a few were still quite close, they began to sink into the mud, some with their heads foremost and their hindquarters sticking high in the air, while others only showed their heads and forelegs, just as if they wished to harangue the remainder and warn them not to advance. Our first impulse was to follow them ; but when we saw what was happening we thought better of it, and merely made efforts to prevent those that

were still on the stone highway from following the rest.
But the stupid animals would not obey, and they all ran
down and sank.   While we stood there bewailing what
had happened, a division of infantry came marching by.
We begged them to help us ; but the men laughed in our
faces, and drawing their knives proceeded to cut from the
haunches of those beasts whose hindquarters were upper-
most in the marsh, large steaks and fillets of beef, where-
at the poor martyred creatures which had their heads
sticking in the mud, began to bellow fiercely like mire-
drums.   At length I could no longer endure the harrowing sight, and as my duty had come to an end here, I
spurred my horse and rode hastily away, reaching Astorga,
the rendezvous of the army, towards evening.

Chapter 8

I FOUND the gate of the town barricaded with great beams, so that only one man or one horse could enter at a time. At the Town Hall or *Ayunamiento*, on the great square, where the billets are distributed, I met Mr. Kearney, the commissary, who seized hold of me and ordered me to assist him in rationing the cavalry. The chief commissaries, Erskine and Kennedy, had apparently already gone ahead, in order to make the necessary arrangements on the way.

On the morning of the 31st December, I was despatched on all sorts of errands. I was to harass the Junta about provisions and forage for the cavalry ; I was to do the same at the slaughter-houses outside the town, where it required an enormous amount of art to secure anything ; and, finally, I was to go to the town to spy out the stores of corn. Chaos reigned everywhere. The majority of the inhabitants had flown, and all the shops had either sold out to the army passing through or else had been plundered. There was not a particle of bread or chocolate to be had anywhere. At the Junta they snorted at me angrily. "What do you English think ? " they cried. " You are retreating, and yet we are expected to supply you with provisions ! To-morrow the French will arrive, and we shall have to scrape something together for them unless we want to be hanged ! " This was certainly an *argumentum ad hominem !*

Meanwhile I noticed a good deal of activity among our infantry. Regiment after regiment marched slowly off. In the evening a portion of our rearguard appeared, consisting of a light brigade of infantry, as also the 3rd (German) and the 7th, 10th and 18th (English) Hussars ; some of them entered the town and the rest halted all round it. I ran anxiously back to my quarters, and found them occupied by hussars, while on the table there was a note to the effect that, as Mr. Kearney had been given permission to ride ahead to see about supplies for the cavalry on the road, would I have the goodness to remain behind with the cavalry and try to provide them with all the victuals and fodder I could find in the place ! " Very much obliged for the honour of this delightful proposal ! " I cried, swearing terribly ; for I was not such a fool as to be blind to the fact that the suggestion made to the general was only a trick. Mr. Kearney, who expected nothing good to come from stopping here, only wanted to get out of a mess—that was it. On the other hand, he had recommended me to Lord Paget as an assistant of his own who was to remain with the cavalry and would see to everything ! God forgive him for it ! Why, he had even taken with him the meat and bread which I had managed to collect that morning, at the cost of great pains and many digs in the ribs, for our joint rations, and had not left behind a crumb for me ! The honour was great, but how I was to prove myself worthy of it I could not see. I was young and inexperienced, and had not attained to that skill in the creation of endless resources which a war commissary acquires only at the end of many campaigns. Moreover, I had no money, no assistants, no food and no transport, for I could only rely on the Junta, and I was shut up in a town full of troops, where there was nothing to be had. My rage was only just beginning to subside when the quartermasters began to call upon me.

Fortunately, that morning I had accidentally noticed, on looking through a wire grating up which I climbed, that in the lower part of a certain house, which was all locked up, every room was full to the ceiling with rye. For in Astorga, as in all the hilly parts of Spain and Portugal, wheat and barley cease, and only rye is grown. As, however, rye is not good for horses, I had not given the matter much consideration. But now I thought better of it, and as the Junta had told me I could take whatever I found, I led my quartermasters thither. We went to a smith's, borrowed an enormous hammer, and broke open the door. They were a little sad to find only rye instead of oats or barley, for rye purges horses ; but

while all of us were contemplating it hesitatingly, a jolly
young fellow in the 3rd Hussars cried : " What does it
matter ? Why think about it any longer ? Let's take it :
here it is, eat or starve ! " And thereupon all of us
stepped up to our necks into the corn—for we had neither
the time nor the appliances to weigh it out—and filled the
sacks with it. In a second down all the streets leading
from this house you could trace long tracks of spilt rye,
which had been scorned and trampled under foot by the
horses bivouacked in the open thoroughfares. I imagine
thousands of bushels of rye must have perished in
this way. " *C'est la guerre !* " I thought to myself ;
" if we hadn't taken it the French would have done so."

Almost killed by the dust and the tumult, I soon
quitted the place, and taking a hussar with me went in
search of wine. There was enough meat to hand, for we
had only to shoot down one of the jaded cart bullocks in
the street, and our wants would be met. At last, not far
from the gates of the town, we found a strongly bolted
and undisturbed cellar, which we opened by force, and a
light having been fetched from a neighbouring house, to
my great joy I discovered on a bar above some casks of
wine, two turkeys, which, quietly roosting there, seemed
to be philosophising about the turmoil in the town. I
took possession of everything I found, and placing a
hussar with his sword drawn as a guard over the place,
sent another to the quartermasters to tell them that they
might detail the necessary number of men to come along
to the wine casks with their camp kettles. It took an
age ! All of a sudden I heard the sound of drums and
much shouting in the streets. It was the remainder of
the Marquis de la Romana's army—about 5,000 men—
retreating through the place. Hardly had the Spaniards
espied the open cellar *en passant* than they began to fall
rather than climb down the steps in large numbers. My
hussar, who tried to stop them, was pushed back by the
throng so that he could not move, while at the same time
he and I were threatened with hundreds of bayonets, one
of which was even pointed at my breast by a caracho.*

* This is a corruption of *caranga* (louse), and was a nickname for the infantry.—Tr.

In the midst of this tumult the lamp which we had borrowed and placed on a ledge in the wall, fell to the ground and went out, and we were all plunged in darkness. The turkeys, leaving their perch, fluttered about over our heads, but they were immediately seized by the Spaniards, who, amid mad yells, fought so long for their possession that in the end the birds' feathers, blood and entrails were strewn all over the cellar. Almost asphyxiated, I succeeded in struggling through the throng and out of the cellar, just as the hussars arrived with their camp kettles. " Now see to it that you get the wine ! " I cried angrily, and then ran home, in order to take care of such articles of property as my horse and my valise, which were no longer safe now that the Spanish army was passing through the town.

Scarcely had I reached my door when an aide-de-camp appeared, summoning me to appear before Lord Paget. "This evening," said the latter, " I have invited all the officers of the rearguard to dine with me. Get me some bread and some wine, the rest I can supply." I told him all my experiences, and he ordered me to appeal to the Junta. They would find ways and means ! The Junta sent a deputation to the general to apologise to him and to assure him that to the best of their knowledge there was no bread or wine at their disposal. I was then ordered to search the town to see whether I could not find some. We ran round all the streets and visited a number of houses in vain, until it grew quite dark. It had been misty the whole day, and our rearguard had found it difficult to observe the approach and position of the enemy. The night was dark, stormy and wet. The remaining inhabitants of the town, alarmed by the retreating army, and even more so by the rapid approach of the French, ran about the streets in desperation, bemoaning their lot. Marauders rushed noisily out of the houses and store-cellars, which they had entered by force, while the streets were thronged with baggage, wagons, horses, bullock carts, cattle, soldiers, and moaning natives. Now and again the light of a torch of straw and resin would pass quickly by, or a fire, fed with the fragments of a broken ammunition wagon would suddenly shed its harsh light upon the scene of disorder and misery, only to leave it in darkness again a moment later. Meanwhile, the chatter of the muskets in the distance, and the monotonous staccato calls of the bugles, mustering the scattered rearguard together, mingled with the cries of the women praying to the Virgin and the uproar created by the cursing of the military close at hand ; and the whole town presented such a ghastly spectacle, that in the end, feeling feeble and exhausted, I left Lord Paget's dinner to its fate, and went in search of my quarters. But peace had departed from Astorga !

Eleven o'clock had just struck, when suddenly one of the hussars in my billet, springing up as if electrified, cried, " Get up, get up ! The trumpets are blowing ! " and ran out into the kitchen, followed by us all. But before I could even bridle my horse these centaurs were already galloping out of the yard. All you could hear in the streets was the ominous clatter of horses' hoofs, the cries of command, and the sound of general flight. In a great hurry I wanted to bridle my horse, which, by the bye, had remained saddled the whole night, but forgetting to tighten his girth, which I had loosened to let him feed more easily, I fell, saddle and all, on to the floor at his feet. Fortunately the beast stood stock still. I was obliged patiently to unfasten the valise, one of the straps of which was broken, so that it hung askew, and to loosen all the other straps, and put the saddle on afresh. It was pitch dark in the yard. Never shall I forget the despair which I felt at this accident. From sheer rage I did nothing but swear disgustingly or weep like a child. Moreover, I was in such a hurry that I did not know what to do first, and thus lost much time. At last I succeeded, and forthwith scampered out of the house.

But the hussars had vanished, the streets were dark and deserted, and I did not even know out of which gate the troops had gone. My position was desperate. At last through the darkness I caught sight of a few English servants in white overalls who were riding spare horses ; and joining them we rode out of the town where we kept

to the left of a broad highway. We had not gone far
before we encountered a number of men of the 18th
Hussars, who told us that if we had not had the good
fortune to meet them we should have taken a bee-line
to the French army ! I then heard that Lieutenant
Heise, who with thirty of the 3rd Hussars (German
Legion) formed one of the extreme outposts of the rearguard, had informed Lord Paget that the French, having
received substantial reinforcements, had so far only been
prevented from advancing by the mist, but that they
would certainly attack Astorga at dawn. Towards
evening, however, Heise had reported that the French
were pressing upon us in superior numbers, and that
he must therefore ask for reinforcements. Whereupon
twenty hussars under a lieutenant were despatched to
him ; but overwhelmed by the superior strength of
several squadrons of French cavalry, he had been forced
to retreat slowly, and had reached Astorga at 11 p.m.
While the bulk of the army retreated, our rearguard
remained in Astorga until four in the morning. It was
pitch dark, and the road taken by the army ran to the right
across the mountains. We passed a filthy little village,
and reached a highway, where a regiment of hussars were
posted with a battery of horse artillery. The gunners
had unlimbered and seemed to be awaiting the enemy.
Together with various detachments of troops, I rode
forward the whole night, and in the mountains we came
upon glaciers or roads which were so deep in snow and
ice that the horses could not stand, and we were obliged
to dismount. I passed by a number of glowing bivouac
fires which, flaring up now and then, illuminated the wild,
desolate, wintry scene, the expressive stillness of which
was gruesomely broken by the retreating army. The
sausage I had had for supper made me feel dreadfully
thirsty; and my horse, too, badly wanted a drink. But
there was no water; everything was frozen hard. Both of
us therefore ate the snow. I slept while walking, for the
road was too steep and slippery to ride, and it was too cold
to sit in the saddle.

At last the day broke and we found ourselves in the

mountains that join Galicia and Asturias to Leon.   The
road was incredibly bad, and we sank knee-deep in mud
and snow.   On the mountains hung clouds of driven
snow which from time to time the wind blew in our faces.
My horse grew tired.   Not far from Manzanal, three to
five leguas from Astorga, we reached at dawn the serpentine road which from this point follows along the mountains.   It is a noble piece of work, broad, frequently cut
through the rock, and marked by milestones after the
manner of a great highway, and leads from here to
Corunna, a distance of 160 miles without a break.   It
winds its way about so much in the mountains, however,
between valley and peak, that it makes one feel one is
making no headway.   Where the mountain streams are
most violent, bridges are placed, and they are built upon
foundations consisting of huge boulders of rock.   The
road itself, though possibly hard enough in summer, was
now, owing to the march of the troops, and particularly
of the cavalry and the guns, the melted snow and rain,
and the loam washed down from the mountains, like a
huge lake, on the bed of which, still hard as it was, men
and beasts walked up to their knees in water.   Among
these mountains, and particularly in Manzanal, there are
many traces of the Moors, as the strange gipsy clothing
of the people and their dark-brown complexions plainly
show.   The Marquis de la Romana's army is constantly
getting in our way.   All the houses, huts and villages are
full of his troops.   When we reached Manzanal there
were some ghastly scenes.   The Marquis de la Romana's
men demanded straw, forage, bread and wine.   The
wives of these descendants of the Moors, whose husbands
were all away at an annual gathering of shepherds, raised
a loud outcry when their doors were broken open, and
tearing their hair, they endeavoured to defend their
property tooth and nail.

I looked into one of the huts.   The fireplace was in the
middle, and the smoke went whither it listed, up to the
roof or out at the door.   The fuel consisted of moist
heath ; they do not burn any light through the long
winter nights, but illumine their huts with their heath

fires, the smoke of which makes the eyes smart horribly. The family in this particular hut consisted of a tall old black and yellow witch and three ugly children, of whom two were suffering from a hectic fever. Everything was extremely dirty ; their hair was matted together, and they seemed never to have washed since the day of their birth. Round the woman's neck hung a rosary in three strands, enriched with sacred medals, and she wore two huge earrings. She did nothing except sit over the fire and shake with cold and misery, and the whole place presented a picture of the most appalling wretchedness.

For several more miles now the road was knee-deep in mud and snow, until we reached the village of Sevadon, and the mountain of that name, from the summit of which a stormy wind blew clouds of snow and sleet down upon us. The road now led a zig-zag course along the edge of deep precipices. If these passes were adequately defended by an army, it would be impossible for any enemy to force its way into Spain on this side. During the march, and up to this point, there had been much murmuring among the officers about the defective rationing of the army ; but the men themselves, who knew of no restraint, complained openly of being allowed to go hungry amid such great exertions. Situated as we were, however, it was impossible, even with the best will in the world, to relieve our privations ; for the cause of our suffering lay in the fact that we were a large army, all pursuing the same narrow road through the mountains, and could not avail ourselves of the resources which would have lain to our left and our right had we been marching in three or four separate and parallel columns over roads covering a larger area of the country. Even if, owing to the special care of the commissaries in Corunna, provisions had been sent out and deposited at various points along the road—as, for instance, at Villa-franca—these measures would have proved nugatory owing to the impatience and unbridled state of the foremost troops, who, in their masses, and with the wildest tumult and noise, literally stormed the stores depots. All orderly distribution was at an end. No officer, commissioned or non-commissioned, was respected. The storekeepers and other Spanish officials were driven from their posts at the point of the bayonet ; every soldier took what he liked, everything was plundered, carried away, and trampled under foot ; the casks of wine were broken open, so that half their contents were spilt over the floor, and the general fury and unruliness of these hordes of men was such that those officers who attempted to maintain order had to make haste to fight their way out of the crowds, if only to save their lives. Aye, towards the end, the men even used to fight among themselves and kill one another, and one frequently saw a regular battle fought over the *débris* of a stores depôt. But this is the difference between an army that is marching towards, and one that is retreating from, an enemy. In the first instance everything is in order, everyone is inspired with courage, hope, and a sense of honour, while in the latter, the soldier shows his dissatisfaction with his leaders ; and the failure of his prospects, shame, discouragement, contempt of discipline, and unaccustomed privations, make such a change in his character, that he is no longer recognisable. When an army is situated as ours was, no pen can describe the horrors which follow in its wake.

Truth to tell, at Benevente a general order was indeed issued to the effect that the army was not to retreat to Corunna, but was merely waiting to take up a better and stronger position ; but the common soldier was not so silly as to believe this, for he read the contradiction of it in every step that was being taken. He realised that all hope of measuring himself against the foe in open warfare had been abandoned, and he likened himself to a bull tied to a stake and worried by a dog. Worn out by privation and vain hopes, he respected the rules neither of war nor of life ; all he sought was to snatch enough for his immediate needs, no matter what the morrow might bring. The road we followed showed all the traces of the horrors and destruction that war leaves in its path. Starving inhabitants of the country fled in front and past us with faces distorted by fear, despair and vindictiveness ; and the weaker among them, the aged, the children and the women, laden with their belongings, and perishing from fear, and from the rain, the storms, the snow and the hunger to which they had been exposed night and day, sank in the mire at our feet imploring in vain for help, which we could not give even our own men.   But the road was not only strewn with human corpses ; horses, mules and draft-bullocks suffered the same fate.   They collapsed beneath their load, and in order that their misery might end and they might not fall into the enemy's hands, they were shot and their corpses left as obstacles in our wake.

All the way from Salamanca snow and sleet fell day and night ; the roads offered no foothold, the swollen waters of the streams flooded the valleys and plains, and turned them into swamps or bogs through which the whole army waded up to the knees.   The transport wagons stuck, the soldiers' boots were torn from their feet, and there was no fire to warm the men who were crippled with the wet and the cold, nor any fortifying nourishment either.

At last, when the French had taken 200 mules with supplies from us near Valderas, and the rearguard had faced about once or twice to exchange a few gun and musket shots with the enemy's advanced guard and had driven it back, ; also, when the guards and the cavalry had fought a battle near Villa Bol, both friend and foe seemed to be in need of peace.

Things grew quieter, and at midday on the 2nd of January we reached Bembibre—a wretched, filthy little hole.   At the cost of great pains I was able to stable my horse, or rather wedge it into one of the houses packed to the attics with men and beasts ; while I myself crept into a dreadful house, where there was hardly enough room left to allow me to lie down and rest.   I had brought with me a handkerchief full of rye, and on this I fed.   I had also been able to procure a little bread on the road from a native to whom I gave a dollar to fetch it from some hiding place he had.   With this I now refreshed myself.   Then laying myself resignedly on the bare floor among a number of exhausted stragglers, I wrapped myself in my cloak and was soon fast asleep, despite the fact that my boots and

socks were wet through, and my teeth were chattering
with the cold.   From midday until about six o'clock in
the evening, the rearguard and everybody who marched
in front of it were able to take a rest ; then suddenly the
trumpets sounded.   " Get up, get up ! " was the cry.
I ran to find my horse ; but in the gathering gloom of the
evening I could not find the stables where I had left it.
The confusion was appalling, and I was in despair.
Everybody was running hither and thither.   Foaming
with rage, I dashed from one stable to another, and had
already made up my mind that I should never look upon
my horse again, when at last I found the right door.   I
mounted, and once more rode forth into the night.

Villafranca del Bierzo, which I reached towards the
evening of the 2nd January, lies in a small valley at the
foot of fairly lofty mountains.   The River Vallcarso flows
between the town and the mountains ; and an old castle,
belonging to the Marquis of Villafranca, commands the
Pass of Galicia.   My first care was to find a billet for
myself, but the presence of two divisions of infantry, and
a large force of cavalry and artillery in the town under
Generals Hope and Fraser, together with numerous
officials, who had already established themselves here,
made the matter of finding quarters very difficult.   Nevertheless, I succeeded in discovering something in a small
house, and I took possession of a minute room which I
shared with a hussar officer of the Legion.   The rooms
below were occupied by about thirty Jägers of the 60th
Regiment.   My friend, Mr. Kennedy, had once again
managed to escape.

General Moore, who always remained with the rearguard and shared all their dangers, has not yet arrived.
The commandant of the town was Major Cavell, of the
76th Regiment. I was very much pleased to reach the town
and to get a little rest ; for all the way from Astorga I had
had to make my way knee-deep through snow and mud,
and often on foot, partly because my horse was exhausted,
and partly because I feared lest I might sleep and fall out
of the saddle.   By walking, I warded off sleep and also
kept myself from freezing in my wet clothes.   My boots

were torn, and my socks all perished.   There were plenty
of stores here, so that at first rations were distributed in an
orderly fashion.   We had particularly large quantities of
salt fish and biscuits, and a convent on the far side of the
bridge was full of them.   But two-thirds of the army were
still behind us on the road, and every hour fresh detachments of various regiments arrived in the most deplorable
condition.

On the following morning I heard that the enemy
in dense formation had attacked our rearguard near
Cacabelos, and had skirmished with it until quite close
up to the defile that begins at Villafranca ; but that the
sharpshooters of our rearguard had repelled the French
advance with such heavy slaughter, that the enemy had
been forced to retire.   This affair was one more laurel leaf
in the wreath of cypress which the angel of death had
already suspended over our road.   It was fortunate that,
owing to the precipices, the enemy was unable to attack us
on our flank, and could not send more troops against us than
the width of the road, and the shelves and crags of rock on
either side of it, which we occupied, would allow.   Thus
they were obliged to wait until it pleased us to retire still
further ; but I also heard that at Lugo, towards which
another French army was moving, we should be exposed
to much greater dangers, if we hung back here too long.

Although Villafranca is not small, every corner of it
was soon full of men.   You could hardly turn round in
the place, and many regiments had to bivouac.   Most of
the mules and draft-bullocks and pack-horses seemed only
to have lasted out up to this point, and now fell down and
died.   Very soon we could neither drive nor ride through
many of the streets.   The rations came to an end, but, amid
the chaos that reigned, could in any case no longer have
been distributed.   Fresh troops were always streaming in,
the stores depots were also violently raided, and the
commissaries were no longer able to perform their duties.
In the end Villafranca was literally plundered, and the
drunkenness that prevailed among the troops led to the
most shameful incidents.   Down by the river the artillery
destroyed all their stores, and lighting big fires burnt all

their ammunition wagons, which they broke up for the purpose. They also threw all their ammunition into the river. Several hundred horses, which could go no further, were led to the same spot and shot. Day and night we could hear the sound of pistol fire. Everything was destroyed. Discipline was at an end, and the officers were no longer heeded.

In the kitchen at my billet I saw on my arrival that various pork sausages and hams were still hanging in the smoke of the chimney. On the second day of my stay they had all gone. Fortunately I had already bought one of the former, and intended keeping it for the continuation of the retreat. But when I awoke one morning it was to find that some of the Jägers who were lodged below, and who had marched before dawn that day, had crept up to our room before leaving, and while I was asleep, had not only robbed me of one of my pistols, but had also taken the sausage, a bottle of rum, my biscuits and my gloves, together with the provisions and many other things belonging to the officer of the 3rd Hussars who shared the room with me—a discovery which upset us both very much. Meanwhile, we of the commissariat were on our legs night and day. All the ovens in the place were occupied and we had flour ; but what was the good of all our baking, when we could not deal with the riotous throng ? Besides, we were badly treated while performing our functions, and any sort of organisation was useless, seeing that we expected every minute to be told to decamp again.

On the morning of the 3rd January, the troops, consisting of infantry and cavalry, having marched out on to an open space inside the walls of the town, a detachment of the 18th Hussars, who were on foot, brought out one of their own men, and I was told that General Moore had arrived, and was so much exasperated by the relaxed discipline and the excesses that had taken place that he was going to make an example of the fellow. It appeared that in a certain house three hussars had broken open a case, and extracted a ham and other things from it. Thousands of others had done the same, and much worse.

Unfortunately, however, General Moore happened to be riding through the street when the Spaniards raised their outcry over the ham, and these three fellows had had to draw lots for their lives. The man who lost was led out, and placed in a kneeling position with his face turned towards a big tree. A detachment of twenty men stood behind him with their carbines at the ready. In a loud voice the adjutant cried, " Fire ! " and the poor devil was dead ; whereupon all the troops were made to march past the corpse.

After this execution headquarters and the bulk of the infantry marched out of the town, and most of the cavalry and artillery, who could not be used in the narrow defiles and gorges, went also. Only General Baird's light division, and a little cavalry under Lord Paget, took post on the other side of the town, in order to keep the swiftly approaching enemy at bay and to cover the retreat. In the town itself, however, there were still a bustling throng of people consisting of men who were too tired to proceed, some wounded, and stragglers who had fallen out of the ranks in order to plunder. What I actually did during our stay here has remained in my memory like a nightmare. I had to be everywhere ! At one moment a Commissary-General appeared and shouted, " Mr. Schaumann, come here !—you stay here—you make sure that this and this is done ! " Hardly had I begun when someone else turned up and yelled : " Mr. Schaumann, you come with me ! " " But I mayn't." " What do you mean, you mayn't ? Who gave you the order ? " " Why, So-and-so ! " " Oh, nonsense ! I am in command here. You come with me, immediately ! " Scarcely had I moved a step with the last gentleman, than the Commissary-in-Chief, Mr. Erskine, would appear, and exclaim : " Mr. Schaumann must go there, and do this and that ! " I always answered, " Very well, sir," and ran like a greyhound. As for anything to eat or drink, it wasn't to be thought of until eleven o'clock at night. There were moments when I thought I should never survive it.

On the afternoon of the 4th January, some sharp

firing, intermingled with gunshots was heard just outside
the gate of the town. Many of the rearguard marched
in, and told us as they went by that things were very warm
out there. " But we popped them off, whenever they
showed their ugly faces, like mice in the sun," said one of
them. A sapper officer then galloped through the streets
shouting that by six o'clock everybody was to be over the
bridge as it was then to be blown up. Now the uproar
began ! Women, children, the sick, and baggage wagons,
all tried to get across at once. The troops making their
way across by force, slowly marched away regiment by
regiment, while other troops, fresh from the battle outside, arrived in the town. At that moment I happened
to be at the quarters of Commissary Moore, where the
tumult was at its worst. He had his gig brought out,
and tried to get his luggage on to it, but owing to the
tumult he could not succeed, and being a notoriously
choleric person, he went almost mad with rage. His
wife, a fat woman, who was looking out of the window
implored him to be more patient, and urged him above all
to be calm and keep his presence of mind. But she was
nicely rewarded for her pains ; for never in my life shall
I again hear such a flow of choice invective as this fellow
Moore poured forth against her. Now, however, it was
her turn to lose patience, and she retaliated with such a
volley of exquisite abuse—she was an Irishwoman—
which, by the bye, she punctuated by flinging down all
sorts of missiles, consisting of cups and pots and pans,
upon his head, that all those who were standing by, even
the wounded, were contorted with laughter.

Just at this moment I was caught by Commissary-
General Kennedy, who, pointing out six large Spanish
mule carts, and ordering me to take them to a street,
which he vaguely indicated, told me that I would find a
convent there and a store of flour, which I was to transfer
to the mule carts and bring along in the rear of the army.
Then, putting spurs to his horse, he rode hurriedly away
with his escort, who did not seem to envy me in the least.
I was terrified, for he might just as well have said to me :
" You will stop here and allow yourself to be taken

prisoner ! " The worst of it was that it was quite impossible to get these carts out of their corner until the army and the rearguard had marched by. Moreover, before we could reach the convent a number of dead horses would have had to be moved out of the way. We had to wait therefore, but the Commissary-General had not even left a guard to protect me. So I drew forth from my saddle the only pistol I had, and assuming a threatening attitude, swore that I would kill the first man who dared to run away or refused to obey orders. For, the moment there is any danger the first thing the Portuguese and Spanish bullock and mule drivers do, is either to cut the traces, or throw down the load, and ride off with the spare animals. I also feared lest these drivers, when they had me alone at the convent, might draw their knives and, stabbing me on my horse, gallop away. My situation was in every respect hopeless. For the moment, all they did was to implore me frantically to let them go. " *Por amor de Dios y todos los Santos !* " * they cried. Then they added that beyond Villafranca there was a terrible defile, several miles long, and that even if we succeeded in leaving the town and getting the flour across the bridge before it was blown up, we should be sure to find ourselves between the French advanced guard and our own rearguard in the defile. We should only block the way, and be robbed of our load, our mules would be unharnessed, the carts flung down the precipice, and we ourselves killed or for ever ruined. I found all this most illuminating. The fellows were right. But what about the order ?

While I was thus wrestling with myself regarding what I should do, the sun sank towards the horizon. The fire of the skirmishers became so fierce at the entrance to Villafranca, where I happened to be standing, that the bullets rattled on the surrounding roofs. The rearguard poured in in masses. One or two sapper officers ran hither and thither, urging everybody to proceed to the bridge, for the gate of the town was not going to be held after the bridge had been blown up. Now all who still happened to be in the town made haste to escape, and it

---

* " For the love of God and all the Saints."

was at this point that I lost courage. Why should I be sacrificed ? What purpose could it serve ? " *Mucha-chos !* " (Boys !) I cried to the drivers, as I returned my pistol to its wallet, " *Vamos fugir !* " (We're off !) Not losing a moment, the fellows quickly released their mules, and thanking me effusively, fled hurriedly away, leaving their carts standing. I also made for the open country. On the bridge, which was somewhat elevated and narrow, I and my horse were carried shoulder high by the throng, and were frequently almost crushed by the ammunition carts. At last I reached the other side. A number of barrels of salt fish, which were stored in a convent on the far side of the bridge, were rolled out, opened, and their contents left at the disposal of the passers-by.

Night soon fell, and we marched slowly forward in the darkness. A loud report in the direction of Villafranca announced that the bridge had been blown up, and at the same moment the horizon was illuminated as if the town were in flames. At the entrance of a certain defile, we all marched higgledy-piggledy or rather pushed each other forward through the darkness in one compact mass. Never shall I forget the heartrending cries of some wounded men, when their cart broke down, and they were deposited in a shed on the road and left behind. These poor devils implored us fervently not to leave them to the mercy of the French advanced guard ; but the whole procession marched on unfeelingly. Some of the senior and more experienced officers were completely astonished at the speed with which General Moore made the army retreat, and were of the opinion that if it were continued at one stretch as far as Corunna, two-thirds of our troops would be left lying on the roadside. Others defended the General, and declared they had heard that a French army was on its way across Leon with the view of cutting us off near Lugo, in which case the utmost speed was imperative. In the end it was the latter who proved to have been right.

As far as I was able to tell in the dark, the road we were taking ran through a deep valley, with enormous ravines and precipices on either side, round the bends in which the River Vallcarso rushed down from the moun-

tains.   The slope to our left was covered for miles with
tall chestnut and oak trees, now all bare of leaves.   The
road itself is a so-called *Camino Reál* (high road), which
runs from Astorga to this place, and has with infinite pains
been cut through the solid rock.   Towards morning,
after I had been obliged to halt owing to the constant
checks which, with an army marching at night, are as
tedious as they are unavoidable, I reached the village of
Heresias,* five leguas west of Villafranca on the 5th of
January.   Here the road climbs gently up the mountains,
and crossing the summit of the highest peak in Galicia,
ends near the villages of Los Royales and Constantino.
As far as Heresias,* where one enjoys an extensive view
of the surrounding country, the wild chaos of the mountain scenery is somewhat modified, and there are also signs
of human habitation and cultivation.   In the valleys, and
on the hills between the rocks, small enclosures can be
descried, and here and there a hut with a slate roof ;
while there is not a square yard of earth, however unprofitable, that has not been used by the industrious and hardy
natives.   From this point onwards the mountains rise
ever higher and higher.

Many of the soldiers, worn out with hunger and
fatigue, had fallen out of the ranks during this rapid
march, and had flung themselves in despair in the midst
of the mud and filth on the side of the road.   Insubordination was noticeable everywhere.   The men regarded
the retreat as an indignity, and many bitter remarks were
made, all of which usually ended with the following
prayer : " Give us something to eat ; let us just take a
little rest, then lead us against the enemy, and we shall
beat him ! "   As for any order on the march, or regular
halts—such things were not even thought of ! He who
could go no further, stood still ; he who still had something to eat, that ate he in secret, and then continued
marching onwards ; the misery of the whole thing was
appalling—huge mountains, intense cold, no houses, no
shelter or cover of any kind, no inhabitants, no bread.
Every minute a horse would collapse beneath its rider, and

---

* Schaumann means Herrerias, the village of the blacksmiths.—Tʀ.

be shot dead. The road was strewn with dead horses bloodstained snow, broken carts, scrapped ammunition, boxes, cases, spiked guns, dead mules, donkeys and dogs, starved and frozen soldiers, women and children—in short, the sight of it all was terrible and heartrending to behold. In addition, the road frequently followed a zigzag course along the very edge of a precipice. We often reached small villages completely deserted by their inhabitants, and anybody who at night succeeded, by dint of many appeals to the soldiers, in being given a tiny bit of space either in a stable or a sty, in which to lie down and rest, together with a small fragment of bread, considered himself lucky.

On the 6th January we were climbing the mountains again. The army was now retreating along a road which had been very much deteriorated by the bad weather, and through mountainous country, intersected in all directions by swollen mountain streams, and utterly devoid of all human food. It was, moreover, constantly exposed to rain and stormy weather, and its progress was incessantly hindered and arrested owing to the many wounded and sick, and the wretched women and still more wretched children. Discipline became ever more and more relaxed, and horrible deeds of every description shed a black stain upon the fair fame of the British soldier. Every hour the misery of the troops increased. We were working our way through open, naked mountain country, covered all over with snow, but wonderfully sublime in aspect. Unfortunately sublimity is not nourishing ! Our road, which wound round the mountains, was often bounded by the most forbidding precipices, or else flooded by torrential forest streams. Many, who were too weary to resist, were flung down the former by the powerful and violent gusts of wind that would blow up quite suddenly ; while others were constantly being washed by the current into the mountain torrents. Much time was spent in climbing the steep mountain slopes, and in travelling over the increasingly bad roads ; and then night would fall— pitch black night ! At every step we took, we waded through snow and mud over the bodies of dead men and horses.   The howling wind, as it whistled past the ledges of rock and through the bare trees, sounded to the ear like the groaning of the damned ; and while the darkness certainly concealed all the horrors of our plight, it only made us the more attentive to the moans of the dying and the execrations of the hungry.

Having reached Puerto, we soon got as far as Cabrera, whence we ascended to the summit of the snow mountains, where the army again suffered the most terrible hardships. Everybody was so drunk with lack of sleep that again and again one of the throng would stop, and in spite of all appeals and warnings, drop down and fall asleep and freeze, and never awake again.   Many wounded and sick men, whom we had brought all the way with us, met with their end now.   Beasts of draught and beasts of burden gradually sank in ever greater numbers beneath their load and died of hunger, after they had devoured the snow in the hope of slaking their thirst.   I saw one bullock cart, belonging to the Paymaster-General's department, loaded with six barrels full of Spanish dollars, standing on the side of the road, with its back resting against a rock.   The bullocks were lying on the ground under their yokes, utterly exhausted.   A soldier with bayonet fixed stood guard over the treasure, and with a desperate air implored every officer that passed by to relieve him of his duty. But of course no one dared to do so ! If only those dollars had been bread ! Now, however, nobody paid any heed; the most confirmed thief passed by unmoved.   Further on a Portuguese bullock driver lay dead beside his fallen bullocks.   A soldier's wife had sought shelter beneath his cart, but she, too, was lying lifeless ; and the tragic part of it was that her child, who was still alive, was whimpering and trying to find nourishment at her frozen breasts ! One or two officers had the child taken from her, and wrapping it in a blanket, carried it away.

Among the disasters that befell us while ascending this dreadful mountain, was the fact that we found ourselves compelled to rid our wagons of the load of Spanish dollars which constituted our war treasure.   Most of the mules and bullocks that were drawing it had fallen down dead, and we had no fodder for those that still remained. The speed with which the French were pursuing us, moreover, left us no time in which to take any measures to save this money. A hussar regiment had, indeed, been furnished with bags, in order that they might carry some of it on their saddles ; but as the men could not endure the load, they put as much of it as they could in their pockets and flung the rest away. As, therefore, it was impossible to conceal the stuff, the barrels containing it were rolled over the side of the precipice, where they smashed to pieces, and hurled their bright silver contents ringing into the abyss. And there, when the snow melted, many a poor shepherd or peasant must have found his fortune.* For much the same reasons we had been obliged, when two miles beyond Villafranca, to abandon seventy to eighty wagonloads of arms and equipment intended for the Spanish army, which were either plundered by the body of a hundred Spanish patriots escorting and protecting them, or, what is more likely, taken by the French advanced guard.

The road now became more terrible than ever. It was so stormy that we could hardly stand against the wind and snow, and it was horribly cold. A division which had been unable to continue on its way had evidently bivouacked here on the previous night, and had left melancholy traces of its sojourn. To the right, at the summit of the peak, we saw by the wayside, under the shelter of a ledge of rock, an overturned cart with the mules lying dead beside it. Under the cart lay a soldier's wife with two babies in her arms, evidently twins, which could not have been more than a day or two old. She and a man, who was probably a canteen attendant, lay frozen to death, but the children were still alive. I halted for a moment to contemplate the wretched group. A blanket was thrown over the bodies, and I had the pleasure of witnessing the rescue of the infants, who were handed over to a woman who came along in a bullock cart, to whom a few officers

* Napier gives the amount of the treasure abandoned at £25,000 (*op. cit.*, Chap. V., Book IV.). Blakeney also gives an interesting account of some of the circumstances preceding the sacrifice of this money (*op. cit.*, pp. 78–81).

offered a substantial reward for taking care of them. It was a most harrowing spectacle. The enemy did not need to inquire the way we had gone ; our remains marked out his route. From the eminence on which I stood I saw our army winding its way along the serpentine road, and the motionless blotches of red, left and right, upon the white snow, indicated the bodies of those whom hunger and cold had accounted for.

The dark, almost polar night fell early, and concealed these dreadful sights from our eyes. Amid a deep silence, which was broken only by the howling of the storm and the groans of those who flung themselves left and right on to the ground, never to rise again, we staggered forward. How many will not be missing when day breaks ! The day dawned just as we were descending the western slope of the mountain, and coming upon a road along which we were forced to wade knee-deep in mud, we reached the village of Honorias, which, almost buried in snow, lay on the edge of an oak forest. It was pouring with rain and snow, and I and my poor horse could hardly move a step further. So we crept into a house and forcing our way between hundreds of horses and men, at last succeeded at the cost of many curses and threats, and much abuse, in finding a resting place. I had brought a bag of barley with me from Villafranca, with which I fed my horse, and I gave him water to drink in my hat. But my own biscuits I had to eat in secret in order that I might not tempt my starving comrades to plunder my store. We were told that we should find victuals here, but the bulk of the army, which had passed through the place already, had devoured everything. Here, to my great joy, my old interpreter, Falludo, joined me ; for he had been left behind by Mr. Kearney in order to keep watch over some provisions for the cavalry. But the guards had plundered the whole place. We therefore continued on our way together. As the road was sometimes as hard and rough as granite, and at others knee deep in mud and snow, the soldiers' boots, which had possibly lasted out until this moment, now hung round their feet in ribbons.

After we had ridden gently uphill for a few miles, we

reached, on February 7th, a magnificent bridge composed of three arches, which looked like an aqueduct, and led across an abyss through which foamed a mountain torrent. Both the ravine and the bridge were regarded by many as a bulwark which, the moment the bridge had been blown up, would protect us for a few days from the French, who were hard on our heels. And, indeed, we actually found a party of sappers with an officer there, who had bored two holes into the centre of the bridge and were now engaged preparing to blow it up. Unfortunately, as we heard later, this operation failed, as it had also failed in the case of the bridge leading from Villafranca ; and that was why the French were able to follow us so effectively and so fast. A good deal of fun was poked at the English sapper officers, owing to their obvious incapacity and lack of skill ; and it was deserved, for it was unpardonable and caused our army an incalculable amount of harm.

Many people will feel inclined to ask how it was, if the English army suffered so severely and almost perished through this rapid retreat, that the French, who were also human, and who, moreover, had to march through country already devastated by us, appear not to have suffered, but, on the contrary, to have been able to follow us at great speed and without respite. It sounds odd ; but truth to tell, it is not so ; for, in the first place, the only troops that followed us were a corps of cavalry, light infantry, and field guns ; and naturally we never knew how many of them were left behind. The bulk of their infantry and their artillery came along at a comfortable pace behind. Secondly, an army corps was marching along a side road from Leon to Lugo, to outflank us, which never suffered at all, but marched quietly through country overflowing with provisions of all sorts ; and it was really this army corps which was the cause of our excessive speed. *Hinc illæ lacrimæ !*

When we were across the bridge, we noticed in the dusk a group of small houses, lying some distance from the road, in one of which, together with a number of exhausted soldiers, we took shelter. As we now thought ourselves safe, we unsaddled our horses, and, in ex-

change for money and a few kind words, with which my
friend Falludo, all in secret and confidentially, plied our
host, a poor linen weaver, we received on the quiet some
of his hidden store of barley, a loaf, and a garlic sausage,
which we had to eat clandestinely.   Then we fed our
animals, and at last stretched ourselves on our blankets
under the weaving loom to try to get a little sleep.   It
certainly struck me as strange that this ideal resting place
had not already been seized ; but it lay between rocks
at some distance from the road.   Concluding that the
whole army had already gone on ahead, and that only the
rearguard and those who had fallen out from fatigue still
remained behind, and believing, moreover, that if the rearguard came across and blew up the bridge, we should be
certain to hear the explosion, we felt completely reassured
about our safety.   Soon the whole lot of us lay packed
together on the ground like herrings, and the house-door
being barricaded up, as we were all so dead tired we fell
asleep immediately.   It seemed to me, however, that I
had not slept very long before we were awakened by a
most appalling noise.   It was a portion of the rearguard
that had crossed the bridge and come up with us.   In a
moment our peaceful door was being hammered with the
butt-end of their muskets, and curses were heard, which
were forcibly answered by the men lying all round me on
the floor.   " Open ! " they cried.   " No ! " we replied,
" we are full up here, and we have the first right to the
place."   " Burst open the door ! " shouted an officer ;
and in a moment it was bombarded with heavy stones and
soon crashed inwards, followed by the whole of the 28th
Regiment, who proceeded to stamp across our bodies.
The adjutant was even beast enough to come inside and
ride over the bodies of those who were not able to get up
immediately.   As I crept from under the weaving loom
and out at the door, I, too, got between the horse's legs.
Enraged at what had happened, I overwhelmed that
adjutant with a veritable flood of abuse, and threatened
to shoot him if he took another step forward.   This had
its effect ; swearing heavily he reined back his horse, and
beside himself with rage, he yelled : " Who are you ? "

while every moment I interrupted his curses with similar ones of my own. My one object was to save my blankets and my valise, and to work my way to our horses. Having at length succeeded, at the cost of much swearing and pleading, in reaching them, we mounted, turned out into the street in the most appalling rain mixed with sleet, and strapping on our valises, rode grumbling away.* While we were bridling up, the 28th Regiment had imprudently lighted a number of fires not only on the floor of the house, but also all round it, so as to warm and dry themselves, and before we had gone a hundred yards the whole house burst into flames. Then there was the most frightful tumult and outcry, and the 28th in its turn had to take to its heels and flee from the house, which gave us much secret satisfaction ; and, feeling avenged, we pursued our way more contentedly. Hardly had we gone a mile before my good Falludo had such a severe attack of colic that he was obliged to dismount and lie down behind a hedge. In vain did I endeavour to procure him some relief, but I had nothing with which I could help him, and I therefore pushed on, and reached Lugo at ten in the morning. It is a rather large town situated on a plateau, close to the source of the River Minho.

* Blakeney, who was at the time a subaltern in the 28th Regiment, does not mention this incident, but he mentions so many like it, in which he declares that the 28th had to perform the onerous duty of rousing and urging on the stragglers (*op. cit.*, pp. 69, 89), that it is not unlikely that this incident was only an example of the kind of thing that happened when the rearguard was compelled to drive the stragglers forward. Schaumann, who had fallen among stragglers on this occasion, seems to have misunderstood the intention of the 28th.—Tr.

Chapter 9

THERE was a great throng at the billeting office, but I managed to get a billet at the house of some working people, where my horse was comfortably installed, and where I, too, rejoiced in a bed which they made on the ground for me. It was said that the army would bivouac outside the town, muster, and after having been reorganised, give battle to the French. From my landlord I obtained some fresh pork, some onions, and a little bread and wine for myself, and some barley for my horse. He was among the few kindly people in this country, and, in exchange for payment of course, drew forth for me from some secret hiding place a number of things which, seeing that the inhabitants had fled and had buried everything, were difficult to obtain even for cash. In the town itself, the most hopeless confusion reigned. Numbers of Spanish recruits were brought in and armed ; but as soon as it grew dark they threw away their muskets and deserted. Many more of our horses were shot here. The army has taken post along a strong position, about three miles away, on the crest of a chain of hills. Headquarters are at Lugo. Here we are awaiting the arrival of our reserves and the cavalry. The Brigades under Generals Crawford, Alten and Fraser have gone to Vigo. We, on the other hand, are to go to Corunna, the ultimate goal of all our suffering, where our best friend, the sea, with its ships, more hospitable than the Spaniards, will take charge of us. The apathy with which the inhabitants of this mountain country, who are usually so warlike, have witnessed our misery, is revolting. They were to be seen in large armed hordes, far away from us in the mountains, and deliberately turning away when, in view of their familiarity with the passes and other conditions, they might have been very useful to us, and have covered our retreat. But not only did these puffed-up patriots—or rather patriotic tub-thumpers—give us no assistance, but they also took good care to remove all cattle and all food-stuffs out of our way, emptied and locked their houses, vanished, and, in addition, murdered and plundered our own men who fell out left and right along our road.

Truth to tell, had these hill-folk risen up and joined themselves with us, had they occupied the passes and held foodstuffs in readiness for us, the French would never have dared to follow us into the mountains, where, covered by Corunna, we should have stood firm, and need never have embarked at all. But we had been shamefully forsaken in every way.* Owing to the dearth of transport I understand that we are going to leave all our unfortunate wounded and sick behind in this place, and entrust them to the mercy of the enemy. Hundreds of exhausted soldiers arrive here every hour, but we have no victuals, and I therefore believe we shall soon have to move on.

On my way to my quarters I met the good and faithful Falludo, who, having quite recovered, had already been scouring the town most anxiously for the last few hours to find me. His joy at discovering me again was indescribable. We went to rest, and I know not how long I had slept when the sound of sharp musketry fire woke me up again. I sprang up hastily—I always slept fully dressed—and called Falludo and my landlord, who helped us to saddle up and led us to the gate of the town. It was dark ; the bulk of the inhabitants had fled, and the ring of our horses' hoofs was gruesomely echoed by the deserted streets and open houses. When we got outside, I cast one more look upon the decayed and blackened walls of the town, which loomed darkly above the glowing embers of the fires that had been made with broken-up ammunition wagons. On the other side of the road which we took, there stood the 3rd Hussars of the Legion and the light artillery. As the French columns that were trying to outflank us had already advanced

---

* Oman pleads very eloquently on behalf of these very hill-folk (*op. cit.*, Vol. I. p. 577).—TR.

so far, and as it was considered that to give battle here would merely occasion useless delay, the army had suddenly been ordered to strengthen the bivouac fires and to retire slowly. The French, who were expecting a battle on the following day, and were at first deceived by this *ruse de guerre*, halted in order to concentrate their forces ; when, however, they at last realised our intentions they attacked at once; hence the firing which had roused us. It was, therefore, high time for me and my Falludo to leave the town. Had we slept an hour longer we should have been lost. Silently we rode into the night, the darkness of which was slightly relieved by the bivouac fires that glowed here and there. It began to rain again.

Towards eleven o'clock at night we at last reached a number of large houses close to the roadside. We pressed our way into one of them. Hundreds had taken refuge in it ; the ground floor rooms were packed tight with horses, and it was only after much pleading and cursing that we were able to obtain a little space to rest in. It was quite impossible to get near the fire. But in the end we fell asleep from sheer exhaustion, and neither the stone floor on which we had squatted down, nor our clothes which were wet through, could keep us awake. Our teeth were chattering with the cold, but we were lying so tightly wedged that in the end we warmed each other. It must have been quite one o'clock when one of the hussars called out : " God bless us ! There comes the rearguard ! " " What's the matter, what's the matter ? " I cried. " Get up ! Get up ! " was the reply, " the bugles of the rearguard have just sounded." We had all been told that when the rearguard passed by houses and villages they would blow a blast on their bugles in order to warn those who might be sheltering inside that they must decamp. And now we all scampered head over heels out of doors, and into the darkness, the rain and the storm.

It was just dawn on the 9th January when we reached a branch of the Minho, whose deep banks were spanned by a bridge which a party of the staff corps were preparing to destroy. After a night of gentle rain there blew up such a terrific storm of sleet and hail in the morning that we could hardly keep on our saddles. When it struck our faces the hail stung like drops of molten lead. The army, which had spent this appalling night, almost without rations, in a cold bivouac, were marching slowly in the direction of Quitterez, in a straggling throng, weary, discouraged, hungry, wet to the skin and covered with mud. All the inhabitants had flown ; all the villages were deserted and were therefore immediately plundered. Many of the soldiers lay down completely exhausted in the ditches, never perhaps to rise again. Few women were still to be seen, the majority lay behind somewhere between Villafranca and Lugo. In one of the villages through which we went I saw one of them sink up to her waist in a bog, whereupon, the mud and slime preventing her from rising, she fell, and the whole column marched over her.

Having reached Quitterez, I jumped from my horse, but was so stiff and numb that on dismounting I fell backwards, and was only able to stand up again with great difficulty. We pressed our way into a house, watered our poor horses as best we could, and refreshed ourselves with some bread which Falludo had managed to purchase secretly and at a fabulous price from a peasant along one of the side roads. Here was also dealt out a small ration of salt fish and rum ; but as we had neither fires nor kettles, the salt fish was eagerly swallowed raw, while the rum, of which everybody, by the bye, did not get a portion, was poured down afterwards. The combination of the two in empty stomachs resulted in the death of many of the men on the spot, while several others went mad. One of them took up a defiant attitude, *à la* Fabius, in the middle of the road, and with fixed bayonet shouted that he was General Moore, that the army was to halt, turn and give battle, and the first man who dared to pass him by and disobey his orders he would kill outright. And, by standing there with legs wide apart, in the middle of the highway, brandishing his bayonet, he barred the way to me, a colonel, and several other officers. When at last coaxing words proved of no avail, the whole lot of us crashed forward and rode over him.

We rested whenever we could—wherever we found a shelter or a little grass for our horses. And so it went on throughout the day. Late in the evening, when we were almost dead with cold and fatigue, we reached the town of Betanzos, where headquarters lay. We were now not far from Corunna, and were given quarters which seemed to us like Paradise. The house where we were billeted lay a little way off the road, so that we ourselves and a few officers who joined us in the evening, remained comparatively undisturbed. The town which was not small, had not been much disturbed by the army, part of which was still on the way there, or had been quartered in the neighbouring villages, convents and summer houses, and the remainder of which was bivouacked. Our first concern was to have a good fire made in the kitchen, after which our host regaled us with a plentiful and excellent supper.

From the officers we heard that the march from Quitterez had proved a greater trial than all former marches to the troops.* Officers and men of all regiments came along in groups, or alone, jaded, exhausted, starving and numb. Their feet were swollen, frostbitten, and bleeding, from walking over roads consisting chiefly of granite, quartz, or deep mud. A soldier's wife, probably the last to have got so far, also collapsed and died just outside Betanzos. Here the army was quickly mustered again, put into better order, and then marched off towards Corunna.

A sad affair took place at the bridge over the Minho. A party of about 500 stragglers and exhausted men came up who wanted to cross it, and found it already blown up. Just at that moment the French advanced guard and the Polish Lancers of the Imperial Guard suddenly appeared, and raising a loud cry and brandishing their lances, prepared to charge. But our stragglers from all regi-

---

* According to Napier (*op. cit.*, Book IV., Chap. VI.) the march from Lugo to Betanzos cost the army in stragglers more than double the number of men lost in all the preceding operations.—TR.

ments were not dismayed, and electing a sergeant as their commanding officer, formed square, and with a cheer opened fire on the lancers.   This kept the enemy at a respectful distance for some while, and it was only when several other French regiments appeared that they were compelled to capitulate and allow themselves to be taken prisoners.

We slept like drunkards.   I was constantly dreaming that I was still riding along the edge of terrible precipices and over rocky heights, and every other minute I would jump into the air with fright, as if in the delirium of fever, constantly imagining that I heard the bugles of the rear-guard.   On the 11th January there was too much tumult and noise in the town for me, and mounting my horse I rode away.   The town of Batanzos is three leguas from Corunna.   It lies upon a peninsula formed by two rivers. Across one of these, the Mandea, there is a bridge of fourteen arches, and a mine had been laid to blow it up as soon as the army had crossed it.   How my heart leapt for joy, when, standing upon a height, I beheld a strip of the blue sea upon the horizon, and, about a mile this side of Corunna descried the masts of a few ships ! " Thank God ! We are now safe ! " I cried, and everybody about me heartily agreed.   The road now wound round the slope of a mountain, and marching through Inas to Burgo, we came to a bridge at which we again saw a party of engineers laying a mine.   There was also a detachment of the 60th Regiment established here, which all this time had been acting as a bodyguard over the stores.   God ! how well fed and smart the fellows looked beside us.

As I was riding through the suburbs of Corunna, past a convent called Santa Lucia, I met a number of the inhabitants who were fleeing and taking everything portable with them.   Then I passed through the gate, and went along fine, smoothly paved streets to the commandant.   I was given a billet in that part of the town known as the Citadel, where I had to ride through another gate, and was quartered in the house of a wealthy gentleman called Don Bernardo Mascoso.   We were led into a beautifully furnished sitting-room, which seemed to us like heaven ; then we were shown another charming little room with two beds, and were given a glorious meal. Feeling very happy I smoked a few cigars and drank mulled wine with Falludo, and went early to bed.

On the morning of the 12th January we looked about us. From my window we had a view of the harbour, where only Admiral de Courcy's large man-o'-war and a few transports lay at anchor. The rest of the fleet had gone to Vigo, but had been recalled by express messengers sent by land and sea. Corunna lies on the narrowest part of an irregular peninsula, and is protected by a chain of bastions. At one end stands the Citadel, which forms a sort of horn or arm encircling the harbour. At the other, which is called the San Diego Point, there is a fort, in the middle of which on a rock there stands the castle of St. Antonio. To the south of the town there is a double chain of hills, along the lowest and flattest of which our army will take post.

The next day it was high time for me to go down into the town to report myself to the Commissary-General ; but the first person I met in the streets was my old bug-bear, Mr. Commissary Kearney ! " Good thing you are here ! " he cried. " Come with me at once to my office ; there's plenty to do." I told him about my experiences with the cavalry, and referred somewhat bitterly to the way in which he had increased my difficulties and left me in the lurch. But he pretended not to be listening. My assistant, Falludo, who wished to travel by land to Portugal before the French surrounded Corunna, had had his account settled, and was preparing for his journey. He bade a touching farewell to me. " Oh," he exclaimed, as the tears flowed down his cheeks, " *Vostra Senhoria sempra me tratta comepay ! Vostra Senhoria e humanjo, viva Vostra Senhoria muitosannos !* * I made · him a present of my horse, and he went away. A large number of troops have arrived, and have filled all the houses. A major and four other officers of some Highland regiment

* " Your lordship has always treated me decently and humanely. Long live your lordship ! "—Tr.

have been quartered in my house, and the hospitality of my host seems to have declined in consequence. The bulk of the army is bivouacked on the hill outside the town, without tents, in the rain and wind.

On the 13th January I was sitting in my office attending to some orders, and three hussar quartermasters were standing in front of my table, when suddenly two such fierce flashes of lightning and claps of thunder burst over the town that my windows flew into our faces in a thousand pieces, the doors sprang open, the slates rolled from the roof, while I, who had just been rocking myself in my chair and talking, was flung backwards by the gust of hot air that poured in at the window. Even the quartermasters, who believed that a bomb had fallen in the room and burst, ducked under the table. We were almost deaf and the house had been, so to speak, shaken in its foundations. Pulling ourselves together, we stared at each other in dumb amazement, when the streets were suddenly filled with piteous cries. The whole population, particularly the women, who perhaps believed that an earthquake was going to swallow them up, dashed out of their houses with despair written on their faces, and shouting like maniacs, tore the hair from their heads. On inquiry we heard that these appalling shocks, which I had taken for lightning and thunder, had been caused by the blowing up of two powder magazines, containing 24,000 lbs. of gunpowder, which the Spaniards had destroyed on the heights of Santa Margaretta, so that it might not fall into the hands of the French.* The day was fine and calm. The column of smoke that rose from the ignited powder was therefore magnificent. It rose up to the heavens like a rock of black marble as big as that of Teneriffe, and did not move, and its edges, like white basalt, were dazzlingly illuminated by the sun. And it was over an hour before it began to bend and sink gradually down to the earth.

The inhabitants here are very friendly. Several officers who have been with General Spencer in Cadiz say

---

* Napier also gives an account of this explosion (*op. cit.*, Book IV., Chap V.). (See also Blakeney (*op. cit.*, p. 110–11).)

that the people there are just as liberal and enthusiastic in spirit as they are here.   Everybody, young and old, rich and poor, alike—aye, even the women and girls—are busy on the ramparts helping to throw up entrenchments. Whole troops of young and beautiful girls go in procession with baskets on their heads, carrying ammunition into the forts and to the batteries, and it looks wonderfully fine. Had the Spaniards been as patriotic everywhere else, things would have gone better, and we might possibly have still been standing our ground at Salamanca.   The majority of the officers have lost everything.   I have only two shirts, and no other clothes than those I am wearing. I therefore look quite charming.   My clothes are all torn and caked with hard mud, my shirt is hanging through my breeches, and my decayed socks are showing through my boots.   The first things I bought in Corunna were boots and socks.   In fact, I took good care to freshen myself up, and to compensate myself for the sufferings and privations I had undergone.   When I was not on duty I spent my time in the cafés and confectioners' shops.   I spent my evenings laughing and joking in the company of ladies, and often had drinking bouts with other officers.   Almost the whole of the cavalry horses have been shot on the march, partly because, owing to the lack of shoes, they went lame on the granite roads, and partly because they could go no further through want of fodder.   Large numbers of artillery horses have also perished, as the result of dragging the guns over the great heights between here and Astorga.

Many people blame General Moore very severely for having made his army retreat so fast across mountains and passes, which might have been so splendidly defended, and for having in this way allowed everything to go to ruin.   Others say that he was obliged to do it, if he did not want to be cut off, enveloped, or starved to death.   The wild mountains had neither corn nor bread ! True, but there were flocks of sheep and goats among them, and there were also our horses, mules and draftbullocks.   With these we might at least have been able to hold out until the sick, the wounded, the ammunition

and the war treasure had been sent to the coast in safety.
God knows who is right ! *

It is believed that our general will have to give battle
here and drive the French right back, if he does not wish
to expose himself to the danger of allowing them with
their usual craftiness to wait until one half of our army has
embarked, in order to fall upon and annihilate the other
half.   The whole bay and all our movements can be
watched by the French from the heights, and that is bad.
Our losses are said to amount to 6,000 men,† and half a
million pounds sterling in cash, horses and war material.
On the 14th and 15th of January the fleet arrived from
Vigo, and sailed into Corunna.   The sick, the wounded,
a good deal of artillery, and the cavalry are already on
board.   Since the 24th of December we have marched
370 miles, without halting, in fantastically bad weather,
across lofty and inhospitable hills, and through ice, snow
and mud.   Hunger, plague and death, those companions
of war, entered Corunna with us.   Our artillery and
cavalry horses that have reached Corunna and its environs
were so weak, worn out, and lame, that some of them
dropped dead in the streets, and numbers of others have
had to be shot in order to be put out of their misery.
Their putrefying bodies, swollen by rain and sun, and
bursting in places, are lying under the colonnades in
front of the public buildings in the market place, on the
quays about the harbour, and in the streets ; and while
they offend the eye, they fill the air with a pestilential
stench of decomposition, that makes one ill.   Over 400
of these wretched animals lie about here, and the
discharge of pistols, which are adding to their numbers,
continues incessantly.   Hundreds of horses were killed
on the bay outside the town.   Many of the cavalry
officers who were embarking could not bring themselves
to kill the horses which had been their companions—aye,

---

* See Oman (*op. cit.*, Vol. I., pp. 570–571, and 600–601), who has some
interesting remarks on this point.   Among other things, he suggests that " Moore,
shocked at the state of indiscipline into which his regiments were falling, thought only
of getting to the sea as quickly as possible."—Tr.

† Napier gives the number as 4,000, including those lost in battle (Book IV., Chap. VI.).
Oman (*op. cit.*, Vol. I., p. 582), speaks of 5,000 men who " had perished or been taken
during the retreat."—Tr.

and even their means of salvation—throughout so much suffering ; and they allowed them to run free. And these noble animals, many of which are genuine blood horses, now roam about the town and eat the cabbage leaves they find in the gutters and in the refuse heaps. One of these poor brutes followed the boat which bore its master—an officer of the 18th Hussars—to the transport, and twice swam like a dog from the shore to the ship ; but it could not be taken on board.* All those who witnessed this incident had tears in their eyes. A general order did in fact appear to the effect that all horses were to be delivered to an officer specially appointed to take charge of them ; but, as everyone felt sure that they would not be embarked, but only left to die of hunger or to fall into the hands of the French, nobody took any notice of it. The artillery wagons were thrown over a cliff into the sea. Many of our stores depots were only partially emptied, and the guttersnipes of Corunna got hold of a number of large English hussar swords, with which they trooped about the streets playing at soldiers.

The Spanish governor of Corunna was a good honest man. Mounted on an Andalusian stallion, he galloped round the streets, and wherever he found some Spaniards standing idle he would harangue them, and with mingled kindness and authority urge them to go to the ramparts and help build trenches. Huge mortars were brought up, and the gate of the Citadel was restored by English pioneers and engineers. In short, the turmoil was terrible.

On the morning of the 16th January there was some firing by the outposts. The French having received substantial reinforcements, a battle was believed to be inevitable. It had taken the French some time to concentrate behind Betanzos, and the crossing of the River Burgo, the bridge over which was, after all, wholly destroyed by our engineers, assisted from Corunna, contributed not a

* See p. 97, *ante*. Schaumann means the 18th Light Dragoons. In 1805 the 18th Light Dragoons were clothed and equipped as hussars, but continued to be called light dragoons. In 1813, for the first time, the regiment appears in the Army List as 18th Regiment of Light Dragoons (Hussars).—TR.

little to the delay.   It was only on the 14th January that
the enemy succeeded in restoring it, and in bringing over
his artillery.   General Moore availed himself of this delay
in order to establish order in the army and take up a
position one and a half miles outside the town along a
range of hills, across which the high road passes.   The
British left wing rested on the high banks of the Burgo,
while the right, which was covered by the little village of
Elvina, at the extreme end of the range of hills on the
crest of which the army stood, being less favourably
situated, was supported by General Fraser's division,
which was posted in echelon at a favourable point about
half a mile to the rear.   The reserve, under General
Paget, was formed up close behind the British centre.   At
one o'clock, just as I had finished luncheon and was going
to the office as usual, the sound of sharp firing could be
heard coming from the direction in which the armies
stood, and the noise attracted a large number of people,
who collected on the quays.   From the windows of the
houses it was almost possible to get a view of the battlefield.   At two o'clock the gunfire grew more fierce, and
it was quickly followed by the most terrific musketry fire,
which veiled the heights and adjacent valleys with clouds
of smoke.   All the roofs, windows, balconies and ships'
masts became black with spectators looking towards the
battlefield, and I ran out of the town in order to watch
the fighting from the Santa Lucia height.   It looked
terrible.   The whole valley was clouded with powder
smoke, through which shone the flash of the guns and
muskets.   The firing was unusually fierce, and the
thunder of the guns roared incessantly.   Again and again
we were able to see the English regiments quite plainly
charging the French at the point of the bayonet, and with
a loud cheer forcing them to run uphill under the protection of their guns.

Among many wounded men who were borne past us
into the town there appeared at about four o'clock a party
of several aides-de-camp and officers, marching very slowly
and sadly behind six soldiers bearing a wounded man in
a blood-stained blanket slung upon two poles.   Two

doctors walked on either side of the litter, and repeatedly cast anxious looks inside it. It was General Moore. A cannon shot had shattered his shoulder. He was still alive, but those who followed him entertained no hope of his recovery. Deeply grieved I followed him into the town to the door of his quarters, where a large crowd of people, both English and Spanish, soon gathered. There they waited in dead silence, and with much anxiety and solicitude inquired of everyone who left the house how the General fared.* A number of slightly wounded officers who came into the town told the following story :

On the morning of the 16th, the enemy, having received reinforcements, had increased his force to about 20,000 men. At about two o'clock in the afternoon his whole line was under arms and in battle formation, and under cover of a wood and supported by artillery, a strong column immediately attacked the village of Elvina on our right wing, which was commanded by that brave soldier General Baird. The first onslaught of this huge column was violently repulsed by General Moore in person and by General Baird—a most gallant Scotch officer, who had seen arduous service in the East Indies and all corners of the globe, and who subsequently fought under the Duke of Wellington in every battle, including Waterloo†—at the head of the 42nd Regiment, and Lord William Bentinck's brigade. The village was vigorously defended, and it was here that General Baird lost an arm. Lord William Bentinck's brigade met the enemy with a well-directed shower of bullets, and gave three loud cheers. Then the 52nd, 42nd and 4th Regiments, with bayonets fixed, charged into the midst of the enemy, and so much increased their confusion that they were forced to retire. Sir John Moore had just completed his splendid and

---

* As most students of the Peninsular War are aware, no English general has ever been more severely criticised than Sir John Moore for the campaign that ended with the Battle of Corunna. Perhaps, therefore, it may not seem out of place to quote here Mr. Fortescue's eloquent tribute to him. Mr. Fortescue says (op. cit., Vol. VI., p. 413) : " No man, not Cromwell, nor Marlborough, nor Wellington, has set so strong a mark for good upon the British Army as John Moore."—Tr.

† Schaumann is wrong here. Corunna was Sir David Baird's last battle. There was a David Baird at Waterloo ; but he was the famous general's nephew, Ensign David Baird, of the 3rd Foot Guards. He became Sir David on the death of his uncle in 1829.—Tr.

masterly plan of defence and attack, when he, too, at the very moment when he was shouting encouragement to one of the brigades then charging, fell mortally wounded by a cannon shot. But our troops, undaunted by this event, pressed forward, and forced the enemy to yield and bring up reinforcements. At this moment, Lord Paget, making a movement with the reserve, placed himself at the head of the 95th Regiment and of the 1st Light Battalion of the 52nd, and sweeping everything before him, gained the enemy's left flank, where he was supported by General Fraser's division. Unable to make any headway in this quarter, the French now formed again, and attacking our centre with greater vigour and determination than ever, were now repulsed by Major-Generals Manningham and Leith, who were stationed here with their divisions. Then came the turn of the left wing ; and the enemy attacked with such violence that they actually entered the village that lay across our line, and through which runs the road to Madrid. Here they established themselves in the houses, but were instantly attacked with such ferocity by the 14th Regiment under Colonel Michels, who drove them out at the point of the bayonet, that it seems that some of them were seen to jump out of the windows. The streams of blood in the houses and in the streets is said to have been terrible. At five o'clock the enemy had not only been driven back at all points, but the English had actually advanced.

At six o'clock, under cover of a heavy bombardment and the lively fire of a swarm of skirmishers, the enemy troops withdrew, and gradually all was still. The regiments that suffered most severely were the 4th, 42nd, 50th and 81st. General Sir David Baird lost an arm, Lieut.-Colonel Napier of the 92nd Regiment, and Majors Napier * and Stanhope were left on the field, and Lieut.-Colonel Wynch of the 4th Regiment, Maxwell of the 26th, Fane of the 59th, Griffith of the Guards, and Majors Williams and Miller of the 81st Regiment,

---

* This was the eldest brother of the famous author of the History. He was commanding the 50th Regiment, and was badly wounded. He was subsequently treated with great generosity by Soult. (See Napier, *op. cit.*, Book IV., Chap. V.)—Tr.

together with a number of subalterns, were either wounded or killed. Everybody is particularly distressed about General Moore. I returned home almost wild with sorrow at what I had seen and heard. At ten o'clock in the evening, the victorious English troops gradually marched into the town in the finest order to embark. They were all in tatters, hollow-eyed, and covered with blood and filth. They looked so terrible that the people of Corunna made the sign of the cross as they passed. After as many of the wounded as possible had been collected, and the dead buried, our piquets resumed their advanced position, and the army prepared to embark. The whole of the night of the 16th–17th was occupied in this way, so that by daybreak everybody, except the brigades of Generals Hill and Beresford, was on board. The piquets now withdrew and were embarked with their regiments, and while all this was afoot, the enemy lay perfectly still. They had learnt to know us. General Beresford occupied the ground near St. Lucia, and General Hill the heights in front of the Citadel. Meanwhile the inhabitants did all they could to facilitate our embarkation, and thus, after all, we became reconciled to the Spanish character. In the night of January 17th–18th, the brigades of Generals Hill and Beresford were also embarked. The moment the enemy were satisfied that we were all on board they began to move forward, and, occupying the heights of St. Lucia, erected batteries that swept the harbour.

General Sir John Hope now assumed command of the troops.* He was a handsome man, with a bold military air. I saw him charging through the streets like mad, fresh from the battlefield, issuing orders right and left. The death of his friend, Sir John Moore, is said to have left him inconsolable. A French officer who had been taken prisoner said to one of our own officers : " Neither you yourselves nor your general, knows how very near you and all your army came to falling into our hands ! " " How's that ? " inquired the Englishman. " No Englishman would ever have been capable of such

* He had naturally succeeded Sir John Moore long before this.—Tr.

treachery ! " " I readily believe that," the other replied,
" but I do not mean through one of your own men, but
through your friends and allies—that is to say, through
General Morla, who sold Madrid to the French." This
anecdote shows how correct had been the judgment
which our unfortunate and much misunderstood general,
Sir John Moore, had formed of the Spanish character.

A very touching incident occurred at my quarters
yesterday. When the English troops under General
Baird, which afterwards joined us at Benevente, first
embarked at Corunna previous to the great retreat, a mule
belonging to my host was requisitioned and given to an
English officer. Now this mule must have collapsed
from hunger on the retreat, and then, finding itself
recovering, must have got up and followed the army, and
probably swum several rivers and found its way along
various bye-ways ; for it suddenly appeared in Corunna
without either a saddle or anything on its back, and,
staggering into its master's stables, dropped down
exhausted. The whole family assembled round it, and
did their best to help the poor brute ; but it was too far
gone, and it died to-day.

Even my landlord seems to be suffering from the
events of the last few days. He has become gloomy and
bad-tempered, and told me that he could no longer provide
luncheon, particularly as a number of Highland officers
had joined our party. Hitherto I had always supplied
him with fresh meat, but towards the end this was no
longer possible, for we had no more bullocks, although
there was plenty of horse-flesh to be had. The lady of
the house has fallen ill from fright and grief, and is lying
in bed ; and my host does not leave her for an instant.
Meanwhile I have been able to lay aside a store consisting
of 12 lbs. of chocolate, some sugar, a few cigars, two
bottles of brandy, and some tea, and have packed it all
in a small box. I bought the chocolate from a wonderfully pretty girl who, with tears in her eyes, exclaimed to
me : " *Ay nosotros infelices !* " (Woe to us wretches !).
" What will happen to us when the French come in ? Oh
how lucky you English are to have your ships here and

to be able to get away ! " This young lady seemed to be very anxious to accompany me, and the temptation was great—but Schaumann was reasonable !

On the 18th January I saw, among other regiments, the 32nd march in. It halted close to me. I rushed up to Colonel Hinde and begged him to take me under his protection. " It will give me much pleasure," he replied, " to take my good old marching companion and former commissary under my wing. Just come here and stick to me ! " My old servant, Pat, who was still among the living, caught sight of me, and falling out of the ranks, expressed his joy at seeing me again. I begged him to take my box containing provisions, and undertook to carry the valise myself. The order " Quick march ! " suddenly rang out, and we marched along the quay, and then down some steps where we pushed everyone violently aside and passed under a vaulted arch to the water's edge. The sloops from the men-o'-war were already waiting, and we were just on the point of boarding them, when on the height of St. Lucia there was a sudden terrific outburst of fire, and it seemed as if the Day of Judgment had come. Shot and shell whistled about our heads, and striking first the water, then the sloops, and anon the ships themselves, made hearing and seeing almost impossible. It was the French, who at this very moment had opened fire from their batteries, in order to shell and bombard the harbour and the fleet. Then followed a scene which I shall remember to my dying day. Riding peacefully at anchor in the harbour were hundreds of transports, and at least twelve battleships—the *Ville de Paris*, the *Victory*, the *Barfleur*, the *Zealous*, the *Implacable*, the *Elizabeth*, the *Norge*, the *Plantagenet*, the *Revolution*, the *Audacious*, the *Endymion*, and the *Mediator*,* under Admirals de Courcy, Samuel Hood, and Bowen, and the boats from the battleships were being rowed backwards and forwards, embarking the troops. Up to that moment

---

* This list corresponds exactly with that given by Brenton in his " Naval History " (see Vol. IV., p. 332), except that he does not mention the *Zealous*, while Schaumann does not mention the *Tonnant*. The *Revolution*, however, should be the *Resolution ;* for up to the time of writing no British man-of-war has, as far as I am aware, been named in the way Schaumann suggests.—Tr.

everything had been quiet and peaceful, but the minute the bombardment started, and the shot dropped among the shipping and sent splinters whistling all around us, there arose an extraordinary tumult and outcry. In a moment a man-o'-war of seventy-four guns opened its portholes, and returning the French fire, bombarded the heights until the very harbour shook. Unfortunately, however, our shot had no effect, for the French were securely entrenched behind the rocks and only had to fire blindly among us in order to be sure of hitting at least one of our ships. All the transports immediately cut their anchors and began to get under way. They ran into one another, and damaged and smashed one another's bowspits, rigging and yards. Five ships which attempted to escape between the island of St. Antonio and the Citadel got into such terrible confusion that one of them ran up on a bank in the direction of the French and was stranded, and had to be abandoned by its crew and blown up. Most of the transports sailed out of the harbour and made for the open sea, so that only the men-o'-war remained, and they had to take many thousands of troops on board.

At last one of the shots ricochetted over the water and struck the wall quite close to us, whereupon, owing to the fact that we were so closely crushed together on the steps, one of the naval officers called to us from the boats, and told us to turn back and march through the town to the lighthouse, where we would be more protected, and where they would await us. Just as another shot whistled over our heads, one of the men, grinding his teeth and shaking his fist at the French, suddenly exclaimed : " Ah, you mad beasts ! " At which everybody laughed. We therefore marched out towards the Citadel to the opposite shore, which was very rocky, and over which the breakers were beating furiously. The sloops from the men-o'-war could not come up close, but were kept at a safe distance from the rocky boulders by means of their oars, while we had to go to the edge of the rocks which were being washed by the surf, and then, with the water splashing over our heads, take hold of one of the oars. Then we were grasped by the mighty fists of the sailors, who were leaning overboard, and seized and dragged in like sheep. The naval officers commanding the sloops shouted and swore like mad when any one of us brought luggage with him. The orders were that only men were to be saved—no baggage ! Every piece of luggage we brought with us, therefore, was thrown overboard without ceremony, and there was already a whole variety of valises, chests, parcels, and such-like tossing about in the surf. At last my turn came, and closing my eyes, I plunged into the breakers. The water rose above my head, sealing both my ears and my eyes, and I felt myself being seized. My valise, which held all I possessed, was on the point of being consigned to the waves, when I angrily clasped it to my breast and cried : " I am a commissary, and this valise contains public papers and money ! "   " Well, then, stick to it and be damned," exclaimed one of the officers. We started off immediately, and were flung head over heels on board the first transport we came across, which was already under sail. Far away on the shore I saw the remainder of the 32nd Regiment, and on a ledge of rock, my faithful Pat who had lost me in the crowd, was standing with the small wooden box on his shoulders containing my chocolate, brandy and cigars. This sight went like a stab to my heart. I never saw either Pat or the box again.

While we were sailing out of the harbour, the thunder of the Spanish batteries, of the English men-o'-war, and of the French guns continued as violent as ever. But I cannot express the joy I felt at being out of all danger, and having been spared through all that peril. We all embraced and congratulated each other. Triumphantly I glanced back towards the French. " If ever we should happen to meet again," I muttered to myself, " I devoutly hope you may go to the devil ! "

I took off my soaking wet clothes, hung them up to dry, and rejoiced at finding in my valise a pair of dry socks, which I had bought in Corunna. I handed my valise to the captain to keep for me, assuring him as I did so, that it contained things of great value. He laughed incredulously. " Yes," I said, " in addition to certain official papers, it contains fifty Spanish dollars, which is all I have in the world !" "Poor fellow !" he replied.

Our ship, the *Nimrod*, was a three-master, and was packed to overflowing with troops of every description. Twenty-two officers and 220 men were on board, in addition to the crew and the servants. There was not enough water or provisions on board to supply half of them for a fortnight. But the wind had meanwhile become very favourable, and was blowing towards England. Although the admiral had signalled from his flagship that no transport was to make for England until the whole number were ready to start under escort of a man-o'-war, our captain thought that with such a throng of starving men on board, and with such an inadequate supply of provisions, he would be justified, in view of the favourable wind, not to wait for the convoy. He therefore decided to risk it, and crowding on all the sail he could, we took flight.

It was evening. Corunna lay hidden by a thick mist, through which the gleams of the lighthouse and the flames of a burning suburb projected a faint glow. The bombardment had ceased ; only now and again could we hear the report of one of the great French mortars. At last the blackness of night fell upon the coast and the sea, and the past lay behind me like a nightmare. At bedtime there was the utmost confusion in the cabin. Officers of the rank of Colonel Alten and Major Hay, of the 18th Hussars, for instance, had taken possession of the bunks, while the rest of us had to lie packed together like sardines on the floor. As there was very little room we had to assume the following order : three rows were formed ; the first row spread out their legs and allowed the second to lay their heads between them, and the third row lay with their heads between the legs of the second.

We were given private soldiers' rations, and were not allowed to use drinking water to wash with. But it was impossible to wash with sea water, because soap will not dissolve in it, and it does not remove any dirt. In the morning we received a pailful of porridge or gruel, with a large lump of butter floating on the top of it. We were all so famished that this pail was besieged as it was being brought down the stairs that led to the cabin. Nobody had any plates, knives or forks. Some borrowed a spoon and a cup, or a fragment of china from the sailors, or did as I did, and made themselves a spoon, which they dipped into the bucket. At midday we had peas and salt meat, with a portion of rum, which looked quite black, and at night we had a little hard cheese and some ship's biscuit. We felt the need of tobacco badly. With much pain and silent sorrow I bethought myself of my box containing chocolate, cigars, tea and sugar. If only I had had it with me, how they would have envied me ! And how they would have made up to me in order to get something out of it ! Meanwhile we drove away care, and forgot our privations, either by playing cards in the cabin, where two or three whist parties were constantly engaged, or by going on deck and teasing a monkey belonging to the captain. We had a few showers of rain on our journey, but the wind was favourable throughout, and we drove before it in a direct line from Corunna to Portsmouth.

How Mr. Augustus received Orders to go to Portugal, and with a heavy Heart leaves England—Life in Lisbon—Portugal's Political Condition—On the Road again—How the English Army escapes the Pursuit of the Enemy near Montelegre, and Mr. Augustus goes to Braga with the Cavalry.

[TRANSLATOR'S NOTE.—Schaumann describes the landing of the troops in England, their deplorable condition, and their hearty reception by their fellow countrymen. He spends a few weeks in London, to recover from the exertions of the campaign, and after applying for further military employment, General v. d. Decken promises to think of him when the next vacancy occurs.]

ON the 31st March, 1809, I received a short note from Mr. W. F. Dunmore, the Deputy Assistant Commissary-General, in which he asked me whether I would like to join a fresh expedition to Portugal. I need hardly say with what joy I accepted this offer. On April 3rd I received another note from Dunmore, in which he commissioned me to look round London to see if I could not hunt up a few German bakers and enlist them for the commissariat.

6th April. My appointment is now definitely settled, approved by the authorities, and I have been entered in the lists by the Treasury.*

12th April. I reported myself to Mr. Gauntlet, the resident war commissary at Gravesend, and then hurried to the transport office, where I was ordered to go without delay and embark on the *Indefatigable*, commanded by Captain Wills, which was lying at anchor in Stokes Bay. With all possible speed I purchased the necessaries for the journey, and taking a boat went on board. Twenty-eight artillery horses and their drivers had already embarked.

On April 17th, 1809, we were on our way, and after a somewhat tedious journey, we passed the Berlengas on the Portuguese coast on April 25th, and reached the bold promontory known as the Cabo da Roca, but usually called Cintra Rock. We sailed down the hilly coast of

* Schaumann's salary, however, was not increased. He was still to be paid 7s. 6d. a day.—TR.

Portugal, keeping Cape Cintra always in sight. The air is so soft and warm, so balmy and bright, that we are beginning to recover from our rough passage. We shall reach the Tagus this evening.

In the Tagus, April 26th, 1809. It is a lovely day ! What a climate ! The sky is such a deep blue, and it is so bright and warm, and the most fragrant breezes are wafted from the coast. There is plenty doing in the harbour. Boats laden with oranges, lemons, vegetables or poultry, come out to meet us. They want threepence for fourteen large oranges. The moment one lands in Lisbon the beautiful vision presented by the white houses as they gleamed afar off in the sunshine is soon horribly dissipated by the badly metalled and steep roads, the heaps of refuse, the dogs, a dead horse covered with flies and in the last stage of decomposition, soldiers, monks, sailors, civilians in their cloaks, ragged townspeople, whores, the smell of fish fried in oil, and broken windows with no shutters. And yet the Portuguese say :

> " *Quem não tem visto Lisboa*
> *Não tem visto cousa boa !* " *

In the evening I dined with the men of our department in Belem. We drank heavily. Some pretty girls who were watching us from their windows were invited to join us, and we joked and sang. It was already late when I returned to the ship. I again went into the town on April 27th, and for the express purpose of having a good lunch. I found Lisbon, and all the surrounding forts, full of our troops. General Beresford was the governor. At twelve o'clock the whole fleet fired a great salvo to celebrate the victory gained over the French fleet at Rochefort, and many a bottle was emptied in honour of the occasion.

28th April. To-day I landed with all my luggage, and took up my quarters at the American Hotel Ruo do Corpo Santo. As I heard, however, that no one was to be allowed to take more luggage with him into the field than

---

* " He who has not seen Lisbon
Has not seen a good thing."

a small hand-valise, I took care before I left the ship to pack all my beautiful miniatures and studies, which were now quite a fair collection, together with my precious paints, my drawings, and my superfluous clothing, and addressing the whole to my landlady in London, handed the parcel to the captain, who promised most faithfully that, as all empty transports were to return at once, he would see that my things were handed to the post in Portsmouth. The cavalry are already disembarking, and from what I hear, we, too, shall be marching in a day or two. In order to find out what is happening I often go to the Commissary-General's office, or take a walk. Opposite our place is a house full of pretty young girls. I am very busy putting my things in order, and, as a sort of horse fair is being held outside the town, I am trying to buy a mule ; for, according to all accounts, I am supposed to be going on a secret mission with Mr. Commissary Downey. The mules and horses that were offered for sale were, however, either lame or blind, or excessively dear. All the good ones had been purchased by the army already on the road.

As to what happened in Portugal during our retreat to Corunna, I heard the following account : The story of the unhappy events that had taken place in northern Spain were first made known in all their horror in Lisbon, together with the disturbing news that three French armies were concentrating in order to march into Portugal —one in Galicia under Marshal Soult, one in Salamanca under General Lapisse, and a third under Marshal Victor on the banks of the Tagus, at which nearest point the French advance was most to be feared, as the only protection at hand on this side consisted of a few fugitive troops which General Cuesta was trying to reorganise. This news occasioned the greatest unrest and alarm. The garrison and all stores were withdrawn from Almeida, the forts and batteries on the Tagus were left without means of defence, and the English troops were concentrated and held ready to embark at a moment's notice.

Fortunately for Portugal, Bonaparte, in order to make ready for a war with Germany, returned to France with

15,000 of his best troops, and this, by putting a stop to the progress of the French army, afforded an opportunity of making more careful preparations, of which the Allies availed themselves with great energy. General Beresford, who was chosen for the purpose by the British Government, was made a marshal and appointed Commander-in-Chief of the Portuguese Army, and English officers were at the same time placed in the higher ranks of every battalion. By this means a uniform system was introduced throughout the army in matters of 'discipline and subordination, which was what it chiefly needed in order to place it on a war footing. For the fact that it did not lack native courage, and was well able, under good leadership, to fight against the French had been proved by the legion which had some time previously been formed, entirely of Portuguese troops, by Sir Robert Wilson. Thanks to these demonstrations of strength on the part of the inhabitants, the whole country had been filled with new hope, and as England had not only taken 20,000 Portuguese troops into her pay, but had also increased her own army in Lisbon to 14,000 men, the old feeling of confidence had gradually been restored before any fresh complications had arisen.

I hear that I am not to go with Mr. Downey, who is going to take an interpreter with him, but I am to meet him at headquarters in a week. After having waited six hours at the office of the Commissary-General for instructions, I was told to remain in Lisbon under the orders of Commissary-General Dunmore. I was not at all pleased at this news, for I am not fond of office life, and much prefer active work in the field. Very soon, however, I was recalled to the central office, where I found that all my previous instructions had been cancelled, and I was to follow headquarters to Oporto ! Good ! Nothing but orders, counter-orders, and disorder ! I am to march this afternoon, and to Rio-Mayor forsooth, where I am to take over the stores, so that I have still a thousand and one details to attend to. As I have not yet been able to obtain either a horse or a mule, I am relying on my luck and on the requisitioning system, and have decided to set off on foot. I therefore went aboard a boat in the afternoon with Mr. Gibbon, in order to sail up the Tagus as far as Villa Franca, by which means we saved a good deal of time, and spared ourselves much trouble. Wind and tide being both favourable, and the banks of the Tagus delightful, we reached Villa Franca in the evening, and stayed the night there.

After having requisitioned a mule from the magistrate, we started off on the 30th for Alcantara, five leguas further on. We got there late and had to cover another two leguas to Azambuja.

Travelling *viâ* Santarem, I reached Rio-Mayor on the afternoon of the 3rd May, and the moment I had been given a billet, I called on Mr. Vanstock, the resident commissary, who was just about to sit down to a meal and kindly invited me to join him. I accepted with pleasure, and proceeded to explain to him that to my great regret I had been ordered to take over his duties, and handed him my credentials. In return, however, he gave me a letter addressed to myself, which had been left by the Commissary-General on his way through the town, from which I read exactly the reverse. It was to the effect that I had been so warmly recommended to him as a capable man, that he intended to give me more important duties than the charge of a small stores depôt on the lines of communication. I was therefore to follow headquarters without delay, and report to him there. Now, all this would have been excellent if only I had been mounted ! As, however, all horses, mules and donkeys in this small town had already been requisitioned for the public service, and were not to be had even at a high price, I was at a loss to know what to do. Two officers, Mr. Hornsby, of the Scotch Fusiliers, and a doctor, who have arrived here, are in the same predicament. We shall all travel together. Mr. Vanstock is doing all he can to make us comfortable. His wife and children are in Oporto, where, he says, the French are perpetrating the worst horrors. We comforted him, and all went to bed a little top-heavy.

[TRANSLATOR'S NOTE.—With great pains they at last manage to procure two post mules, and two donkeys. Schaumann, Hornsby, the doctor and the postillion take it in turns to ride the mules and the donkeys, and travel in very hot weather *viâ* Leiria, Pombal Condeixa to Coimbra. Schaumann stays four days in Coimbra, then proceeds *viâ* Prelano de Camino to Agueda and Villa Nova. On the way he hears that the English Army has taken Oporto by storm.*]

Having reached Oporto on the evening of the 13th, I dined and went immediately to the Commissary-General, Mr. John Murray. He had been anxiously awaiting me, and had already appointed me commissary to the 14th and 20th Light Dragoons, which, however, had marched in pursuit of the enemy on the previous day. I was to return at eight o'clock to receive my instructions. Aghast at having to undertake so important and fateful a duty, I left the office with a face as long as a fiddle, and walked about the town. It was both large and beautiful, but the French had dealt most severely with it. There were some French prisoners in an underground cellar, and they were looking through the iron grill and laughing and joking, while a crowd of street ruffians with angry gestures and drawn knives were demanding to be let in to murder them, which, of course, the English guard did not allow them to do.

At eight o'clock, according to instructions, I returned to the Commissary-General. It was raining heavily. I had to wait a long time. At last his red-haired adjutant, Mr. Coffin, with the honey-sweet expression of a Judas, told me to cross the river to Villa Nova, the suburb of Oporto, and to call on a Mr. Nesbit, a Commissary, who by rights should have marched with the light cavalry, but had shrewdly reported himself sick. From him I was to obtain my instructions. Damn him !

Having failed in my attempt to reach Villa Nova that night, I set off in the direction of the suburb at seven o'clock on the following morning, and crossing the river once more, found the said commissary, who did not seem to be ill at all. In any case, I was unable to load the rations, which another commissary, Mr. Lobo, was to give me for my two regiments, for I had no carts. I spent the whole day running up and down any number of

* This was on the 12th May, 1809.—Tr.

extremely bad and hilly roads, in the sweltering heat, from the stores to the Commissary-General, then to the Regidor, and on to the Provedor and the Juiz. At last, at midday, the carts came, and then I had to draw salt fish, ship's biscuit, oats and rum, and see them all loaded. When at length I had completed every formality and got the carts across the river and on the march, it was five in the afternoon. I had had nothing to eat since seven o'clock, was saturated with perspiration, and was so tired after all that running about that I could hardly stand up. Mounted on a bad requisitioned mule, without any help, money, or office, and lacking even the means of taking the necessary writing materials and books with me, I was expected not only to overtake two cavalry regiments which had had three days start in pursuit of the flying foe, but also to satisfy all their wants, and, in addition, to cross the hills over most appalling roads, with fifty bullock carts loaded with provisions and forage! When Mr. Coffin smilingly handed me my final instructions at the Commissary-General's office, and wished me a pleasant journey, I had to summon every kindly feeling I possessed not to break out in a torrent of reproaches, and thus be guilty of insubordination.   I bit my lips in my rage, hurried home, ate a scanty meal, and mounting my mule, left the city of Oporto accompanied by a guide.

Penafiel, May 15*th*.   Here I am, and I am quite desperate ! I had hardly been on the road an hour when it began to pour like fury, and the roads became like rivers. I caught up a Portuguese, called Senhor Domingo Antonio Minho, who was interpreter to Mr. Melville the commissary of the 26th Dragoons, and who was going my way.   After we had travelled about three German miles,* it became pitch dark.   It was stormy and raining in torrents, and the roads between the rocks were so dangerous that at the village of Alvator we were obliged to take shelter in a big house which the French had plundered, and which was tenanted only by soldiers.   I installed my mule as well as I could in a large stable, and repairing to the kitchen, wrapped myself in my blankets,

* 13½ miles.—Tr.

and laid down with several others on the floor beside the
kitchen fire. I told my young muleteer to lie down
beside me, and resolved to stay awake and keep an eye on
him. I was so overcome by the day's exertions, however,
that before I knew what had happened, I had fallen fast
asleep. The day had hardly dawned when, starting up,
I called my boy by name. There was no answer. "He's
gone to the stables and is saddling the mule," I thought,
and ran downstairs. But heaven help me !—the boy,
the guide and my mule had all disappeared ! The devils
had stolen away from the fire while I was asleep, and
creeping into the stables, had told the soldiers there, who
had questioned them, that they were going to water the
mule, and had thereupon fled. I was so mad with rage
that I would have shot both of them on the spot if only
I could have caught them up. When I had calmed down
a bit, I sat down at once and wrote a long report of what
had happened to me to Mr. Murray, the Commissary-
General, and gave the letter to a Portuguese dragoon
who happened to be passing through the village with
despatches for headquarters. And now what was I to do ?
It was impossible to get another mule in the plundered
district. I therefore hired a man to carry my valise, and
bearing my own small despatch case with my writing
materials myself, for it contained things of value, such as
my instructions and my diary, I set off on foot for
Penafiel.

[TRANSLATOR'S NOTE.—At Penafiel Schaumann succeeds in getting a
pony and a guide. At Marosos he encounters a rich Spaniard who treats
him very hospitably, lends him a mule, and travels with him *via* Guimaraes
to Egregia Nova. Here the Spaniard suddenly changes his attitude, and
insists on returning home together with the mule he had lent Schaumann.
The latter again continues the journey on foot.]

At midday on the 17th May I passed a field where the
French had bivouacked. All the furniture and even the
crockery had been taken from the houses of a neighbouring
village, and had been brought into the field. The beds
and the mattresses lay in rows in the mud. The drawers
from the various articles of furniture had been used as
mangers. Wardrobes had been transformed into bed-

steads and roofs for the huts ; all the crockery and glass lay in fragments on the ground. The chairs, staircases and window frames had been used partly as fuel for the kitchen fires, and partly to feed huge bonfires which had been lighted when the French had withdrawn. The unfortunate inhabitants stood all around lamenting their plight. All the crosses and statues of the saints on the road had been thrown from their pedestals, and the alms-boxes in front of them broken open and plundered, while all the altars and chapels had been ruined and polluted. In the churches even the graves had not been spared, and the sanctuaries had been rifled. Altar candlesticks, and arms and legs of apostles and saints, torn vestments chalices, prayer books, and the like, mixed up with straw and filth, lay all about them. In one chapel there were a number of French prisoners with an English guard over them. I saw one well-dressed Portuguese at the head of a band of peasants offering the English sergeant ten gold florins to give the prisoners up. The cruelties perpetrated at this period by the Portuguese hill-folk against the French soldiers who fell into their hands are indescribable. In addition to nailing them up alive on barn doors, they had also stripped many of them, emasculated them, and then placed their amputated members in the victims' mouths— a ghastly sight !

Towards evening I reached the bridge of Saltador, and shortly afterwards I passed two farm houses and Campa Ruivas, where I intended to spend the night. But all the houses were chock full of men of the Coldstream Guards and the light cavalry, together with General Wellesley's staff. Here at last I reached the 14th Regiment, and reported myself to its commander, Colonel Hawker. It was quite impossible to obtain either provisions or forage for the troops. All around there was nothing but hills and rocks, and every house for miles had been plundered by the French. Anybody who had anything to eat could have a meal. I comforted my dragoons with this assurance.

At last, after much trouble, in company with the commissary, Mr. James Ogilvie, I found shelter in a ruined house, where, for want of chairs, we installed ourselves on the floor by the fire, and supped off ship's biscuit and water. We were wet to the skin and covered with mud. The water was oozing from our boots. We were so tired that we both lay down on the wet stones and fell asleep. At midnight I was awakened by the cold, my teeth were chattering, and the fire had gone out. The hours went by like years, and everybody longed for the morning. At last the dawn broke, and with it the bugles sounded. We all got up, yawned and stretched, then, shaking ourselves like dogs, decamped.

Ruivas, 18*th May*. All the streets in the village are full of troops, who with pale and famished faces are standing up to their knees in mud, waiting their turn to march out. I received a few bullocks for my dragoons, which, with the help of one or two men who had lost their mounts, I managed with great trouble to drive along, for the brutes were wild and intractable. What made them more particularly timid and unwilling to advance were the many naked and bloody corpses of French soldiers that were lying in the road, and the sight of broken bridges across roaring forest streams, which they had to cross, and which had been repaired with brushwood and trees.

The hills seemed to be getting ever higher and bigger, and the roads ever narrower and more impracticable. Our cavalry suffered severely. I was lucky enough to obtain some Turkish wheat and some Portuguese milho * for my dragoons. Not far from Villa Nova, the cavalry halted to feed. In Villa Nova we got a little bread, meat and corn, and then continued our march.

After I had climbed a very high hill that fatigued me so much that I often had to stop and take a little rest, I caught sight of a few lights and fires gleaming through the darkness, and feeling utterly exhausted and feeble, for I had walked thirty-five English miles that day, I at last found myself in Montelegre.

The French had left the place only that morning, and had plundered the whole town. The inhabitants had fled, and all the houses were deserted and empty. I took

* This appears to be millet.—Tʀ.

shelter in the first house I could find.   Here in the hills
one sees hardly anything but goats and rye.   The
English soldiers, and particularly the officers, pull
dreadfully long faces over the rye bread.   " It lies sour
on the stomach ! " wailed Colonel Hawker.   Even the
horses could not get on with rye, for it purged them
violently.   On the other hand, the Germans were as
delighted as children with the rye bread.   It appears that
we are to remain in this wretched hole, stuck between grey
shelves of rock, until General Beresford has attempted to
overtake the French from the other side, and to cut them
off from the Spaniards—which he will not find an easy
task.

May 20*th*.   Another wretched night.   According to
all accounts we shall soon leave this place.   At nine
o'clock this morning an Englishman mounted on a mule
halted at my door and announced that he had been sent
by the Commissary-General as a clerk to assist me in my
duties, and to work under my orders.   I was badly in
need of such assistance, and was therefore very much
pleased at the sight of this prospective companion and
attendant, who seemed a nice fellow, but none too young.
He was a Mr. Bailey.   It is raining incessantly here, and
I am cold, tired, and peevish.   I purchased a nice mule
from a sergeant, complete with saddle and bridle.   It had
been taken from the French, and I paid him 80 piastres
for it.   So I am now happy again, and have a mount.
At twelve o'clock to-day, orders came that we were to
march back the way we had come.   The troops will not
march till to-morrow, but as I always have to be ahead of
them, I left this hateful spot at four in the afternoon, in
very high spirits, accompanied by Mr. Bailey.

Passing through Salamonde on the 21st May we
reached Braga, eight leguas from Oporto, at twelve
o'clock on the 22nd.   After dinner I went to General
Payne, who was commanding the cavalry, and reported
myself.   I told him with all due respect, but quite frankly,
that I hoped his reproaches were not directed against me,
for I had only been appointed commissary to the 14th
Dragoons when the regiment had already been two days

on the road; that my mule had been stolen from me on the journey, which was not my fault ; that the regiment had not been too badly off as far as goats and rye bread were concerned, and that the horses had also had rye; that in the midst of the mountains, where rye alone was grown, it was impossible to conjure wheat or oats out of the soil, and that it was impossible to send provisions after a regiment of light cavalry which was pursuing the enemy night and day at such speed across the mountains and over impracticable roads.   I also said that I thought I had done my utmost, and that it was not right to expect too much of a commissary, who, like myself, had been left with no money, no assistance, and no office.   I added that if failure there had been, it was due to my superiors, and not to me.   " Very well," he replied, " then I forgive you ; but in that case allow me to sh—— and spit on your Commissary-General, who is squatting comfortably in Oporto, while he leaves us here to starve ! "   I withdrew as quickly as possible, and conveyed the general's rage, together with the expressions he had used, in a long letter to Commissary-General Dalrymple, dated Braga, the 22nd May, 1809.

Chapter 11

[TRANSLATOR'S NOTE.—Schaumann leaves Braga at 4 a.m. on the 31st May, and reaches Villa Nova de Tamalicao at ten. Then continuing his journey to Oporto, which he reaches at eight in the evening, he stays there three days. Setting off again, he reaches Thomar on the 17th June, having spent four days in Coimbra on the way.]

THOMAR, June 19th. My cousin Gustav marched with the 1st Hussar regiment to-day. To my great regret they have had to move to another station owing to lack of forage. The 14th and 16th Light Dragoons are remaining here with the staff. Every day I have to forage for my regiment in the surrounding fields, which are allotted to me in turn by the magistrate, and I have to cut the poor people's corn down. The latter stand by lamenting, howling and crying, and tearing their hair, begging me, often on their knees, to spare their property ; but alas ! in vain. When one of the townsmen from whom I was taking forage this morning saw that his prayers were of no avail, he went mad with rage, and fetching a gun from his cottage, was on the point of firing at me when he was seized by the arm by his wretched wife and one of my dragoons, and was just prevented from hitting me, the ball flying into the air above my head. What a horrible thing war is ! Often, when I am thus engaged my eyes are streaming with tears ; but I cannot help it. I am compelled, both by my position and my instructions, to answer for the horses being in fit condition to do their work. It is part of my duty to supervise the cutting down and the loading of the corn, and to compensate the poor people for their loss by giving them a requisition receipt on headquarters, based upon a valuation of what I have taken from them. As a rule they assure me that they either fear the magistrate will keep their money—a not uncommon occurrence in this country—or that they prefer their own corn to our cash, for they cannot so easily purchase fresh supplies of the former, and the latter is not edible. Furthermore, it is my most solemn duty to enter the town every day at the head of the regiment, laden with corn and the curses of the inhabitants.

[TRANSLATOR'S NOTE.—On the 23rd of June, Schaumann hears that he has been appointed an Ensign in the 7th Battalion of the King's German Legion, the appointment to date from April 5th, 1809. He is very proud of this, and is heartily congratulated by the whole garrison in Thomar.]

Ever since the beginning of the year Spanish affairs had taken a very favourable turn. No moment, therefore, could be more opportune than the present for making headway against the enemy, particularly as Bonaparte is engaged in a war against Austria, and has just suffered a heavy reverse near Aspern and Esslingen on the Danube, which make it impossible for him to support his Spanish armies.

At last, on the morning of the 2nd of July, 1809, we left Thomar and marched to Villa del Rey, and then on the 3rd of July to Cortizados. The road which stretched away across the hills, was bad in parts, but good on the whole. Large herds of goats were grazing on the heights all round, while in the valley you could see a plough drawn by bullocks, laboriously tearing up the parched ground. It was a picture of beautiful contrasts, a wild, and at the same time, cultivated landscape. In Cortizados we found a horrible place with buildings hardly worthy of the name of houses. The inhabitants were obliging and friendly, but complained bitterly of having been robbed of all they possessed by the French, when the latter had marched to Lisbon. We were therefore obliged to content ourselves with their goodwill, and satisfy our needs with what we had brought with us. Here, as elsewhere, we were shown with great triumph pieces of clothing and arms belonging to French soldiers who, having fallen into the hands of the peasants one by one, had been miserably murdered.

I fear that this sort of revenge constitutes the only energy of which the lower-class Portuguese are capable.

One hears no other patriotic sentiments from them than joy over the liberation of their precious selves from French molestation and lust of booty.   National freedom on a grand scale, whether in the political or religious sense, and the desire for a national constitution, and the limitation of the power of the priesthood, are matters in which they are not interested.   If only they are allowed to live in their accustomed indolent way, unmolested by the military, they are entirely satisfied.   I am quite convinced that if Napoleon's generals had only treated Portugal with greater gentleness, and had endeavoured to win the confidence of the country, everything would have been very different here.   When the French, however, showed themselves capable only of oppression, plunder, robbery and murder, the nation which felt itself weak sought the protection of the British flag.

July 4th.   After marching five leguas we reached Sarzedas.   At some distance from Sarzedas we entered a strongly protected pass which might easily have been defended by a handful of men against a large force. Four forts built on the heights commanded the whole stretch of country in front, as well as the only road which leads to the river that flows along at the foot of these hills. In winter this river, which is hemmed in between the rocks here, gets swollen with rain, and flows so fast that it is difficult to cross.   Regardless of all this, General Junot marched through here during the winter, for the Portuguese had taken no steps, as they might so easily have done with only a few men, to resist his advance into their kingdom.   When he found that the bridge had been washed away by the force of the stream, he ordered his cavalry to swim across, and it is said that two squadrons were drowned in the attempt.   Thanks to the dry summer we found the river fordable in many places ; as, however, the smallest downpour of rain causes it to swell, it is always dangerous for an army to march across the mountains of Portugal.

[TRANSLATOR'S NOTE.—Schaumann now proceeds to Castel Branco, Lodoceiro, Zibreira and Salvaterra to Moraleja, which he reaches on July 10th.]

Most of the Spanish towns are situated in the plain, or, like those of Portugal, on dizzy heights. But the Spaniards are not so friendly as the Portuguese, and, although they are our allies for whose freedom we are sacrificing blood and treasure, they are cold, haughty, inhospitable and reserved,* in return for which we English repay them with compound interest, and by settling for everything in cash, heap coals of fire on their heads. It was only when I was collecting forage from their fields that I rejoiced, for then, by way of paying them out or chastising them, more of their corn was trampled down than actually consumed.

On the 11th we diverged from the direct route, and taking a zig-zag course, partly owing to lack of forage and provisions, and partly to avoid contact between the various columns, we pushed on to Coria, a large tumble-down place where there was some particularly good wine to be had. Here, in the afternoon we had a bull fight, for the Spaniards liked to amuse themselves by taking the bullocks which were to be slaughtered for the British troops, and goading them to fury in a large square. The entrances to the square were blocked by carts. A large doll of rags and straw, with feet made of lead so that it could not fall over, was placed in the middle of the arena, and this was tossed into the air again and again by the infuriated animals. After having played all manner of other pranks they at last wanted to secure one of the bullocks by means of a long rope attached to its horns, and to take it back to the stables. Just as they were leading it out, however, it tore itself away and bolted, followed by a crowd of delighted guttersnipes and raga-muffins, into the fields. They then proceeded to hunt it down, and at last it was killed in a cornfield.

I called on General v. Langwerth while I was here, and found him at luncheon with his aide-de-camp, von Zerssen, while his horses stood saddled at the door, ready for marching. I thanked him most heartily for my promotion.

At last, on the 13th, we reached the valley in which the

* See p. 68.

beautiful town of Plasencia lies. The road thither leads across a plain which stretches for miles, and is surrounded by lofty mountains whose gigantic snow-capped peaks look proudly down upon the old walls of Plasencia. This plain, which is watered and fertilised by the River Jerte, winding picturesquely through it, is covered with olive and cypress woods, vineyards, and fields of melons and corn. The innumerable white buildings, churches and chapels of the town, together with an old castle tower and the cathedral, rise above the groups of trees close to the bank of the river, in whose bright mirror-like surface the ancient and decaying forms of the buildings cast beautiful reflections. A bridge of noble proportions, looking as if it had been restored and repaired by modern hands, but still revealing in many of its parts such traces of antiquity as to proclaim it of Roman structure, spans the river.

It appears that Joseph Bonaparte, with the garrison of Madrid, the guards and Sebastiani's corps—in all 25,000 men—is in the neighbourhood ; while Marshal Victor, with 35,000 men is near Talavera de la Reyna, on the banks of the Tagus and the Alberche. The Junta in Seville gave us the most wonderful promises that vehicles, mules and provisions would be held in readiness for us. But of all these splendid supplies we have so far seen but little. It is said that the Spanish generals with their armies—that is to say, General Cuesta at Almaraz, General El Duque de Parque in Ciudad Rodrigo, and General Venegas at Valdepenas, are not agreed among themselves, are jealous of Sir Arthur, and contrary to his advice, are holding themselves out of range of the firing ; they also make beautiful and grandiloquent proclamations, and devour all the provisions that belong by right to the English army, on which the hopes of all Spain are fixed.

In the circumstances, therefore, we were obliged, as far as possible, to carry our provisions with us. We were seldom able to get corn, hay or straw for the horses regularly delivered by the Spanish authorities, and that is why every day, before we retired to our night quarters, we rode into the fields, where each of our dragoons placed two sheaves of barley on his horse's back, and marched off

with them.   But the Spaniards never forget to claim
requisition receipt notes for this corn from me.   Bread
and wine, it is true, were occasionally delivered—always
for cash, of course—in the towns ; but often enough the
ship's biscuit which we carried with us in bullock carts
as a reserve had to supply all our needs.   No trouble
whatsoever was taken to supply us with transport or
mules.   We almost always bivouacked in the open ; but
if we did happen to get shelter, the Spaniards hardly
offered us a glass of water.

On the 16th of July at midday, Sir Arthur Wellesley's
cavalry mustered, and the army began to move forward
in columns.   Our brigade of light dragoons also
marched.   On the 17th of July the heat was infernal,
even in the early morning.   From my window I could
see one or two infantry regiments laboriously ascending a
hill in the sweat of their brow.   I shuddered as I thought
that in a few minutes I, too, would have to leave my cool
room and take the same road.

Our road ran for four leguas through a desolate and,
towards the end, wooded district.   Again and again we
rode through the winding River Jerte.   A number of
dogs which had contracted a warm friendship for our
regimental butchers and had followed them out of
Plasencia, remained howling and whining on the town
side of the river.   I nearly had a bad accident here, for
a tired soldier asked me to let him mount behind me and
carry him across the river.   Hardly was he up, however,
when my horse, unused to such treatment, reared and fell
over with both of us.   Fortunately the thing happened
on the edge of the river, and we fell on soft ground
without injury.   We bivouacked on the banks of the
Jerte, under beautiful cork trees, oaks, chestnuts,
beeches, and poplars.   Both men and horses, almost
suffocated by the heat, now plunged into the milk-warm
water of the river, and washed and bathed themselves.

July 18*th*.   At three in the morning we moved on
again.   The road was dusty and wearisome, and the heat
terrible.   We had to march four leguas, and at last after
many halts for watering and food, we reached our bivouac.

My brigade of carts, together with the bullocks for slaughtering, which were tired and feeble, came up later. The bread on the carts was covered with dust, and looked as hard as stone. The wine had come to an end, and we could only distribute a small rum ration. With this frugal fare we had to bivouac on the ground beneath huts of brushwood, and as the icy night wind whistled through them the heavy dew dropped down from the leaves on to our noses. During the night my horse, which was tethered to my hut, *à la* Robinson Crusoe, took fright at something and tore itself away. I got up immediately and ran after it, and fortunately succeeded in securing it again ; but I shall never forget the fright I had, for what would a poor devil like me have done without a horse!

With the first signs of dawn on the 19th of July the bugles roused us as usual to water, feed, pack up, saddle and harness, and be off. Meanwhile we quickly cooked a little chocolate in water, and ate some ship's biscuit with it. In a few minutes there came the command " Mount," and away we went. Our customary companion of the road—a heavy cloud of dust—quickly formed, my ungreased cart wheels began to squeak as they revolved, and my bullocks ambled bellowing along. To-day we approached a remarkable section of the Sierra Estrella,* a chain of mountains on which one can distinguish every season of the year at once. High above the clouds the mountain peaks can be seen covered with snow ; the second stratum, in the clouds, showed the bronzed leaves of autumn ; below this there was the fresh green of spring and at the foot of the Sierra, the hot and dry summer prevailed. The world just here seemed to be encircled by a weird screen of mountains from whose snow-clad peaks, however, there descended a cool breeze, which, the closer we came, seemed to mitigate the burning summer heat. Even the oak trees appeared to be stronger, the grass greener, and we seemed to be transported to a more northern clime. The road was flat but desolate, and no houses or villages could be descried, nor was there a soul to be seen. We camped on the banks of the Tietar,

---

* This is the mountain range that runs N.N.E. from Leicya to Macal.—Tr.

which winds its way along the foot of the mountains, and
we all bathed. We could not make any huts, as there
was nothing but grass and rushes on the river bank ; so
we all bivouacked under the open sky. During the night,
not far from my bed, one of the dragoons was stung in the
arm by a scorpion or a viper. There was a great to-do,
and a doctor was fetched. If I remember rightly, the
poor devil had to have his arm amputated because the
wound festered in the great heat.

July 2*oth*. Aurora was just on the point of opening
the portals of the East with her rosy fingers when Bailey
and I were already in the saddle. We rode alongside of
the Tietar. Bailey was trying to water his mule in the
river, when the somewhat steep bank, consisting of loose
sand and loam, suddenly gave way, and both mule and
rider fell head over heels into the water. When the
latter, who clung to the pommel of his saddle, threw out
his legs like a frog, and pushed his bald head through the
rushes—for he had lost his hat and wig—he looked and
snorted so much like a walrus, that at first I could not
dismount and go to his help because I was laughing so
much. At last, both the mule and his rider were rescued,
but poor Bailey, who was as wet as a drowned cat, had to
ride on in the fresh morning air, his teeth chattering with
cold. We halted near Alcanessa, a small deserted place,
where I was able to purchase some wonderful goat's milk
from a goatherd. Then we crossed a wilderness or moor,
three leguas in breadth, where we fell in with the Spanish
army of General Don Gregorio de la Cuesta, which
Sir Arthur Wellesley had just inspected. They were on
the march, and for a while we proceeded alongside of
them, to the cry of " *Viva, viva Inglaterra !* " As we
were moving away from the mountains the heat became
oppressive once more. All the vegetation was scorched
by the sun; there was not a bush or a tree to be seen until
we approached Oropesa, where, at last, we again saw some
cornfields and a few trees. We cut down the former for
forage, and while we were thus engaged, old General
Payne raved and annoyed us as usual ; for he deplored
the fact that we commissaries could not perform the

impossible feat of carrying home 100 sheafs on our backs and stuffing the beloved dragoon horses with it. In the evening we at last retired to our bivouacs.

The 23rd Dragoons joined the army to-day, and were brigaded with the 1st Hussars. Wellesley's and Cuesta's headquarters were in Oropesa.

July 21*st*.   At midday to-day the whole of the Spanish cavalry, 7,000 men, marched past in front of Oropesa. In the afternoon, our army, which is 25,000 strong, was inspected by Sir Arthur at a distance of half an hour's march from the town, on the great high road to Madrid, amid fields of wheat, ghastly clouds of dust and appalling heat. The Spanish general, Cuesta, and his staff, who witnessed the inspection, are said to have cut somewhat poor and incongruous figures, and to have stared in astonishment at the rigid, calm and imposing bearing of our troops.

July 22*nd*.   At three in the morning we marched onwards as usual. On both sides of the road we saw large groups of Spanish soldiers mixed up with women, mules and carts, who had doubtless fallen out of the ranks on the flimsiest pretext, and were now standing round large kitchen fires, comfortably smoking cigarettes and staring and yawning at us. It was a sight that gave us but a poor impression of the discipline and courage of our beloved allies. After we had covered about three leguas along the high road to Madrid, we again met General Cuesta's army, waiting for us in a large plain, and amid loud cheers and cries of " *Viva Inglaterra!* " we united on the road. Immediately afterwards there came the sound of guns and musketry fire. For the rearguard of Marshal Victor's army had taken post in front of Talavera de la Reyna, but had been attacked and routed by the Spanish advanced guard, who, knowing that we were behind them, had for once shown a little courage. I saw the first dead French soldiers lying near a little chapel on the road. The heat was intolerable, the dust appalling, and we were tortured with thirst. Even Sir Arthur is said to have dismounted and taken a drink at a pool. The cavalry and the artillery had to proceed at the trot.

The moment we came in sight of the town of Talavera,
General Anson's brigade, the 23rd Dragoons and the
1st Hussars, under the command of General Payne, were
quickly despatched round a rocky height on the left of
Talavera, to attack the enemy on his right flank.   Mr.
Myler, Mr. Bailey and I, out of curiosity, attached ourselves to this corps, and went forward with them, and
halting in one of the villages which had been plundered
by the French we refreshed our horses at a spring.   As
soon as we learnt at this point that the last French guns
had stolen into the town, and that the Spaniards, under
the command of General Sargus and the Duke of Albu-
querque were engaged in pressing on behind them,
we also hurried forward, and posted ourselves not far
from the gate, in order to watch the drama.   All the
balconies, windows and roofs were full of people, great
jugs and buckets of cool water and wine were carried to
the doors of the houses and held in readiness.   Then
came the horse artillery, followed by the blue Spanish
dragoons, backed in their turn by the green dragoons,
and they rushed into the place with such speed and rage
that one saw and heard nothing but sparks and the
snorting both of the horses and their riders.   To judge
from their expressions, they looked at that moment as
if they would make mincemeat of the whole of the French
army.

The inhabitants greeted them with deafening yells of
" *Viva Espanha ! Viva Espanha !* " and while the women,
waving handkerchiefs, were almost hysterical with enthusiasm, the priests were particularly conspicuous for the
idiotic and fanatically truculent attitudes they assumed.
It was with much laughter that we beheld this Spanish
display of bravado, and galloped quickly behind them to
see how they would continue to distinguish themselves.
But oh, the pity of it ! For hardly had they debouched
from the town than the fatal guns of the French rearguard
began to thunder forth again ! Of course they halted.
They were flabbergasted, and taking time to reform, they
all calmly sat down at last, and before ten minutes
had elapsed, left the English cavalry, which had gone

round to the left of Talavera, the honour of continuing the pursuit. " May God be merciful ! " we exclaimed, and riding back with much laughter, we inspected a French mainguard station, and read the jokes scribbled on the walls. Then we bought some wine and bread, listened to the rodomontade of the Spaniards, and as soon as the Spanish army filled the streets, we rode out of the town to find our regiments.

On the way we visited a beautiful French bivouac, consisting of very good huts, arranged in the form of perfectly straight streets. Owing to the heavy cloud of dust which rose in front of their columns, and also the smoke created by the corn and dry grass which they burnt on their way, it was possible from a height to follow the retreat of the cavalry. We found the brigade posted among some olive and cork trees between the Alberche and the town. Our infantry, which could not advance as quickly, was still in the rear. But in the afternoon they, too, appeared, and occupied a valley full of large olive woods, lying not far from the Alberche, between a mountain ridge and the town. On the other side of the Alberche lay the French, who had thrown up entrenchments.

At ten o'clock on the morning of July 23rd the English army marched forward with the object of attacking the enemy in his strong position on the Alberche. But nothing came of this undertaking ; for the bigot, General Cuesta, owing to the fact that it was a Sunday —*o sancta simplicitas !*—refused to give battle. After standing under arms for a few hours, therefore, we returned to our position. What was the result ? We had not only lost a magnificent opportunity of defeating the enemy piecemeal, but we had also given Marshal Victor time to withdraw quite peacefully and join up with Sebastiani's and King Joseph's corps, by which the French strength was increased by at least 50,000 men. Quite contrary to his true nature, Sir Arthur Wellesley on this occasion showed himself unjustifiably weak, for he ought to have protested with all his might and main against the ridiculous attitude of the Spanish general, by which means he would at least have escaped the suspicion of having also been in favour of observing the Sabbath. For this much is certain, if Generals Venegas, Wilson, Cuesta and Wellesley had attacked on this Sunday, as they should have done, Victor would have been done for, and not a man of his whole corps would have escaped. Mr. Myler and I, with all our retinue, repaired to Talavera de la Reyna.

An Unsuccessful Attack—Mr. Augustus lives from Hand to Mouth and goes out Looting—General Venegas's Insubordination—Great and Bloody Battle of Talavera.

WE were given quarters in a street close to the town gate. Our landlord, who had taken to his heels, leaving the house in charge of a servant, was a literary man, for in one of the rooms there was a large library of dusty books bound in pigskin, and the titles of the books were written on their backs in Gothic letters. We slept on magnificent mattresses spread on the floor. Our horses had a comfortable stable, and in the yard there was a well. As, however, everybody came in and out for water, and slammed the large coach-house door incessantly, it proved rather a nuisance. We entrusted one of our men with the cooking, and the other, owing to the predatory character of the Spaniards, had to keep a vigilant eye on the baggage and horses. When once we had settled down in this way, we scoured the country all about in order to find provisions for the troops. Immediately opposite our house there was a store at which a few Spanish regiments were regularly rationed, while ours had to pine with hunger. Every day Myler and I would take the dragoons with us, and like the robber barons of old, living from hand to mouth, we would way-lay and raid the Spanish convoys, force their escorts to take flight, and then bring back to the bivouac in triumph as much as we wanted. Of course we did not forget ourselves on these occasions, and thus two huge skins of wine somehow found their way to our quarters. On the market place in the town things went on in the same extraordinary way, for the moment the peasants had taken up their position with their bread, wine, onions, melons, red pepper, or loins of pork, they would be besieged, stormed and hustled this way and that by thousands of customers. Everybody wanted to be served at once, and held out his money, crying : " Me first !

I want bread, I want this, I want that, here's the money!" until the poor peasants were overturned with all their goods, and then trampled upon and plundered. In fact, the wretched devils thought themselves lucky if they escaped alive. On the morning when this happened I myself gave a Spanish dollar, equal to two florins of convent money, for a loaf and some onions. But the peasants did not turn up on the following morning, and at midday there appeared a general order enjoining upon all the British troops a more humane and less violent treatment of the peasants who came to market, and particularly forbidding the commissaries any longer to plunder the Spanish convoys, as General Cuesta had lodged a complaint about this. It appears, however, that on this occasion Sir Arthur Wellesley spoke very plainly to Cuesta and the Central Junta, who had fulfilled none of the solemn promises they had made concerning our supplies, and told them that while he certainly would not touch their provisions, he refused to take another step forward in Spain, and would retreat on Portugal.

A propos of this affair, I cannot refrain from commenting upon the ghastly methods that characterised the Spanish Government. Every poky little hole has a junta, a deputation, and privileges of its own. These smaller juntas ought, strictly speaking, to have obeyed the Central Junta of the kingdom, but owing to false provincial pride they would never recognise its authority. This was the case between the above-mentioned juntas of Seville, Badajos and Plasencia, and the result was that the power of the Government was split up into innumerable juntas and privileged bodies, and was never able to initiate a general policy. On the contrary, it was always flouted by these minor bodies which, animated by jealousy, cordially detested one another, thought only of their own particular interests, and always undertook to wreck any general schemes that had been devised for the good of the country. This foolish system must be ascribed to the lack of co-ordination existing between the various provinces, and even between towns that lay cheek by jowl, so to speak. For instance, when the French advanced into Castille, the men of Biscay did not move an inch away from their mountains to support their neighbours, and *vice versâ*. There is no spot on earth more badly in need of reform than this miserable country, Spain.

And the Spanish military are in complete harmony with this state of affairs. The generals, in uniforms covered with gold lace, surrounded by immense staffs, on which the priests play the most important part, are men who, though usually of good family, are both headstrong and conceited. As Sir Arthur Wellesley afterwards discovered, they think nothing of disregarding orders from a higher authority ; and altogether there is about them too much talk, too much church-going, and cigar-smoking. They have three big meals a day, and their sleep after luncheon is to them the principal concern of their lives. Whenever they are confronted by the enemy they reveal a lack of caution and of tactics, and (except be it well noted on Church holidays) they advance with stupid daring right into the field, after having made the most absurd battle formation. The French have literally annihilated their whole armies in a single day.* The common soldier behaves better in forts, but this avails him little ; for the commanders of fortresses, except those of Saragossa and one or two other places, have always acted in such a way as to make it impossible to tell whether they were traitors or cowards. In addition to this, most of the higher Spanish officers in possession of extended and absolute power—particularly the Captains-General of Provinces—are, as a rule, unusually uncouth, and treat all those who have the misfortune to displease them with truly revolting cruelty.

The rest of the Spanish officers are mostly ignorant and ill-mannered. It is impossible to find a gentleman amongst them. The few of them who have attended a military school, generally under the direction of priests, are very conceited and very deficient in the knowledge of their art. They are chiefly concerned with their uniforms, the cuffs of which reach back to the elbows, their enor-

* Cf. Fortescue (*op. cit.*, Vol. VI., pp. 160, 161, and Vol. VII., pp. 207, 214. For cowardice of Spanish cavalry, see Vol. VII., p. 213.

mously large hats, their long Toledo swords, which they do not wear at their sides but carry under their arms, and with loafing about public walks and cafés, smoking cigars and eating and drinking and sleeping a great deal.   As far as manners, military efficiency, writing and arithmetic are concerned, a Prussian or Hanoverian non-commissioned officer is infinitely superior to them.   Among all the Spanish officers I had the opportunity of meeting, only a few were worth knowing.   And they seemed to feel this, and shunned English officers.   Even the Spanish ladies did not hesitate to take exception to the ill-breeding, coarseness and arrogance of their own military men. " *Son brutos,*" they would say.   As the majority of Spanish officers hail from the lower orders, and feel themselves drawn to common and ordinary associates, they have no notion of inspiring respect among their subordinates.   One frequently sees officers hobnobbing quite familiarly with their men, drinking out of the same glass, or smoking the same cigar in turns.   There is, therefore, not much discipline.*

The administrative *personnel* of the armies is just as bad.   There is either a deficiency of money or bread. If they have powder, they have no flints ; if they have plenty of provisions, uniforms are not to be had ; and if muskets are plentiful, there is a shortage of guns.   When the men want to fight, the officers are not keen ; and if a battle does take place, then the whole crowd takes flight. If an army corps has to be formed, the first thing they do is to organise a huge staff, deposit it in a large town, and leave it to the municipality to provide them with quarters and rations.   And this staff may, and frequently does, remain inactive for months, while no soldiers are to be seen.   Truth to tell, if in my time the Spanish armies were efficiently equipped for service, this was solely due to the shiploads of uniforms, arms and ammunition, to the value of millions of dollars, which the English never wearied of landing on the coast, and which were consigned for nothing to an ungrateful country.

* For interesting confirmation of Schaumann's views, see Oman (*op. cit.,* Vol. I.), particularly pp. 98–99.—Tr.

Meanwhile, all English commissaries were given orders no longer to meet the needs of their own regiments alone, but to deliver everything they could obtain to Commissary-General Dalrymple, at a general stores depôt. Accordingly, I took a corporal and ten dragoons, and started off to seek my fortune over the other side of the bridge at Talavera, and to reconnoitre the country beyond the Tagus for bullocks for slaughtering. We had been riding about for an hour or two, and everything seemed deserted, abandoned and lifeless, when at last, feeling very tired, we halted in a narrow valley at the foot of a rather lofty chain of hills. We heard nothing, and there was no movement anywhere. Then suddenly it occurred to one of the dragoons, an Irishman, to climb to the top of a height, lay himself flat on the ground, and place one end of the ramrod of his pistol in the ground, and the other end to his ear, and listen. He had not lain there long, when suddenly he sprang to his feet, and swore by St. Patrick that he had heard the lowing of cattle and the clanging of cow bells on the other side of the hills. At this we all raced up the hill as if we were storming a fort, and we had hardly reached the plateau at the top of it when, at the end of a quarter of an hour, we beheld a very narrow valley entirely surrounded by hills, and in the midst of it, to our great delight, a quantity of all kinds of cattle— bullocks, cows, calves, pigs, about 6,000 sheep and goats, a wooden shed, a well, and also some dogs and a few herdsmen armed with long firelocks. As we approached the dogs attacked us savagely, and the herdsmen seemed thunderstruck. I got my dragoons to surround them, and then riding up to them alone, with my pistol in my hand, told them that they must follow me with all their cattle to English headquarters, where their herds would be properly valued, and where they would be paid to the last penny in good money. I added a word or two of explanation and of comfort, and told them to have patience —which is the Spanish expression for making the best of a bad job. After a good deal of violent and prolonged resistance, lamentations, tearing of hair, protestations, prayers and appeals to the saints, they exclaimed at last :

"Yes, yes, the misfortune is ours," * whereupon, sighing heavily, they fetched their packs, called to the dogs, and herded the cattle together. "*Vamos!*" I cried, and we marched away.

Night was falling when we returned to the bridge of Talavera. About forty Spanish troopers, who had just watered their horses, rode into the midst of my sheep without asking my leave, and seizing one or two of them by the fleece, lifted them without ceremony on to their saddles, and wanted to make off with them. But we put them to flight at the point of the sword, and hunted their spoil down again. We had hardly entered the first streets of the town when I saw a woman standing before the door of her house, contemplating the cattle with amazement. Then she uttered a piercing shriek and wildly tore her hair. Thereupon several other women rushed out of their houses and joined in the chorus. In a moment I was surrounded by hundreds of such furies, and ultimately a number of threatening men as well, all of whom stormed me with prayers and curses, and begged me to spare their cattle—Lord Jesus, the cattle of the town of Talavera! Implying that this was not possible, I replied, "It's impossible, there is no help for it ; have patience ! Only the Commissary-General can release this cattle of yours." † And I made a few other such glib remarks, continuing to urge the cattle on meanwhile, until at last we reached the coach-doors of the great courtyard where Mr. Dalrymple lived. The women now lifted up their voices in chorus again. I found the Commissary-General anxiously conferring with the Lisbon purveyor, Senhor Sempayo, who had a large number of bullocks on the way from Portugal to Spain, which had not yet arrived. Hardly had I reported my find than both of them embraced me with delight, and assured me that I had saved them from a most appalling dilemma. Whereupon, commending both the crowd waiting downstairs and besieging the staircase, and the lowing and

---

* "*Si, si, es la nuestra disgracia.*"
† "*No puede ser, no ha remedio, tened paciencia. Solo el Commissario General puede desembargar el vuestro ganado.*"

bleating cattle tightly squeezed into the courtyard, to the Commissary-General, I turned smartly away and fled. Other commissaries, not wishing to come empty-handed, had brought pigs, turkeys, geese and ducks ; and later on I saw the quartermasters, each with four bullocks, one pig, fifty sheep, ten goats, ten turkeys, and twenty ducks, all higgledy-piggledy—a sight which caused great amusement.

July 2 5*th*. General Cuesta has pushed on to Santa Olalla and Torrijos, whilst Sir Arthur refused to do so owing to lack of provisions. Our advanced posts have also pushed forward to St. Olalla, but only in order to keep in touch with the Spanish army, and the Lusitanian legion under the command of General Wilson in Escalona. I was again detailed—this time with one sergeant, a corporal and twenty dragoons—to make a raid beyond the Tagus for flour, or bread, and wine. Although I had already gone foraging with the regiment at three o'clock that morning, and was thoroughly tired and jaded, I was nevertheless obliged to ride out of Talavera again in the blistering midday heat. My way lay over the bridge across the Tagus, where I thought I should most probably find provisions. We reached a wide and desolate heath, where we could obtain an extensive view of the country. After some hours we descried a few poplars and shrubs, and down an incline, a small town. We halted and held a council of war. I sent two men left and right to the flanks, and advanced cautiously towards the place ; for although the French were on the opposite side of the Tagus, they might easily send foraging parties across my tracks. I had, therefore, to set very carefully to work.

As we entered the town we were surprised to see that the inhabitants fled along the streets like mad, and hid themselves in their houses. An old woman who could not get along very fast, believing, as the rest of her towns-folk did, that we were French, and wishing to do the right thing, cried : " *Viva, viva Franceses ! Viva la Francia !* " But she opened her eyes when we replied with a laugh, " *Maldita sea la Francia, viva Inglaterra, viva Espanha !* " At these words many of the house doors were thrown open, and no sooner did the people see the short tails of our mounts—which were then the universal sign by which both the French and the Spanish recognised English cavalry in the distance—when they cried out shyly : "*Viva Inglaterra!*" The moment we reached the market-place, however, we were surrounded by jubilant crowds. The Alcalde appeared solemnly, with one or two notabilities of the town ; and, after I had explained my mission to him, I showed him, as a guarantee of good payment, the doubloons * which the Commissary-General had given me. It appeared that the French had not been there yet. This seemed to me incomprehensible, for, although the Tagus lay between us, its low water allowed of its being forded. Both armies stood very close together. But the sight of my doubloons had electrified the Alcalde. All the inhabitants were given the order to bake all night, and deliver up at once all the bread, wine and cattle they had in stock. One of the inhabitants begged me most urgently to put up at his house ; but my quarters were not so very.brilliant after all. The dragoons' horses were installed at an inn on the small market-place, and I gave orders that as soon as they had been watered and fed they were to be kept ready saddled and bridled.

In spite of this precaution, however, I made a frightful blunder which might have cost us a good deal. I forgot to post sentries outside the town, and to have the place patrolled. After I had settled my business with the Alcalde and one or two priests—who in this country poke their noses into everything,—expressed my pleasure over the quick deliveries of bread, and settled about the carts which had to be ready to start off at break of day, I returned home with my landlord for a meal. In addition to a stew and the roast, we also had cucumber and eggs on the table, and I was just on the point of cutting the cucumber to make a German cucumber salad, when we suddenly heard the sound of running footsteps in the street, and cries of "*Franceses!*" "God help us!" (*Valganos Dios!*), cried my host, growing pale and making the sign of the cross. The knife I was holding and the

* The doubloon was a Spanish gold piece worth about one guinea.—Tr.

cucumber fell out of my hand ; nevertheless, I pulled myself together, and fled like lightning out of the house to mount my horse which was in the stables with the dragoons' horses. In case defence was out of the question, for the moon was shining brightly, I resolved to escape by keeping to the shaded side of the houses. The dragoons dashed helter-skelter out of the stables, and were just about to mount when a loud clatter of horses' hoofs rang out in one of the streets, and forty horsemen tore into the market-place—but they wore red uniforms and three-cornered hats (helmets ?) aslant on their heads, and there-fore looked very much like our 4th Dragoons, the Queen's Own. And, indeed, that is precisely who they were. Thus, instead of a deadly affray, there followed a joyful gathering. This detachment was led by a Don Quixote the Second, a colleague of mine, the acting assistant commissary, Mr. John Downie. This was the man who, later on, and chiefly at his own expense, raised a Spanish corps dressed in the old Spanish garb, for the purpose of liberating Spain. He was presented by the Pizarro family with the sword of the conqueror of Mexico, lost part of his jaw through the bursting of a bomb at Merida, had all sorts of adventures, spent his whole fortune in the service of Spain, and finally, when the war was over, was pensioned off by Ferdinand VII., and made governor of the castle of Seville.

Over his commissary's uniform he wore a heavy dragoon's pouch-belt, and carried a loaded carbine at full cock in his hand. He was immensely pleased to see me, but declared that he had proved my rescuer on this occasion, for not far from the place he had fallen in with a strong patrol of French chasseurs, who intended to come here, and he had driven them off, killed one of them, and captured a colleague, a French commissary, and one other man. And it was true.' When we had placed the two prisoners in the local gaol to save them from the anger of the populace, and given quarters to the rest of the men, we proceeded with pen, ink and paper to the gaol in order to examine the prisoners, and then to despatch them with our report to Sir Arthur Wellesley. Such a huge crowd had gathered in front of the prison, angrily clamouring to have the prisoners let out to be murdered—a request we Englishmen could never grant—that we could hardly make our way inside.

The hearing began, and I was the clerk of the court. The captured colleague was a man from Alsace who spoke a little German, but never was there a more impenitent delinquent. He answered unimportant questions fully and promptly, but to every question concerning the strength of the French and their movements, he responded with obstinate and gloomy silence, or with a " *Je ne sais pas.*" It was a funny sight to see the bony six-footer, Downie, astride a chair, now flourishing a long Spanish cane angrily in the air, and then allowing it to rest coaxingly on the prisoner's shoulder, while ever and anon he exclaimed : " Do you hear, my friend, how the crowd are raving outside. Confess, or we will let you loose, and then you will immediately have fifty daggers in your body." The friend in question laughed at this, and was of opinion that, as Englishmen, we would never sanction such a horrible thing. And he was right. Wearying at last, he gave in, but whether he told us all the truth or not, will never be known. Nevertheless, his statement that the French army, now united, was turning round and would attack us on the morrow, proved correct. At twelve midnight, when the crowd had dispersed, the prisoners were sent off to Talavera with a despatch. Meanwhile, Downie's landlord, a gentleman of means, whose son was an officer in Cuesta's army, had prepared a wonderful supper for us on a massive old silver dinner service. We drank and talked until far into the morning, then slept for a while in our chairs ; and, hardly had the dawn broken, when, making ready for a speedy flight, we returned without mishap to Talavera, laden with provisions.

July 26th. On reaching home we heard that, owing to the fact that the Spanish general, Venegas, either from cowardice or out of defiance of Sir Arthur Wellesley's views, had, instead of going forward to prevent the concentration of Joseph's, Victor's and Sebastiani's armies, as had been arranged, remained in La Mancha, Cuesta's army had been attacked and defeated at Torrijos. For that foolish man, Cuesta, had expressly begged Sir Arthur to allow his army to form the advanced guard. Very soon this army came back in the greatest disorder, and only the English advanced guard—that is to say, a division of infantry and a brigade of cavalry—remained at Cazalegas on the road to Madrid. By evening the French began to skirmish with these troops.

Early on the morning of the 27th July the alarm was given ; and, as a battle seemed inevitable, I rode out to watch it. I saw on a wooden bridge an old-fashioned coach drawn by six gaily caparisoned mules. A man of about seventy years old, in brown clothes and a bob-tailed wig, who, if he had not carried so many orders, might have been taken for an old German shopkeeper, descended from it accompanied by several officers, crossed the bridge, inspected it, noted that there was a hole in it, and then sat down on the steps of an iron cross standing by the road-side. The officers of his staff stood round him and smoked cigarettes. It was Don Gregorio de la Cuesta, the Spanish Commander-in-Chief !

The enemy had that morning advanced in heavy columns along the road to Talavera. General Sherbrooke was in command of the advanced guard at Cavosleguas,* and it consisted of the divisions of Generals Mackenzie, Sherbrooke and Anson. They were all ready for battle, when Sir Arthur recalled them, and their retreat was carried out and covered in a highly exemplary fashion by Anson's cavalry, Colonel Donkin's infantry brigade, and the German sharpshooters of the 60th Regiment. When General Sherbrooke saw that the bulk of the English army was still about two miles to the rear, he continued his retreat to the Alberche. The French pursued him quickly and followed close at his heels. He was provided with plenty of artillery. On the other side of the Alberche I found our army, looking most wonderful, formed up in squares—*en échiquier*—and slowly retreating according to signals, under the fire of the artillery.

* Schaumann means Cazalegas.—TR.

It was a beautiful sight.   On the hill to the right was the Spanish army, formed into three tiers, while on the great plain to the left the English army was manœuvring as if on a parade ground.   While all this was in progress a very fine French bivouac, consisting of neatly built huts, full of furniture taken from Talavera, and capable of accommodating 20,000 men, was set on fire by a detachment of English soldiers, while a number of cornfields in the neighbourhood were also ignited ; and the crackling and the flames of the conflagration, together with the huge clouds of smoke that rose from it, added considerably to the majesty and terror of the scene.   Feeling very cheerful, and rejoicing at having the opportunity of witnessing and experiencing such things, I was riding about in the midst of it all, when our General Payne happened to gallop past, and catching sight of me, sent an aide-de-camp in my direction to ask me whether I was aware that the spot on which I was standing was a highly dangerous one.   I was informed that the general gave me the friendly advice to go back across the Alberche without delay.   Much astonished, I looked about me, for I was not aware of any such immediate danger.   However, I rode my horse through the Alberche, grumbling as I went, and made for the 14th Dragoons, who had formed on the opposite bank.   Guns were drawn into position to give the French a good welcome.   As soon as the army had got across, and it became clear to all that no battle was to be expected that day—for Sir Arthur wanted to fight on the north, and not on the south bank of the Alberche—I rode back slowly through a large olive grove, in which a division was already making itself at home, and past an old ruined convent teeming with redcoats.

It was five o'clock, and I had scarcely reached Talavera when I heard the sound of terrific gun and musketry fire in the direction of the Alberche.   It appeared that the French had marched up on the other side of the Alberche, as if they intended camping there, and then, under cover of the olive groves, which are unusually thick here, they had sent a light corps across a shallow part of the river, and followed it up by several more.   These troops had crept up under the shelter of the olive trees, and, if the truth be told, had actually surprised our light division under General Mackenzie, who, overcome by the superior forces of the enemy, had retreated across the plain, where he joined our army.   And now the enemy pushed on so far that they even succeeded in dislodging General Hill from the height on which he stood, but this was only for a few minutes ; for, by means of a bayonet charge he soon regained possession of the ground.   This combat, which was watched by the Spaniards with the utmost calm, and which was fought with great fury and bitterness by both the French and the English, proved very costly to both sides,* and we had a most grievous loss in General Mackenzie, who was left on the field.†   Even during the night the French made several attempts to regain the height, but each time they were driven back with heavy losses.   The last attempt, which was again unsuccessful, wâs made towards morning.   Then the Spaniards, who did not know the courage and endurance of the English, lost heart, and forsaking their bivouacs and trenches in masses, fled with a good deal of their baggage through the town.   Mr. Myler and I kept our horses saddled that evening, and till a late hour of the night sat together, smoking cigars and drinking wine, discussing the events of the day and the results we might expect from them on the morrow.

On the 28th July, 1809, dawn at last broke on a day which to me will be unforgettable, and as the sky grew ever redder and redder in the east—that is to say, in the direction of the enemy, we were awakened by a fierce rattling of musketry accompanied by bursts of gun fire. We quickly packed up and rode out.   To the left there lay a somewhat low chain of hills, on the right was the town and the Tagus, and in the centre a plain and a lofty height occupied by our troops.‡   In the rear of the hill was our cavalry, consisting of the 14th, 16th and 23rd

* Napier gives the losses of that day at about 800 English and 1,000 French.—Tr.
† Schaumann seems to be making a bad mistake here, because Mackenzie did not fall until the next day.—Tr.
‡ Schaumann's left and right evidently stand for north and south in this passage.—Tr.

Light Dragoons, the 3rd and 4th Heavy Dragoons, and the 1st Hussars of the Legion. The position was about two and a half miles in breadth, and was shrouded by a cloud of grey smoke. The left wing rested on the chain of hills, and was covered in the second line by the height occupied by General Hill. Towards eight o'clock the English were attacked along their whole front ; it was a terrible onslaught, but the enemy were driven back by our troops.

At eleven o'clock in the morning the enemy attacked once more against our right wing, and to my astonishment the Spaniards bravely resisted them. The thunder of the artillery, combined with the whizzing and whistling of the shot in such an attack, resembles a most dreadful storm, in which flashes of lightning and claps of thunder follow one another in quick succession, and cause the very earth, not to mention the heart in one's breast, to shake and quiver. The eminence so stubbornly held by General Hill had been supplied with a few guns during the night, and it was also defended by several divisions. Even Sir Arthur spent most of the day there, for the fate of the battle depended upon its being held. At midday, owing to the insufferable heat, the fire on both sides was somewhat abated ; but at two o'clock the French again opened a fierce attack supported by small and heavy guns. A Spanish powder magazine blew up in front of our cavalry, and with it a gunner was flung aloft, and sailed through the air with arms and legs outspread like a frog. At the same moment—about three o'clock—strong enemy, columns pressed forward against the height on which Sir Arthur Wellesley was standing. They advanced in all their strength and seemed determined *à tout prix* to take by force the hill so heroically defended by the British. They sent three powerful and dense columns to the entrance of the valley that flanked our position, and advanced against the hill and against our centre with an enormous mass of men. But for a few cannon balls that fell here and there, a gruesome stillness prevailed during this manœuvre. " Heavily they came on, covered in dust—like a huge storm cloud. The sound of their marching echoed across the dusty plain as they approached their wild adventure. Halt ! And the rigid word of command held the regiments as if in a vice. Not a sound was heard along the whole front ! "

At this moment an aide-de-camp appeared, bringing General Anson's light brigade the order to attack the foremost of these columns. At the command " Mount ! March ! " under the eyes of both armies these troops plunged forward at the trot, in the most perfect order ; Generals Payne and Anson, with their staff riding at the head of them. An ear-splitting yell arose from our own and the Spanish armies, cheering them on. When the trumpeters blew the charge, a cloud of dust arose, and in a moment an indescribable and terrible scene was enacted. A sort of ravine or hollow cleft, of which there were many hereabout, starting on the left of the chain of hills and running right across the path of these eight squadrons, suddenly held them up just as they were in full swing and cheering at the top of their voices. Some of the leaders succeeded in jumping across it, but many fell in. Nevertheless, nothing could curb the boldness of the 23rd Dragoons, who were in the van, and in spite of this obstacle, they swept along, formed on the other side of it, and were on the point of cutting their way into a dense French square when, greeted by a deadly burst of gun and musket fire, almost all of them fell on the spot.

The 1st Hussars, profiting from the experience of their comrades, turned sharply about at the ravine, and came back, having suffered only trifling losses. Owing to the thick cloud of smoke that seemed to obliterate everything during a moment's gruesome calm, I was unable to observe what followed. All we could see was here and there a riderless horse appearing through the smoke, and dashing across the battlefield. Meanwhile the furious though unsuccessful attack, which had revealed the true mettle of the English cavalry, had so startled the French that they not only ceased storming the hill, but a portion of their cavalry took flight, and thus gave our artillery the signal to pour a withering fire into the French squares. Very soon after this the brigade of heavy cavalry, under

General Fane, with Spanish artillery under his command, was given the order to push right up to the enemy's lines in order to rescue the survivors of the 23rd Dragoons, a body of only 119 men out of the original 600.* Having reached its objective, the heavy brigade spread out and allowed the artillery to dash through ; whereupon the latter opened a murderous fire upon the dense masses of the French army. In reply to this attack of ours, the enemy made a counter-attack, but, being threatened on his left flank by our cavalry, was afraid to deploy. Thus he left the hill which was held by our men, most of whom were either exhausted, wounded, or dying, in comparative peace, and directed his attack against our centre ; but he was so effectively repulsed by Campbell's division, supported by a portion of the Spanish cavalry, that the attacking troops left fifteen guns, a few eagles, and many dead and wounded behind them.

I was trying to ride back into the town when I overtook one or two bandsmen of the legion, who, with sad and solemn faces, were escorting a dead officer thither. His head was swathed in a handkerchief, and his body, which was clothed only in a shirt, a pair of pants, and some socks, hung athwart a horse's back. He was the man who had done so much for my promotion, General Langwerth von Simmern, and the sight of him upset me terribly. His aide-de-camp, Captain von Zerssen, had been wounded. A German sharpshooter of the 5th Battalion of the 60th Regiment, looking quite black in the face from the sun, the dust, the gunpowder and perspiration, ran from the raging battle and flung himself on the ground in an exhausted condition, assuring me that he had fired off sixty charges. His tongue was cleaving to his palate with thirst; he was unable to fight any longer, and hardly ten of his company were still alive.

I rode through Talavera to see how matters stood with the Spaniards. It was impossible to see what was happening in the olive woods, but the firing within it never ceased, and now and again a detachment or a patrol

---

* Cf. Oman (*op. cit.*, Vol. II., p. 550), who gives 207 killed, wounded and missing out of a total of 450. Napier's figures are the same (*op. cit.*, Book VIII., Chap. II.)—Tr.

would march out of it, or a party bearing wounded would
appear, and ever and anon a few Spanish soldiers crept
stealthily away.   I saw only one Spanish battery, posted
in front of the gate of the town to the right, on a hill
formed by the accumulated municipal refuse of years.
The guns were directed against the olive wood, which the
Spaniards seemed to be watching with eager and anxious
eyes.   I had to laugh heartily to myself when I saw the
vent holes of these guns covered with the three-cornered
hats of the gunners instead of the usual leaden caps.   I
also met two officers who had arrived that morning by
means of post-horses.   They had breakfasted at my
quarters, and though they had not yet received uniforms
and still wore civilian dress, for they had only just been
given their commissions, they had gone straight to the
battlefield and joined their regiments.   For, as they
bravely declared, with a touch of Irish humour, they did
not wish " to lose such a sweet and beautiful opportunity
of getting promotion."   Each of them had secured some
sort of weapon on the field, both had fought gallantly,
both had been wounded, and one of them showed me his
sword, which, by God ! had been all bent and twisted in a
bayonet charge against the French.

Hardly had I reached my quarters in order to refresh
myself and my horse a little, after eight hours of fasting,
before a terrific outburst of gun fire announced the opening
of a fresh attack on the left of our centre under General
Sherbrooke.   This general's left wing rested on a high
hill which was in a line with the town.   It was between
these two points that we had taken post.   Even the oldest
veterans could not remember ever having witnessed an
attack delivered with such desperate fury ; and for a
moment it succeeded.   But the English guards and the
battalions of the German legion again, with the utmost
gallantry, repulsed the enemy at the point of the bayonet.
Both sides displayed the most marvellous heroism, which,
of course, greatly increased their losses.   The English
guards, in particular, suffered very severely, because they
advanced too quickly without waiting for support.   The
German artillery of the legion, under Major Hartmann,

Captain Heise, and Captain Braun, is also said to have fought with conspicuous bravery.

The Spaniards, unaccustomed to the endurance of the English, and losing heart at the sight of the furious attack, did not wait to see the end of it, but dashed headlong in masses through the town, and mixed up with vast quantities of baggage, blocked the streets. Even the Spanish battery above mentioned also came along, without having fired a shot, and, galloping madly forward, ran over everything in its way. I watched this appalling tumult and confusion with amazement from my window.* Even the inhabitants were packing and taking flight. Just opposite my quarters there lived a wonderfully beautiful married woman who, with the help of her family, was trying to load and mount a mule. Every time she attempted to mount, however, the madly hurrying throng would swing her mule and its load so sharply round that the load always fell down beneath the animal's belly. It was interesting to watch this woman's passionate rage ; screaming, tearing her hair out, weeping, scratching, biting and wailing, and imploring all the saints to hear her moving appeals—her expression changed every moment. If only I could have reached her, I would gladly have rescued her ; but at length a Spanish officer came on the scene, and, lifting her on to his saddle in front of him, rode off with his gorgeous booty.

Once more we rode out to see how things were going. Night fell, and the firing ceased. Only now and again the flash of a gun was seen on the hills by our left wing. Apparently the whole French army had taken part in the last attack, but had found in John Bull a tough and powerful obstacle. Nevertheless, our situation seemed to be very critical. The thinned ranks of the English army stood exhausted under the weight of their arms. True, the French had retreated, but they were still hovering, as it were, about our position, every inch of which they knew, and seemed only to be awaiting the dawn in order to attack afresh. Some even said that they

---

* Schaumann is not confirmed here, either by Oman or Napier. He must have seen a body of runaways and exaggerated their number.—T<small>R</small>.

intended to take the town during the night.   Mr. Myler,
Mr. Bailey and I, therefore, held a council of war, and
decided that instead of exposing ourselves to a sudden
attack, we should do better to bivouac.   The moon was
shining dimly down upon the ghastly battlefield, swathed
in the smoke of the guns and of the dry grass that had
caught fire.   There was not a sprout of any sort on the
bald stubblefields, to which one could tether a horse.
I therefore took my horse's saddle off, tethered him to it,
and used it as a pillow.   As, however, the brute insisted
upon grazing and wandering about in search of grass, he
was constantly pulling the saddle from under my head,
and consequently I had a restless night.   In addition to
this we were all wet with the dew and frozen with the cold.

At dawn on the 29th July we heard some troops marching along quite close to us.   It was Craufurd's division
which, coming up from Lisbon, had covered twelve
Spanish miles* in twenty-four hours, in order to
be able to take part in the battle.   The sight of these
reinforcements cheered our hearts.   They went forward
as outposts.   As soon as we heard that the enemy had
retreated to Santa Olalla in the night, with the object of
covering Madrid, we rode back to the town again.   But,
heavens !   What did our quarters look like !   They had
been plundered by the Spanish soldiers themselves.   All
our boxes and cases had been burst open, and their contents   strewn   over   the   ground,   robbed,   broken   or
hacked to pieces ;   our beds had been cut open and the
feathers and horsehair had been shaken out and stolen,
and our bookcase lay in the middle of the room with the
shelves   piled   on   top   of   it.   We waded knee-deep in
feathers and plunder of every description, while all about
the floor lay broken crockery, pots, books and written
records.   It was only with great pains that we were able

* Taking the Spanish mile to be 7,090 yards, this would be equal to forty-eight and a
half English miles.   Napier gives the distance covered by these troops as sixty-two
English miles.   He says that it took them only twenty-six hours, and that they left only
seventeen stragglers behind.   Each man carried 50 to 60 lbs. weight upon his shoulders
This, however, does not appear to be correct.   The distance covered was forty-three
miles, and it was covered in twenty-two hours.   Schaumann appears to be more correct
than Napier.   See Oman, *op. cit.*, Vol. II., p. 561.   Fortescue (*op. cit.*, Vol. VII., p. 265)
says the distance was forty-five to fifty miles, and the time about twenty-five
hours.—Tr.

to find a saucepan in which to prepare our usual breakfast of thin chocolate and water and ship's biscuits.   We made a fire out of an armchair, a few histories of the saints bound in pigskin, and a number of crusty old legal authorities.*

After we had refreshed ourselves in this way, we hurried off to find our regiments.   The battlefield presented a shocking spectacle.   Corpses lay thickly all about for many miles around, particularly on the hill which our troops had so bravely defended.   Here, indeed, the dead were so plentiful that it looked as if several battalions were merely sleeping there.   Our own men could be distinguished by their red coats, and fifty paces off could be seen the blue and grey uniforms of the enemy.   Altogether, 5,000 English and about 8,000 French had perished.†   A number of French wounded who had been left behind cried plaintively to us for help, and begged us to move them away so that the Spaniards could not cut their throats.   We were particularly touched by a finely-built French grenadier who, sitting with philosophic composure amid the ruins of a powder chest containing case shot that had blown up and smashed his leg above the ankle, greeted us in a friendly way.   We gave him a gulp of wine from our bottles and comforted him.   Every trace of vegetation, and all trees and houses in this area had been burnt, and the ground was all singed black.   At six o'clock on the previous evening the dry grass and shrubs had caught fire, and most of the badly wounded men who had not been able to move from the spot had been singed or roasted alive.   In addition to all this devastation, there was also the burning sunshine, which greatly aggravated the trials of the combatants. Not a trace of shade or of coolness, or of water was to be found over the whole length and breadth of this wilderness, except under the olive trees on the Alberche and

---

* It was this perfidy on the part of the Spanish soldiers—plundering the British army while fleeing treacherously from a battle in which their allies were still engaged—that was adduced by Sir Arthur Wellesley as one of the reasons why he refused ever again to co-operate with the Spaniards in battle.   See Napier, *op. cit.*, Book IX., Chap. IV.—Tʀ.

† Napier gives the total at 6,268 British, of whom 5,422 fell on the 28th July.—Tʀ.

the Tagus. The rest of the country round Talavera was desolate, naked and devoid of trees. Many a man wounded on the 27th had died of hunger and thirst. Amid the thousands of fallen warriors there were also dead and wounded horses, weapons of all kinds, broken carts, ammunition wagons, chests, harness, shakos, light dragoon helmets, grenadier busbies, shreds of clothing, ammunition pouches, scattered all over the ground. In a barn not far from the hollow cleft above mentioned, I found the men of the 23rd Dragoons who had fallen—all young and fine-looking fellows— lying dead in three rows. They had been carried thither for burial.

We found our regiment on the Alberche, where they were camping out under the trees and foraging amid half-ruined cornfields. Our sentries were posted on both sides of the river. I took the squadron quartermaster with me, in order to send along all the bread, meat and wine I had been able to collect. In the town the troubles of the commissariat began afresh. We had to find food and there was nothing there. At last a few belated convoys, which had been left behind, began to appear in the town, and we were able to begin our deliveries. For three days I had subsisted only on water, chocolate, biscuit, and a little wine. I felt completely exhausted, and almost dried up with the heat. Both face and my my lips were blistered and smarting. At night, in our plundered quarters, we had to sleep on the bare ground.

On the 30th July we were busy on our legs the whole day, and only at midnight were we able to take a little soup and meat. But this late supper did not disturb us ; for, in spite of it, we slept like logs on the bare ground. Early next morning each of us returned to duty. Towards midday I stood at the entrance of the town and saw the wounded, both friend and foe, being brought in on bullock carts. It was a distressing sight. Many who had been taken prisoner had escaped in the night ; among them two officers of the 23rd Dragoons, Captain Drake and Lieutenant Anderson. These men, who had cut their way into the centre of a French square and had been seized by the enemy, had found their way back, and could not tell us enough about the ill-treatment they had received at the hands of the enemy.

While on an errand in the town I passed a convent where the wounded were having their limbs amputated and dressed. Never shall I forget the heartrending cries which could be heard coming from the windows in the front of this building ; while from one of the windows the amputated arms and legs were being flung out upon a small square below. In front of the door lay the wounded, who had been deposited there as fast as they arrived, awaiting their turn. Many of them were already dead. The total losses in dead, wounded and prisoners were 5,367 English and 3,000 Spanish.* The French lost 12,000 men and numbers of guns and ammunition wagons. They had had whole brigades annihilated. According to information given by one of the captured officers, they marched up to the Alberche on the 22nd July with 47,000 men commanded by Generals Victor, Jourdain and Sebastiani, with Joseph Bonaparte as Commander-in-Chief. On the afternoon of July 30th Victor is said to have complained bitterly that he had been left in the lurch by Soult, who should have marched from Plasencia to strike us in the rear. The French generals, Merlot † and Lapisse, and a great number of their officers had fallen. The French had, moreover, declared that during the battle they had not regarded our allies, the Spaniards, as dangerous ; they had not once been properly aware either of the latter's position or their strength ; for they knew that when once we had been beaten, the Spaniards would take to their heels. In ourselves, however, they had encountered soldiers of the right kind. And I have no hesitation in believing them. King Joseph is said to have ridden away

---

* See p. 191, *ante*. Oman (*op. cit.*, II., pp. 555–556), gives the British casualties as 5,365, and the French as 7,268. *Cf.* Fortescue (*op. cit.*, VII., p. 256.)—Tr.

† There seems to be no confirmation of this, nor is it easy to discover whom Schaumann means. There was a General Morlot with the French Army in Spain, but he appears to have been with Suchet when Talavera was fought. The French only had two officers of distinction slain,—Lapisse and von Porbeck of the Baden Regiment.—Tr.

from the battlefield in a very miserable and desperate mood.

On the morning of the 31st July I once again rode round the scene of the battle. Two battalions were still busy gathering the dead into heaps, and with the view of preventing pestilential smells and of saving time, partly burning and partly burying them. Here and there, however, one could see arms and legs appearing above the soil. Many corpses, both of men and horses, had been burnt brown by the sun, and, swollen to an immense size, filled the suffocatingly bad air with the most poisonous stench. In the afternoon various auctions were held in the bivouacs. At the auction held of the belongings of Colonel Gordon, who had been killed by a howitzer, I bought, for a mere song, his extremely fine dark blue overalls with two rows of buttons. And I wore them a very long time. The town is full of tumult. Eight to ten thousand wounded of all nations occupy all the churches, convents and houses. They are all shouting for help, but the doctors cannot be found. The inhabitants have fled. But what seems almost incredible is that, according to all accounts, this evening the English army, owing to lack of transport and provisions, is not going to push forward, but is going to retreat.

August 1st. This is indeed the case. This morning orders were issued to the effect that the army should be ready to march at any moment. For instance, it is said that Marshal —— is marching along the same road from Plasencia as we ourselves took, and that the English hospital is to be left in our rear, under the protection of Cuesta's army, but conducted by English doctors and commissaries. Furthermore, it is rumoured that the French have already turned about and are again on the Alberche (a lie). The unfortunate wounded, who are firmly convinced that the Spaniards will take to flight at the first sign of gun fire, and will leave them to be taken prisoners, are quite desperate at this sad news. Towards midday some of these rumours were confirmed, and all the sick and wounded who were capable of being moved were carried away in carts and on mules. The remainder, who were more severely wounded, stayed behind. Wailing, horror, and a terrible tumult filled the streets. The chief physicians and many of the people doing duty in the hospitals, who seem to have had no desire to be sacrificed, sneaked hurriedly away in secret. Wounded and sick men who, a moment previously, one would have thought incapable of moving, suddenly recovered the power of their legs and staggered, limped and hobbled away, so that they might escape falling into the enemy's hands. But rescued from Scylla they will only fall into the jaws of Charybdis ; for many of them, if they do not remain behind with the bulk of the wounded, will only be killed by the Spanish marauders and stragglers, or by Spanish peasants, who always scent money and heresy whenever they espy an Englishman.

This strange turn of events remained a mystery to every one. Nobody could explain how it was that the very army, which had so bravely defended Talavera and driven Joseph to retreat, was obliged to leave this important and beautiful position in such a hurry at the end of a few days, in order to take up a strong position at Deleytosa on the other side of the Tagus. And it was only some days later that the matter was cleared up as follows : On entering Spain, Sir Arthur Wellesley had arranged with General Cuesta that the passes of Baños and Perales should be defended by the Spanish—the former by the Marques de la Reyna, and the latter by the Duke del Parque. The importance of the latter pass had, moreover, induced Sir Arthur Wellesley to instruct Marshal Beresford to keep a vigilant look out upon it with the Portuguese under his command, while he considered the Puerto de Baños adequately safeguarded. But two days after the battle, news had already reached Sir Arthur's headquarters at Talavera, that two enemy armies 60,000 strong, were threatening us. One, under Soult and Ney, was in our rear, in the direction of the Puerto de Baños, and the other, under Mortier and Victor, on both our flanks. General Cuesta, who was also very anxious about those points, had proposed to Sir Arthur to send the English general, Wilson, thither with his corps. Now this general happened to be in Talavera in person, but his legion was in the hills of Escalona, and his advanced posts had already approached within five hours' march of Madrid. They had established communications with that city, and had discharged other important duties, which made the Commander-in-Chief reluctant to recall them. He had, therefore, made the counter-proposal to General Cuesta to send a Spanish corps thither. But, while Cuesta was forced to recognise the usefulness of Sir Robert Wilson's legion in the district where they were, and also realised that the pass needed reinforcement he was, nevertheless, equally unable to resolve to despatch thither a portion of his own army which was fulfilling no useful purpose in Sir Arthur's neighbourhood.

On the 30th Sir Arthur repeated his demands, but with just as little success as before ; and then, on August 2nd, the news reached us that the French had already pushed on as far as Bejar, fifteen leguas away. General Basse-court, with a portion of Cuesta's army, was therefore despatched to the pass ; but, as was only to be expected, it was too late, and the pass had already been forced. On the same day further news arrived to the effect that the Marques de la Reyna, with a few troops consisting of only 600 men, had abandoned his post, and without offering any resistance, had retreated *viâ* Plasencia, to the bridge of Almarez, which he believed he had destroyed in his rear. At this General Cuesta proposed to Sir Arthur Wellesley that half of the army should be despatched in the enemy's rear, and that the other half should remain at Talavera. To this Sir Arthur replied that he could not separate his troops, but that he was ready either to defend the position of Talavera with his whole army, or to resist the intentions of the enemy, and to march with this object. Cuesta apparently expressed the wish that Sir Arthur should himself decide what to do, whereupon the English Commander-in-Chief resolved to march, to give battle to Soult, and to leave Cuesta behind in Talavera to cover his rear. And with this arrangement Cuesta seemed to be very well pleased.

On August 3rd the army began to move out

of Talavera, and we stood for about an hour under arms before we quite knew whether our direction lay forwards towards Madrid, or backwards. Very soon, however, all doubts were at an end, for debouching from the grove of olives we marched along the road by which we had come, in the direction of Oropesa, where we bivouacked.

Chapter 13

AS day dawned on the 4th August, the infantry struck camp. At ten o'clock I halted in the van of the army, on the heights of Oropesa, with the whole of the cavalry, and every regiment ready to mount. A few rations were distributed. Sir Arthur and his staff also halted here, and with their telescopes scanned the plain. Eleven o'clock arrived. Nobody knew what the halt meant. At last we perceived huge clouds of dust beginning to rise above the Estrella hills and the Tietar, along the same road which we had taken from Plasencia. It was the French under Soult. " Mount ! " was the command, and the cavalry marched away. We halted frequently on the way, and foraged among the fields ; for, on the principle that where there is nothing the Emperor has no rights, General Payne had had to hold his tongue in Talavera, but he now began to harass us poor commissaries all the more. Among other tactless remarks he would declaim as follows : " A commissary who, situated as we are in this country, does not fail to supply the troops under his care with full rations and the necessary transport—that is to say, who does his duty, is a man whom I would idolise, and to whom I would raise my hat if I met him." Possibly ! But such a commissary would need to possess divine powers, and also the gift of being able to feed a thousand men with five loaves. Or, again, he would say : " Owing to the exertions it would entail, a commissary who did his duty in this country could not possibly remain alive. He would be forced to die. Of all my commissaries, not one has yet sacrificed his life ; consequently they are not doing their duty ! "

N.B.—Most Englishmen of high position, particularly when they are serving in a hot climate, are always a little mad.

In the afternoon we reached the Tagus and the bridge of Arzobispo. Over this bridge there now began to pour a throng consisting of the most motley assortment of infantry, artillery, baggage, wounded, mules, bullocks, donkeys, women, and vehicles of all kinds, among them, of course, the ungreased bullock carts ; and members of three nations, English, Spanish and German, squeezed, crushed and cursed one another as they proceeded across. This procession had gone on since the morning, and yet the cavalry had to wait until evening before they could continue their advance. I, too, wanted to cross the bridge, and was just about to do so, when, alas ! I was seized by Commissary-General Dalrymple, who, possibly labouring under the delusion that the English army was going to hold the bridge, asked me in a friendly way whether I would ride into the village of Arzobispo on this side of the river. There I would find a few bakers of the commissariat, all of whom I was to take under my command, and then I was to requisition all the ovens and see to it that bread was baked all day ! I was obliged to obey, and therefore replied, " Very well, sir ! " On reaching the village I found it completely deserted, plundered, and in ruins ; there were a few drivers and bakers there, it is true, but they had no flour, wood or kneading troughs. The windows and doors of the houses might, at a pinch, have provided the latter commodities, but what about flour ? This should have been delivered to us by the Spanish authorities ; but they had no flour ! When I saw how bad things were, I quickly decided what to do, and as soon as it grew dark and the army had crossed the river, and had spread abroad a rumour that the bridge was to be blown up, as the French advanced guard was expected any moment, we mounted our horses and crossed the bridge too. And yet, as in similar circumstances in Villafranca during Moore's retreat, nobody inquired what had become of me, of the bakers, and of the flour in Arzobispo.

We rode along with the crowd until ten o'clock, when we reached a stony heath, with woods of pine, oak and olive trees under which the army bivouacked. On this heath we marched in the dark into a vast herd of about 20,000 merino sheep, but whither they were going has to this day remained a mystery to me. Probably they were being driven to a place of safety before the French came up. Hundreds of soldiers ran out of the bivouacs, and sprawled over the crowded herd, so that three or four sheep fell beneath one man ; then seizing the best they carried it away. Thousands of fires began to flare in the bivouac, and the bleating of the victims, taken by violence, strangled and then killed under the knife, was heard on all sides. It was a regular Eve of St. Bartholomew on a small scale. As I could not find the regiment I fastened myself on to the first group of men whose camp kettle I saw spluttering invitingly over the fire.

The camp broke up early on the morning of the 5th August. An enormous number of sheep had been killed during the night, and apparently the men had suddenly grown so particular that they had eaten only the hind quarters, for, in the bivouacs through which I rode, whole fore-quarters lay about in great confusion with the fleece still on them, while legs of mutton were to be seen even on the bayonets of the men as they marched. To-day we marched six leguas along bad roads through a wilderness, and the heat and dust were intolerable. At last we bivouacked between Val de la Casa and the little river Gualeja. General Payne established his bivouac close to a small brook not far from a large ruined convent. He was in such a rage that no one dared to approach him. Bread, meat and forage were beginning to run short. But we got good drinking water from the River Gualeja close by.

August 6th. We continued the march early in the morning. We came to a hilly district, and for some while rode along a road that wound about the hills. As the infantry and artillery moved forward very slowly in front of us, and could not cross the hills fast enough for us, the cavalry frequently had to halt in the grilling heat. I believe it was during one of these halts that I came across my friend Dr. Heise, to whom, as he complained of hunger, I gave a small loaf. In order to eat it in secret, he went behind a bush, for if the famished men had seen him with it he would have run the risk of being half killed for a piece of bread. At two o'clock we again went forward over frightfully steep hills. The dust raised by the cavalry was suffocating. It was dark when we reached a small town on the banks of the River Ibor, and we found shelter in an uninhabited house, where we slept on the bare floor. Fatigue parties were busy until late in the night dragging the guns one after the other over the steep heights.

On the 7th August we marched through romantic scenery. The mountains began here, and the heights were much steeper than the day before. The road ran alongside a precipice. Often it rose at such a sharp angle that one felt as if one must slide backwards off the saddle. Two teams of horses and fifty men usually pulled at a gun, and thus, one after another, the pieces of artillery were hauled over the loftiest heights. Many shattered carts and dead horses and bullocks lined the road. The heat was stupendous, and the troops, who had been practically without bread on the 5th and the 6th, began to lose heart. I felt particularly sorry for a poor bullock driver who kept crying most piteously : " I am dying of hunger, I am dying of hunger," * but was only beaten unmercifully with sticks by the soldiers, who shouted at him, " *Arrivo*, you beggar ! " and drove him on. In the evening we halted in a valley by a small expanse of water, a mile from Deleytosa. Most of the villages of our Spanish friends and allies which we passed through were deserted. By way of thanks we plundered them, and carried window frames, doors and furniture to the bivouacs as fuel, for Spain is very poor in wood. In this way whole villages were deprived of their roofs, doors and windows. There was nothing to be had. Occasionally we found a little corn in sheaves, lying on small cultivated areas among the mountains ; there was a little ship's biscuit, which, so long as the carts held out, I was able to keep for my regiment ; and one or two bullocks that fell into our hands during our foraging

* " *Eu morre de fam.*"

excursions ; and with these things we managed to continue our march as best we could.

On August 8th we reached the highest ridge of the mountains near Deleytosa, and then began to descend. In the afternoon a funny incident occurred. The cavalry were bivouacking in a valley where there was a good deal of barley lying about in sheaves in the fields which, fenced round by bushes and hedges, surrounded a village standing on a hill. I had been obliged to ride out with a portion of the regiment to forage, and was standing in the shade, supervising the foraging operations, when a soldier bearing upon his shoulder a stolen bee-hive wrapped in his cloak, was just breaking through the hedge with his booty when he ran panting almost into the arms of a general and his staff who happened to be riding down from the village. " Halt, scoundrel ! " the general roared with rage. " What have you stolen there ? Provost Marshal, arrest that man at once, and make an example of him. Sir Arthur has forbidden all plundering on pain of death." The soldier, as if thunderstruck, contemplated the general for a moment, and looked paralysed with fear. In a second, however, he recovered himself, flung the hive violently to the ground, tore his cloak away from it, and quickly took to his heels. Meanwhile, however, the bees, outraged by the treatment they had received, swarmed angrily over the general, his staff, the provost marshal and his assistants. They even reached my foraging party, and we were all obliged to gallop away at top speed. But the soldier, whose presence of mind I admired, came off scot free. It was one of the funniest scenes I have ever witnessed.

We marched to Truxillo, where General Payne was quartered at the house of the famous Pizarro family.

One day in Truxillo I was commanded by Commissary-General Dalrymple to take a herd of wild Spanish bulls to Aldea del Bispo, and to divide them among the troops quartered in that neighbourhood. These brutes, which were all pitch black in colour, were confined in a corral—an enclosure surrounded by a high wall—outside the town. As soon as I arrived, and after a few tame cows had been placed in front of them, they were cautiously driven out, with repeated cries of Ho ! Ho ! by a few mounted Spaniards who carried long lances and had dogs with them, and whose horses had on a sort of protective harness. I did not feel very comfortable about the business, for I had no wish to participate in a bull fight. Meanwhile, everything went off very well until, as darkness fell, we reached the bivouacs. Here the bulls began to be startled by the number of camp fires ; they gave dreadful snorts, ploughed up the ground with their horns, and raised their tails in the air. I retreated on to the nearest rock. At last, by dint of much coaxing, my assistants succeeded in calming the brutes and getting them to move on again. My idea was to confine them for the night in one of the corrals in Aldea del Bispo, behind the bivouacs. We had just reached a piece of ground between the bivouacs, when, unfortunately, the bugles sounded the " lights out." Hardly had the bugles ceased when the whole of my corps, with their tails in the air, rushed snorting and bellowing through the bivouacs, overturning camp kettles, huts, and even one or two horses belonging to the 14th and 16th Dragoons, and then disappeared into the darkness and gloom. All this created a most horrible tumult, and the Spaniards with their dogs galloped *ventre à terre* after the fugitives. I gave up everything for lost ; but to my intense surprise, I was informed at midnight that the bulls had been brought back and were shut up in a corral in the middle of the field.

On the following morning I gave all the commissaries and quartermasters the word that they were to come to draw bullocks. Four heavy dragoons were stationed before the door of the corral, holding thick staves cross-wise in front of it. The moment I received from one of the commissaries a receipt note—say, for ten bullocks—the door was opened, whereupon the whole herd, mad with hunger, would make a dash for it ; but, instead of ten, fifteen would break through and take flight across the fields, and the said commissary, with his butchers, would dash after them, cursing and swearing. A regular hunt would then take place, and the brutes would be killed wherever they were caught.

The worst of these bivouacs was that the large muddy pools of water that were to be found close to them were full of leeches, which clung inside the nostrils of the horses and the mouths of the men. Moreover, not only were the horses, bullocks and donkeys watered at them, but the pigs of Arzobispo were also occasionally driven into them to be cooled, and dirty clothes were washed in their waters. The heat increased every day, and there was not a drop of rain to refresh us. If a storm rose in the west the distant mountains held it off, and while it increased the heaviness of the air, not a spot of rain came our way. The drought was so intense that our eyelids smarted ; the ink thickened on our pens as fast as we wrote, and our skins, burnt by the sun, peeled off our noses and upper lips. Shaving and washing, and particularly drying ourselves with a coarse towel, became extremely painful. Every soldier stuck an olive leaf or a piece of paper on his under lip to prevent it from bursting.

In addition to this, the long dry grass in which we had bivouacked often caught fire owing to carelessness while cooking. Then the tumult was just as great as when the fire alarm is rung in a town. Such fires occurred twice among the 1st Hussars of the legion, in one of which the commanding officer, Colonel von Arentschildt, lost his tent and all his baggage. The 23rd Dragoons lost over 100 saddles in one of these grass fires, and all their cartridge pouches were blown into the air. It was after this that the regiment was disbanded. Once the fire broke out in the artillery bivouacs, and they had to fly from the place with all their ammunition wagons, which led to the alarming rumour that the French had forced the bridge of Almaraz. These fires would spread before the wind for miles, and would creep like gigantic snakes in long lines over hill and down dale, making a terribly fine spectacle.

The bivouacs themselves were full of vermin ; there were large green lizards, eighteen inches long, that lived in the hollows of the trees ; spiders, mosquitoes, scorpions, snakes, ants and flies. All our clothes and linen suffered accordingly. Many carts full of equipment had been left standing on the mountains, because the bullocks had been slaughtered for food. The soldiers' wives, who as a rule went about decently clad, and were most faithful to their husbands, now rode round hungrily in rags on starved donkeys, and gave themselves to any one who wanted them in exchange for half a loaf of bread. Sick and wounded poured in daily, looking famished and cadaverous. Many of them had had nothing but water for three days. The whole army was suffering from fever and dysentery. The horses grew ever thinner and more debilitated, and suffered from a bleeding at the hoof in the region of the coronet. Owing to the hardness and heat of the dry ground their hoofs also grew brittle and cracked.*

At last orders arrived that we were to march to Portugal. " Thank God ! " cried every one ; and before dawn on the 21st August we moved on for five leguas across low hills, and then bivouacked. All the sick, the dismounted troopers and the debilitated horses were sent ahead. Early on the 22nd we resumed our march, and crossed a wilderness between Caceres and La Roca. Owing to lack of provisions the army had separated from us at Aldea del Bispo, and the bulk of it had gone *via* Merida. Nothing was now to be found in the fields. Everything had either been gathered in, or was dried up, and that was why we searched the villages and plagued the poor Alcaldes. Many horses were shot on the way. I had an example of the crafty way in which they know how to conceal provisions from the enemy in this country, when we passed through the last villages before reaching Badajos, where we arrived on the 27th. A sort of well or cistern was opened in the middle of the road, from which, by means of buckets, lowered to people inside it, a large amount of barley was brought up. How many a famished French trooper must have ridden over that well without suspecting its contents !

* This appears from Schaumann's description to have been the disease known as " sand crack."—Tr.

[TRANSLATOR's NOTE.—Schaumann marches with the 14th Dragoons *via* Montijo, Badajos, Elvas, and Borba, to Villa Viçosa.   On the way he exchanges his mule for a cream-coloured mare.]

On September 1st at Villa Viçosa, where I found myself in company with one half of the 14th Dragoon regiment (the other half had remained at Borba) and the staff, I relieved the commissary, Mr. Strachan.

What a joy it was to have good food again, to live in a cool house—for the heat was still severe—and to sleep in a bed and no longer on the bare floor.   True, I had a lot to do here, but that didn't matter.   My assistant, Mr. Bailey, and I, as well as our poor horses, now believed that, worn out as we were by all our exertions and privations, we had at last come to a haven of rest, more particularly as it did not seem likely that Sir Arthur would move out of Portugal again for some time.

But man proposes and God disposes ; and on the 4th September I received orders to go to Badajos, where I was quartered with a very decent family.   The Spanish live very frugally.   They believe in plenty of vegetables and water, which, in so hot a climate is, at all events, very sensible.   In the morning they have chocolate, toast and water.   At midday they eat a stew or soup consisting often of two kinds of meat, in which they also put a kind of small meat sausage (*Salchichas*) strongly flavoured with pepper and garlic, some bread and red pepper, or bread and water, oil, or, instead of that, the fat of fried bacon, and onions made into a sort of pulp.   Or they eat a couple of eggs fried with ham, poultry cooked with rice, rabbits, a good deal of pork and mutton (very rarely beef), salad, vegetables, small flat peas (*Garvanzes*), dried beans, green cabbage leaves, and drink very little wine.   Both among the rich and the poor, these are the favourite forms of food.   At my quarters here we were usually given a stew, as well as a dish of rice and chicken.   The fact that we Englishmen ate so much meat, drank so much wine and so little water, were constantly on our legs, and never slept after the midday meal, and yet remained fresh and healthy withal, struck the Spaniards with horror and amazement, and was always a riddle to them.

They always said they could not emulate us there.
" They're devils ! " * they exclaimed.

Meanwhile I went about the town a good deal. On
Sunday I went to the principal church in the large square.
They were celebrating the feast of some saint. What a
lot of tinsel there was, and excessive splendour ! All the
columns and walls were covered with red velvet hangings,
and at intervals of four feet adorned with gold lace. The
floor was of marble, and the altar was magnificent, and
decorated with pictures. The Spanish women who went
to mass there were all dressed in black—the wealthy in
silk, the others in camel's hair, trimmed with velvet and
lace. They wore white silk stockings and shoes, white
gloves to the elbow, and short skirts with fringes six inches
in length. Their calves were pretty, they had small,
kissable feet, and wore black veils which they held with
two fingers in such a way as to conceal half their faces,
and to leave only room for their dark eyes to flash between.
Their hips were well developed, and their arms and breasts
very full. But their waists made one long to clasp them,
and their whole figures were charming, well rounded, but
slender. Their gait was regal. The bells were pealing
the whole day, but they were well tuned and not unpleasant.

* " *Son Demonios !* '

Chapter 142

Elvas—Commissary in Viçosa—Heavy Duties—Mr. Augustus is made an Assistant Commissary—How he travels about the Province of Alemtejo, is welcomed and entertained by many, and returns Home safely after many Adventures—Events in Abrantes—Sudden Orders to March to the Banks of the Mondego.

FROM Badajos I rode to Elvas, where I spent a week, and then I returned to Villa Viçosa, where I was quartered first in the Rocio de San Paulo, a large open square, on which there were a few convents, and afterwards in the Rua de Cambayo. There was a great deal for me to do here. In addition to a fine hospital, there were the depots of the light infantry regiments, which, together with the generals and officers, accounted for an enormous amount of forage daily, and worried me terribly. This place was, moreover, a post on the lines of communication for all detachments destined either for the army or headquarters. Within a radius of ten miles I had requisitioned all available supplies. Every blessed day I had to ride out to Badajos, Elvas, Borba, Redondo, or Estremoz. Even in the town itself I had not a moment's peace. I had to keep baking and slaughtering. At one moment I was with the Juiz de Fora, at another at the food purveyor's or the magistrate's ; then, anon, I had to go to some general or other, after which I was obliged to go in person to this or that place, either preparing lists, writing letters, or making up accounts, so that when evening came I was so tired I could hardly stand on my legs. Villa Viçosa, the former residence of the Dukes of Braganza, which lies in a fairly well-cultivated valley, is a very beautiful place of only moderate size. Its regular streets are well paved, the houses are fine, and it has three large squares and an old castle, where a portion of the 11th Dragoons were quartered, and where some very fine knights' armour was on view.

In Elvas I visited my friend, Lieutenant Ernst Poten, of the 1st German Hussars, who having been shot through the breast at Talavera, was suffering from a dangerous wound.   Just outside Badajos, too, I generally called on my friend Dr. Heise, who was camping with the artillery of the legion on this side of the bridge over the Guadiana. It was true that they had very fine huts, but owing to ague they lived, as the saying is, with snakes amid roses.   For the banks of the river and the morasses beyond, which are flooded in winter and exposed to a grilling heat in summer, were so unhealthy that very soon there was an outbreak of ague and typhus, to which thousands of the English army succumbed.   The epidemic was so virulent that men died from it in twenty-four hours.   I myself witnessed the case of a very healthy-looking gunner of the legion.   He came back to his hut one day and told Heise that he was ill.   After he had been examined and told to go to the hospital at Badajos, he left his hut, and Heise said to me : " That apparently robust man, who does not, after all, look so very ill, will be a corpse the day after to-morrow."   Apparently the Spaniards had warned Lord Wellington about the banks of the Guadiana, which were proverbial, and which had been known to be bad in other wars ; but he would pay no heed.

The heat lasted until the beginning of October, and then at length we had a few showers, and the air and the country were both refreshed after a drought of four months.   The fortifications around Badajos did not seem very considerable, and here and there they were actually in ruins ; but by means of trenches, barricades and *chevaux de frises*, they had been so much strengthened by French engineers, that many an Englishman, who laughed at them then, lost his life in the deadly night assault of the town that took place in 1812.

The people who made the most stir in Villa Viçosa were the officers of the 23rd Dragoons, who, having lost most of their comrades at Talavera, were due to return to England.   They did not know what pranks to be up to in order to kill time and relieve their wanton spirits ; for instance, they all wore the large round hat of the Portuguese peasant and carried a spiked stick, six feet long, like that of the bullock drivers.   They had their heads tonsured as if they were priests.   They ended their mess or their dinner every night by all getting drunk and flinging the dinner service, and finally the chairs and table, out of the window. One morning, just as I was sitting writing, I heard the trampling of feet in the street, and a crowd of people collecting, and, at the same time, all my neighbours threw open their windows and their balcony doors. When I asked what had happened, I was told that an English bishop had arrived and was going to pass through the town. True, I laughed in their faces when they told me, but lo and behold! at that very moment the alleged bishop really did make his appearance, riding solemnly down the street on horseback, accompanied by all the officers of the 23rd Dragoons, bearing their helmets reverently in their hands. The bishop (a captain of the regiment) was clad in red velvet breeches, white gaiters trimmed with lace, a long skirted red velvet jacket, an English flannel dressing-gown trimmed with black, a large Spanish collar *à la* Van Dyck, with a clerical band, a wig, a moustache, an old-fashioned hat with a large tassel, and gauntlet gloves. In his left hand he carried a sceptre, on which a huge lemon was stuck, surmounted by a cross. With his right hand he blessed the people. And thus they marched in solemn silence through Villa Viçosa to Borba, at which place they intended to take luncheon. The whole town was in an uproar. Everybody wanted to get a glimpse of the English bishop. The extraordinary part of it was that no Portuguese would believe that it was only a joke. The whole crowd shouted : " *O Bispo Inglese ! O Bispo Inglese ! tem visto O Bispo Inglese !* " I only wished that Lord Wellington might by chance have encountered this cavalcade ; how quickly it would have dispersed !

On the 20th November I had the pleasure of finding in a general order dated the 19th of the month, 1809, that I had been promoted to " Acting Assistant Commissary." And thus I was now not only an officer of the legion, but also an officer in the commissariat.*

* In the G.O. in question, he appears thus : " Mr. Showman is appointed an acting Assistant Commissary till His Majesty's pleasure is known." (" General Orders Spain and Portugal," Vol. I., p. 222.)—Tr.

Meanwhile I was busy preparing accounts, as well as with making various drawings of Villa Viçosa. Unfortunately, however, I lent the latter to friends and they went astray. On the 22nd November I received orders to go to the country to buy barley, and Mr. Belson gave me 2,000 piastres, and a few dragoons as escort. Now it just happened that Captain von Bischoffshausen, who had received his discharge, and was returning to his estate in Germany, was travelling a portion of the way with me, and after we had made the necessary arrangements, and had taken leave of friends, both male and female, we set out on November 26th in high spirits for Redondo.

On the 27th November we pushed on further to Evora, where we stopped in front of Bischoffshausen's quarters, which were in the house of a noble Fidalgo. Bischoffshausen ordered the groom of the establishment to remove all his master's mares from the stables, as his English stallion was a fiery and restless animal, and might cause trouble. The groom, however, refused to obey, and was insolent. But when Bischoffshausen began to belabour him with a branch of young oak, the mares were speedily removed. After I had had a look at my own quarters and established my horses and staff there, I returned to Bischoffshausen, and wandered about the town with him.

As my quarters seemed strange to me, I stayed the evening with Bischoffshausen and had dinner with him. After dinner we invited the ladies of the house to join us ; for the master was away. They came—a very beautiful woman, with fair hair and blue eyes (a rare occurrence in these parts) just risen from child-bed, her sister, and a young and good-looking Portuguese in Jäger uniform, who played the guitar. All three sang divinely. Bischoffshausen had brewed some punch, to which full justice was done ; and we two, who had both fallen in love and were in the seventh heaven of delight, did our best to make the two ladies understand how reverently we worshipped them. They, for their part, were accepting our attentions very well indeed, albeit with perfect innocence and ingenuousness, when, in the midst of all this merry love-making, we suddenly heard the sound of angry words downstairs, and an ugly little man in a grey coat stepped into the room. He took not the slightest notice of us, but turned wrathfully upon the women, who had both grown very pale, and ordered them out of the room. Then, snatching the guitar from the hands of the young man, he smashed it on the ground, and stamping upon it with both feet, behaved like a madman. I was on the point of asking Bischoffshausen whether we were to put up with such treatment when he, a little top-heavy with love, wine and punch, seized hold of the dwarf, twisted him round, gave him several kicks in the backside, threw him down on a chair with such violence that he made it crack, pulled him up again and lifted him high in the air, tearing his coat in two as he did so, and then, finally seizing hold of a heavy chair with both hands, he would have broken the skull of his host—for such he proved to be—if I had not shouted to him : " Bischoffshausen, are you mad ? No violence here, or we are lost ! " This brought him to his senses and prevented the blow. Nevertheless, my friend's violence resulted in the grey gnome fleeing away from the room like lightning, and leaving the ladies trembling and weeping in our hands. They wanted to follow him, but we did not allow them to do so, saying that it would reflect upon our honour. They must remain with us. Thereupon the husband was summoned to appear, and assured that no harm would overtake him if he did. Ultimately, after a long discussion, he came snarling in, with his sly cat's face, bowed and cringed, and then quickly pleading that he was tired after his journey, begged us to allow him to go to bed. He also added that as English officers and men of honour, he would gladly allow us to enjoy the company of his wife and sister-in-law for a little while longer, under the surveillance of the young Portuguese. His request was granted.

Shortly after this I wished Bischoffshausen farewell for ever, for early on the morrow our ways were to part—he going *viâ* Lisbon to Germany and home, I going onwards to my destiny. Although I was feeling a little giddy after the wine and love-making, I remember, nevertheless, that

I kissed the hands of the ladies, who lighted me down-stairs, on nearly every step.   And as I tramped home through the dark, deserted streets, it was not without certain qualms concerning the stiletto of the husband in the case.   It was with some difficulty that I found my quarters, but when I reached them there was a supper waiting for me in a large, lonely hall, furnished in an old-fashioned style.   In order not to offend my hosts, who were very kind, I sat down and for their sake ate another supper.   Thereupon I was shown my bed in a little old-fashioned room adjoining the hall, likewise furnished in an antiquated style, and the door of which would not close. I therefore pushed a chair against it, inspected the walls for secret doors, laid my pistols by my bed, and soon fell fast asleep.

It was midday on the morrow before we were able to mount and set off, and at ten at night we reached Portele. I was quartered with a priest, who, under the designation of housekeepers, cousins or dairymaids, kept at least seven concubines.   As he had no stabling, we were obliged to take our animals to another place, where we had almost to force the stables open by violence.   My host was very friendly, chatty, courteous and hospitable. The Juiz de Fora, Senhor Joze Silvestre de Mocedo, was also a pleasant and obliging man, whose extremely kind attentions I shall never forget.   My host gave me a very delicious supper, but it did not interest me nearly as much as a good-looking little girl of fifteen, who waited upon me, and whose roguish coquetry, mingled with innocence and temperament, played havoc with my poor heart.   She was one of the seven girls mentioned above.   Maybe she was still only a novice in this ecclesiastical association.

I concluded my business with the Juiz de Fora, from whom I had purchased 500 Alquieres [1,000 gallons] of barley, had a good luncheon, and rode for seven hours beyond Portele, reaching Marmesar late at night in a storm of rain.   It is a poverty-stricken place, but its priest, who bears the title of prior, received us with extraordinary heartiness.   His living did not seem to be a particularly good one ; but what little he had he did not conceal. His only companions were an old manservant and a tom cat. Contrary to the custom of other priests, he, though in the prime of life, had no housekeepers. When our horses had been installed in a huge stable, up to their bellies in fragrant hay, he had a large fire lighted in the kitchen, around which he himself, my dragoons, my muleteers and I formed a comfortable circle. The old manservant acted as cook, and turned a lamb on the spit. Meanwhile we smoked cigars and spun the most impossible yarns to our host, who, in this out-of-the-way corner of Portugal, obtained but little news.

While he, all agog with curiosity, was listening attentively and open-mouthed to all we said, a messenger arrived to say that an old woman was dying and required extreme unction. I have never laughed so much as I did at the absurd fury of our host, when he saw that our narrative was to be interrupted so prematurely. " Let her wait ! The devil won't come to fetch her ! " he snorted angrily at the messenger. " I cannot leave my house now, I have people billeted here ; and I don't want to break my neck in the dark ! " he exclaimed. And then he added : " And yet ! " and suddenly recollecting himself, continued more gently : " Yet, after all, Antonio, give me my cloak ! Confound it ! " he cried, growing angry again, " an old hag like that always imagines her hour has come ! O Lord of my days ! *Sanctissima mai e todos os Santos !* * What a plague old women are ! They want to be confessed, confirmed, anointed and absolved every ten minutes ! She can wait. The devil will not come to fetch her ! " Then more gently, he added : " I mean, he shall certainly not come to fetch her. I'll see to that ! " Then, again angrily : " Pooh ! Why not now at once ? Let her wait ! And yet——" But once more his voice softened, and he said : " Antonio, give me my boots ! " Whereupon, finally, he tore himself away, and promising to return as quickly as possible, soon left the house, grumbling, cursing and complaining.

On the 2nd December I pushed on to Beja, a moderately large town, where I was billeted on a rich priest. He

* " Holy Mother and all the saints ! "

inhabited a fine well-appointed and comfortably furnished house. Superfluous means were apparent in every corner. But he was not as conscientious as the poor prior of Mamesar, for he kept three cousins under his roof. One, a person of Junonian proportions, a typical Flemish Venus, directed the household and was the Sultana, while two slim and elegantly dressed girls sat by the kitchen fire, and seemed to be apprentices. I had said a few flattering things to the Sultana, and had been vouchsafed several favourable and encouraging glances. But the priest watched over the girls with jealous Argus eyes, and it was impossible, in so short a time, to pull off an intrigue, although I was longing to do so.

On the 17th December I was suddenly given orders to repair at once to Olivenza, in order to join the 16th Light Dragoons as their commissary ; and on the 18th I went to Elvas, where I lunched with my friend Commissary Callow. We allayed our hunger so barbarously that I could hardly sit up in the saddle. It was consequently late when, on my way to Olivenza I passed a lonely farm, from which three huge sheepdogs or wolf-hounds charged at me so furiously that I was obliged to fire my pistol among them. One of them was wounded, and the brutes took to flight with a howl. As, however, I heard human voices close by, I put spurs to my horse, and fled with all possible speed.

[TRANSLATOR's NOTE.—When once the regiment had reached Olivenza, Schaumann travelled *via* Aviz and Ponte de Sor to Abrantes, which he entered on the 2nd January, and took up his duties as commissary to the 16th Light Dragoons.]

I was quartered in a very fine house, containing two features with which I was particularly pleased. There were two pretty girls, and a little room with glass windows, where I made myself at home. My host was a clerk at the city court and central billeting office, where his son, who was quite young, was also employed. I had little to do, for there was a large stores depôt here, and I obtained all I needed for the regiment without much trouble. But I was anxious to avail myself of this interval of peace to get my accounts in order ; and the rest of the time I spent walking about, eating, drinking, sleeping and love-making, in which last occupation my host's two pretty daughters, Rosa and Joaquine, as well as their friend, Senhora Angelica, ably assisted me. In the evening my friend, Captain—then Lieutenant—Baertling, of the 1st German Hussars, used to visit me. He had fallen in love with one of the young women at my quarters, and while their father and brother were at market, Baertling and I used to go to the girls' rooms and entertain ourselves with our three graces in that time-honoured fashion which was popular even in the days of Paris and Helen.

[TRANSLATOR'S NOTE.—Schaumann was not destined to remain in Abrantes long, for on the 20th January he is ordered to leave the 16th Dragoons and repair at once to Barquinha, where he takes over the 4th Dragoons, and engages a secretary, a Senhor Isidro Gomez, at a salary of five shillings a day. On the 15th February, a general order appeared announcing that the army would soon march again, and on the 17th a letter from General Fane urgently summoned Schaumann to Gallegao, where to his surprise he finds that marching orders had arrived in the night.]

Chapter 15

New Cantonments and Unpleasant Duties—The Cavalry Horses are still thin—Mr. Augustus is Harassed on all sides, but Defends himself like a Spiteful Dog—He discovers why the Horses do not Improve—His Domestic Arrangements and Merry Life.

I MARCHED with the 4th Dragoons to Temtugal and Montemor Velho. The district we now occupied, close up to the banks of the Mondego, was very beautiful. There are several grassy islands in the river at this place, on which one occasionally comes across a small farm. Temtugal itself is a small town on the banks of the Mondego. It has a few convents, and is picturesquely surrounded by a number of large farms, gardens, orange and olive groves, and fields, with hills in the distance. It lies between Coimbra, Montemor Velho, and the seaport town of Figueiras, at the mouth of the Mondego. In the winter this valley, twenty-eight miles long and one and a half broad, is usually flooded by the Mondego, which, like a miniature Nile, covers it with about five feet of water. The ground is consequently very fertile. There are also great numbers of water fowl in the neighbourhood, which are hunted in small boats in which two men and a *pederero* work great slaughter among them. Fish, particularly the old-time delicacy, lampreys, are to be found in abundance. When I arrived at Temtugal, I and my staff were quartered in a large uninhabited house in the yards surrounding which, lemons, bay and fig trees grew lustily out of the old dung and refuse heaps.

The maize that grows in the district was given to the horses of both regiments, and they ate it with a good relish. But, in spite of all our care and good food, they remained very thin. At every inspection the generals would raise an outcry, and ascribed their condition, first to the maize, then to insufficient food, and anon to the fact that the grass we gave them was too moist. Old General Payne therefore gave orders that green forage was always to be gathered a day ahead, and not given to the horses moist, as it came from the meadows. As, however, moist grass grows very hot if it is stored over night, and acquires an unpleasant taste which the horses do not like—a fact which I was able to point out and give abundant proof of—things went on pretty much as they were before. I was dismissed with scornful smiles, and told that they must continue to eat the heated and sour-tasting grass or else leave it. They elected the latter alternative. Then bran was ordered, and things became very hard indeed for me. But I had to bear it patiently. (O, ye English cavalry generals !) One day, however, when I was talking to the Juiz de Fora of my trouble, he smiled and said : " If your horses grow thin it means that the people in my district grow all the fatter, and surely that is a good thing ! " Very much astonished, I begged him to interpret these cryptic words. " Well," he said, " this is how it happens. Hardly have the dragoons drawn their corn than hundreds of old women appear on the scene with bottles of brandy or wine concealed in their aprons, with which they bargain with the men for the return of the corn. Your horses have hardly any corn, although they have probably had heaps of straw and grass."

A light suddenly dawned in my mind ! I thanked the Juiz de Fora, and mounting my horse, galloped off to General Payne at Coimbra, and triumphantly disclosed my discovery, adding, by way of revenge, that such horrors had never been heard of in the German cavalry, where nothing of the sort had occurred. A furious general order was immediately issued and circulated, according to which, when the trumpet blew for feeding time, officers were to be present to superintend, and were not to go away until the horses had devoured the last grain of corn in their presence.* Some officers even had their horses fed in the street in order to be able to keep them better in view. As, moreover, in all cases of a breach of this rule, the dragoons who were caught *in actu flagrante*

---

* It would be interesting to know whether this was the origin of the custom now prevailing in all the mounted regiments of the British Army, and certainly observed with great regularity by the artillery all through the late war, according to which one officer at least always had to be present in the lines or stables at feeding time, and had even to give the order to feed.—TR.

were court-martialled and flogged—that is to say, unmercifully cut to pieces with the cat-o'-nine-tails—the horses grew fatter, and the poor townsfolk thinner.

The English cavalry soldier looks upon his horse as a machine, as an incubus, which is the cause of all his exertions and punishments. He ill-treats it. And even when forage lies within his reach, he will not, of his own accord, lift a finger to get it. The commissary must procure everything, and actually hold the food to his own and his horse's mouth. Even the officers do not give a commissary the smallest help, and grumble when they have to hand him over a few men even as a protective escort. From the colonel downwards, all they can do is to find fault with the forage, and every day they repeat the remark : " I shall report it."

How different things are in the German cavalry regiments of the legion ! Every officer and man tries to help. " Provided you pay," they exclaim to the commissary, " we will see that it is procured." Whereas all the English cavalry regiments were going to pot, the German were distinguished from the first to the last moment of the campaign by their fine efficient horses and men. Nevertheless, I must do justice to the 14th and 16th English Dragoons, by admitting that they were an exception to the rule, that they at least acknowledged the efforts I made, and that their active, useful, courageous and skilful officers, eagerly supported me, even in the matter of detailing parties for foraging. But enough about my duties ! Let me speak of my domestic or private life. Here in Temtugal, my adjutant, Senhor Fereira's first concern was to obtain a good though ugly cook. Then a pretty servant girl, Maria Brada, was also engaged. The latter Fereira kept for himself, and as my bed was not far from the wall of his room, I was able to bear witness every night to the ardour of their passions. But I had another love affair with an exquisite child called Joaquina Cavaleira. Her excellent mother brought her round to me every evening, decked out like a bride, and then fetched her in the morning. It is no good worrying one's head about the customs of different countries!

The fishermen, on pain of excommunication, were supposed to deliver all their lampreys to the bishop and the high priests of Coimbra. But, as a rule, they laughed at excommunication, and taking our English gold, gave us the fish. These lampreys were about fifteen inches long and three inches thick, had nine holes on one side of the head like river lampreys, and their flesh was extremely tender and delicate. There was also plenty of poultry in our yard, and game, particularly wild duck and snipe, were brought to us by the peasants. I did not like to go to the officers' mess, partly because I should only have felt embarrassed there, and partly because a commissary is very soon regarded as the general cook and bottle-washer of such an institution, who gets no thanks and all the outlay and vexation. I therefore kept aloof from it, which certainly got me into evil odour.

In order to complete my princely establishment, Fereira had provided musicians and dancers who, like East Indian dancing girls, diverted us with dancing and string music during our evening meal. The performers consisted of our newly engaged fat and very ugly cook, a jolly shoemaker, and the barber of the place, who sang and accompanied himself on the guitar. As, owing to my duties, I lunched very late, a large number of officers joined our mess almost every day, to drink a glass of wine, to enjoy my convent jam,* and to spend the evening drinking grog and smoking cigars. The Juiz de Fora, too, always turned up every evening, and was highly delighted by our entertainment. The shoemaker, an arch-buffoon and born jester, first made his jokes and performed his tricks, accompanied in a casual way by the barber's guitar. But the moment we cried, " *Fandango !* *Fandango !* " the cook and the shoemaker took up a position face to face, the barber struck up on his guitar, and then the fun began, until all of us rolled on the floor with laughter. I cannot describe the positions and scenes that occur when common people dance the *Fandango*, but what I cannot understand is how these dancers did not do

* This consisted of very good preserves with which the nuns of a local convent provided Schaumann in order to induce him to spare their fields.—Tr.

themselves some serious internal injury. For when the
two of them, who were both corpulent, short and dispro-
portionately broad, *chassé* towards each other, first their
bellies and then their hindquarters would collide with such
violence, *dos à dos*, that they both croaked and rebounded
like shuttlecocks to the opposite walls of the room. The
shoemaker, moreover, cut an extraordinarily comic figure,
with his leather apron decoratively lifted on one side, his
black string cap on his head, the long tassel of which, as
he danced, beat time to and fro upon his corporation
swathed in a waistcoat of blue plush decked with two
round patches, and his bare brown legs ending in shoes
with enormous buckles. The evening generally ended
with every one going to bed a little top heavy and full of
sweet grog.

In Coimbra, whither I repaired occasionally, a variety
of pleasures awaited me. As a rule I stayed in the house
of Commissary Gordon, who, however, as a travelling
depôt-commissary, was almost always absent. I had
fallen in love with his alleged wife, a beautiful woman
who ruled the household ; and I may say that she returned
my love ; for, whenever we came across each other in
after years—and even in Paris in 1815—she always
showed me the most tender attachment. She had come
to Portugal as the wife of a man in the 3rd Dragoons, but
endowed by nature with extraordinary beauty and talent,
she soon felt that she was not in her proper place. Mr.
Gordon, who came across her while acting as commissary
to the regiment, took her, with her husband's consent,
and in return paid the man a solatium. When this man
was killed in a small engagement, and Mr. Gordon
entered the Spanish service, she married Commissary-
General Boyes, and it was as Mrs. Boyes that I saw her
again in Paris. She was fair, and had the most beautiful
blue eyes I have ever seen in my life. She was well
developed, her cheeks were like peaches, her mouth and
teeth quite perfect, and her skin beautifully white. She
was extremely vivacious, and was quickly able to acquire
the most refined manners. Nobody would have suspected her of being the wife of an ordinary dragoon. Her

maiden name was Anne Luke. My two clerks had also become attached to two young and pretty Portuguese girls, and Mrs. Gordon had her meals with them whenever Mr. Gordon was absent. Whenever I came to Coimbra she had a merry guest the more, and we would eat, drink, joke and laugh until late at night. She and I were naturally inseparable. To this very day I think with joy of the gorgeous hours I spent with her. What days and what nights ! She would have made a magnificent model for a statue of Venus.

Medicine, surgery and the treatment of illness are still in their infancy in this country, although the Portuguese doctors will not admit it. On the contrary, they claim that Coimbra is now the rival of Paris, Montpellier, Pavia, London and Edinburgh ! As far as my own experience goes, I can testify to the fact that I have come across many doctors here who were quacks, and have, as a rule, found their surgical instruments obsolete, rusty, and few in number. They seem to know nothing about the latest discoveries. And these quacks always appealed to the regimental doctors either of the English forces or of the legion, whenever an operation had to be performed, or a bungled case had to be set right. Even the apothecaries were not much good, for although a parchment diploma ratified by the king and the university declared the holder to be proficient in his science, the matter remained doubtful, seeing that these documents could be bought for money.

My domestic peace in Temtugal was only once disturbed. I had often had to reprove my man John, who seemed to be living on the most intimate terms with my English housekeeper, Mother Pegg, for his insolence and carelessness, and also for having, in my absence, laid violent hands upon Senhor Joaquim, my friend Ferièra's brother. Now both of them took this in bad part, and one morning, when John did not appear with my washing water and failed to clean my things, the circumstance struck me as so odd that I went with the two Ferieras to find out what it all meant. But we could find neither John nor Pegg. As, however, nothing was

missing, and the stable was in order, and the large outside
door was closed, we calmed our fears and went down into
some cellars where the stores were kept ; and here, in a
small room we found that a board had been removed, and
on it there stood a ladder which led into an upper room.
In this upper room we found two unmentionable memen-
toes of the couple, lying symmetrically side by side, and
we realised from this that they must have absconded.
But, as my housekeeper, Mother Pegg, had taken her
husband's savings with her by mistake, and he was a
dragoon, he pursued the couple, and caught them at
Figueiras, where they intended taking ship to Lisbon.
He proceeded to take everything from them, but being
surrounded by a crowd of people who threatened him
with daggers and stones, he drew his sword, and charging the mob, fought his way through it and returned
triumphantly to Temtugal.   He and I were both quite
pleased to be rid of the couple.

The leader of my mule brigade was a well-to-do
Castilian peasant, and an exceedingly honest man—a
Spaniard whom one could send any distance with gold or
treasure, and who would not run away with it as 90 per
cent. of Spaniards would have done.   He was a short,
thick-set person, and people called him my Sancho Panza.
Among his brigade of mules he had some magnificent
beasts, which I rode by preference.   The whole of the
mule-breeding industry in Spain and Portugal is on a very
high plane of excellence.   I have never seen such fine
and powerful beasts.   When they are on the road they
are decked with numbers of bells which tinkle melodiously
in the distance.   If they have not got these bells, the
leading mule, at the head of the column has a bell, or
rather a cylinder, slung round his neck, the constant
clanging of which makes the rest follow.   According to
the cruel Arab custom, neither horses nor mules are
allowed to lie down in their stables, and they are given
high-sounding names such as Queen, Frigate, Coney,
Count, Princess.   Their endurance, strength, unexacting
wants and gentle pace, and the fine manner and certainty
with which they climb up and down the impracticable

mountain roads, in which the country abounds, are incredible. I have often travelled as many as forty-five miles with them in one day, and they carry the largest loads day after day, on long marches, and patiently and unwearyingly subsist on the most exiguous supplies of food and water. They even constitute the only transport for the Portuguese mountain artillery ; one mule bears the falconet, another the carriage, and another the ammunition. By means of some shears which were easily adjusted, the gun is lifted from the mule without difficulty, put together, and replaced.

When ladies travel on mules, two often sit together, one on either side of the mule, which looks very picturesque. If wool is being transported, it is impossible to see the poor brutes ; all one can perceive are three enormous sacks, one on each side almost trailing on the ground, and one on top, and they look as if they were moving along automatically. The price of a mule depends on its size, strength and beauty. Fifty to sixty guineas are frequently paid for a first-class mule. The muleteers form a large and hardy class of men. They seldom change their clothes or sleep under shelter throughout the year ; they are always on the road, and are very merry and constantly singing. When their mules are hired out for riding they are able to run alongside them at a trot for ten miles at a stretch in the greatest heat without getting tired. While running along in this way they fling their arms about, and this seems to give them great relief. They are very temperate, but also greedy and devoted, and I had many in my brigade, who, if I had wanted it, would have faced death for me. More than once, on retreats and marches, while in charge of my baggage and public funds, and when everything was in confusion, they were separated from me, and might easily have escaped and made their fortune by so doing, but they always turned up sooner or later. They wore large black felt hats with tassels, short jackets, a mantle, a blanket with a hole in the middle for their heads, blue plush breeches, and spats or sandals. On arriving at an inn or public house, they are very smart in finding accommodation for themselves and their beasts. Eggs cooked in oil, cod-fish, garlic, sardines, bread, and a measure of wine, are then prepared, and round this meal they sit, to the accompaniment of much noise and smacking of lips.   In the morning, before they start on a march, they always like, if possible, to attend mass at the nearest chapel or church.   But, towards the end, the war had turned them into such radical free-thinkers that, not only did they cease to trouble about mass, but actually assisted in the plundering of churches, and decked themselves and their beasts in the vestments of the priests.

Chapter 16

Unpleasant Duties in Cea—Don Louis Bernardo—Life in Cea and other Curiosities—Thoughts about the Future—Mr. Augustus grows Economical and the French grow Restless—Disposition of our Army—Ciudad Rodrigo is taken—The Fall of Almeida—Masséna concentrates all his Army—Attack on Portugal.

[EDITOR'S NOTE.—Schaumann leaves Temtugal on the 29th April, 1810, and marches to Cea.]

AT midday we reached Cea, which, together with a white palace belonging to Don Louis Bernardo, that stands in front of the town, lies picturesquely on a hill, with the lofty walls of the Estrella mountains in the background. We obtained good quarters. The Juiz de Fora, Senhor Xavier da Costa, was a courteous, obliging and amiable man. My stores were established in an old deserted chapel on the slope of the hill, opposite Don Louis Bernardo's palace, where Colonel Lord Charles Somerset was quartered. Since we had come closer to headquarters, as also to the army and the enemy, victuals were more scarce here, and the dear old troubles of the past began afresh. I had to ride about so much that, as a rule, I succeeded in exhausting one or two horses or mules every day. At one moment I had to go to Virsen, at another to Mangoalde,* and then later on to Alorico and innumerable villages. Things were wanted here, there and everywhere. First I was summoned to Lord Charles Somerset, then to Sir Granby Calcraft, and then to General Grey or Major Leighton. First one man wanted to speak to me, then another. One wanted this, another that. One wanted hay and no straw ; the other straw and no hay. One would not accept maize, either for man or beast, another complained that the wine was not good enough, and a third that he did not like the meat. One party asked for the tongues of the slaughtered bullocks, another begged for kidney-suet for his pudding,

* The first-named place may be a misprint and stand for Vizeu ; the second is usually spelt Mangualde.—TR.

and yet another for marrow bones for his ox-tail soup.
Fortunately, very precise rules were laid down as to how
much each was to have according to his rank. I was also
tormented by the officers' mess, and when the mess-
servant, an impertinent fellow, once came into my room
with his hat on, I threw him out again. Shortly before
this, the same man had seized a cask of wine which I had
bought for my store and had taken it to the mess. I had
complained of this in pretty outspoken terms to Lord
Charles Somerset, who was the mess president, but he
categorically forebade me to interfere. I was consequently in evil odour with the whole mess, especially as I
absolutely refused to be a member of it. But I did not
care. If they will behave like churls, I thought, then so
will I. But I lived very well on the whole. We had
plenty of garden produce, such as salad and young peas
and beans. True, the peas were only of the so-called
sweet or flat variety, which are eaten in their pods, and
which my Portuguese cook knew how to prepare in an
excellent fashion, according to the custom of the country,
with poached eggs. Otherwise our principal dishes
consisted of good marrow-bone and vegetable soups with
roast beef, roast joints of mutton which came from sheep
fed entirely on the aromatic herbs of the hills, and were
extremely delicious, and hill rabbits or pigeons. For
desert we had a cold preparation of rice known as *Arroz
doce*, some excellent milk cheese with cinnamon and sugar,
and wonderful cherries and peaches. Every third day,
moreover, I used to send some one on a mule into the
mountains to fetch snow for myself and for the mess,
with which we cooled the wine and made lemonade.

My duties took me almost weekly into Celrico, Viseu
and Mangoalde, where I usually spent the night. There
resided in Viseu, in addition to my Mr. Gibbon, the three
Commissaries Macgreen, Unwin and Cooper, who lived
on the fat of the land there, and also Mr. Gordon, together
with his beautiful alleged wife, with whom I had once
been so intimate in Coimbra.

In Mangoalde I found Mr. Hughes, my second clerk.
He, too, was leading a fine life, and not only kept a

girl, but also two horses, two hunting dogs and a groom. He wore a huge Portuguese hat with a large flat brim. He was a good fellow, but exceedingly sensual and lazy at his work, and I often had to reprimand him most severely. If, however, I could not enjoy the pleasant home life of Viseu, I had at least other things to feast my eyes upon, for in this place there were numbers of the prettiest girls one could wish to see. One of them, called Maria, particularly attracted my attention. She was only fifteen, but she was beautiful and well-developed. Unfortunately, with all her youth and ingenuousness, it was impossible to assume that she was still innocent, for the owner of the palace where Colonels de Grey and Sir Granby Calcraft were quartered—a wealthy man who had travelled much in England and France—shared with his brother the evil reputation of having deflowered all the girls of their large village the moment they grew up. What the eye does not see, however, the heart does not feel, and as the girl pleased me, and I her, I took her with me on the back of a mule that was carrying produce to Mangoalde and Cea. I rode on horseback beside the mule. The girl was perfectly built, with beautiful chest development, snow-white teeth, delightfully small mouth, black and fiery eyes, full of voluptuousness, and the daintiest of hips. Even in our love-making she always retained a certain modesty, and at the first cockcrow she would flee from me.

Among the many matters that occupied my mind at this time, were thoughts about my own future. Hitherto I had not been able to save or lay anything aside, because my salary of 7s. 6d. a day did not permit me to do so. Now, however, that with my pay as a lieutenant I drew almost three times as much, and had done nothing that I needed to regret, I began to think seriously of securing a bright future for myself. · The old paymaster of the 4th Dragoons, Captain Peterson, gave me the address of Messrs. Hopkinson and Sons, Army Agents, St. Alban's Street, London, and never shall I forget my childish joy when I got their first letter, in which they informed me that they had received my remittance of £150, and had invested it for me in 4 per cent. stock, then standing at

£78. From that time onwards I held my nose somewhat higher in the air, and even grew a little mean, for every dollar I could save found its way to London.

While the English army was recuperating and gathering strength in its cantonments, the Portuguese army under General Beresford, had been so thoroughly put in order by English commissioned and non-commissioned officers, that it was possible to incorporate her strong, well-drilled, and finely equipped regiments in the English army. These fellows, with their dark brown faces, really looked quite martial. Thanks to rest and good living, the army recovered all the spirit and pluck which it had lost on the retreat from Talavera. Little heed was paid to the external appearance of the troops. Whether their breeches were of a light or dark shade did not matter, provided the men themselves and their arms were right. Wearing jackets of blue, black, green or crimson velvet, with round silver filigree buttons *à l'espagnol* as large as plums dangling from small chains, and with breeches of a green, azure, or brown colour, the officers considered themselves perfectly attired for mess. All these fashions, together with the cut of the small hats with the tuft of cock's feathers—an object of mockery and horror to the French and Spaniards—hailed from headquarters. Generally speaking, the uniforms of the English army were of a very practical design for service in the field— that is to say, comfortable, ample, and as loose as sacks. That is why the French prisoners were so much amused by them, particularly by the uniforms of our heavy dragoons ; and caricatures of them were published in Paris. Later on, instead of hats, the dragoons were given helmets, from the back of which hung a tail of black horse-hair. The light dragoons wore blue uniforms with red, yellow and white facings, gold or silver braid, and black leather helmets ornamented with a bear's tail, which gave them a very fine appearance. Later on they were given shakos.

According to a regulation emanating from Lord Wellington, which had been circulated everywhere, all the inhabitants were enjoined, as fast as the enemy approached, either to take flight with their belongings and cattle into the inaccessible parts of the mountains, or else to retreat with our army. By this means all the ground between us and the enemy could be devastated, and all mills destroyed. At about this time these measures began to be enforced more and more rigorously. It appeared, however, that the English and Portuguese Governments were agreed that the poor people should be compensated for their losses. Irrespective of this regulation, however, we commissaries were, of course, strictly bound to pay in promissory notes, bills of exchange, or cash, for everything we took. Many families from the neighbourhood of Ciudad Rodrigo took flight along the valley of the Mondego.

On the 4th July General Craufurd was driven back by the enemy, and it was on this occasion that Captain Krauchenberg of the 1st German Hussars distinguished himself so gloriously. With only his own squadron he held back thirty enemy squadrons at a bridge across a small river this side of Gallegeos, until such time as a battery of English horse artillery was able to retreat across it. The news of this feat was received with great rejoicing by the whole army.* On the 9th July the French took the suburbs of Ciudad Rodrigo, and the convent of San Francisco by storm, and the same night they sprung their mines. Nevertheless, the brave Spanish governor, General Herrasti, would not hear of surrendering. But, in the end, though only after all breaches had been made practicable, and the French were preparing a general assault on the place, the white flag was hoisted. In the town itself it is said that not a single house remained undamaged, and over 2,000 men were killed or wounded. On the 12th July my old companion and interpreter of the Corunna campaign, Senhor Antonio Falludo, called upon me and wished to be taken on again ; so I wrote recommending him in the warmest terms to the Commissary-General.

---

* See Beamish (*op. cit.*, Vol. I., pp. 276–278), where it will be seen that not a whole battery of horse artillery but only two guns were concerned in this exploit. See also Napier (*op. cit.*, Book XI., Chap. IV.), where, by-the-bye, the German officer's name seems to be given wrongly as Kraüchenberg.—Tʀ.

On the 17th July the army began to grow restless, and we were warned to be on the alert, as marching orders might be expected at any moment. I therefore took all the necessary steps. These rumours were confirmed by a letter from the Commissary-General dated the 18th July, and at ten o'clock on the morning of the 19th July orders arrived that we were to march early that day. Now there was plenty to do ! Fortunately my mules had just arrived back laden with corn, and after I had settled my accounts with the Juiz de Fora both here and in San Romao, and had received the most friendly and substantial assistance in procuring the necessary bullock carts, I began to take leave of my friends. First of all, amid heartrending wailing, lamentations and tears, we had to wish good-bye to the women of our household and to all superfluous servants ; on the other hand, standing on the balcony, we asked Master Joaquim Jose de Moria,* who lived opposite, and in whom we had learned to recognise a useful and crafty customer, whether he would like to come with us as a convoy conductor. He sprang into the air with joy at this suggestion, and throwing his leather apron and his lasts out at the door, declared that he would be ready in five minutes to follow us to the end of the world. First of all, however, he was prevailed upon to accompany my Senhora Maria, laden with presents, and riding on a mule, back to her mother at Mangoalde. Then the office was closed, and all the luggage sent ahead, and we bade farewell to all the families whom we had frequented during our stay. The whole of Cea was in mourning over our departure. They were good people. We also took leave of Don Louis Bernardo and his family ; he seemed very sad about the future, and was filled with qualms.

At last we were free and galloped through San Martinhao, where we greeted our three beauties once more, and then on to Gouvea, which lies picturesquely on the rocks at the foot of the Estrella mountains. Here, for the first time, I saw a Portuguese brigade of so-called

* This is doubtless the shoemaker mentioned above as one of the dancers of the *Fandango.*—TR.

mountain artillery pass by ; the mules they used were enormously strong.   This artillery was intended to taunt the enemy from impassable mountain heights, and then to fire upon them.   From Gouvea, where Don Louis' brother was bishop, and owned a conventual estate, we went on to Mello, an almost deserted place, where we halted for a while.   Quite close to Mello there was a brook of crystal-clear water, picturesquely overhung with rocks, which sorely tempted us to bathe.   We climbed down to its banks, undressed and plunged in.   Suddenly, however, on the other side of the rocks there appeared a number of local village beauties, who, having come to fetch water and discovering us here *in puris naturalibus*, shrieked and shouted with laughter.   Far from feeling ashamed or running away, they calmly sat down and began to make fun of poor Fereira because of his brown skin, and compared it with my own—very much to my advantage.   Fereira, who, as a rule, knew how to look after himself, could not silence these nymphs, despite his coarse jokes, until he pretended to be a faun about to seize them.   Whereupon they all ran shrieking away as fast as does.

[TRANSLATOR'S NOTE.—Schaumann stayed some days at Gouvea, then, *viâ* Linhares, he reached Barracal on the 30th July.]

Most of the inhabitants had fled, as any moment the French were expected to surround Almeida and attack us. We therefore took up our quarters in the rather large church, in which we also deposited our stores.   Like all Portuguese and Spanish churches, it was alive with fleas, which were brought in by the women, who squatted oriental fashion on the floor.   We did not make our beds on the grave-stones, through the crevices of which there rose unpleasant odours, but in a more exalted fashion upon the high altar ; the two Fereiras taking the altars of side chapels, and Quartermaster Allen settling himself on a bench.   The butchers kept their scales, knives and choppers in the chancel.   A large door was taken from the vestry and used as a table on which to stand the altar candlesticks.   Under the altar we found a drawer containing a number of candles, some of which were enormously thick—as thick as a man's leg—and had been presented to the church by pious people in fulfilment of a vow, or as a sin offering. We burned these candles on our table at night, but, owing to their thickness, the wick did not melt the wax through, but sunk a hole in it, so that ultimately it stood all round the light like a lantern. Our kitchen was established in a shed outside the church.

The first evening many hungry officers joined our party and dined with us ; but they showed such scant reverence for the church and the consecrated candles that shone on our table that they all got drunk and made the most shameful uproar the whole of the night. As the church provided us only with uncomfortable and unwholesome quarters, and the houses all around were uninhabited and had been left in a filthy condition by the troops passing through, we preferred to camp out in huts in a fine field not far from the church, where we kept our store of straw.

Meanwhile, a certain gentleman called Senhor Magelhaes, who had fled from the district, turned up again just to see how things were going. He was a foolish person, clad in old-fashioned violet clothes, with pearl buttons as large as plates and a three-cornered hat ; and he carried a Spanish cane. In order to deceive the marauders he had succeeded in giving his house a brokendown and neglected appearance, and had barricaded it to make it look uninhabited ; and he pointed all this out to us with great triumph. With all his slyness, however, we had stolen a march upon him ; for not only had we climbed into his house and made an inspection of it, but my cook, who had dug up onions in his garden, had also found his crockery and taken it for our use. When, therefore, he showed his surprise at seeing such beautiful earthenware basins and jugs in front of our bivouac huts, and china dishes and plates in our field kitchen, and even joined us in eating meals off the latter, without guessing that they belonged to himself, his repeated expression of astonishment always made us laugh uproariously. We soon left the field, however, and took up our abode opposite the church in a peasant's house, the inmates of which had taken flight, but had now returned from their exile. They were good, honest folk, and were delighted to find such bright, pleasant and generous people billeted on them. They had a very pretty daughter, and I was rather fond of the young thing. When, however, on one occasion I saw her lousing her mother and licking her finger-nails after killing the vermin and then wiping her fingers on her bodice, she disgusted me. Even the Juiz de Fora had taken flight, and did not seem inclined to return, although he knew that friends had come to the place. To punish him we took the beds and furniture from his house to add to the comfort of our quarters, and we also took from his cellar, which he thought he had craftily walled up and concealed, a quantity of rye, potatoes, walnuts and a large jar of honey. A pretty young woman, who with an older female had been left in the house, helped us in our search.

What increased the hardship of the situation, particularly for me, was the fact that we had to sleep in our clothes. My packed valise was used as a pillow, my cloak as a blanket, while my hat, sword and pistols lay at my side. At dawn of day we marched out to the alarm post, the baggage was sent a legua to the rear, and we only went forward again when the patrols had returned. This business of marching out and marching onwards lasted until the 7th August, when, instead, we had to have our horses saddled at break of day and all the baggage packed, so as to be able to mount at the first sound of the trumpet. It all depended on the circumstances. If we were not attacked early in the morning, by midday we felt quite safe owing to the terrific heat. The whole of our system of defence and of retreat from here to Lisbon in case of need, was most accurately and prudently thought out, and every position was selected and every general, instructed. On the 4th August the Portuguese Government published another proclamation, calling upon the inhabitants of Almeida and the surrounding country to leave their houses and estates and to remove with all their

portable effects into the mountains. And now again
everybody began to take flight. Much wine, corn and
straw were offered to me for sale, and all cornfields were
cleared of their crops. The siege of Almeida had not yet
begun, because the rocky nature of the soil complicated
the task for the French. In this deserted spot, with the
enemy close at our heels, all the trouble about forage
started afresh.

I had enough riding to do at this time, and was constantly going either to Mr. Routh at Minhocal, or to
Celrico. In the latter place a signal station had been
erected on an old ruined Moorish castle, which was
directed by Colonel Elley, Quartermaster-General, by
means of which signals could be sent direct to Almeida.
I also visited my cousin, Gustav Schaumann, a lieutenant
in the 1st German Hussars, who were bivouacking under
chestnut trees in Maçal da Chão. I begged him, as well
as Lieut.-Colonel Arentschildt, to seize the first favourable
opportunity for proposing me as commissary to the
regiment. What a magnificent regiment it was ! In
all matters connected with bivouacking, the management
of horses, patrols and sentries—in short, in regard to
everything that a hussar ought to be when he is on duty
with an advanced post, the English might well have taken
a lesson from them. But in this matter the English were
so deficient* that it was nothing new for a French bearer
of a flag of truce, together with a trumpeter, to ride
between the English sentries without being noticed, and
actually to arrive in a village and inquire where the officer
in command of the guard was to be found. Among other
cavalry regiments, this actually happened to the English
heavy dragoons, known as the Royals.

On the 21st August it seemed as if the army were about
to move forward to relieve Almeida, but our expectations
were not realised. In spite of English discipline, the
inhabitants of a country cottage just outside Barrancal
were robbed and severely injured by two English soldiers

* This view, confirmed by Sir C. Oman, also receives support in Tomkinson's " Diary
of a Cavalry Officer, 1809–15." See p. 135 : " To attempt giving men or officers any
idea in England of outpost duty was considered absurd, and when they came abroad, they
had all this to learn."—Tr.

who had disguised themselves. The poor people came howling to Lord Charles Somerset, and, just as everybody began to bewail the fact that the culprits would be hard to find, a certain young subaltern, named Gregory, exclaimed : " If any one in the 14th Dragoons has been guilty of this crime, it can only be two particular Irishmen. They are the only men who I think would be capable of it." " Then let investigations start with them ! " cried Lord Charles Somerset. And forthwith they were discovered to have been the perpetrators of the outrage. The stolen property lay hidden beneath the straw in the stable, a pistol was found that had not been cleaned after use, and there was blood on the sword-hilt of one of them. The two men were despatched to Celrico.

On the 24th August we struck camp and marched to our right in the direction of Lagiosa, a pretty but deserted village. We deposited the stores in the church and kept our straw in the churchyard. I lived with the whole of my staff higgledy-piggledy in one house ; for the Portuguese infantry were also in the place. In the fields there were a large number of melons, of which I partook too greedily and made myself ill. Our house belonged to the Capitao Mor of the place, who had taken flight, and we ransacked his cellar, in which we found some good strong brandy. In the familiar drawer which is to be found under every altar, and which, therefore, we naturally found in the church of this village, we discovered a number of wax candles with which we illuminated our abode. Quartermaster Allan also found hidden under the altar a case bound like a book in red velvet, and in it a rich piece of golden embroidery representing the crucifixion. This was declared to be treasure trove, and was taken with us ; while some fine ecclesiastical vestments found by my muleteers were kept by them to be used as State coverings for their mules. We knew that if we did not take them they would be seized by the French. At all events, everything seemed to have been concealed by the inhabitants in a very puerile fashion ; a child would have been able to find the lot ; how, then, could the French, who were known to have acquired considerable virtuosity in this matter in Spain, have overlooked them ?

While here I visited our German artillery and my friend Dr. Heise, who was with them.   On the 26th August my assistant Fereira asked for leave to go to Santarem, to acquaint his mother of the French advance, and to take measures to save his belongings.   I also gave him my accounts to take to Lisbon.   On the 27th we heard some exceptionally heavy gun-fire in the direction of Almeida ; the weather had grown stormy, and there was some rain.   This continued on the 28th, when, towards morning, after a burst of gun-fire there followed a terrific explosion.   All of us sprang up from our mattresses and wondered what on earth it could be. Suddenly, at 10 a.m., we were ordered to march to Assores.   On the following day we heard that the powder magazine in Almeida had been blown up, and that the fortress had capitulated.   It appeared that the explosion had been brought about through the treachery of the Portuguese Governor and Tenente del Rey, Don da Costa, and Barreiros, the officer commanding the Portuguese artillery, who, according to the report of the brave English Commandant, Colonel Cox, had not behaved at all well during the siege.*   It was said, moreover, that they acquainted the French with the fact that, owing to the explosion, ammunition was short in Almeida.†   Nevertheless, Colonel Cox was able to obtain fairly good capitulation terms, which, however, Masséna broke by taking prisoner 600 men of the Portuguese infantry, instead of letting them go.   But most of them escaped and came over to us.

The destruction in Almeida seems to have been terrible.   The casemates that had contained the powder, as also the neighbouring houses and churches, had completely vanished.   A number of guns were put out of action, and a large number of soldiers and inhabitants were killed.   As, owing to the fall of Ciudad Rodrigo and

---

* Though it is true that da Costa and Barreiros were not loyal, the explosion appears to have been an accident.   See Oman, *op. cit.*, Vol. III., pp. 272–276.—Tr.

† Barreiros it was who divulged the hopeless state of Almeida to Masséna.—Tr.

Almeida, the French no longer had any obstacle in their way, they now prepared for an attack on Portugal. They formed their columns, and we formed ours. All peace was now at an end, and we had to be ready to move any minute. On the 29th August we reached Maçal da Chão, where we stayed only two days. On the 1st September we returned to Assores ; and here we had an unpleasant encounter with Captain Holmes, who wanted to have my quarters, and whom I therefore charged before Lord Charles Somerset. I ought to mention that a most unsatisfactory rule prevails in the English army, by which an officer of higher rank, or a senior according to his commission, can turn a junior officer out of his quarters, with the result that the latter may often have the misfortune to be obliged to change his lodging six times in a day. Now it was difficult to apply this rule in my department, and with my business, for I could not close my office at a moment's notice and go elsewhere, as a subaltern with his valise could. But, in any case, it was a piece of insolence to expect a civil department to go out into the streets, while the dragoons, like fine gentlemen, took possession of the best houses. Many complaints had already been lodged at headquarters about this, but Lord Wellington, that inflated god almighty, had never thought it worth his while to make the smallest regulations about the matter, and our Commissary-General, Sir Robert Hugh Kennedy, was, in this respect too, such a pitiably stoical or feeble man, that I have often seen him, together with his whole staff of twenty-four clerks, install himself and his office in a broken-down hovel without any windows, writing by artificial light in the day-time, while Lord Wellington's youngest volunteer aides-de-camp, including the provost marshal, or executioner, occupied the best houses. And all this to please head-quarters !

It was here in Assores that the two dragoons above mentioned met their tragic end.* They were sent back by headquarters to their regiment, accompanied by Wallenstein's words, " Let the beasts hang ! " and in the

* See p. 236, *ante*.

afternoon were taken in a bullock cart to a group of olive trees. The regiment formed a circle, the cart was driven under one of the trees, the men were made to stand on a wine cask lying in the cart, and after the ropes had been placed round their necks the peasant was given the sign to drive the cart away. But the unfortunate man, paralysed with fright, did not dare to do so, but stood with his mouth open and his hair on end, staring upon the whole scene. At last, the adjutant, Mr. Chantry, tired of mute signalling, roared "*Arrivo!*" whereupon the peasant, as if in despair, prodded the bullock in the belly with his goad, and not daring to look back at the wine cask or at the two poor dangling sinners, dashed off at top speed, while every one roared with laughter.

On the 7th September we again marched to Lagiosa, where we remained in comparative peace with the regiment in bivouac until the 14th. Early on the morning of the 15th I had ridden into Celrico on business, and was just on the point of asking Colonel Elley, our Quartermaster-General, a question, when a dragoon, with his horse covered in foam, halted before the house and delivered a letter. Colonel Elley had hardly opened it before he cried, " Schaumann, get back to your regiment at once ! The French are advancing." I did not waste any time, but, mounting my horse like lightning, galloped back. Before reaching Lagiosa I already heard the fire of the skirmishers, and when I was dashing into the place, and turning round a corner behind which my quarters were situated, whom should I see but my head driver, the shoemaker Joaquim, also galloping along, but on a mule and bearing a large pan full of cold rice pudding which he wanted to save. Unintentionally he dashed at full tilt right into me, and with such force that the pan of rice flew into the air. " Jesus Maria ! " cried the shoemaker. " *Filho da puta !* "* I replied, " where is all our baggage, where are the stores, where are the mules ? Turn round. Don't run away like that. *Vmoe naõ tem vergonha ?* " † Follow me ! " And the poor shoemaker had willy-nilly

* " Whoreson knave ! "
† " Are you not ashamed of yourself ? "

to turn back. I found all my servants and assistants running about like mad. Only half of the things had been packed. At last, by sheer dint of cursing, exhorting and kicking, I established order, and, giving a hand myself, succeeded in getting my baggage off. Nothing was forgotten except a few magnificent apples and some cigars and other trifles in a table drawer.

I ran from my quarters to the stores in the church, where Mr. Allan, the quartermaster, had in my absence had the kindness to see to the loading of the mules as quickly as possible. Then, with a stone we broke open the wine casks and let the wine flow out, set light to our small stock of straw in the churchyard, and just as we were ready and mounted, and our own and the French skirmishers had already reached the churchyard on one side of the village, and the balls from their muskets were whistling and rattling about the walls and roofs, we galloped away. Amid the constant chattering of the skirmishers' muskets, now close at hand and anon far off, interrupted by the deeper notes of the horse artillery guns, which here and there had been unlimbered to fire, we at last reached Celrico at sundown. Here everybody was making ready to move on, and the traces of war began to be noticeable. Innumerable carts, bearing our sick and a few of our wounded, and the belongings of the inhabitants who were fleeing, moved slowly forward with us, accompanied by streams of women and children running alongside of them. The Estrella mountains loomed majestically in front of us, and the villages acquired a more genial aspect. On the 16th, after I had obtained 3,000 lbs. of barley in Celrico, we again went forward across the bridge over the Mondego and bivouacked behind a pine wood. I had the good fortune to find a deserted farmhouse in a vineyard, where I established myself with my movable stores depôt and my bullocks, and where I had one or two bullocks slaughtered in the dark. We slept on the bare floor, wrapped only in our cloaks.

Our army might well have made a stand near Celrico, for the place stands on a height and provides a favourable position.   But to do so would have served no purpose, as owing to the number and superior strength of their columns the enemy could have outflanked us on all sides. The first village we reached beyond Celrico was Cortizao, a mile from Villa Cortez, whence we could see Coral, while Linhares, buried deep in the ravine, lay concealed to the left.   At dawn on the 17th September we marched back again for two leguas, accompanied by the same music as on the previous day, to Villa Cortez.   We were so hard pressed by the French that Lord Wellington considered it necessary suddenly to confront the enemy ; and attacking them, we repulsed them with such slaughter that, after that, they behaved more discreetly.   We heard here that the French army was advancing into Portugal in three huge columns at three different points, and that it had already outflanked us at Viseu.   I spent the night in a bivouac, and suffered terribly from the cold.

At dawn on the 18th September we marched on to S. Pago, a pretty, romantic spot, with a finely built church on the river Mello, across which a bridge leads to Gouvea. A few years ago an Englishman established a cotton factory here, but after the surrounding country had profited from his industry, and people had learnt the tricks of his trade, he was murdered as the result of jealousy and Christian gratitude.   There is a formidable-looking monastery just outside the town.   It has been plundered by the French, and is now used as a hospital by the English army.

Early on the 20th September I was awakened by the clatter of horses' hoofs, and the rattle of baggage wagons and artillery being drawn along the rough and hilly streets of San Romão.   A heavy mist had fallen, and the sentries on the summits of the hills looked like phantoms. The regiment had bivouacked beneath chestnut trees. Up to that time our regiment had always marched close up to the Estrella mountains, but now we left them and cut straight across the Mondego valley.   On the way we fetched along our beautiful, large and fat friend Dame Angela of Cea, who, meanwhile, had been freed of her ugly, miserly old husband, and was now a widow.   She

walked arm in arm with the local priest, who had long
been her lover, and who had now thrown off his priestly
garb, partly in order to avoid offence, partly to save himself
from a violent end in case he should fall into the hands of
the French, who were the ruthless enemies of all priests.
He was, therefore, attired in a fashionable frock-coat and
a round hat, and walked very lovingly at her side, whis-
pering sweet nothings into her ear. This charming
couple walked along in such a smug, cheerful and leisurely
manner that they might have been out merely to take the
air. In front of them two bullock carts bore their children
and the more valuable of their belongings. They wanted
to find a little place of safety far away from the din of war.
I advised them not to stroll along so slowly and not to bill
and coo so much, as the French were not far behind. At
last we reached Gallizes, where we found shelter in
S. Ginhelda and the neighbouring villages. It was sad
to behold the fugitives arriving from all directions. They
marched wailing along in families, carrying bundles and
packages ; the children, the sick and the aged packed on
donkeys and in bullock carts. They had no time to lose,
for if they had been caught by the French, death and
plunder would have been their lot.

Before dawn on the 23rd September we were already on
the march and were about to cross a river when we were
obliged to turn back, as the French columns advancing
from Viseu were trying to cut us off from Coimbra, and
were already too close. We therefore forded the
Mondego near Ruivals, where it is possible to cross the
river on horseback. At last, in the afternoon, we halted
and bivouacked beneath thick pine bushes on a broad
green heath, picturesquely surrounded by villages, pine
woods, and mountains. We deposited our stores in a
stable inside a farmyard, and made excellent beds for
ourselves with the beautiful clean straw. I immediately
requisitioned all the loose straw and corn I could find for
the cavalry, and allowed it to be plundered. Our whole
army lay in and about this district, concealed in bivouacs
behind large pine woods.

The hills and shrubbery in front were thickly occupied

by light troops, and batteries of horse artillery were distributed among the advanced guard. Headquarters were in Morteagua*, where in the morning a portion of the 1st German Hussars had had a fierce advanced guard action with the French close by the church. The French had suffered severe losses and had had to give way. Towards evening my friend Senhor Fereira, to my great joy, returned unexpectedly from Lisbon, laden with coffee, sugar, brandy, wine and confectionery ; and behind the pine trees, where we had established our kitchen, we had a jolly meal.

When all the interesting activities peculiar to a huge bivouac were over—the fetching of water, the watering of horses, the building of bivouac huts, the transport of baggage, the drivers of which are looking for their particular regiments or masters, the procession of mules with their muleteers singing the long notes of their hymn to the Virgin Mary through their noses, the squeaking of ungreased bullock carts, the shooting and slaughtering of bullocks, the weighing and distributing of victuals, the return of detachments of cavalry with their commissary at their head bringing in bundles of forage on their horses' backs, the lighting of fires, the cooking operations, the running hither and thither of aides-de-camp and officers of the general staff with their orderlies—when, as I say, all these activities were over, and I had done my writing and had sat myself down, I smoked a cigar by the side of a fire with a few chosen friends, and then crept into my straw bed. On the 24th we were still there.

On September 25th at daybreak all cavalry commissaries were ordered to the front to forage ; so I, too, went out with my brigade of mules, a few empty carts, and ten dragoons in the van, and took to the hills on my left with Lieutenant Philips to assist me. After proceeding along the most appalling roads, at last, at ten in the morning, we reached a few villages in which no soldier appeared to have set foot till then, for we found heaps of corn, chickens, eggs and onions. We eagerly seized the whole lot, and were on the point of loading it on our carts, when we

* This appears to be Mortagoa.—Tr.

heard the sound of gun fire. Listening attentively, we found that the noise came from the direction of the heath and that it grew louder every minute. In a moment we abandoned all that we had not yet loaded, and hurried back to the army. A good genius had directed our movements, for we found the French advanced guard engaged with our rear guard, and the whole army under arms and already on the move. All baggage had already gone on. Our troops were standing formed up in large masses, while the French, whose muskets shone in the evening sunlight like distant lightning, were coming on in dark columns slowly down the hills and getting into formation. We could actually see one of their generals on a white horse, for he was particularly conspicuous as he rode up and down the dark lines. It was a grand, but at the same time gruesome, sight. Probably the French had been held up in the hills by some obstacle, and were now trying to make up for lost time. Lord Wellington, whose inflexible will the French did not yet know, endeavoured to show them that he was only prepared to retire when he thought it was policy to do so, but that he was not in the least inclined to let himself be hunted down. Hence the artillery were distributed among our rearguard, which in the matter of material, horses and *personnel*, were far superior to the French, and gave the latter short commons whenever they attempted to annoy us.

The 14th and 16th English Light Dragoons and the 1st German Hussars had until now borne the whole onus of covering our retreat, and had therefore performed a very tiring, trying and difficult duty. Moreover, the French light troops of the advanced guard had endeavoured by skirmishing the whole afternoon to drive us back ; but in vain. I strongly suspect that our army, spread out in masses between the pine woods, and resting with its flank upon the Mondego, had from the hills presented a formidable spectacle, and had deterred the French from attacking us in this position. Well, we held them until nightfall, whereupon we quietly withdrew brigade by brigade. As I was leaving the bivouac I noticed on the spot which had been occupied by the 95th

Regiment, a man who was so drunk that he could neither walk, stand, speak nor allow himself to be transported. As a punishment his uniform and arms were taken from him, and he was left behind. We were soon marching through a defile, and in a moment it was pitch dark. We marched the whole night—oh, what an interminable, horrible, harassing night ! The whole army was in one column, all of us close on each other's heels, and every ten minutes there was a halt, or rather a stoppage, the cause of which remained unknown. Drunk with sleep, we then dropped on to the ground, but hardly had we closed our eyes when we were kicked in the ribs and told to get up. Once more we mounted, only to dismount ten minutes later and drop on to the roadside. Sometimes I actually slept in the saddle like a hare with open eyes, and dreamed that I was walking through the crowded streets of a large town with huge and brilliant palaces on either side of me ; or else I fancied that I was walking between two roaring torrents over bridges and in the direction of smiling gardens.

It is a curious fact, but nevertheless true, that many officers to whom I recounted my experiences assured me that they, too, had had similar visions when, drunk with sleep, they had been on the march by night either mounted or dismounted. In order to keep in good spirits I used to amuse myself by thinking of the joy of lying in peace far away from the tumult of war on downy pillows in a great four-poster. I would also take the solemn vow that when once peace had been declared I would recover the time lost and have my sleep out.

Towards morning on the 26th September a bitterly cold wind sprang up and made marching very unpleasant. We were proceeding through wooded country and a deep gorge across a lofty mountain. Here we caught up the Portuguese infantry. They were all looking thoroughly tired and drunk with sleep, and had pale, drawn faces. The mountains we were crossing were the Serra de Busaco, at the foot of which, on the other side, were some green fields, where we bivouacked at nine in the morning When I had discharged the duties of my office, I thought

I would refresh myself by shaving, washing, changing my clothes, and then having a meal and going to sleep. The latter, however, proved to be impossible, probably owing to the fact that the night march and the frequent potations of rum had overheated my blood. In the afternoon, therefore, I rode to the top of the Serra to see what was happening. Close by the wayside the 1st German Hussar Regiment was bivouacking among the bushes and trees, and in clefts in the rocks. Having reached the ridge of the mountains where the English infantry was bivouacked, I was but little prepared for the scene which met my astonished vision. For, as far as the eye could see, I could discern three dark columns of a colossal army (75,000 strong)* advancing under cover of clouds of dust, and gleaming with the glint of arms. Below, at the foot of the Serra and beyond a ravine, enemy pickets were already stationed. At last the huge mass seemed to break up into small regular clumps as the army went into bivouac. At some distance beyond these foremost groups, and behind the left wing of the enemy, one could discern the huge bivouacs of their cavalry, and still further away, almost too far for the eye to see, a black mass, consisting of wagons, carts, mules, ambulances and the commissariat, could be divined. And so this was the famous French army, the terror of the world, the con-queror of Italy, Spain, Egypt and Germany! It had been victorious at Jena, Austerlitz, Marengo, Ulm, and Vienna, and on the morrow we were probably going to try conclu-sions with it. Even including the Portuguese, our army was not half so strong, nor could we always reckon upon holding a position like our present one. Our courage, moreover, was not at its best, for an army in retreat is conscious of its weakness and loses confidence in itself and in its leaders. Indeed, several English officers were so firmly convinced that we should have to take to our ships that they had already informed their families in England that this was our certain and ineluctable fate. And by this means the news had actually got into English

---

* Cf. Oman (op. cit., Vol. III., p. 593), who gives 62,538 men as the exact fighting force of the French at Busaco.—Tr.

newspapers before the retreat had started.   Other officers had written to their friends in Lisbon begging them to collect provisions for them to consume on board.   The French, too, regarded our defeat as so certain that they were following in our rear rejoicing over their superior strength, and assuring everybody that they would drive us into the place where we belonged—the sea.   Turning these things over in my mind—and they were not very comforting, for I remembered Corunna—I returned to the camp somewhat downcast, and joining a few officers by a fire, drank two or three glasses of grog and then retired a little top-heavy to bed.

AT six o'clock on the morning of September 27th I was awakened by the roar of gunfire mingled with the chatter of musketry. The trumpets were blown and the cavalry marched out and formed. We waited thus in great suspense the whole morning, and only portions of regiments at a time were allowed to fall out in order to feed and water their horses. The enemy's principal attack seemed to be directed on two points, our right and left wings ; but though they were particularly fierce they were not repeated. For some while afterwards only a few stray shots could be heard, and very occasionally the sound of a gun. At nine o'clock we marched back, and after I had breakfasted and discharged my official duties, I rode as quickly as I could with Senhor Fereira to the top of the Serra to see how things stood. On reaching the ridge I found an infantry battalion quietly drawing their rations of meat, and Lieutenant Riefkugel, of the artillery, posted on the edge of a rock with two guns, which he had surrounded with a breast-work of stones. He described the state of affairs to me as follows : Masséna, who had not noticed the arrival of General Hill's and General Leith's divisions, and thought that our position was occupied only by a weak force, had attacked us early that morning with two strong columns under Generals Simon and Graindorge, covered by a swarm of skirmishers. The attack on our right wing, which was commanded by General Picton, was made by two divisions, one of which succeeded in reaching the summit of the rock, though it was immediately driven back again at the point of the bayonet by the 88th and 45th English, and the 8th Portuguese Regiments. The other division only got half-way up the height, and was also repulsed at the point of the bayonet by the 74th English and two Portuguese regiments.

The attack on our left wing was executed by three divisions, of which only one climbed the hill.   All three, however, were thrown back with great slaughter by the 48th, 52nd and 93rd English and the 3rd Portuguese Regiments.   The Portuguese fought with conspicuous courage, and did great credit to Marshal Beresford, who had trained them.   They also proved a tribute to the masterly soundness of Lord Wellington's military policy, for he had attached a couple of Portuguese regiments to every English division, and brought them into a position where, for the first time, they could prove their mettle and stand the test of battle.   He had thus inspired them with confidence in themselves, which always leads to deeds of daring.   They behaved just like English troops, and, indeed, fought with such valour that the French believed them to be Englishmen disguised in Portuguese uniforms. As usual, of course, Lord Wellington displayed extra-ordinary circumspection, calm, coolness and presence of mind.   His orders were communicated in a loud voice, and were short and precise.   In him there is nothing of the bombastic pomp of the Commander-in-Chief sur-rounded by his glittering staff.   He wears no befeathered hat, no gold lace, no stars, no orders—simply a plain low hat, a white collar, a grey overcoat, and a light sword.

After the first attack had been repulsed, Wellington galloped past with a numerous staff, and shouted only the following orders to General Hill.   " If they attempt this point again, Hill, you will give them a volley, and charge bayonets ; but don't let your people follow them too far down the hill." *   I now looked about me.   Below there was a deep ravine, and that side of it which lay behind us was studded with the brown Portuguese *Caçadores* (sharpshooters), the other, on the opposite side, with enemy skirmishers, who, concealed behind rocks and withered bushes, were shooting at each other.   In this, the Portuguese displayed extraordinary bravery and skill

* According to Sidney's " Life of Lord Hill " (p. 143), these are the very words used by Lord Wellington on this occasion.—Tr.

—nay, they were even comical ; for when they got a successful shot, they laughed uproariously, as if skirmishing were a source of great amusement to them. Below, to our right, there was a village teeming with the French, and a little beyond, the height where the attack had taken place. The ravine close to the said village, where the columns had formed for the attack behind the houses and had been met by the deadly fire of our artillery as they debouched, was full of dead bodies. Opposite our position, and far away in the distance, isolated groups of pine trees could be seen, in and out of which the French were busily running ; on a slight eminence the great marquee representing enemy headquarters was also visible, and finally, columns of infantry could be discerned marching away to the left in their grey cloaks. With the help of my telescope I was almost able to distinguish each man. In the ravine there was a small stream, at which, with the most profound harmony, and as if nothing had happened, both French and English soldiers fetched water, and, as a sign of very special mutual esteem, exchanged their forage caps.

While I was standing there entertaining myself, an enemy sharpshooter must have taken aim at us, for a bullet whistled between Riefkugel, Fereira and myself. We therefore withdrew to a respectful distance, looked at the prisoners that were being transported behind the line, and also at the chapel in which General Simon, who was a prisoner, had been quartered for a while; and then we went to the monastery. The road thither led across the rocks and was so uneven that the jolting caused the French wounded, who were being carried up in bullock carts, great suffering. The fact that there were many Germans fighting in the ranks of the enemy could be inferred from the plaints of the wounded. For instance, I remember one who, his face contorted with pain, exclaimed : " *O Gott ! O du verfluchter Pisang von einem Bauer, fahr' sachte ! *"* The monastery, with its beautiful garden, had a rich and imposing appearance. As, however, Lord Wellington's headquarters were here, we did not dare to

* " Oh God ! Oh, you confounded savage of a peasant, drive more gently."

enter to inspect the inside of the building.   One of the chapels was full of wounded.   Thus ended Masséna's foolhardy attempt to break through an English army in a strong position.

My friend, Lieutenant Ernst Poten, arrived at midday with a mixed detachment of the 14th and 16th English Dragoons and the 1st German Hussars.   His pelisse and fur cap were all in tatters from sword cuts, while both he and his men and their horses appeared to have suffered a very fierce attack.   When I asked him what had happened he told me the following tale.   I shall repeat his exact words.

" On the 21st September, 1810, our corps had retired behind the River Mondego, and on the 22nd we marched to Morteagua* along the high road from Coimbra to Viseu, where, after a long while we again encountered some infantry and artillery.   Up to that time the 14th and 16th English Light Dragoons and the 1st German Hussars had alone been responsible for covering the retreat, and we were therefore very much exhausted.   On the 23rd a portion of our regiment had had a very serious outpost encounter near the church of Morteagua, in which the French suffered heavy losses.   On the 24th, with my mixed detachment, consisting of men from three regiments, I went to Ferrigo to cover our right flank, and my orders were to retire only if the enemy's strength proved too much for me.   The French columns marched the whole of the night and following morning on my left flank, on their way to Busaco, without attempting to interfere with me.   At last, at two o'clock in the afternoon of the 25th, a column of French cavalry wheeled in my direction, and, as on my right flank, which I had been ordered to observe with special care, I had many patrols, I was obliged to make a stand at this point until they returned.   I succeeded in this, but the moment I gave up the defence of the ravine in front of me·the whole mass of the enemy charged down behind us, and attacked us furiously.   A hill that lay in our rear, and which we had to climb, utterly exhausted our horses, and a column of

* This appears to be Mortagoa.—Tr.

French infantry which had been posted on the other side of the ravine, poured down a murderous fire upon us. Well, it seemed all up with us. Many of my dragoons who were badly mounted—for at that time the English cavalry was notorious for its inferior horses, the majority of which were not even shod—sprang from their horses, in order to save themselves on foot. Meanwhile, with a few of my men, and in order to allow my exhausted men and horses time to retire in safety, I charged about a dozen times into the French, who were pressing forward in ever greater numbers. In one of these charges I had the good fortune to cut down the leader, a captain of chasseurs ; while in another of the *mêlées*, when my reins were severed and I was surrounded by six Frenchmen, I only succeeded in saving myself by a mighty spring of my horse across the bed of the ravine which lay alongside of me ; and thus I was able to reach my men again. It was in these charges that they cut my pelisse and fur cap to rags, though, fortunately, they did not injure my bones. And then I continued my retreat for two and a half leguas, the whole of the time over open country, and constantly charging at the enemy's front, until, having come close up to the position at Busaco, I came under the protection of an English infantry post. I had lost six men and five horses, in dead and wounded, out of my detachment, which numbered twenty-four men. General Picton thanked me for having held the enemy up so long on this road. He ordered me to repair to the rear of his division in order to rest my weary men and horses ; and there I was afforded the pleasure of witnessing at close quarters an infantry battle at night."

Here ended my friend Poten's narrative.

In the afternoon we received orders to march, and proceeded towards the road along which the French were expected to come ; then we encamped partly in the isolated houses, and partly in the fields and olive groves in and around Pedreira or Povo de Pereira. Of the enemy, who had to take a long circuitous route in order to outflank us, we saw and heard nothing. Early in the morning on September 28th we marched in the same direction to Mealhada. English troops, army baggage, and wailing inhabitants, with their cattle and belongings, were already retreating in confusion through this place. Here, too, one of my most ardent wishes was gratified, and I was told to leave the 4th Dragoons and to take up my duties as commissary to the 1st German Hussars. As I had no time to lose in seeking out my new regiment, which was suffering from every kind of privation, I soon made ready to trot off slyly with my stores and mules, when Lord Charles Somerset, to whom the matter had been reported, rode up in a towering rage, placed a guard over the carts, and compelled me to go off without anything. Going in search of the 1st German Hussars, therefore, accompanied by my aide-de-camp, Senhor Fereira, I found them bivouacking on some uneven ground in front of Mealhada, close to a village near the road to Oporto, where the enemy was expected. They were all ready for marching. I reported myself to the commanding officer, Lieutenant-Colonel von Arentschildt, and was kindly and warmly welcomed by him and the other officers.

That same evening the regiment marched still further back, and I with them ; on the way we passed a pine wood which had been set alight by the bivouac fires of the army, and the crackling, sparking and crashing of the falling trees, combined with the bright red glow of the setting sun, presented a dramatic spectacle. On September 29th we continued our march, and heard the fire of the skirmishers. Later we learned that the enemy had appeared in front of our advanced guard early that morning, and had fiercely attacked and sorely pressed the 1st Hussars, together with the 16th Dragoons, but that our men had, in order to hold them up as long as possible, stood their ground with stubbornness and courage. One of the hussars, who had been shot through the body, was brought back on a cart by a comrade who had lost his horse in the engagement. An English infantry doctor, who happened to be passing, probed the wound, laid an adhesive plaster on it, and spoke a few words of comfort to the wounded man and then allowed him to go on ;

but he told me afterwards that there was no hope for the poor fellow, as his bowel had been pierced. At nine o'clock on September 30th we heard the skirmishers firing, and mounting our horses we marched towards Fornos, and other small villages not far away, where the large fields begin which are sown with maize, alongside the banks of the Mondego. The French followed in our wake, but halted. The whole of our cavalry was mustered here, with the hussars and the 16th Dragoons in front. Colonel Elley, our Quartermaster-General, stood bent over a large telescope the whole afternoon. He had laid it across the branch of a tree that stood on a hill, and with it he observed the roads along which the French were supposed to come.

A new reign of terror now began for Portugal. Her defenders, driven back by superior forces, had to leave the Mondego, whose fertile banks would be at the mercy of the enemy. But the French had not been expected so soon in these parts ; truth to tell, they were thought to be marching only against Oporto. Some of the officers assured me, however, that in two small villages, that included a convent, which lay to their left and rear in the direction of the road to Oporto, in which they were cantoned during the attack on Busaco, a large annual fair had lately been held in perfect peace. The maize harvest had not yet begun. All the fields and many of the barns were full up, and as there was a shortage of carts and mules the poor inhabitants were forced to leave behind everything they could not move, and were only able to save their children, cattle, and a few portable treasures. Their flight was carried out partly in pursuance of orders, and partly from instinct ; for they knew the French and their lust for murder and plunder, and were only too familiar with the ill-treatment that awaited them. As a serious and formidable attack was expected on the morrow, all commissaries were ordered to transfer their stores to a place of security beyond the Mondego, and I accordingly started off again in the direction of Coimbra. The sun was just sinking when I tried to make my way through the streets of this town, crammed as they were with infantry passing through—particularly General Craufurd's division—artillery, the tail of the Portuguese army's baggage convoy, marauders, and the refugees from perhaps fifteen of the neighbouring villages. Old people, lame and sick people, women just risen from childbed, children, and whole families with all their belongings, packed either on bullock carts, mules, horses or donkeys, were to be seen mixed up with all kinds of beasts, among which pigs, owing to their unruliness and horrible cries, were most conspicuous. And this throng, marching to the wailing and lamentation of the fugitives both from town and country, presented a scene which I shall never forget. Now and again the cry would arise that the French were at the gates, and then the young girls would implore all those who were riding to help them up on the saddle with them. At one moment an old grandmother, riding a donkey, supported by two old women, could be seen passing through the throng, and a little later she was knocked down by a mule bearing a load of camp kettles, and, amid piteous cries, trampled under foot. Ladies who, according to the custom of the country, had perhaps never left their homes except to go to Mass, could be seen walking along, hand in hand, three in a row, wearing silk shoes and their heads and shoulders covered only with thin scarves. Monks and nuns who had left their monasteries and convents, were walking out of the town in procession, not knowing whither they were going.

I had great difficulty in making my way through with my brigade. Fereira led them on, a few hussars rode on either side of them, while I brought up the rear. At last we reached the bridge, and the crowd became denser than ever. A pretty girl, who had lost her family in the throng, and was standing in the middle of the stream of people on the bridge, called to me for help. I worked my way towards her, pulled her on to my horse, and rode away with my fair spoil. It had grown quite dark when we reached the houses on the other side of the river. In the midst of the tumult, the refugees, as well as the marauders and the soldiers who were escorting the baggage of the Portuguese army, took advantage of the confusion in order to plunder the goods that were packed on the backs of the mules, under whose bellies they crept in the dark in order to slit open the sacks they bore. Every moment I heard the curses of my muleteers and their cries for help, and ever and anon I heard the rattling of the dry ship's biscuits as they poured out on to the ground ; but I could do nothing, for I was so much hemmed in by the crowd that I could only move forward a step at a time, and nobody cared a halfpenny for my threats, curses or anger.

At last we reached the open country and bivouacked on fields of stubble not far from Casas Brancas, to the right of the road that leads to Condeixa. When we unloaded I found that I had been robbed of 300 lbs. of ship's biscuit. Then a fire was lighted, the tea kettles were placed upon it, and beef-steaks and bacon were fried ; and, while all this was going on, a hut was built for me (for the night wind was very cold) the walls, roof and furniture of which consisted entirely of sacks of ship's biscuit and of maize.

Feeling tired and jaded by the exertions of the day, I withdrew into this quaint palace, which reminded me of fairyland, in order to sup. A small piece of candle as thick as a man's leg, which had been stolen at Baraçal, served as our table illumination. The young lady who had placed herself in my charge, and who cried and laughed alternately, was highly pleased with all this, but she was even more delighted when I gave her a glass of sweet wine and the remainder of the Lisbon confectionery. She told me that her name was Eufemia das Neves, that she was the daughter of a doctor, and that her father had gone to Lisbon in order to try to find a lodging for them in case of invasion. She was just following him thither, accompanied by her mother, a maid and a man-servant, when she lost her people in the throng. I consoled her with the assurance that we would find her people on the morrow. After our meal, I prepared for her and myself a sort of couch, the mattress of which consisted of dusty biscuit and maize sacks and the cushions of horse blankets. Then I left the hut in order to give the girl time to undress and get to bed, and, returning later, discreetly lay down in a corner. As, however, Eufemia did not cease wailing about the cold, I regarded it as a duty and obligation to warm her in the suitable way. And this I proceeded to do with so much love and devotion that, although she resisted me at first, she soon became very happy, and I was very sorry indeed when my servant tore me away from my beautiful dreams by the cry : " It's time to get up, sir ! "

At five o'clock on the following morning, which was October 1st, while my brigade was busy loading we heard the firing of skirmishers and the roar of guns. It was the French who, forcing their way through Forres, were attacking our cavalry in superior strength, and the latter were slowly retiring across the maize fields towards the Mondego. I let my men continue their loading. While we were sitting eating our breakfast we were able, without the help of glasses, to obtain a distinct view of the whole of the battlefield in the plain, and, as our troops approached the Mondego, to hear the sound of the cannon balls whizzing across the river. It was just as if they were falling close at our feet. This was musical entertainment during our meals and spectacular accompaniment with a vengeance, but, although terrifying, it was grand. I then ordered my men to proceed with the cattle, the stores and the baggage towards Condeixa for the time being, and to await me on the high road just outside the town. Meanwhile I rode along the Mondego to watch the issue of the combat. In the suburbs of the town my former clerk, Mr. Hughes, called to me from the window of a house, and invited me up. He had spent the night more comfortably than I had in superbly furnished rooms, and he introduced to me a young and beautiful woman with fiery black eyes, who in the tumult had placed herself under his care. Little did I think at that moment that a few months later this young lady would capture my heart, and that I should elope with her. Her name was Maria da Rosa Barbosa.

Suddenly I perceived that our skirmishers were marching through Coimbra, that our cavalry were fighting their way across a ford in the Mondego, and that a French column was approaching the town. An indescribable medley and throng of troops of all kinds, with their baggage and strings of mules, bullocks, carts, refugees from Coimbra, and all the other places in the neighbourhood, were coming along the high road ; some were mounted, others were on foot. They had their baggage and their cattle, and the dust they made was suffocating. I looked for my people and stores in the vicinity of Condeixa, but they had been seized by panic and had gone farther on. In Condeixa the streets were so much congested that I was driven into a by-way, where I had to wait two hours before I could move. Here a supply of victuals, shirts, boots and horseshoes was distributed among the troops marching through, and what was left was burned. It was already dark when I halted one legua beyond the town.

On the 2nd October we again went forward to Pombal. The road was just as thickly congested as on the previous day. I do not know what terrifying rumour had spread among the mule brigades (even among those carrying ammunition), but all of them certainly fled—probably, however, only to take a short cut to the left over the hills. I heard that even my lot had gone the same way. I wanted to follow them, but the track was too steep, and I turned back. And thus I continued my journey without my baggage, and went along very sadly in the dust and the heat, feeling both hungry and thirsty. On reaching Pombal, however, to my great joy, I found my people again ; but my delight was greatly mitigated by the news that my beautiful Eufemia had found her family again and had gone off with them.

We found shelter in the house of the once famous minister named Pombal, which was now in ruins. Here he had lived in exile when banished from the court of his sovereign. The house had been abandoned by its present tenants, and in it we found a number of things lying about, of which many, as the saying goes, suited our taste. We refreshed ourselves, and then continued our journey for a few leguas more, until we reached a field, where we bivouacked. We made a tent out of a rug we had taken from the house in Pombal, and being dog-tired laid ourselves down to rest in it. In this southern part of the country the dust and the heat increase daily, but the nights are cool, and even cold. The bulk of the English army reached Pombal on the 2nd October, and camped out for miles beyond this place on the road to Lisbon. Innumerable kitchen fires flared up, fed by many a precious olive tree, and, illuminating the country for miles around, created a wonderful scene. On the morning of the 3rd October, we marched to Leiria. This once beautiful town looked terribly devastated. The Government's order that all inhabitants should take flight with the most valuable of their belongings had also reached this place, and, as in Coimbra, it had to be carried out with the greatest speed. False rumours had caused the inhabitants to be in too great a hurry, and many ne'er-do-wells, taking advantage of the confusion, had entered the houses before they were empty, and, under pretence of helping people to obey the order, had robbed and plundered under the very eyes of the owners themselves. In the midst of the tumult, however, Lord Wellington had arrived, and had immediately imposed the severest measures of justice ; and, indeed, the first objects we saw hanging from an olive tree before the gates of the town were the bodies of two soldiers, one English, the other Portuguese. The place was completely deserted by its inhabitants, and offered to the troops passing through the greatest temptation to plunder. But, as I have mentioned already, Lord Wellington had, on this very account, issued the most barbarous orders. For instance, a sergeant of the legion, a fine, handsome fellow of good family, was caught by the provost marshal just as he was fetching one of the carters under his command out of a shop, where the latter had gone to steal sugar ; and, in spite of his innocence and his protestations, he was flogged on the spot like a common soldier. The carter, however, together with an English soldier's wife who had stolen a little flour, were immediately hanged in front of the house. The Portuguese soldiers are believed to have done most of the plundering. Quantities of spilt coffee, sugar, chocolate, corn and flour, still lay about in the streets, together with rags, broken crockery, and paper. At the chemist's shop all the jars had been destroyed.

We quartered ourselves in a farm beyond the town, and here I met my cousin Plate, with his independent company, and had lunch with him. The town itself, except for a few sick people and a few also who had gone mad through shock and grief at having their homes plundered, was entirely deserted, and the houses stood open. I found a quantity of corn and had as much loaded upon my mules as I possibly could. From the 4th to the 5th October our cavalry had a rest day between Pombal and Leiria, but they also had a skirmish with the French advanced guard, which they repulsed, and kept the enemy in check until their own infantry arrived on the following morning ; whereupon the cavalry marched towards evening and bivouacked in a wood beyond Leiria. Hardly had we made ourselves comfortable, however, than the enemy advanced again, and we had to retreat one legua to the rear. The French now remained quiet and confined themselves to posting a few squadrons in front of our picquets. The high road between Cavaleco and Rio Mayor runs straight across the plain for six miles and is broad and good. But as no water is to be found along the second half of this road, the pangs of thirst suffered by both man and beast throughout the night will readily be understood. I would willingly have given a sovereign for a glass of water. I reached Rio Mayor early in the morning of the 6th October. The place was terribly crowded and it was difficult to find a lodging ; but I was fortunate in running across my cousin Plate here again, and, as he had good quarters, I breakfasted with him.

On the following morning, the 7th October, our cavalry had a sharp encounter with the enemy in the region of Batalha, in which Captain v. d. Decken, who was stationed near an isolated post-house with a picquet consisting of a squadron of the 1st German Hussars and another of the 16th Dragoons, was attacked by the enemy in superior numbers and driven back three leguas. The regiment bivouacked about three miles from Rio Mayor. Everybody in Rio Mayor, therefore, hastened to get up and flee. The retreat of the Anglo-Portuguese army from Coimbra to the fortified lines, over a stretch of thirty leguas, presented a sad spectacle. The roads were littered with smashed cases and boxes, broken wagons and carts, dead horses and exhausted men. Every division was accompanied by a body of refugees as great as itself, and rich and poor alike, either walking, or mounted on horses or donkeys, were to be seen, all higgledy-piggledy—men and women, young and old, mothers leading children or carrying them on their backs, nuns who had left their convents, and, quite strange to the world, either wandered about helplessly, beside themselves with fear, looking timidly for their relations, or else, grown bold, linked arms with the soldiers and carried the latters' knapsacks. Monks, priests and invalids—everybody was taking flight. The nearer the procession came to Lisbon, the greater was the number of animals belonging to the refugees that fell dead either from fatigue or hunger ; and very soon ladies were to be seen wading in torn silk shoes or barefoot through the mud. Despair was written on all faces. It was a heartrending sight. This wretched vanguard of the divisions was followed by a herd of bullocks destined for slaughter, among which those refugees who were unable to proceed were constantly becoming involved. Behind these came the mules laden with bread, corn and rum ; then followed the baggage, transported partly on mules and partly on donkeys, together with tired, sick or wounded soldiers, either in carts or on foot. Then came the guard with the provost marshal and the prisoners, the divisional artillery, and, finally, the divisions themselves, many of which numbered 10,000 men. The tail of the procession was made up by exhausted, weeping and wailing refugees. The cavalry remained several leguas behind in order to keep the enemy from advancing too quickly.

Now, just as I was riding out of the town I passed an old church on the left of the road which had been used as a so-called army store, and it occurred to my head driver—the shoemaker Joaquim, whom, owing to his peculiar gift for unearthing hidden forage, I had appointed my bloodhound or magician—that possibly in the hurry something had been left behind here, and he decided to inspect the place. I had waited barely two minutes when I heard his cries of joy. The storekeepers, seized by panic and probably also owing to lack of transport, had left heaps of things behind, including—and this is what electrified my shoemaker—several sacks full of new English boots. Now, as these goods were bound to fall into the hands of the French in a few hours, I allowed Joaquim to take them and to load them on our mules ; but what amused me most about the whole business was his exorbitant joy and gratitude. He kissed my hands and also the hem of my coat, called me the creator of his fortune, his father, his angel, and behaved generally like an idiot.

In a few hours we reached a convent, in the vineyard of which we spent the night, making ourselves at home between the large wine-vats in the vintage house. We made a wine soup with eggs beaten in it, and fried some steak and onions, after which we drank grog by the kitchen fire and smoked cigars. Feeling a little top-heavy, we made splendid beds with our blankets and valises inside the large cistern used for collecting the juice of the pressed grapes during the vintage, and quietly went to sleep as if the enemy were miles away. The regiment bivouacked this side of Rio Mayor. On the 8th October our cavalry was attacked by the French, and things might have gone pretty badly with them. It all happened so suddenly that a dinner service that was standing on a table for the general's luncheon, together with a turkey that the cook had just hung upon the spit, were discovered later on just as they had been left. The French, however, secured no booty, though a number of their horses certainly galloped riderless away, and they themselves received many a wound in the head. In the Thirty Years' War an attack of this sort was called "breaking up quarters." If our 1st Hussars had formed the picquet on this occasion the affair would never have taken place ; but the English were, and always remained, bad on outpost duty.

On the 9th October our cavalry retreated to Quinta do Torre. In the course of the day Captain Aly's squadron of our regiment inflicted a severe defeat on the French, in which the latter lost seventeen men in addition to wounded. This affair was our bloody revenge for the bad time which the French, in superior numbers, had given that morning to a squadron under Captain v. Linsingen. On the other hand, through the imprudence of General Slade, who led them against the whole of the French infantry, the English Heavy Dragoons, known as the Royals, lost ten men and four horses. These were the last engagements fought by our cavalry in front of the entrenched lines. It rained continuously the whole of the day, and I was wet to the skin. On the way I passed the Brunswickers who, dripping with the rain, were wading through the mud ; and I reached Villa Franca in the evening. Here, too, the whole life of the town had ceased, as the place lay outside the fortified lines. Most of the inhabitants had already gone, but had left a good many belongings behind to be shipped to Lisbon. It rained incessantly. The deserted houses were broken into without ceremony by the Brunswickers and Portuguese troops who spent the night here, and beautiful beds with silken hangings were used for sleeping accommodation.

The first familiar face I saw was that of my cousin Plate, with whom I took up my abode in a nice house that had been deserted by its owners. The regiment bivouacked in the mud and the rain on the right of the town. It poured the whole night, and I felt sorry for the poor Portuguese refugees, who with their wives, their children and their cattle, had set out in piteous plight to paddle along the muddy roads. It was on the morrow, however, that the confusion and lamentations of the people of Villa Franca reached their highest pitch ; for the wind being unfavourable, the ships that were to sail to Lisbon with the best of their belongings were held up.

The enemy was reported to be close to the gates of the
town.   While the confusion was at its worst, we left the
town and proceeded to Alverca.   Here we obtained the
first glimpse of the fortified lines which Lord Wellington
had built upon a chain of hills which seemed to have been
destined for this purpose by Nature herself.   Running
from Alverca to Peniche on the sea, they encircled Lisbon
completely, and had been studded with batteries, mines,
trenches and barricades.   As far as the eye could see there
was nothing but gun embrasures.   Earthworks on the
hill and barricades made with wine casks, boxes and even
trunks filled with earth and stones, formed the entrance
to Villa Franca ; every means of access was blocked.   A
few 24-pounders frowned darkly upon the road.   To
the left on the Tagus lay a respectable-looking fleet of
gun-boats manned by English sailors.   All garden walls
had been thrown down, and trenches ran to the very
edge of the river.   As up in the north with the army we
had not heard of these prudent measures of defence, our
surprise at what we now saw may well be imagined.   I
sang Lord Wellington's praises, and feeling that I was in
clover, took possession of a house lying on the high road,
which was already occupied by a number of Portuguese
officers and men ; and installing my people in it, I
deposited my stores in the cellar.

It was dark, and we had gone to bed, when a whole
division marched up, and proceeding to break open the
doors of all houses, took possession of mine also.   In vain
did I protest that royal stores were deposited in it.
Fortunately, however, the colonel of one of the regiments
appeared, and immediately inviting him to be my guest,
I told him to consider my quarters as his own.   Thereupon all the men had to turn out, and gradually the place
grew quiet again.   I treated the officers to wine, soup,
cold roast meat, grog and cigars ; then all the mattresses,
palliasses, chairs and sofas in the house were collected, and
having made beds of them, they retired to sleep in their
wet clothes.   Many lay on the bare floor.   But sleep was
out of the question, for the troops that passed down the
road all through the night in the pouring rain would

hammer at our barricaded door, demanding either admittance or water to drink, or else would ask whether we had any wine, brandy or bread. Every other minute we had to get up and look out of the window to shout to them that the master of the house was not at home, that the place was full of troops, and that we ourselves had nothing to eat. Cursing and swearing, they would then continue their journey in the mud and rain. One of the Portuguese officers in the house had a pretty girl with him, and, as I was unable to sleep owing to the incessant banging at our door, I entertained myself quite pleasantly with her while he slept.

At last the day dawned, and everybody in the house got up, stretched, gave themselves a cat-lick—that is to say, washed their noses with the tips of their fingers—and then marched off drearily just as the bugles were blowing. Only I remained behind with the pretty girl and my retinue to have breakfast, and she and I availed ourselves of this opportunity in order to demonstrate our mutual regard to each other. We withdrew to the bedroom, and, bolting the door, had the place all to ourselves. Seldom have I enjoyed an hour of more perfect bliss than I did with this young woman, and I would gladly have taken her with me, but that was unfortunately impossible. We therefore parted amid a final shower of kisses, with the promise to meet again ; but we never saw each other after that day.

At midday we marched to Mafra, which I reached in the evening after having been soaked to the skin by the drenching rain. I had caught cold and was suffering from a bad headache. Not knowing where I should go to find shelter, I rode past the great castle and along a number of streets, grumbling as I went, when suddenly I ran across Fereira who, feeling anxious about my failing to appear, had ridden out to meet me. My quarters were outside the town, but very good. I changed my clothes, had supper, and while smoking a cigar, drank a bowl of mulled wine with cloves, and felt very comfortable. I was so tired that I could hardly stand. Anyone who, like myself, has lived in a constant state of alarm for two months, marched the whole day on horseback, and lain at night on the bare floor in deserted houses or stables or out in the open, will be able to picture my feelings as I stepped into a clean little room here and saw a comfortable, soft snow-white bed. I dropped into it at once and hardly had time to think : what joy ! before I was already asleep. Good night !

How Mr. Augustus runs many risks with the Outposts and with Foraging Parties, but lives a Happy Life all the same—Retreat of the French to San-tarem—Events on the March thither—Rio Mayor and San Joao de Ribiera.

FROM the 11th October to the 1st November. Ten o'clock had hardly struck when I was waked by the melodious chimes of the clock in the castle tower. I spent the morning writing letters, book-keeping, arranging stores, receiving and distributing victuals and seeing to my domestic affairs. The first thing I did was to engage the wife of a hussar who, as I afterwards discovered, certainly knew very little about cooking. We stayed at Mafra until the 21st October. I rode to Senhor Cammarata in Goadil, the wine merchant who supplied the regiment, and who had the most beautiful wine it is possible to get ; his white wine in particular sparkled like gold as it poured out of the tap of his huge earthenware vat. I also gave all the officers here a sumptuous lunch, on which occasion my hussar's wife, who, as the saying is, was a better bed companion than cook, did me but small honour. The officers, too, gave dinners. If we wanted venison, a hunt was organised in the castle grounds, and a deer was shot. In the evening we had large parties at which we smoked cigars and drank barbarously. Not once did any of us go to bed sober.

While we remain here in such peace the enemy, to our great surprise, also keeps quite quiet. But the reason is this. Situated as Lisbon is at the extremity of a peninsula formed by the sea and the Tagus, it is only natural that if an army is posted right across the neck of land joining the peninsula to the mainland, the enemy cannot reach the city without making a frontal attack on the obstructing army. It was with this knowledge that Lord Wellington conceived the plan of the lines covering Lisbon. Nature herself helped with the peculiar features of the country, and art completed her work and converted those features into a strong defensive position. A piece of country thirty miles long, reaching from the mouth of the Zizandre on the sea to Alhandra on the Tagus, was chosen as the scene of action. The slopes of the hills were cut vertically, rivers were dammed up, and some of the country was flooded ; all roads that might be used by the enemy were destroyed, and others were built which facilitated communications between the defending troops ; the weakest features were strengthened and fortified by means of formidable entrenchments, and at all points where an attack might take place a large number of guns were mounted for defence in inaccessible places, so that the position was equally strong along the whole line. Moreover, no pains were spared, and no precautions neglected, to make offensive operations from the positions as easy as defensive ones. Thus was the ground prepared on which on the 8th October the army at last retired and again took post.* On the following morning it was joined by 6,000 Spanish troops under the Marquis de la Romana.

As the ground was uneven, and a sudden attack was quite possible, horses remained saddled all night. We all rose an hour before daybreak, and the officers had to parade on some open ground in the middle of the village, where Lieutenant Colonel von Arentschildt called out their names. Woe to any man who had overslept himself and did not turn up. In the early days his friends answered " Here ! " for him ; but in time the old man found this out, and then there was trouble. Except for the commander of the regiment and Captain Aly, the officers were quartered in a house where the mess was held, and their beds were made on the various stolen mattresses and straw. I also lived in this house. And thus our idle existence came to an end, and we were again faced with unpleasant and dangerous duties. I lived in Torres Vedras, but visited Ramalhal from time to time to see to my business there, and sometimes stayed the night. At night everybody had to sleep fully equipped and with his weapons beside him. All this was not

---

* While Lord Wellington may have been responsible for the conception of the lines of Torres Vedras, it should be remembered that it was Sir Richard Fletcher, of the Royal Engineers, who undertook and carried out their construction.—Tr.

pleasant, but the mood and the *esprit de corps* in this regiment, which was an example to the whole of the English cavalry, was so great that everybody discharged his disagreeable functions on outpost duty *con amore*, and with a cheerful heart and much fun and laughter.

My duty was to clear the ground between us and the enemy of all victuals as quickly and as thoroughly as possible. Accordingly, I was given a detachment of hussars from time to time, with which I carried out raids. My people followed us with mules and empty sacks. When we reached a village we sent patrols to the left and right of it ; then we would go forward, post sentries, and proceed to plunder the houses and barns which had long lain deserted by the inhabitants. As a rule, the owners had concealed their property badly ; everywhere one could see from large damp patches on the walls that something had recently been walled up just there ; or from hollow sounding places in the gardens that things had been buried. In all these matters my shoemaker, Joaquim, displayed the utmost virtuosity. We often found large supplies of corn, wheat, oil, flour, ham, pork, sausages, and vegetables ; unfortunately, however, we also found clothes, beds, linen, and furniture, and I was not always able to prevent either my own people or the poor devils who had been left behind, from making off with these articles. Often the alarm was given that a French foraging party was advancing towards us. But as soon as they ascertained that we were already busy loading up in the place they would halt and patiently wait until we had finished and gone away. Naturally we reciprocated these courtesies if we came to a place already occupied by the French. If, however, we had met unexpectedly, or on a reconnoitring patrol, we would have fought to the death.

As the enemy left us in peace we had jolly times, particularly in the mess, and afterwards at Ramalhal ; we drank, feasted, and sang until late at night, played *lansquenet* for Spanish dollars, and were up to all kinds of jokes.

But quiet as the French were in the mass, their patrols

were constantly disturbing the neighbourhood. Almost
every one in our regiment had an encounter with the
enemy. Our plucky friend, Strenowitz, among others,
came with his patrol across a small detachment of infantry
that had withdrawn inside a mill. Strenowitz immediately dismounted his hussars, stormed the mill at the
point of the sword, and took the whole detachment
prisoner. The French did not even scorn to use unaccustomed and treacherous means. For instance, they must
have had a corps of sharpshooters using air guns, for my
cousin declared that on one occasion when he was on
patrol numbers of bullets whistled about his ears, although
he never heard the report of a musket. The whole
neighbourhood had been deserted by the inhabitants, and
the wet and stormy weather, which was then seasonable,
made the roads impracticable. The enemy's army in front
of our lines was in a critical condition. Every day the
raiding parties under General Miller and Colonel Trant
brought back numbers of Frenchmen who had been sent
out in search of victuals. Deserters who gave themselves
up to our outposts were also plentiful. They complained
that they were forced to starve, that practically all they had
was what we chose to leave behind, and that they subsisted
chiefly on maize which they ground between stones and
usually fried in a pan. On the 25th October, 1810, the
army celebrated George III.'s birthday, and the fiftieth
year of his reign. At midday a salute of guns was fired
from the lines and the gunboats on the Tagus, and the
sound could not have been pleasant music to the French.
While we thus pursued our happy existence amid much
varied entertainment, a rumour suddenly spread that
Masséna was preparing to withdraw his army, now much
weakened by sickness, privation, desertion and death.
On the 13th orders were issued that we were to be ready
to march at a moment's notice, and the French having
retired on the 14th, we received our marching orders on
the morrow.

I marched off at midday in gloomy rainy weather ;
the roads were slippery and deep in mud. We passed
Sobral, where the French had destroyed everything.

Here we made inquiries about Quinta da Torre, where, according to all accounts the regiment was to spend the first night in bivouac. Nobody knew of the place. They said it was on the Tagus ; so we took the road in that direction. Night came on and we did not meet a soul. At last we reached a small house, and found the road barred by a wall of rubble. We pulled part of it down and jumped over it. In the house we found a fire the embers of which were still glowing, and also an old French uniform all torn. We rode on towards a place where a light was gleaming, but were suddenly pulled up by a strong barricade of casks and boxes filled with sand. After we had made a breach and climbed through it, we came to a bridge, the passage of which had been blocked by such huge trees, which had been cut down and allowed to fall across it, that not even a dog could have found its way over. In order to reach the village, therefore, we had to find our way round this obstacle, and ride into the place by the road by which the French had left it. The village was large and had some fine buildings, but only one inhabitant remained behind, whom, after much shouting and ringing, we at last summoned before us. He led us to one of the best houses and brought a light. The house had been completely plundered. We then proceeded to make a fire and prepare the food we had brought with us ; and amid much laughter over our quaint situation, as masters of a great deserted village, denuded of inhabitants, we wrapped ourselves in our wet cloaks and laid ourselves on the floor to sleep.

At dawn we rode on to Alemquer ; and here and there on the way we passed spots where French cavalry piquets and bivouacs had stood, paths made by sentries, small entrenchments, huts, burnt-out watch fires, bones, rags, and broken utensils. Close to Alemquer we found a number of French soldiers lying in a trench. They were a party of sick men whose cart had broken down and they had been left behind helpless by their comrades. The peasants had cut their throats. At Alemquer, which is situated on a hill in a fertile district, we entered a house in order to prepare breakfast with the provisions we had

brought with us.   Our host could not tell us enough
about the desolation and misery of the French.   At first
they had lived in luxury, and wasted everything and
trampled it under foot ;   but ultimately they had been
reduced to eating their pack donkeys, then their sick or
fallen cavalry horses, and finally dogs, cats and rats.
Instead of vegetables, moreover, they had to eat cooked
maize, fig and cactus leaves, and thistles, while many of
their men, when marauding in the district, had been killed
by peasants in ambush.   Here, where the French headquarters had been established for a long while, it looked
terrible.   The houses were covered with filth from cellar
to attic, the streets were strewn with the gnawed remains
and bones of horses, mules and donkeys.   All the
furniture in the houses had been smashed up.   On the
doors the name of the occupier was written in chalk, and
on the walls of the rooms in which we were quartered
there were caricatures drawn in charcoal and invectives
against the Portuguese, as also grandiloquent remarks
such as :   " *Le premier qui fut roi fut un soldat heureux !
Un bon soldat doit avoir le cœur d'un lion, la vigueur d'un
cheval, l'appétit d'une souris, et la férocité d'un tigre.*"
   At midday we again moved on in the direction of the
Tagus.   As the opposite bank of this river was being
watched by our observation corps, and was made unsafe
owing to the presence of gunboats, the French had
transported from Abrantes the pontoons for a bridge
across the Zezere near Punhete, and we found one of these
on a bullock cart abandoned in the middle of the high road.
It was a strange and ludicrous sight.   In the streets and
houses of the village we saw many French soldiers and
horses lying dead :   they appeared to have died of disease.
The whole neighbourhood was deserted, and it was filled
with a pestilential stink.   As we could not discover here
whither the regiment had gone in pursuit of the enemy,
we made for Cartaxo, where we heard that headquarters
had gone.
   While I was passing a lonely house on the roadside
beyond Azambuja, I was called by a lady at one of the
windows.   She was Maria da Rosa Barbosa, whom I had

met on the retreat from Coimbra, and the friend of my
former clerk, Mr. Hughes. She had stopped here to
have some luncheon and to feed her mules. She was very
vivacious, young and beautiful. Deeply in love, and having
secured her permission to call on her shortly, I rode away.

I reached Cartaxo very late in the evening after an
extremely fatiguing march. I was tired out, and found
the whole place full of troops. Thousands of bivouac
fires illuminated the district. We managed with much
difficulty to find shelter in one of the plundered houses
of this extensive town, in which a few hussars of our
regiment were already quartered. I admired their
domestic economy. Each of them had a bag hanging
from his saddle, in which there was a small metal saucepan
together with some ground coffee, chocolate, pepper and
salt. The streets of the place were deep in mud, in which
thousands of fragments of house furniture, flung out of
the windows by the French, were swimming about. All
the houses had been plundered ; our horses were standing
in the ground-floor rooms of our house, and looking out
of the windows. The inhabitants had returned, and a
most dreadful crowd filled the town. The regiment
marched on the following morning towards Rio Mayor
and San João de Ribiera, in order to act as advanced guard
to a small corps which was to observe the enemy's right
wing. I remained behind to collect my stores which had
not yet arrived and to add to them and put them in order,
and I followed at midday. The terrible rains had flooded
everything, whole stretches of country lay under water.
With great pains in the dead of night we reached an
isolated house close to San João de Ribiera, which was
already full up with some of the regiment's baggage;
but owing to the floods, the darkness and the rain, we
were obliged to spend the night here. It was a wretched
billet to spend a night in ; every corner of it was full up.
There was no room to lie down to sleep. I got out of the
difficulty, however, by going to a Spanish woman, the
friend of one of the native drivers of the baggage carts,
and she received me with open arms, and generously
compensated me for all my woes.

That night I found better quarters, and two days later I moved to a house on the other side of the river and quite close to it. I had established a small stores depôt in Rio Mayor, where Major Otto was stationed with Captain Aly's squadron, and placed one of my head drivers in charge of it. The French had deserted everything here. In the houses, which had to be cleansed by our men before they could be used, dead bodies of French soldiers and animals were found in a state of decomposition. All domestic utensils had been destroyed, the altars and the churches polluted, and the graves opened. A pestilential stench pervaded the deserted streets ; the whole of the olive harvest lay rotting beneath the trees, and all the inhabitants had fled either into the woods or else to Lisbon. A few, however, did, as a matter of fact, return in a day or two and opened a small market at which they sold chocolate, chestnuts and pepper.

The country round Rio Mayor was thickly wooded, but quite beautiful, although it was made most unpleasant by the wolves which at night attacked even our hussar sentries and could only be kept at a respectful distance by carbine fire. The situation of sentries posted in lonely wooded gorges and upon hills, with the enemy in front of them and all around them howling wolves, was gruesome almost beyond endurance at night.

In addition to one squadron of our regiment there was also in Rio Mayor a squadron of the 16th English Light Dragoons and three companies of Portuguese sharpshooters (*Caçadores*) under the command of that brave German soldier Captain Schwalbach. These troops had to keep the road to Leiria and particularly the neighbourhood of Alcanede under observation. Some salt works just outside Rio Mayor, from which even the French fetched their salt, often induced the latter to come to the place in reconnoitring parties of 3,000 or 4,000 men. The 16th Light Dragoons were brigaded with the 1st Hussars, and my good friend, Mr. Macnab, a Scotsman, was their commissary. The French were right in front of us, exactly *vis-à-vis*. Every evening, before going to bed, I would look out of the window after having put out my light, and peering through the darkness in the direction of the enemy, would murmur : " I wonder whether those confounded fellows will attack us to-night ? " We did not dare to undress ; our horses were kept saddled, everything was ready packed, and we slept uneasily. We got up at the slightest sound to hear what had happened. The approach of winter, the impossibility of attempting any movement against us, and the difficulty of collecting provisions had induced General Masséna to withdraw to his present new and well-chosen position, and to remain on the defensive until fresh orders and reinforcements reached him from France. Our position was equally favourable. Covered as we were by the lines, and with the stores of Lisbon at our disposal, we could calmly await events, and meanwhile harass the French piecemeal as they ranged the country far and wide in search of victuals. We occupied all the country, towns, villages and hamlets from Barcos on the opposite side of the Tagus, including the river itself, as far as Vallada, Cartaxo, Alcoëntre and Rio Mayor to Caldas.

A detachment of our regiment was stationed at the latter place. According to the orders of the Portuguese Government, all inhabitants on our own and the enemy's side had been obliged to flee with their belongings, and all the villages were empty. Many of the people, however, had not obeyed the orders to the letter, and being doubtful about the future turn of events, had hung back on their estates until the French cavalry raided them and forced them to take flight. Others had buried their belongings so badly that they were easily unearthed, while yet others had only taken their cattle with them. The whole of the country east of Santarem, therefore, was gradually transformed into a desert waste, in which, apart from the military, wolves and vultures were the only living creatures. Moreover, it was some time before the French had thoroughly exhausted the fertile district. Their cantonments were well chosen and well protected, and, as regards victuals, offered the same resources as our own. Many of the inhabitants, driven away by the enemy, reached our lines in a sick and famished condition, and died of bad fevers brought on by privation, inferior food, and the wet weather.   Many were to be seen feeding like beasts off the grass in the fields, or off chestnuts, acorns and rotten olives in the woods.   The most beautiful girls, and even nuns, considered themselves lucky when our hussars took charge of them.   There were derelict stores of corn, straw and wine in the woods, and derelict herds of cattle everywhere.   On our side we took possession of everything.   The hussars, divided into groups of ten and twenty, each had their herd of sheep or goats, which was placed in charge of some Portuguese youth, humorously called a " rompboy "— that is to say, a boy whose duty it is to go out and steal, from the Portuguese *rompere*, *robare*, to destroy, to steal. All the officers had rompboys, and they were smart fellows ; for when they were sent out with canteens and sacks they seldom returned with them empty.

My principal supplies were obtained from some large stores at Vallada on the Tagus.   But, in addition to this I, too, used to go out diligently robbing with a detach- ment ; for we commissaries were actually ordered to go out in these parts accompanied by armed parties, in order to remove all cattle and corn supplies from the enemy's side of the country, and to clear it of all victuals.   These expeditions were frequently accompanied by weeping Portuguese, who wanted to recover their property.   On one of these raids I discovered beyond Rio Mayor, towards the enemy's side, a country estate called Quinta de Pego lying concealed behind some extremely romantic wooded rocks, where, at the risk of being surprised by the French, I spent the night.   Here we found in a number of large casks such a quantity of white wine resembling *Caçavello*, that during the whole of our stay I could not only supply the regulation regimental rations, in exchange for cash of course, but I was also able to allow all the hussars and light dragoons in Rio Mayor to send a number of donkeys with bottles to the place every day to get wine for themselves.   In spite of this the supply lasted to the end.   Quinta de Pego remained a pleasant memory for long afterwards.   Before I made this discovery the hussars in Rio Mayor had supplied their needs from a huge vat of red wine which they found in a farm, but when they reached the bottom of it they discovered to their horror the body of a fully-equipped French soldier. From that day Captain Aly never drank a drop of red wine.

Every three days I had to go to the depôt at Vallada on the Tagus to urge on the loading of my mules. It was a long and irksome journey. There was such a crowd there that at night I was obliged to sleep on the bare floor of the depôt. Mr. Aylmer, the depôt commissary, kept open house. While I was on one of these excursions I met Donna Maria Rosa Barbosa, the young lady already mentioned, who was leading an idyllic existence in a small cottage with her Mr. Hughes, who was stationed there. I was selfish enough to convince her that she would be happier with me—in short, we eloped together, and for a while I lived very happily with her. She had a wonderful figure and a loving disposition, but she was so passionate that even I, insatiable as I was, sometimes grew anxious and frightened. As, moreover, I suspected that in my absence our brigade-major, a magnificent man, fished in my waters, I parted from her amid floods of tears on her part, and the major took her about with him until the day we sailed from Bordeaux. Later on she married a non-commissioned officer in the cavalry of the legion, and even visited me once in Hanover. After the death of her first husband she married another non-commissioned officer, and then I lost sight of her.

In this way we lived very happily, but our sojourn in the damp, cold houses was not pleasant, our drinking water, which had to be fetched from the muddy, slimy river was bad, and owing to the incessant rain the roads were deep in mud. The weather remained mild throughout the winter, and there was no ice ; even when the north wind was at its worst we could bear the windows open all day. I spent Christmas at Rio Mayor.

Before dinner we often rode to a small river where our outpost was stationed. Across this river there was a bridge which was barricaded. On the opposite bank stood the French sentries, on this side our own. On these occasions the French officers would come down and have a chat with us. " *Bon jour, messieurs*," was the salutation from either bank. They admired our beautiful English horses, spoke of our good King George, praised the Marquis de la Romana who was at our headquarters in Cartaxo and who, as a matter of fact, died there ; and they also sang the praises of Lord Wellington and the Portuguese troops. They told us that they had a theatre in Santarem at which every night a piece entitled " The Entry of the French into Lisbon " was acted. We retorted smartly that very soon they would act the piece called " The Flight of the French," at which they all laughed. We also gave them all the news, and they would throw their water bottles over to us to be filled with wine, and we would exchange our English newspapers for their French ones, by tying them round a stone and flinging them across the river. But Lord Wellington, who was told about it by an informer, put a sudden end to this fraternisation—and rightly, too—by a furious general order. In addition to the cavalry outposts our position was guarded by a battalion of Portuguese sharp-shooters. The enemy would send out a number of small detachments to scour the country for provisions, and our patrols used every day to bring back prisoners and even deserters from these foraging parties, particularly when the latter consisted of a certain regiment of the Franco-Hanoverian Legion (mounted sharpshooters in green uniforms with white facings) who were largely recruited in the Göttingen district, and were commanded by Colonel Schenk von Winterstedt, whom I had known very well in my youth in Ricklingen. Otherwise, the French, but for their habit of reconnoitring in strength, did not trouble us much.

I had been invited by my friend Poten to have break-fast with him in Rio Mayor. I reached him at 9 a.m., and we had just sat down to our meal when we heard a clatter and the sound of people running in the streets. At the same moment Poten's servant entered, and

exclaimed, " Sir ! the French are advancing, the bugles
are calling ! " We threw our magnificent breakfast out
of the window, jumped on our horses, which were kept
saddled day and night in the whole cantonment, and
dashed off to the alarm post as soon as I had had my wine
casks broken open at the stores. We saw our sentries
on a hill circling round in an anxious manner—the signal
that the enemy was advancing—and then we saw them fix
their carbines and make a dash to the rear. In a moment
the French appeared in strong columns, and halting on
the heights, examined our position through telescopes.
They seemed to pay particular attention to a formidable
battery which we had mounted beyond the town in front
of a church—though only as a joke in order to take them
in ; for being short of guns, we had erected dummies out
of old camp kettles. If, however, the old kettles could
have done the duty of a gun and swept the high road of
Rio Mayor, the enemy might certainly have entered that
town, though they could never have left it again! Our
Jägers took post at the entrances of the town and all round
it. Brave old Schwalbach stationed himself with his
foremost outposts, and coldly explained to the fellows how
close they were to allow the French to come before they
aimed and mowed them down. The squadron was
posted at the rear of the village and of the battery.

The enemy now deployed with about 3,000 to 4,000
infantry and a few squadrons of cavalry, and as they feared
our battery, advanced cautiously and slowly in complete
order of battle against our kettles. The Jägers opened
fire, and then, being outflanked, immediately withdrew
behind the battery, which so much impressed the enemy
that they continued to keep out of range. At last, seeing
that the battery did not fire, the French *tirailleurs*, taking
courage, stormed the kettles and took them. This little
attack made a pretty picture. The *Caçadores* with the
16th English Dragoons withdraw to Caldas, while we
retired along the road to Lisbon into a thick wood, which
extends behind the heights of Rio Mayor. Hardly had
we reached this cover and halted, and sent the skirmishers
forward, than on the heights just above our heads we

noticed a French general and his staff, accompanied by a cavalry escort, examining our position with a telescope. One of our skirmishers, a hussar named Dröse,* climbed up the side of the hill under cover of the trees, and stealing forward, rested his carbine on the branch of a tree, aimed and fired, and at the same moment the general fell from his horse and was surrounded by his staff and carried away.

After the French had occupied Rio Mayor until night-fall they withdrew from the place, and when we entered it the following morning the first thing we heard from our spies was that the hussar, Dröse, had shot General Junot through the nose, and that one of his aides-de-camp was dead and another badly wounded. Lord Wellington afterwards sent a bearer of a flag of truce to present his condolences to the general and to inquire about his health. The enemy had done a good deal of damage in Rio Mayor. My small stores were plundered ; mattresses, beds and chairs had been destroyed, and flattering messages written in chalk and charcoal had been left on all the tables and walls. We retaliated by lying in watch for their foraging parties and taking them prisoners. And in this our brave friend, Lieutenant Strenowitz, certainly distinguished himself. Day and night he used to speculate as to how he could play a trick on the French. One evening, for instance, he begged for a small detachment of men, and taking with him a few armed peasants, whom he had organised into a guerilla band, and to whom I was ordered by the High Command to distribute victuals, he marched out on a pitch-dark night in the direction of Alcanede. When he approached the French sentries he declared he was a French officer returning from patrol duty ; where-upon, cutting the sentries down, he surprised a strong cavalry picquet which, startled by the cries of his men, got hopelessly confused. Mowing down these also, and taking several prisoners, while his peasants untethered their horses, which were standing under some trees, he then rode quickly back towards our lines with his booty, while in Alcanede the drums beat the alarm. When,

* Beamish (*op. cit.*, Vol. I., p. 317) calls him Dröge.—Tr.

on the following morning our old Colonel von Arentschildt got up and looked out of the window, there was
Strenowitz standing at his door with a score of horses
and men whom he had captured, including the French
officer of the picquet, who was badly wounded about the
head.

Lord Wellington certainly commended Strenowitz for
this deed, but as such surprise attacks did not promote the
principal object of the campaign, and were contrary to the
courtesies of war, owing to the fact that the army was in
cantonments, they were forbidden for the future. The
French, for their part, refused to send along the baggage
of the captured officer, in order to punish him for not
being sufficiently alert. Once Strenowitz took it into his
head to visit the outposts of the Portuguese *Caçadores*, and
finding a whole picquet asleep, he took possession of the
officer's sword and the men's muskets, without their
noticing him, and afterwards reported the officer to our
own commanding officer, who naturally punished the
picquet very severely. Strenowitz knew no fear. Once,
in order to test him, we broke into his house at night, put
out his light, fired a few pistol shots, and cried : " The
French are coming up the stairs ! " and then withdrew.
He got up, seized a chair, held it in front of him, and swore
in French that he would smash the skull of the first
Frenchman who entered, and fling him downstairs. And
I believe he would have kept his word and never have
surrendered alive. The best of it was that on the following morning he told us about it as if it had been a dream.
In 1812 Lord Wellington made him one of his aides-
de-camp and gave him a company in an East Indian
regiment.

We had captured more French horses than we
could deal with, and every day we held a horse fair
and ran races. Let me give just one example of the
eccentric nature and licence of our military life—our old
friend, Lieutenant-Colonel von Arentschildt had secured
a nun from one of the convents, which had been plundered
by the French, and keeping her as his mistress, used
to teach her to ride at the end of a long bridle in the

yard where at night I kept my bullocks for slaughter !
Thus we lived in the style of the old robber barons
of old. Daring deeds, combats, alarms of all kinds,
and the clash of arms, alternated with the clinking of
bumpers, the playing of all kinds of pranks, and love-
making. As for myself, it is true that this merry
existence was frequently interrupted by work, a good
deal of annoyance, and many a wearisome ride to headquarters in Cartaxo.

Meanwhile Masséna did not abandon his designs upon
Lisbon, but made great preparations on the Zezere. He
had boats built for the construction of bridges, fortified
certain points, reconnoitred Abrantes and threatened the
Alemtejo, with which province he would fain have opened
up communications. On the 30th December, General
Claparède, in order to cover Masséna's rear, joined him
with 12,000 men,* and defeated the Portuguese militia.
The latter had become so daring as to have debouched
from the Estrella Mountains near Oslardigas and captured
a strong detachment conveying transport to Masséna ;
and having grown even more intrepid through this success
had attempted another similar exploit, when they were
compelled to take flight near Trancoso. But Masséna
wasted much time in organising his huge armaments.
The provisions available for his cantonments, which at
first had seemed inexhaustible, soon came to an end, and
with appalling consequences. Sickness and death began
to decimate the troops, which, both discouraged and
reduced in numbers, lost all confidence. The skilful
operations of Lord Wellington and his allies, together
with a thousand and one other fatal circumstances,
defeated all his plans.

Lord Wellington, who was only waiting for reinforcements from England, decided to resume the offensive as
soon as the transports with 7,000 men on board came to
anchor in the Tagus on the 7th March. For some time
we had been informed by spies that the French were
growing very restless, and were sending their heavy

* This appears to be an exaggeration. *Cf.* Oman (*op. cit.*, Vol. IV., p. 22), where
Claparède's force is given as 6,000 men.—Tʀ.

artillery, their sick and their baggage back to Spain ; and we also heard that they were burning a good deal of material, a statement which was confirmed by the huge columns of smoke which we saw rising in the direction of Santarem. We therefore received orders to be ready to march at any moment.

Chapter 19

EARLY on the morning of the 6th March, 1811, a few peasants arrived who told us that the French had vanished. In order to deceive our patrols, however, the enemy had employed a ruse of war, and had set up men of straw, clad in old uniforms, at all points where their sentries used to stand. These dummies had shakos on their heads and long sticks in their arms instead of guns. This is what misled us, and it was only at eleven o'clock that we were convinced the peasants were right.

The moment the patrols returned we hurried away as fast as we could, and joined up with the remainder of the regiment from Rio Mayor, beyond Alcanede. The country through which we marched was picturesque, and the sky was slightly overcast with rainy clouds. Not a Frenchman was to be seen, though there were plenty of traces of the ravages of the enemy. In one village that had been completely plundered and deserted by friend and foe alike, we found in a basket near a burnt-out bivouac fire a baby that had been forsaken by its mother, and was still alive. What became of it, God alone knows !

We marched to Pennances. The place had become a mere heap of *débris* and ashes. At eight o'clock in the morning the head of our column came up with the enemy. Our regiment had to go to the front, and as we rode up to the infantry, which had halted, they cheered us loudly. We advanced for half an hour at a smart trot, until we reached the entrance of a wood occupied by a small detachment of French cavalry. Our advanced guard soon drove them back, and then we came upon a column of French infantry, whose vanguard marched up and greeted us with a gunshot or two. The regiment could not, however, come to grips in the wood, and therefore followed slowly behind the column which began to move on again, and forced the enemy to blow up a number of ammunition wagons.   Close to one of these and behind a small wall of earth, we found a Frenchman lying dead. As the trail showed, he had fired the wagon by means of the powder spilt on the ground, but had been killed by the explosion.   On another wagon which we came across a fuse had been fixed and the string to fire it had been attached to the leg of a sick French soldier lying close by.   This man was expected to jerk the line as soon as the first of us approached.   But he did not succeed ; at all events, no explosion followed.

Late in the afternoon, just as I was passing a certain village, two Frenchmen suddenly crept out on to the road through a garden hedge, behind which they had hidden themselves out of fear of the peasants, and begged us with shaking voices to rescue them.   They were sick, emaciated, and numb with wet and cold, and were suffering from dysentery.   As I had noticed an English infantry guard in the village in charge of prisoners, I took them thither, and handed them over to our provost marshal.   A few of our hussars had been wounded; among others, Trooper Schey had been shot through the neck.

On the 9th March we reached a height from which we could see Pombal before us, and on the road thither a column of French infantry and artillery that stretched further than the eye could see.   The head of the column seemed to have reached Pombal.   To the left lay the beautiful town of Leiria, now in flames, in which horrors of all kinds had been perpetrated.

With the object of finding the high road to Lisbon, and also of discovering whether it was already held by the enemy, my cousin Gustav, together with a few hussars, was despatched through a wood to our right.   He told me afterwards that when he had been riding for over half an hour through the wood, he came to an opening from which he saw the great highway, and caught sight of a small troop of French cavalry riding along it.   In order to catch them, he and his men rode quickly forward ; but the Frenchmen dashed full speed ahead, and he

followed as fast as his horse would go.   Then, suddenly
halting and looking round, he saw that more French
cavalry, in considerable strength, were standing to the left
and right, and that a strong troop had broken away from
the rest with the object of cutting him off.   It was only
with difficulty that he reached the wood again, where he
was joined by some of our Jägers who had arrived meanwhile.   A number of enemy squadrons galloped past
these Jägers at full speed towards a height near Pombal,
where a large force of cavalry were assembled.   Meantime three squadrons of our regiment debouched from the
wood, and advanced with open front against the French
rearguard, which, consisting of a few regiments, had
formed in column on the highway.   A detachment of the
16th Dragoons, which had followed the French from
Leiria, then joined up with our regiment.   Major von
Müller at the head of the first squadron, started when he
saw the French advancing to attack him, and cried :
"Halt !"   The wing commanders, however, who were full
of rage and the lust of battle, shouted, " March ! "   The
second command was obeyed, and in a moment the
French were repulsed, and made helter-skelter for their
position, which we were too weak to attack.   The regiment had no casualties, but one or two of the enemy
were killed, and several were taken prisoner.   For this
engagement the regiment received Lord Wellington's
thanks.

As soon as Picton's division arrived on the 11th March,
our regiment, together with the heavy cavalry and the
horse artillery, marched as advanced guard at the head
of the light division ; and in order to expedite our progress, the cavalry carried the knapsacks of the infantry on
their saddles.   The moment we reached the broad highway we broke into a fast trot which made the earth shake,
while the infantry marched at a quick pace.   Thus we
advanced towards Pombal, where we found the enemy,
20,000 strong, still holding the town and the castle.
Our regiment had to turn the enemy's right wing, but as,
owing to the nature of the ground, this proved impossible,
we were brought back again to the centre, which was on

the high road. Our infantry made a frontal attack on Pombal, while our left wing seized the old castle which flanked the town. Lieutenant Cordemann, who was standing with a detachment of our regiment behind the attacking infantry to support them, suffered terribly from the fire. The enemy evacuated Pombal, which was burning in several places, and which our troops, crowding thickly upon the advanced guard, passed by ; whereupon we bivouacked under lofty pine trees three miles along the road to Coimbra.

We marched at daybreak on the 12th March, and found the enemy posted very favourably in a narrow gorge in front of Redinha. It was an imposing sight! Owing to the wooded nature of the country, however, it was difficult to survey the whole of their position. It was therefore necessary to allow a large proportion of our army to draw up for the attack, and the operation occupied several hours. The enemy's rearguard stuck to its position to the last, and then, when we threatened to cut them off, they hurried back to the main body in the greatest confusion. Masséna covered his retreat very skilfully. His rearguard was constantly being relieved and consisted of the best troops. They had to hold the ground until the bulk of the enemy had moved far enough. Lord Wellington, on the other hand, tried every possible means known to the art of war to outflank, harass and cut off the French, to cause them serious losses and to exhaust them. His maxim was never to make a frontal attack, and never to give battle, so that on the Spanish frontier he might present a fresh and efficient army to his discouraged foe.

Our regiment did not take part in the combat, but received a few gunshots as it advanced across a small plain on our left wing. Lord Wellington directed the attack, which opened with a heavy bombardment lasting several hours ; and after a short struggle the enemy was defeated and retired in disorder on Redinha. The French had deposited many of the men wounded in this and previous engagements, as well as a number of their sick, in a few houses in this place, but when they withdrew and the place caught fire, all these men were woefully burnt to death. As, owing to the narrowness of the bridge across the River Redinha, it was impossible to put our light cavalry across quickly enough and in sufficient numbers, our pursuit of the enemy had to be discontinued. In the evening I went over the battlefield, which was covered with dead and wounded, and saw the latter being carried into an old chapel. We made numbers of prisoners. We bivouacked in a pine wood about three miles beyond Redinha, and formed the advanced guard against Condeixa. In order that I might not lose my way, the regiment fixed signposts pointing the way thither.

But here I cannot refrain from describing an incident witnessed to-day by my cousin Gustav, proving how cool-headed Lord Wellington was. Gustav, with twenty-four hussars of the regiment, was ordered to act as escort to Lord Wellington when the latter went to reconnoitre the enemy's position. His lordship rode right into the zone of the French battery fire, and jumping from his horse, examined the position with a telescope. The French battery concentrated its fire on this point, and their shells fell incessantly about the Commander-in-Chief and the detachment of hussars. But Lord Wellington did not allow himself to be perturbed by this, and remained dismounted about a quarter of an hour. One of the aides-de-camp then implored my cousin to move a little to the rear, so as not to draw the enemy's attention too much upon the Commander-in-Chief, which he proceeded to do not at all unwillingly. The detachment lost several horses as the result of the enemy fire.

On the morning of the following day we marched out, but returned owing to a heavy mist. Our intention had been to attack the enemy who had taken post in a strong position on the River Ceira, and had concentrated almost all their forces there. We had hardly gone two leguas when we came up to this position. In front of us lay a small wood, occupied by the enemy ; behind this was a little town, and beyond the town the bulk of the enemy's forces. The French, who were no longer expecting us, and were busy cooking, were almost taken by surprise, and

our division cleared the wood and then the town at the
point of the bayonet.   Lord Wellington, who was standing on a steep hill with his staff, watched the manœuvre
through a telescope.   I was riding a cast hussar horse,
which I had cared for and fed up, and he was now a most
excellent steed.   When, therefore, the regiment, which
was concealed behind a wooded height, was given the
order to charge, my horse insisted with all its strength
upon following its old squadron, and the consequence was
that I charged with the regiment.   A few enemy shells
flew over our heads and burst against the pine trees, and
a splinter from one of them smashed the medicine chest
which was being borne in front of me on the back of a
mule belonging to the English doctor.   The man who
was leading it could not sufficiently display his astonishment at the accident.   " By God ! " he cried, grinning
at me, " look at this ! Isn't it funny ? The whole corner
of the medicine chest has gone to the devil, and we are
safe and sound ! "   As we reached the top of the wooded
height we were commanded to halt, and the Brunswickers
were allowed through.   As they stormed down the hill to
the bridge and joined the fight, their musket fire was terrible.

Here we stood in order of battle until late in the evening
when it grew dark and the rain came down in torrents.
At last we were ordered to bivouac.   As, however, you
could not see your hand in front of your face, the infantry,
artillery and baggage got badly mixed up, lost themselves
in the wood, dashed into trees, the thick branches of which
increased the darkness, and everywhere the cry arose :
" Have you seen this or that regiment ? "   As my baggage
was still in the rear, I joined some men of our regiment,
who with great pains at last succeeded in making a fire
with branches from the pine trees ; and in the end, whole
trees were thrown into the flames.

On the 17th March a thick mist prevented us from
marching before midday, as it was impossible to discover
the road the enemy had taken.   We marched across the
battlefield to the narrow pass through which the enemy
had been forced across the small bridge over the Ceira.
We found the bridge blown up, and the river, a foaming

forest stream, roaring along and swollen with the rain, its bed so full of large, smooth flints, that it was dangerous to ride through it. Here we began to see evidences of the appalling consequences of a too hasty flight. Prisoners assured us that the crowd on the bridge was so thick at the time it was blown up that a number of men had been flung into the air, and about 500 had been drowned in crossing the river. The banks were still covered with dead bodies. A number of exhausted donkeys, horses and mules, which had not been able to wade across the large smooth stones of the roaring stream, and which the barbarians had made unfit for use by either hamstringing them or twisting their necks, were still writhing in the mud, half dead. Among them lay commissariat carts, dead soldiers, women and children, who had died either from want and cold, or through the explosion. Over the whole of this ghastly confusion of bodies, our cavalry and artillery now proceeded to march without mercy, until the whole was churned into a mess of blood and slush. Never during the whole of the war did I again see such a horrible sight.

Our hussars came back with a number of prisoners, and in a chapel we found a poor Portuguese peasant, probably a guide, who for some reason or other had been cruelly cut to pieces. After following the enemy for two leguas, we camped out in a pine wood close to the road. Death and destruction, murder and fire, robbery and rape, lay everywhere in the tracks of the enemy. Every morning at dawn when we started out the burning villages, hamlets and woods, which illuminated the sky, told of the progress of the French. Murdered peasants lay in all directions. At one place, which contained some fine buildings, I halted at a door to beg water of a man who was sitting on the threshold of the house staring fixedly before him. He proved to be dead, and had only been placed there, as if he were still alive, for a joke. The inside of the house was ghastly to behold. All its inmates lay murdered in their beds, but their faces were so peaceful that they looked as if they were sleeping, and some were even smiling. They had probably been surprised at night by the French advanced guard and murdered. The corpse of another Portuguese peasant had been placed in a ludicrous position in a hole in a garden wall, through which the infantry had broken. It had probably been put there in order to make fun of us when we came along.

As on the 19th March we thought the enemy were still occupying their strong position on the Ponte de Murcella, our baggage was sent to the rear, and we marched to the attack at dawn. But we had made a mistake. The enemy had gone and the bridge had been destroyed. The sappers were already engaged in building a light wooden bridge for the passage of our infantry. The cavalry and artillery had to go through the roaring stream, on the stony bed of which many a horse fell. We halted on the opposite bank and waited until a portion of our infantry had crossed, and then continued our pursuit, and found the plain covered with stragglers, dead Frenchmen, arms and baggage. Gradually they were compelled to abandon upon the high road all the silver, gold, valuables, silks and velvets, costly ecclesiastical vestments, monstrances and crucifixes, which they had plundered from the churches, convents and private houses ; and as the Portuguese peasants cut the throats of all the Frenchmen they encountered, the Light Division became the heirs to all their abandoned treasure. The villages through which we marched were nothing but heaps of *débris*. We followed the enemy over five leguas, and Captain Aly, who commanded the advanced guard, made 600 prisoners. In the afternoon we caught sight of some French cavalry, but they vanished again. Late in the evening we camped close to a swamp in which several enemy soldiers and animals had sunk and perished. A few that were still alive were rescued. Among other things our booty consisted of 1,000 bullocks, cows, goats and sheep, which were handed over to me. The rest of the plunder was either sold by auction that night, or else bartered away. In addition to other things, I bought two very sharp amputating knives out of the instrument case of a French surgeon, who was a prisoner; and for a long time I used them as carving knives at table.

When we continued our march we found the small town of Galliges completely burnt and deserted. The ravages of the French on this road had again been terrible. In one of the villages lying in a hollow to our right, they had drowned some of the inhabitants by first binding them hand and foot, and then laying them head foremost in a stream. We marched on to Cea. As I was riding towards the place over some rocks surrounded by bushes I heard a piteous cry, and when I reached the spot whence it came I found a Frenchman, whom a few peasants had stripped quite naked and now proposed to beat to death. The Frenchman dropped on his knees before me and implored me to save his life. The peasants, on the other hand, begged me urgently to allow them to cut his throat. Of course, I did not allow this, but took him with me to Cea, where he was placed among the prisoners.

Instead of Don Louis Bernando's fine palace, I found only smoking ruins in Cea. All my friends, male and female, had flown to the inacessible heights and clefts of the Estrella Mountains. We had a few days' rest here, which Lord Wellington utilised in sending a bearer of a flag of truce to Masséna, in order to remonstrate with him for his barbarous treatment of the poor inhabitants, and also to inform him that if this were not discontinued it would no longer be possible to protect the numbers of French prisoners gathered together in various depôts against the fury of the populace. This had some effect. All incendiarism ceased from that day.

On the 26th March we again marched forward, but we saw nothing of the enemy. Towards evening we passed Celrico, where we found a few inhabitants had already returned. Numbers of dead bodies, which were probably those of Frenchmen killed by the peasants, were propped up against the houses and walls. To-day, this 26th March, 1811, I was promoted Lieutenant in the 7th Battalion of the Legion.

After having been divided up, our regiment was reunited at Villa de Torres,* a wretched village on the left bank of the Coa, to which we marched on the 2nd April ;

* This appears to be Villar de Toro.—Tr.

a division of Portuguese infantry accompanied us. The weather was bad, and everybody tried to crush into the houses for shelter. The French were posted on the other side of the Coa, which could only be crossed at one point. We attacked under a heavy bombardment. Our regiment, with the light division, was ordered to turn the enemy's position. We accordingly forded the Coa, and after a sharp conflict, in which the Light Division had to fight on ground covered with brushwood, we appeared on the left wing of the enemy. At the moment there was such a thick mist that we could hardly see our horses' ears. Everyone therefore stood still. Captain Aly, who was posted on the extreme right wing with his squadron, and was feeling a little anxious about his flank, sent my cousin with six hussars to the right in order to cover it. And now let me continue in my cousin's own words : " I had ridden about a hundred yards when I suddenly found myself obstructed on both sides by walls four feet high. Then, in a moment the road turned to the right, and just as I was about to follow it, I came upon some enemy infantry. They were drummers who had slung their drums on their backs. We all started with surprise. Soon recovering myself, however, I cried : ' Squadron, gallop, march ! ' and I plunged into the midst of them. I soon perceived that I was in contact with a bigger body than I had at first imagined. As, however, all of them jumped over the walls and ran away, I pursued them at top speed. After proceeding along in this way for about ten minutes, the mist very opportunely lifted, and I saw before me a road covered with transport and baggage, and infantry fleeing in all directions. It was the baggage of an army corps, escorted by a battalion of infantry who had lost their way in the mist. With a loud cheer I cut off a detachment of the escort, and made three officers and sixty-five men prisoner. Our booty also consisted of forty laden mules, bearing the baggage of the young General Soult.* One of my hussars, who ventured too far, was taken prisoner. Among the

* This appears to have been Nicolas Soult's brother, Pierre Benoit, six years younger than the Duke of Dalmatia.—Tᴿ.

baggage we found a mule laden with General Soult's correspondence, and that same evening I had the honour personally to hand to Lord Wellington in Sabugal all that General's diaries, letters, maps, plans and orders of the day."* For this, and many other such coups carried out in later campaigns my cousin afterwards received the Guelphic Order.†

The French army retired. Close to the town I admired a number of dead French soldiers who, as a proof that they had defended themselves gallantly, were lying in files. They were all fine young fellows, and had already been stripped stark naked. I also rescued a French officer, by birth a Swiss, who was lying on the heath with a bullet through his leg ; and I talked to him for a while. He showed plenty of *sang froid*, and taking a pinch of snuff, implored me to shoot him dead so that the peasants might not cut his throat. I found a donkey on which he was transported to Sabugal with a few English wounded. On the 4th April we remained at Sabugal, at which place the French had not had time to destroy the bridge across the Coa, and we bivouacked amid delightful scenery. On the 5th April we marched right up to the Spanish frontier, behind the enemy, who were retiring across the Agueda on Ciudad Rodrigo.

We were quartered in the village of Nava de Aver on the Spanish frontier, and here the first auction was held of a portion of the baggage belonging to General Soult, which had been captured by my cousin. In addition to the marshal's baton, the uniforms richly decorated with gold lace, and the other precious belongings of His Excellency, we also found many valuables taken from churches, convents and private houses, and among other things a number of sacks which had been filled in haste with all kinds of articles, such as silver knives and forks, old breeches, an ecclesiastical vestment, ladies' chemises, handkerchiefs, stockings, old boots, worn-out gold and

---

* Beamish (*op. cit.*, p. 324), in his brief account of this affair, says that four officers and ninety men and horses were captured, together with twenty-five mules, and the entire baggage of Marshal Soult.—Tr.

† See Beamish (*op. cit.*, p. 549). It was the Guelphic Order, 3rd Class, that Schaumann's cousin received.—Tr.

silver lace and sheets.   And now let me relate a practical joke that Lieutenant Baring played.   This officer found among the baggage a complete French general's uniform, with thick epaulettes, which happened to fit him like a glove, and having put it on he suddenly appeared in it at dusk before Major Otto.   The latter sprang up horrified, and Baring wanted to exclaim in a disguised, raucous voice : " *Monsieur, vous êtes mon prisonnier !* " but as he was not very good at French, he could not think of these words at once, and rashly concluding that it mattered not much what he said, he cried in a barbarous voice : " *Monsieur je suis un fortune de guerre !* "   At these words Major Otto immediately perceived his mistake, and burst into a loud laugh at Baring's speech. Ever since that day Baring was known among ourselves as " *Fortune de guerre.*"

On the 7th April a portion of our regiment had to go down to the gruesome rocky banks of the Coa and march to the frontier fortress of Almeida in order to join a corps of light cavalry, infantry and artillery, and to drive the enemy, who had made a sortie with the idea of breaking through, back into the place again.   In the evening our hussars returned.   We remained here on the 9th April, when a portion of the regiment went to the Spanish village of Espeja.   Our headquarters lay in Villar Formoso, and both armies stood facing each other on either bank of the Agueda.

And thus the famous campaign had come to an end. Our army had followed close at the enemy's heels all the way into Spain for twenty-eight days, and covered a distance of seventy-five leguas, or 337 miles *l'épée à la main*, as the saying goes.   Now, considering the appalling roads and the weather, this was a very great deal, particularly when it is remembered that, in order to allow our victuals to come along we often had to stand still, and then recover the time lost.   Both horses and men were often hopelessly worn out, and yet we were always victorious whenever the enemy chose to make a stand.   The French, however, then gave vent to their impotent rage in a manner so horrible that there is no parallel to it in the records of barbarism in either ancient or modern times. Towns and villages were literally turned into rubbish heaps, in the smoking *débris* of which sucklings and old people, forsaken by their families, fought against death from hunger or else perished in the flames. Along the roads, and in the houses, there were vast numbers of animals and inhabitants to be seen which had been sacrificed or maimed in the most wanton manner ; and the enemy's acquisitiveness was such that the human bodies were always found stripped of their clothing and exposed in a naked condition in the cruellest weather, and left to groan and moan in company with the sick and wounded abandoned by the enemy.

It is very difficult accurately to estimate the strength of the enemy on the retreat, but it is believed that their infantry alone numbered 40,000 to 45,000 men.* The nauseating heaps of filth and garbage, the remains of the most unwholesome victuals, which offended the eye in every town and village we entered, as also the wretched and dirty condition of the men we took prisoner, and the neglected state of the hospitals, afforded sufficient evidence of the sad plight into which the French army had fallen, and shed some light upon the heavy mortality in its ranks. On the other hand, the distress and losses of the inhabitants were also very great. In a certain area covering 2,000 square miles hardly one inhabitant was to be seen for five months. Everything was converted into a wilderness in which soldiers, vultures, swarms of birds and pigeons grown wild, dogs without masters, wolves and foxes, lived their lives undisturbed. Fifty thousand of the inhabitants had fled to Lisbon. The remainder of these unfortunate people spent the whole winter in the neighbouring mountains and forests, where, exposed to the most inclement weather, they lived on chestnuts, acorns, roots and herbs. And when, as the result of our advance, they were able to return to their homes, not only were their bodies emaciated through privation, but their

---

* Napier (*op. cit.*, Book XII., Chap. V.) gives Masséna's total forces when he repassed the Portuguese frontier into Spain at 45,000. Beamish seems to give a much lower estimate. Oman (*op. cit.*, Vol. IV., p. 202) gives a total of 39,546 sabres and bayonets. —Tr.

minds, too, had been weakened by the constant fear in which they had lived. Troops of these thin, pallid and haggard-looking creatures, with children of both sexes, who had survived the cruel ordeal, wandered by the side of the road along which the army was marching and begged for alms. Even the official French organ of the day, *Le Moniteur*, could not refrain from commenting as follows : " The houses and villages are deserted, the mills destroyed, the stacks burnt, the wine flows down the gutters, even the household utensils are broken up, and no horse, mule, donkey or cow is any longer to be seen."

The unnecessary cruelties perpetrated by the enemy cast a shadow upon the military character of the French which no praise of them as soldiers can possibly remove ; for they acted in this respect not as organised warriors, but as bandits.* And it was in this country that I was expected to act as a commissary ! Verily few people can be aware of the tremendous efforts I was sometimes obliged to make. I was the deity to whom men prayed : Give us this day our daily bread ! The moment we turned into bivouac all eyes were upon me. Even the most appalling scenes of the Thirty Years War, which we know from historical descriptions, are nothing compared with the horrors, the misery and the devastation that I have witnessed.

Masséna had now returned to the same position whence, about a year previously, he had set out to conquer Portugal, and all he had done had been to devastate the country and lose 30,000 men and a quantity of valuable war material into the bargain.† My exertions on these marches had been enormous ; for, owing to the fact that the pack mules, the bullocks for slaughtering and the carts could not proceed as quickly as the main body, I was obliged to cover the same distance like a dog as many as ten times, partly with the object of superintending, and partly in

---

* Any one who has read even Schaumann's own account alone of how the Portuguese and Spanish peasants treated French stragglers, sick and wounded, may possibly wonder whether there is any connection between these two facts.—Tr.

† Schaumann's figures are confirmed by Napier. (See *op. cit.*, Book XII., Chap. V.) Oman (*op. cit.*, Vol. IV., p. 203) estimates Masséna's losses at just under 25,000 men or 38 per cent. of his original force, and these figures are confirmed by Fostescue (*op. cit.*, Vol. VIII., p. 114).—Tr.

order to find and bring along my convoy when, as often happened, it lost its way; and then again at night I would have to discover in which wood or rocky cleft our regiment was bivouacking. It was frequently pitch dark before I was able to find it.

The regiment rested for several days at Espeja ; for the army badly needed to recover from its fatigue. I had a great deal to do to get my affairs in order, and to obtain forage and victuals in the devastated country. The Spaniards began to produce their hidden stores of corn, and started baking. Every morning the yard at my quarters was full of donkeys bringing corn, wine or bread. But everything had to be paid for on the nail. We had to march out at 2 a.m. on the morning of the 16th April to catch a convoy bearing provisions from Salamanca to Ciudad Rodrigo. It was a fine morning, and above the hills across which our road led there hung great clouds all golden with the rising sun. We marched to the left of the road to Rodrigo, towards the Agueda River, where a few squadrons of light cavalry joined us. Then we crossed the river, and soon came in contact with a body of enemy infantry, who immediately withdrew behind the walls of a large ruined farm, and were surrounded by us. A bearer of a flag of truce was sent to them to summon them to surrender, but not only did they refuse to comply, but actually climbed on the walls and, with fitting accompanying gestures, showed us their backsides. Meanwhile the expected convoy did not appear, and as from the towers of the town the French had observed what had happened, and the garrison had despatched a large force to liberate their comrades hemmed in behind the walls of the farm, we were obliged to withdraw after having been twelve hours in the saddle. The French, too, withdrew in splendid formation *en carrée*. It was a badly managed affair.

On the 20th April I took up my quarters in a lonely farm called Quinta de Agila, lying behind pine woods. I stayed there a very long time, was often driven out of it by the enemy, but always returned to it again. My sojourn there is the more vividly imprinted on my memory owing to a love affair I had within its walls. The victuals in these parts were very dear, and it was only by dint of great efforts that I was able to supply the troops with a certain amount of necessaries. As regards forage, the most I was able to obtain was half rations, which consisted of a wonderful mixture of barley, beans, *garvanzos* (a kind of flat pea or vetch), rye, wheat and maize. The enemy were constantly disturbing us with their reconnoitring parties.

Chapter 20

We strike Camp again—Battle of Fuentes Onoro—Almeida—The Army returns to its Quarters.

THE farm where I was quartered belonged to a rich old peasant, Camillo Siego, who lived in it with his family. He had two sons and a very beautiful daughter, Josepha. A few trifling attentions which I had paid her (among other things I gave her a pair of good English scissors out of a housewife I had, and she gave me a lock of her hair) had won me her affection. For a Spanish country girl she was extraordinarily cultivated, or at least seemed to be much inclined that way. She often drew comparisons between the English officers and her own countrymen, and would admire the good manners of the former to the detriment of the uncouth, coarse, gloomy and repulsive ways of the latter. " *Son brutos,*" she would say. When I was at home I usually sat by her side, entertaining her with stories about England and my native land. If she went to the well in front of the house to fetch water, I would accompany her and give her a hand. Josepha was good, full of feeling, tender, very good-looking, and, like all Spanish women, wonderfully well built. Her gait was that of a queen. Her body overflowed with vitality and blooming health ; and her character was also like that of most Spanish women, for she was steadfast, enterprising, passionate and severe, but also faithful. The thought of having one day to marry a brute of a fellow-countryman distressed her, and unconsciously almost we won each other's hearts. The fact that the beautiful Josepha of Fuentes Onoro loved me was soon known throughout the whole area, and all my comrades spoke to me about it and envied me. Oh, it was a gorgeous time ! But it was not to last long, and soon the very war that had brought us together, with all its horrors, was to come between us.

On the 24th April we were positively informed that the French were drawing reinforcements from Ciudad Rodrigo and receiving numbers of Spanish deserters.   On the 27th April Lord Wellington returned from the Alemtejo and took command, with headquarters at Alameda.   Meanwhile, Masséna had done his utmost to bring his army up to strength and ready for battle.   Up to the 1st May our regiment was separated, one part of it being stationed at Espeja, the other remaining at Guinaldo.   When news had been received on the 2nd May that Masséna was marching from Ciudad Rodrigo with 35,000 to 40,000 infantry, 5,000 good cavalry,* and a respectable convoy of provisions, etc., to relieve Almeida and to supply it with victuals, our army, which at most numbered only 36,000, was immediately concentrated, and by evening we were bivouacked in front of Fuentes.   Our supper consisted of some ship's biscuit, rum and water, followed by cigars ; the ground with a few bushes was our bed, and the starry heavens, into which we stared until we fell asleep, our only shelter.

Day had hardly dawned on the morning of the 5th May when the bugles called us to our horses, and to break up camp.   I was ordered to post myself with my establishment near the bridge of Castello Bom, which spans the rocky banks of the Coa.   When I had put everything in order at the bridge, I rode back again to watch the battle. I had not come up behind our right wing a minute, before Junot's corps with its superior strength had already engaged Houston's division and taken the village of Pozo Bello.   A detachment of French cavalry, taking advantage of this opportunity, moved in order of battle to the hill on the opposite bank of the unimportant river known as the Dos Casas.   The trumpets blew the attack to drive them from it, and the 16th Light Dragoons had the honour of opening the dance, followed by the 1st German Hussars. It was hard for the unfortunate horses to scale the height. When they reached the summit the men attacked with a loud hurrah, and there was terrible carnage.   The clash of the swords alone was audible at some distance.   As, however, the French cavalry were not only superior in

---

* Oman (*op. cit.*, Vol. IV., p. 305) says, " the whole force consisted of 42,000 infantry, 4,500 cavalry, and 38 guns."—Tr.

numbers to our men, but had also received reinforcements, and as Lord Wellington's orders had been that, with the object of sparing our cavalry, they were only to fight in single squadrons at a time, our men were obliged to retreat. The enemy cavalry followed them up quickly, and had the boldness to come right up to our lines and slash out at the foremost skirmishers. There, however, they were given such a warm reception by our light infantry and horse artillery, that they were driven back in confusion.

Meanwhile I had gone back to the bridge. A number of wounded had been taken to Castello Bom. The local inhabitants, particularly those of Fuentes, had all taken flight. I even met Josepha here, accompanied by her relatives and the priest of the place. With the view of protecting her I escorted her a part of the way beyond Coa, where she and her companions wished to hide themselves in the rocks. Among the prisoners who were being marshalled on the bridge was a colonel of chasseurs, a fine big fellow, whose enormous bearskin cap, fiery blue eyes, and huge fair moustache, lent him a splendid and martial air. He spoke English very fluently and complained that his guard had not yet offered him any food, although he was hungry. " *Sacré dieu*," he cried, " our men have as much meat, bread and wine as they can possibly carry in their haversacks ; but you beggars have nothing." I pointed out to him somewhat resentfully that, unlike the French army, we English did not live on spoil and plunder, and that an English soldier could not therefore be expected with his ration to entertain a chasseur colonel to a meal. " March ! " I added, addressing the guard. In a great rage he drew his bearskin down over his eyes and walking angrily across the bridge, muttered in desperate tones : " *Bien, en avant donc !* "

After this *intermezzo* I was just on the point of consuming a little cold luncheon, when I heard the sound of heavy gun and musket fire in the direction of Fuentes. In order to strengthen his position, Lord Wellington had concentrated our army, and out of Craufurd's and Houston's Divisions, which had formed in the right rear of our right wing, he had made a sort of wedge which stretched from Dos Casas to Freneda, on the Coa, and in front of which, as in the case of our left wing, he had caused trenches to be dug with a slight slope to the parapet to give them more strength. While our troops took up their position behind these works, the enemy endeavoured to hinder them by all kinds of manœuvres, including at last a futile bombardment. Thereupon Masséna again attacked Fuentes Onoro, the key to our position, and this time he seemed bent on breaking through *coûte que coûte*. In great haste I mounted a fresh horse, and galloped to the place I had occupied on the previous day. The French attack, particularly their gun fire (they usually fired salvos of six), was terrible, and the carnage in the streets of the village was, if anything, worse than on the day before. The whole place rang with the clash of bayonets, the cheers of the men, and the chatter of muskets. Death flew forth from the churchyard wall and from the village church, which had been crenelated like a fortress by our men, and pierced with embrasures. As usual, our side distinguished themselves with the bayonet, and made themselves masters of the village. Among the dead that covered the streets of Fuentes, it was quite a common thing to see an English and a French soldier with their bayonets still in each other's bodies, and their fists convulsively grasping the butt ends of their muskets, lying on the top of each other. At one spot in the village I saw seven, and at another, five, French officers killed by bayonet wounds. We buried 500 of the enemy, and our losses amounted to 198 killed, 1,028 wounded, and 294 prisoners.* Both sides fought with conspicuous bravery, and our Highlanders distinguished themselves above all. Let me give one example among hundreds that could be given : a detachment was skirmishing, and a young Highlander concealed himself

---

* Napier estimates the losses of the Allies at 1,500 men and officers, of whom 300 were prisoners ; thus it seems probable that Schaumann's figures on this occasion are about right. Oman (*op. cit.*, Vol. IV., p. 340) says the total losses of the Allies were about 1,452 officers and men, of whom 192 were killed, 958 wounded, and 255 taken prisoner. See also Fortescue (*op. cit.*, Vol. VIII., p. 171), who gives the numbers extracted from the Gazette, and makes them slightly greater than Oman.—Tr.

behind a rock, and from this cover shot bravely at the enemy. The moment one of the older Highlanders saw this he cried to him indignantly : " Since when have Scotsmen fought in that cowardly manner ? " and seizing the younger man by the collar, he pushed him into the middle of the field, exposed to the enemy's fire, with the words, " When Scotsmen fight they look straight into the enemy's eyes ! " Whereupon he gave the order to continue firing. Without wishing to boast, I, too, risked my life often enough on this day. Again and again I was violently spattered by the mould churned up by a shot which had been aimed too high up the hill on which I was standing; and hardly were the French out of Fuentes than I was in it, gratifying my curiosity.

Among the French there was a small corps mounted on red roans, which was called the French Hanoverian Legion. To-day they tried to measure their strength with the English Hanoverian Legion, and jumping over a wall, advanced to the attack in front of Fuentes with the taunt, " Hanoverian rascals ! " But after they had lost a few men they were soon repulsed and retired as quickly as they had advanced. Almost the whole of this Legion ultimately deserted to our side.

The gun fire lasted until late at night, and feeling very tired, I went in search of our bivouac. To my joy I found a tent pitched (the first, for hitherto I had always slept in huts made of branches covered with tarpaulin, or under the open sky) which I had requisitioned from the stores of Mr. Commissary Haden, of Villar Formoso. In the evening Mr. Commissary Macnab, a Scotsman of the 16th Dragoons, was my tent mate, and he brought with him a Captain Macnab, a fellow-countryman and relative of his, who had lost both his arms. We did all in our power to give this unfortunate fellow a comfortable bed, and to console and refresh him ; and, indeed, he joked about his condition, and drank a glass of grog and smoked a cigar. But although at the first dressing the doctors had spoken hopefully of his wounds, he ultimately succumbed to the acute inflammation that supervened during the night. Commissary Macnab sent the captain's last words and his blood-stained sash to his father in Scotland.

On the 6th May I rode to Castello Bom, a ruined village which, with its old castle, lies gruesomely upon the rocky banks of the Coa, and has been totally deserted by its inhabitants. Apart from the church, it has few habitable houses left, and these, though full of dung and filth, are nevertheless crowded with the wounded of both armies. Among the men who had received strange wounds I saw a private of the 16th Dragoons who, incredible as it may seem, had ridden about for a quarter of an hour with a three-pounder cannon ball in his thigh before he could find a surgeon. True, the ball was probably a spent one. At all events, he died as the result of the amputation.

On the 10th at sunset we heard some more gun fire coming from the fortress of Almeida. It was probably a signal for Masséna, which we could not understand, for at that moment the French corps in front of Fuentes marched back to Ciudad Rodrigo. At twelve midnight, when I was in the depth of slumber, I was startled by an explosion, which sounded like a terrible clap of thunder, and shook my bed quite violently. A few hours later the news reached us that General Brennier, the Governor of Almeida, had blown up the works of the fortress, hurled the garrison at General Erskine's blockading division, surprised and cut down a picquet, and escaped along byeways in the dark, and with only trifling losses had succeeded in passing by Barba del Puerco unobserved, in spite of all the English troops assembled there. It was only when he crossed the Agueda that another English detachment reached him, with the result that in going over the bridge he lost 200 in killed and 200 in prisoners* ; but he then oined Masséna's. corps, and could not be followed any further. Nevertheless, he had executed a well-conceived enterprise, the success of which did serious damage to our drunken old General Sir William Erskine.†

* Napier says : " Many were killed and wounded " and 300 captured (*op. cit.*, Book XII., Chap. V.). Oman (*op. cit.*, Vol. IV., p. 354) says : Brennier " states his loss in his report to Marmont at 360 men out of 1,300, of whom over 200 were prisoners and 150 killed or wounded."—Tr.

† This officer later became insane and finally committed suicide. Larpent in his " Private Journal," third edition (p. 65), writes : " I am told that he [Erskine] had been

Our regiment had gone off in pursuit of the enemy, and I found it on the 11th May bivouacking in a wood in front of the Quinta de Agila.   Masséna now gave up the struggle, and proceeding to Salamanca, soon afterwards left the army.

As the north of Portugal was now safe, Wellington despatched the divisions of Generals Picton and Houston to the Alemtejo to reinforce Marshal Beresford's troops, who were threatened with an attack from the French under Soult, and then, leaving General Sir Brent Spencer in command, followed them thither in person.   He covered the distance (135 miles) in three days, but as he could find no relays for his horse, he rode two to death in accomplishing the journey.   Two of the Dragoons of his escort were drowned on the ride while crossing a roaring stream.   My old quarters, the Quinta de Agila, were in a terrible state.   The French had done an enormous amount of damage to the place.   Josepha had gone with her parents to a house they owned in Fuentes, and for the time being they had given up their perilous position in the Quinta de Agila.   I therefore visited her in Fuentes, and stole many a kiss from her there.   On the 23rd May I rode to Almeida to get a close view of the damage General Brennier had done in blowing up his mines in the nights of the 9th and 10th.   I passed Fuentes Onoro, where swarms of large vultures with naked necks (I mistook them for turkeys at first) were clearing up the battlefield, which was covered with rags and rubbish and imperfectly buried bodies of men and horses.   Then, leaving Villar Formoso and San Pedro to the right, I reached Almeida after a hard ride lasting three hours. From the distance I could already discern the ruined houses and ramparts, as also the ground round the fortress, covered for a breadth of 300 feet with blocks of

---

two years confined, and that he should not have been here as chief officer of the cavalry : it was too great a risk."   He was in the Walcheren Expedition, and according to " The Military Memoirs of an Infantry Officer " (1833), p. 39, recommended as a prophylactic against ague and fever " one glass of brandy before dressing, one at breakfast, one after dinner, and another in the evening."   For further details about Erskine's shortcomings see Fortescue (*op. cit.*, Vol. VII., p. 419, and Vol. VIII., pp. 102, 109, 113, 175, 178). —Tr.

masonry and stone. In addition to the whole of their wagon train, the French, it was said, had thrown about 100 wagons into the moat, and had then blown up the walls and ramparts to such an extent that the *débris*, by falling into the moat, had covered everything up. The carriages of the heavy guns lay smashed on the ramparts. A portion of the walls was still standing where the mines had failed to explode. The gates were shattered, and I was obliged to enter through a vaulted opening that had been made extemporarily. Most of the houses were lying in ashes, and shells and splinters of bombs strewed the streets. All guns had either been spiked, or shot had been fired at them and dented their sides, or else shot had been hammered into their muzzles. Vast stores of entrenching materials had been burnt or otherwise rendered useless, muskets had been broken in two, and, in fact, everything had been destroyed. Some men of the English Artificers' Corps, however, were already busy cutting out the damaged vent holes of the spiked guns in an ingenious fashion and, by means of a screw thread, fitting new ones to them. All the *débris* was still smoking, and as some of the mines had not exploded, it was dangerous to wander about among it.

Let me give but one example to show how war was conducted in this luckless Peninsula. Before their evacuation the French had hidden live cannon and howitzer shells in the ashpits of all chimneys, baking ovens, and fireplaces of the houses and barracks, so that the returning inhabitants or troops might be blown to pieces the moment they began to light fires ! We also examined the spot where the castle and powder magazine, together with two companies of Grenadiers, had been blown into the air during the late siege. A deep crater and the ruins of 100 houses were all that remained of it. Many of the inhabitants had already returned, and one or two shops had opened. Here and there girls in their Sunday clothes could be seen peering from the windows, and endeavouring to attract our attention by frivolous gestures. After I had ordered a new cloth cloak at a tailor's we had luncheon at what had once been a restaurant, the owners of which had gone off with the troops and left behind the most glorious jams, liqueurs and fruit preserved in brandy.

On the 24th May we heard that the portion of the English army which was under General Beresford had won a great battle at Albuera, and that the French had retired on Seville.* We remained quietly in our cantonments in front of and behind Ciudad Rodrigo until the 29th May, when we started marching again with a vengeance, for we had not a moment's rest from May to September. Our movements depended upon the French. According as to whether the French held Ciudad Rodrigo, were besieging or victualling it, or threatened the Alemtejo, or attempted first at one place or another to reconnoitre, cross or menace the Portuguese frontier, so Wellington drove us left or right, forwards or backwards. Marshal Soult certainly kept us constantly busy, and for that he richly deserves recognition.

* This battle was fought on the 16th May.—TR.

Chapter 21

How Mr. Augustus goes on the March again and suffers all kinds of Hardships—He crosses the Tagus, goes to Niza, and camps beyond Portalegre, close to Campo Mayor, amid Scorpions and Typhus —From there he is obliged to retreat on Borba. But hardly does he begin to taste the Joys of Peace when he is again forced to manœuvre about with the Regiment, although he ultimately finds himself once more happily installed at the Quinta de Agila.

AS the result of some such movement on the part of the enemy as I have indicated above, the regiment was suddenly obliged to leave the neighbourhood of Espeja, and to march through Sabugal. On the 5th June we marched to Capinha, a charming open town of some importance, lying between rocks on the road to Castel Branco. Ernst Poten and I shared the same quarters. Our host, a Capitao Mor, seemed to be a decent and wealthy man, for the windows of his house had glass panes. He also had two daughters, who, though certainly fair to look upon, were rigorously guarded by their mother. The moment, for instance, I went into the sitting-room, the girls would flee into a corner; their mother would then stand in front of them, and spreading out her dress as far as she could on either side, like a hen protecting her chicks with her wings from a hawk, she would demand in an angry voice what I wanted.

It was here that my friend Lieutenant Baertling, who, as brigade-major to General Anson, could not very well take a lady about with him, abandoned my former sweetheart, Maria Rosa Barbosa ; and one of my drivers was ordered to take her back to her relatives at Castel Branco. I accompanied the poor child as far as the little river. She cried piteously. In vain did I beg her to stay with me: she was too much attached to Baertling. At last we parted. The following evening, however, she came back, and flinging herself on her knees before Baertling's bedroom door, which he angrily refused to open, proceeded to cry out in such a heartrending fashion that even General Anson took her part and allowed Baertling to take her along with him.

[TRANSLATOR'S NOTE.—On the 9th June Schaumann marched to Lardoza, and as he left Capinha General Slade's heavy cavalry brigade entered the town. On the 11th he went into bivouac at Castel Branco, the headquarters of General Spencer. On the 12th he went to Villa Velha and then on to Niza, and on the 15th he marched with his brigade to Portalegre, where they went into bivouac.]

In addition to my official duties, I was much harassed here by certain affairs connected with the fairer sex. For instance, Mr. Purcel, the commissary of the light division, had eloped with a beautiful girl from some respectable family, and the latter had arrived in Portalegre and lodged a complaint with the General. In order to put an end to all investigations, Purcel sent the girl to me in bivouac in the night, and begged me to conceal her. I therefore installed her in a vintner's cottage lying on a hill behind our bivouac, and, after having made her as comfortable as possible, left a guard sleeping outside the door. Later on Purcel married the girl and reconciled himself with her family. Our Brigade-Major, Baertling, who was travelling somewhere with General Anson, also placed his Maria Rosa Barbosa in my charge. One night there was a most dreadful storm, as if the end of the world had come. Half dead with fright, Maria rushed into my tent. I naturally wished to seize the opportunity to take her in my arms. But she had pangs of conscience and resisted me. At last, however, a sudden fresh clap of thunder terrified her to such an extent that, trembling with fear, she at last yielded. Thus Nature helped us, and I did the rest.

At 3 a.m. on the 19th June our brigade and the Light Division marched into bivouac at Arronches, and it was here that we heard that the siege of Badajos had been raised. On the 22nd June we continued our march, and bivouacked near Torre di Moira, half a legua beyond Campo Major. Our camp, which lay beyond the River Caya, which flows at the back of Arronches, was situated among cork trees, whose prickly leaves afforded no shade, and between hills strewn with stones, under which there were hundreds of scorpions. In the stifling heat it was a horrible place to halt at. As, moreover, with a view to making the ground more comfortable for the horses, the

Hussars moved all the stones out of the way, the scorpions were all dislodged. For these creatures wander about at night, but are in the habit of lying under stones in the day-time ; they were therefore infuriated, and caused a good deal of distress both to our men and our animals.

In the evening we heard that, previous to our arrival, the 11th Light Dragoons and the 2nd German Hussars had suffered a disaster through the foolish stubbornness of Captain Lütjens. It appeared that he had taken a strong detachment of French cavalry, that had formed unobserved by him behind a vineyard, for Spanish troops, and had proudly and discourteously rejected a warning that had been sent to him about them. The result was that he was taken by surprise and surrounded, and eighty-five men and horses of the Dragoons were taken prisoners, and of our own 2nd Hussars thirty-seven men and one sergeant-major, apart from dead and wounded. As both regiments had only just arrived from England, and were beautifully equipped in the matter of horses, saddlery, arms, etc., the joy of the French over their magnificent capture may well be imagined. The finest horses among this lot (worth at least fifty golden louis apiece) were acquired by the French generals, while the others went to the leading cavalry officers of the French army. Lord Wellington is said to have been terribly put out by this event.*

Our life in this camp was by no means pleasant. Every morning between two and three o'clock we had to march out with the whole army, as an enemy attack was expected. Only at nine, when the patrols returned, were we allowed to go back to our quarters. During the day the heat was tropical, with no shade anywhere, and we suffered from eternal dust, mosquitoes and lizards. Dr. Fiorillo had two of the latter animals, which were about 18 inches long and of a bluish-green colour. He had found them in the hollow of a cork tree close to his hut, and had succeeded in making them so tame that when he breakfasted they came and ate out of his hand, and even followed him a

* Beamish (*op. cit.*, Vol. II., p. 7) gives a slightly different account of this ; but Schaumann's is the more detailed and circumstantial. For Wellington's report of the affair to England see Fortescue (*op. cit.*, Vol. VIII., p. 235/6).—Tr.

little way when he went out. They belonged to the species which the Portuguese reapers find when they are harvesting, and which they always surround and drive towards a female reaper. Mad with fear, and not knowing how to escape, the lizard then takes the girl's skirts for a hollow tree, and stealing under them, climbs up her legs, while she utters most horrible shrieks. All day long we were infested by snakes, blowflies, and other vermin, while our water came from a dirty warm stream known as the River Caya, in which the whole army bathed, the cattle went to drink, and dirty clothes were washed. At night we were plagued by scorpions, mosquitoes, and a piercingly cold wind.

If one heard the slightest sound of crawling or wriggling under one's mattress or pillow at night, one called one's servant immediately, and the latter had to get up, strike a light, examine the floor of the tent and the bedclothes, and proceed to kill the scorpion, which had usually crept in under the skirt of the tent. One morning, just as I had got up and was on the point of drawing on my nankeen pantaloons, I thought I saw an object in my tent that looked like a leaf illuminated by a ray of sunshine that was pouring in from outside. I drew back my leg and found that it was a fat scorpion. Even during the day we were not safe, for on one occasion when several officers were lying on a tarpaulin under a cork tree near my tent, drinking grog, we found, when they went up to go, that Captain v. d. Decken had squeezed a scorpion that had crawled under the tarpaulin perfectly flat. But not every one was lucky enough to survive such an experience without a sting. If the beasts were touched with a stick they would get so angry that they would actually tear the stick with the hooks in their tails. We used also frequently to set fire to the dry grass all round a scorpion, and then the little brute would get so furious at finding no way out that, tortured by the heat, it would beat its tail back and sting its own body, and thus kill itself. The troopers of our regiment tried this experiment thousands of times.

In addition to all this, the unhealthy nature of the

district in which the army was bivouacked began to tell.
The banks of the Guadiana that flowed not far away, as
also those of the Caya, were proverbial throughout Spain
as plague spots during the hottest part of the summer.
A Spanish peasant told me: " Where oleanders thrive, fever
thrives also."   And he was right, for the finest oleanders
grew plentifully over all the flat country in the neighbourhood of these rivers.   All kinds of typhus and ague began
to break out.   Numbers of our men fell ill.   Nevertheless, Wellington would not allow us to withdraw to a more
salubrious district.   At last I also began to feel a weakness in my legs, which I could not explain until ague set
in, and then I understood.

The heat was so oppressive that Captain v. Müller,
who was president of the officers' mess, was obliged to find
out the precise spot which at five in the afternoon happened
to be shaded by two old cork trees, so that we could at
least enjoy a meal for a few minutes protected from the
sun.   The table consisted of an oval patch of ground with
a trench dug all round it, into which the diners dropped
their legs.   The Hussars' kitchens looked fine, for they
used the hollowed-out bowls of cork trees for fireplaces,
and the trees themselves as chimneys.   But they were a
little dangerous, for once one of these chimneys, which
had burnt through below, fell over, and not only smashed
all the pots and pans, but also cut Sergeant Meyer's leg off.
But for the drinking bouts we used to have after meals of
an evening, our life was comparatively dull.   Whoever
was not on duty would lie half stripped and perspiring in
his hut, with his legs and arms stretched wide apart.   My
duties did not permit of such comforts.   I had to be in
the saddle all day.   I used to ride to Elvas, among other
places, and visit my former hosts there ; but everything
was very much altered.   I also rode to Campo Mayor,
where Major v. Arentschildt, who was in command of the
Portuguese artillery, once invited me to dinner.   This
amphytrion, who was famous for his eccentric and miserly
habits, gave me poor soup, some roast bullock's heart,
and a couple of potatoes, and added thereto such inferior
wine that on the way home I vowed I would never dine

with him again. His mistress, a young Portuguese girl, dined with us. It was amusing to see Arentschildt with a menu in his hand ordering his old servant to bring in this or that dish, while the latter, already schooled in his part, would sheepishly make the expected replies. For instance, Arentschildt would exclaim : " Any fish ? " Answer : " The fishwife did not come to-day." Arentschildt: " What about the turkey ? " Answer : " John, who was sent for it, has not yet returned." Arentschildt invited many officers to dine with him ; but none went a second time. On the 18th July we at last moved to another bivouac, which was at least fresh.

The heat was now terrible and almost intolerable. Water was scarce, and lukewarm at that. But if the camp kettles were filled overnight and left to hang in the cool night wind, swathed in damp cloths, the water in them was ice-cold the next morning. In the afternoon of the 20th July we saw smoke and flames rising some distance away, and at the same moment perceived that a whole stretch of heath had caught fire, and that the wind was wafting the flames towards us. The regiment was immediately ordered to arm itself with branches of olive and chestnut, and to march out of the camp in the direction of the fire in order to beat it out. And this succeeded. True, the fire spread on either side of our bivouac, but this was not dangerous. But the moment the flames reached fresh stretches of heath it was a sight to see the swarms of insects, locusts, snakes, toads and lizards, some of them already scorched, dashing forward with leaps and bounds as fast as they could. If they grew tired they were lost.

On the 21st July Lord Wellington reviewed the whole army.* These wretched cantonments between the Guadiana and the Caya had cost us a number of men. It was reckoned that 4,000 had either died or been rendered unfit for further duty as the result of typhus and

---

* Speaking of the low strength of Wellington's Forces early in Sept., 1811, Fortescue (*op. cit.*, Vol. VIII., p. 258) says : " The low strength of the red-coats was due to the fact that 14,000 men were on the sick-list, the sufferers belonging chiefly to regiments which had either just landed in the Peninsula, or had taken part in the expedition to the Scheldt, though fever had left its mark also upon all who had been encamped on the Guadiana."—TR.

ague. On the 23rd July we struck camp and marched to our cantonments at Borba, a distance of six leguas. Here I remained with the regimental staff, and occupied the same quarters as Paymaster Longmann. The 1st and 2nd squadrons marched to Villa Viçosa ; the 3rd squadron was stationed outside Borba, and another squadron inside the town. The place was also full of infantry, particularly Highlanders, and the tattoos of the latter, which were carried out at night by eight pipers in old Highland costume, always struck the inhabitants of Borba dumb with astonishment. Also, thanks to the Englishman's innate love of cleanliness, the soldiers on their own initiative swept the streets in front of their quarters every morning, and then sprinkled them with sand, a blessing which will certainly never again befall the good town of Borba as long as it stands. The inhabitants rather opened their eyes at this, too, as if they were living in a beautiful dream and dreaded awakening. Hardly had my fever declined as the result of the few days spent quietly in more wholesome air, in the shade and in a cool house, than on the 17th we received orders to march to Castel Branco.

Happy indeed is he who, far from the tumult of war, remains quietly at home growing cabbages ! Thus thought I when at 5 on the morning of the 28th July I placed my foot in the stirrup, and with sleepy eyes rode sullenly through the streets, which were already deserted by the troops, and followed my regiment. My fever had, unfortunately, started again. On the 1st August we marched from Crato back to Niza, where we met the whole of the 1st squadron. Our new brigadier, Victor v. Alten, joined us here. In the afternoon Lieutenant Armbrecht, of the Legion, paid me a visit, and informed me of the death of my good cousin, Captain Plate, a member of the invalid company.* As the commissary in charge of a store at Ruvains, on the River Mondego, he probably died as the result of too heavy drinking. I had

---

* Beamish (*op. cit.*, Vol. II., p. 646) gives this death as having occurred at Coimbra on the 27th May, 1811. He also refers to Plate as belonging to the garrison company.—TR.

a great deal to thank him for, so I was much distressed by this news.

Early on the 2nd we marched again. On the way we met a large number of sick men from the division in front of us, who were being transported to hospital in Abrantes. They were one of the consequences of our long sojourn on the unhealthy banks of the Guadiana, as also of our incessant and heavy marches in the terrible heat. We crossed the Tagus on a bridge of boats, and then bivouacked close to Villa Velha, where I, surrounded by my cattle and my retainers, after the manner of the patriarchs of old, had my tent pitched by a small stream under the shade of a group of olive trees. On the 3rd August we marched to Castel Branco, and on the 15th into bivouac at Aldea da Ponte, where the whole brigade mustered. Here we heard the fatal news that, through the treachery of one of the inhabitants and his own disgusting carelessness, the lieutenant of the 11th Light Dragoons in charge of a detachment at San Martin de Trebejos (certainly a difficult outpost to hold in the middle of a thick forest) had been taken prisoner with all his men. He had foolishly allowed them to remove the saddles from their horses, and had made himself comfortable in his dressing-gown, when he was surprised by the French, who had come from Moraleja, four leguas away, where the advanced guard was stationed. The six troopers of our Hussar regiment, under Sergeant-Major Gehle, who understood outpost duty better than the English lieutenant, and who foresaw what would happen, warned him again and again ; but it was all in vain ; he merely dismissed them haughtily. They, for their part, had stationed themselves in a barn just outside the place, and had not only kept their horses constantly saddled, but had also posted a sentry. The consequence was that as soon as a shot was fired they quickly mounted, and cutting their way through, succeeded in escaping.*

Meanwhile, at my old quarters in the Quinta de Agila,

---

* This sheds a good deal of interesting light on Beamish's brief account of this incident (*op. cit.*, Vol. II., p. 10). Possibly Beamish feared that it would create bad blood to give the facts as Schaumann does. Or, maybe, Beamish was never in possession of the facts. See also Napier, *op. cit.*, Book XIV., Chap. VII.—Tr.

I was so repeatedly shaken with ague that I was almost desperate. Nothing relieved me, not even the strongest doses of quassia, quinine, or quinine and black pepper mixed. At last I lost patience, and taking no more care about my diet, ate and drank just what I liked, and did my duty as before. On the 21st August the Commissary-General sent me a new clerk or assistant, a Mr. Baldy, a cockney, it is true, but a good fellow. Owing to the lack of forage, my duties were very heavy. I often went to bed not knowing how I should be able to feed 800 horses and mules on the morrow.

In addition to the excursions connected with my duties, I often had to go to headquarters. At these headquarters of Lord Wellington, as in Villar Formoso and Fuente Guinaldo, everything was strikingly quiet and unostentatious. Had it not been known for a fact, no one would have suspected that he was quartered in the town. There was no throng of scented staff officers with plumed hats, orders and stars, no main guard, no crowd of contractors, actors, valets, cooks, mistresses, equipages, horses, dogs, forage and baggage wagons, as there is at French or Russian headquarters ! Just a few aides-de-camp, who went about the streets alone and in their overcoats, a few guides, and a small staff guard ; that was all ! About a dozen bullock carts were to be seen in the large square of Fuente Guinaldo, which were used for bringing up straw to headquarters ; but apart from these no equipages or baggage trains were visible.

The heat was frequently intolerable. When once the trying and exhausting business of the day was over, my fever would return every night at nine o'clock. Then I would creep into my hammock ; but, tired as a dog though I was, I could not sleep. Mosquitoes, fleas, mice and rats then began their pastimes, and drove me to distraction, and even outside in the yard things were not still, for my staff, who were established in an open shed, would sit round their fire, and every night without growing tired would sing a certain Portuguese national hymn at least fifty times over. I have forgotten the words, but not the sad melody, which still rings in my ears :—

Foaming with rage, I would dash to the window and drop a few curses on their heads, whereupon dead silence would reign. Not long afterwards, however, the frogs in a neighbouring swamp would begin to croak, and hungry jackals would start crying and wandering round my slaughter-house, fighting over the offal. Then the mules would neigh, and here and there donkeys would answer them with terrible hee-haws, or the bullocks would bellow, and the horses in the stable would stamp their feet. The fleas partly accounted for all this uproar, because they gave the poor brutes not a moment's peace. Occasionally, too, huge bats would fly in at my windows, which, owing to the heat, I was obliged to leave open, and they would hover round my light and put it out. Or an owl would sit on the window ledge and give us its tee-whit-tee-whoo at such interminable length that, losing all patience, I would fling my boot-jack, which I always kept ready to hand, headlong at the brute and frighten it away. At last Morpheus would take pity on me, my weary eyes would close, and I would fall asleep in spite of the fleas and mosquitoes.

One morning when I was still lying exhausted and jaded on my mattress, after having had an attack of fever in the night, some one knocked at my door. " *Entra usted !* " I cried, and a dirty little fellow entered my room and handed me a little note. Wondering what it was, I opened it and found it came from Josepha.* She informed me that, contrary to her own wishes, her family

* See pp. 298-300, *ante.*

wanted her to marry an officer called Don Julian Sanchez*
of the Guerilla, but that she could never willingly give this
wild and brutal lout her hand.   In her trouble she turned
to me.   I was a chivalrous English officer and her friend,
and as such I would not hesitate to take the part of a
helpless damsel in distress.   In the name of Jesus, Mary,
and all the saints, she implored me to help her.   She
concluded her appeal by kissing my hands.   Fastened to
a piece of bright ribbon in the letter there was a square
piece of silk embroidered in the form of a cross and a
heart.   At first I was somewhat embarrassed by the
contents of the letter, for her father, old Camillo, was a
proud and haughty man, and one of the most respected
and wealthiest inhabitants of Fuentes Onoro.   As a rule
only generals were billeted on him, and he was even in
Lord Wellington's good books, for, owing to the fact that
his house had been plundered during the battle of
Fuentes Onoro, the Commander-in-Chief had given him
a letter freeing him from further services to the army, and
commending him to its protection.   In addition, her
brothers were young and fiery youths, who, with her lover,
the Guerilla officer, would think nothing of waylaying me
and shooting me down.   On the other hand, the girl was
pretty, interesting, good and irreproachable, and seeing
that she had asked me to protect her, who, in the circumstances, could have refused his consent ?   I therefore
handed the little messenger a couple of lines in which I
undertook to serve her, and promised my immediate help
Then I summoned my secret counsel and head driver,
the shoemaker Joaquim—a smart fellow—and discussed
the rest with him.

As a certain amount of bread was baked every day in
old Camillo's house which was intended for the regiment,
and had to be fetched by my mules, Joaquim very soon
had an opportunity of speaking with Josepha ; and he
was able to inform her in whispers that every night he
would wait for her with two mules until eleven o'clock in
a ruined and deserted stable that stood opposite the house.

* This man was a famous guerilla chief.   For some of his exploits, see Oman, *op. cit.,*
Vol. IV., pp. 201, 213, 316, 318, 472, 587.—Tr.

Twice he returned alone ; but the third time I happened just to be going to bed, when I heard a creaking of the coach-house doors and the sound of mules in the yard ; then there was a patter of light feet on the stairs, and Josepha flew into my arms !

Thus the first act had succeeded, but the second, which was much more difficult, yet remained to be accomplished. It was impossible for Josepha to remain with me one moment ; not a minute was to be lost. While, therefore, she was taking a little refreshment, I wrote to my friend Xavier, the Juiz de Fora in Cea, begging him to take charge of the young lady, and to treat her as one of his own family, and I enclosed in the letter a small sum of money which I thought would cover the expenses of her clothes and upkeep for three months. Finally, I enjoined the most absolute secrecy upon him. Then three fresh and fleet mules were quietly saddled, and led out to the door of the Quinta, and Josepha, almost fainting for fright in my arms, was wrapped in a warm cloak, and, with a kiss on her beautiful lips, was lifted into the saddle. I ultimately took leave of her, accompanied by the shoemaker and my groom, both armed to the teeth, on the understanding that the three of them were to ride hard all through the night. They rode off. Soon the dark pine wood surrounding the Quinta concealed them from view, and Josepha vanished from my sight.

She had made her escape as follows : In order to let a load of wood in, the coach doors of her father's house had had to be thrown open late at night, and Josepha, seizing this opportunity to slip out, had been able, amid the confusion in the yard, to vanish into the darkness. Thereupon Joaquim, who was on the alert, immediately lifted her on to a mule and carried her away.

On the following morning I suddenly noticed that a large party had ridden into my courtyard, consisting of old Camillo, his sons and neighbours. They were riding mules with high Moorish saddles, and had strapped their brown cloaks in front of them. A firelock hung from a hook on each of the saddles, and they wore brown gaiters and one spur, which was fastened to their left foot. Great leather girdles with cartridge pouches and knives were round their waists, and they wore large round hats, brown jackets and breeches slit in the usual way. One of them carried a lance. The whole cavalcade was indescribably solemn, and also a little ludicrous à la Don Quixote. Having dismounted, they began to make a search of the whole courtyard and surrounding buildings. At last old Camillo himself came to me and artfully accounted for his visit by the fact that, as the Quinta was badly in need of general repairs, he had come with one or two friends, who understood building, thoroughly to inspect all the rooms to see what required doing. I pretended to be quite innocent, and commended his enterprise.

When they had searched everywhere in vain for any trace of Josepha, and found me behaving so calmly, they were a little puzzled, and, after holding a consultation, mounted their mules again. Unfortunately their appearance had so tickled my men and one or two Hussars in the yard that they all began to roar with laughter, whereupon old Camillo, suddenly becoming furious, behaved like one possessed, and rode away cursing and swearing, and gesticulating wildly. A few days elapsed, old Joaquim had returned from Cea, and Don Xavier's letter overflowed with praise for the beautiful Josepha. All the ladies in Cea had entertained her, and made the necessary provision for her wardrobe. She was happy, was treated like a daughter of the house, and sent me all sorts of kind messages and thousands of kisses. But things were not to remain like this for long. The traitor was not quite fast asleep.

One evening, when I was quietly having tea with Mr. Baldy, a guide rode into the yard and handed me a letter from Commissary-General Kennedy, summoning me to proceed to him at once. I smelt a rat, and begging him to excuse me on account of my fever, I sent Mr. Baldy. He, by the bye, almost broke his neck riding along the bad roads at night, and when he returned the whole matter became quite clear. The Commissary-General had questioned him very searchingly, and had pressed him to confess if he knew where I had carried ou old Camillo's daughter. At first Baldy pretended to be quite ignorant of the whole affair, until—oh God !—Mr. Kennedy produced my letter to Josepha and at the same time exclaimed : " Tell Mr. Schaumann that everything has been found out " (for Josepha had imprudently left my letter lying in her room), " and that Lord Wellington, to whom old Camillo has complained, has ordered that, under pain of incurring the Commander-in-Chief's severe displeasure, the whereabouts of the girl must at once be made known to her parents."

As there was nothing left for me to do but to obey, I summoned old Camillo to my quarters, and in due course he appeared, accompanied by the village priest and Don O'Lawlor, a Spanish colonel attached to headquarters. The latter helped to patch things up. Having made Camillo promise on his honour that he would not punish his daughter for what had happened, that he would, on the contrary, forget the whole business, and not force her into a marriage so repugnant to her as that arranged with the Guerilla officer ; having, moreover, made it sufficiently clear to him how disinterested my behaviour in the affair had been, and told him that I would give him back his daughter as pure as she had been when she came to me, I let him know that I had placed her with a respectable family, and as proof thereof showed him Don Xavier's letters from Cea. The old man seemed much affected. " 'Pon my soul ! " he cried, " you Englishmen are strange, but noble, creatures ! But, Mr. Commissary, when a man loves a girl, he does not carry her off ; he speaks to her parents." " Perfectly true, Senhor Camillo," I replied. " You, however, forget that I did not abduct your daughter in order to marry her, but to protect her. Who can contemplate marriage in these troublous times ?"

I then wrote a letter to Don Xavier, informing him of the unfortunate turn events had taken, and begging him to comfort the poor child and restore her to her parents. Old Camillo took the letter and sent his sons to Cea with it. Ultimately, when Josepha returned home, almost mad, she sank into her mother's arms in a faint, and afterwards refused to speak or take any food. But although the family were true to their word, and abstained from reproaching her with her conduct, Camillo's Spanish blood was not so easily appeased. He could not help wreaking his revenge, if only in a petty way. So one day he rolled up all the fine clothes, veils, silk stockings and long white kid gloves that I had given his daughter, and laying them on a chopping board in the kitchen, chopped them all to pieces and flung them into the fire.

In order to bring this little story to a close, I will anticipate events a little by relating how it ended. After her return to the Quinta de Agila Josepha twice attempted to run away and come to me, but on each occasion she was pursued on horseback by her brothers and caught in the woods lying between the Quinta and Fuentes Onoro, and brought back home. A year later, when, as commissary to the 18th Hussars, I was marching from Lisbon to the Pyrenees, Mr. Haden, the commissary at headquarters, told me that when he was stationed at Villar Formoso, and I was at Alverca, not far away, Josepha came to him and inquired after me. As, however, he was aware of my relationship to her, he thought it would please me better if he did not reveal my whereabouts. He therefore told her that I had left a week previously for Central Spain, but precisely where, he did not know. She left him in floods of tears. Shortly after that, at the very foot of the Pyrenees, I was again reminded of the unhappy Josepha. We had just crossed the Ebro, and a heavy shower of rain had forced me to seek shelter in one of a row of houses on the roadside, which had been deserted by the inmates, but was occupied by numbers of our own men. In the kitchen there were three or four Spanish country girls round the fire, who greeted me as an acquaintance the moment they saw me. Somewhat surprised, I asked them where they came from. "From Fuentes Onoro," they replied. They had come along as the wives of English soldiers who had been stationed there. I straightway inquired after Josepha. "Oh, she!" they rejoined. "Almost every day she goes out to the Quinta de Agila, Senhor Commissary, and looks for you. She often sits for whole days on a stone, refusing all nourishment, and looking up fixedly at the window of your old sitting-room, or she wanders through the empty rooms of the deserted farmhouse, and calls you by name. Only when the sun goes down, the shadows grow longer, the owls begin to hoot, and the bats to fly in and out at the broken windows, does she return sadly to Fuentes Onoro. Her parents let her do as she likes. A student from Salamanca, who came on a visit to Espeja during the holidays, wrote her history in the form of a ballad, and his verses are sung as a sort of folk-song throughout the neighbourhood." (Thereupon the girls sang me the song.) I am not ashamed to admit that while they were telling their story a few tears trembled on my cheeks. At all events, I could not listen to any more, and springing into the saddle, I rode sadly away. Poor Josepha !

*Further Proceedings at the Quinta de Agila—The French make Prepara-
tions to Victual the Fortress of Ciudad Rodrigo—We suddenly strike Camp—
Bloody Cavalry Combat near El Bodon—The Danger of being taken
Prisoner—Our Regiment is moved to Covilhao.*

Chapter 22

ON the 28th August Don Julian Sanchez, the
famous guerilla chieftain, came to my Quinta
with his suite, and begged to be allowed to eat his
luncheon there ; and I gave them my own room. Don
Julian was a short, robust fellow with curly black hair.
Suddenly, in the middle of their convivialities, one of the
guerilla band appeared in the yard, and reported that a
strong French reconnoitring party was approaching the
outposts. Like lightning Don Julian and his staff
mounted their horses and vanished. His men looked
magnificent, were splendidly mounted, and wore their
national dress, to which they had added the huge bearskin
caps of the French chasseurs of the guard which they had
taken from the enemy from time to time, or else picked
up as spoil on the battlefields. They were very much
feared. No Spanish municipal authorities would have
dared to refuse them anything. Even the inhabitants of
small towns submitted to their orders without complaining.
Let me give just one example of this. One of my muleteers had a young and extraordinarily pretty girl with him
(whether she was his wife or not, I do not know). At all
events, he seemed very jealous of her, for he never let her
out of his sight for a moment. One afternoon they were
sitting arm in arm in front of the Quinta, when a guerilla,
dashing past, suddenly halted, and scrutinised the group
with some attention ; then, calling the girl to him, he
peremptorily commanded her to jump up behind him
on the horse's back, and galloped away with her. The
parted couple did not dare to protest against this treatment
by uttering even one syllable of complaint ! As these
guerillas expected no mercy when they were caught, they
did not refrain from retaliation, and woe to the Frenchman
who fell into their hands !

We live on very friendly terms with the Spaniards here, and they are exceedingly pleased with us, for we pay for everything in cash. The most flourishing peasants of the district, who are my suppliers, often visit me, and sometimes even stop to a meal. Our English cooking, our table appointments, and our customs—particularly our heavy drinking—always fill them with astonishment. On Sunday everybody in the neighbourhood puts on their best and cleanest clothes, and in the afternoon the Fandango or the Bolero is danced on one of the open spaces in the village. The beautiful figures, the grace and the expression in the eyes of the Spanish girls, as well as of the young Spaniards themselves, are really enchanting. Many of our officers here have tried in vain to learn these dances.

In order to relieve the monotony of our life in the cantonments, we devised all sorts of amusements. Among other things, those of our officers who were Freemasons had established lodges, and Freemasonry was carried on. When, however, everything was going swimmingly, Lord Wellington put an end to it by a general order, in which it was pointed out that the Spanish priesthood not only felt greatly affronted by it, but out of fear lest we should infect Spain with this devilry (as they called it) had also raised a protest against it. As policy demanded it, Freemasonry was therefore dropped, and pony, mule and donkey races were instituted instead. This led, of course, to all kinds of betting, and the favourite sport was this : two officers had to ride through a district not very well known to them, and across which in the distance a church tower could be seen ; and one betted the other that he would reach that church tower on horseback in a given time, by following an absolutely straight path, and going out of the way neither for swamps, rivers, clefts, walls nor farmhouses—in fact, that he would either walk through or climb over all obstacles ; while the other officer, reckoning on the certainty of some impracticable obstacle, betted him that he would not. Then off they would go. A whole concourse of officers would accompany the one who had accepted the bet, in order to enjoy his embarrassment when he had to ride through a swamp or climb over a house. These bets always provided an enormous amount of fun.

A large barn was also transformed into a theatre, in which the officers acted, and the regimental bands provided the orchestra. In addition to Shakespeare's plays, many favourite English comedies were given. Many of the officers acted extremely well, and I saw one infantry subaltern in particular who as regards costume, mimicry, dancing and singing, impersonated a *prima donna* with such inimitable skill and comicality that he might without fear have appeared on any stage. All infantry brigades had their own messes. But if one happened to be invited to dinner with any one of them, the difficulties were two-fold : first of all, the long distances one had to go to reach them, and secondly, the return home in the dark when one was drunk. On these home journeys one either lost one's way, or plunged into an abyss or swamp, or else was scared by a wolf.

In the middle of the night on the 24th September our regiment suddenly received orders to march, and set off early in the morning for El Bodon. Towards nine o'clock on the 25th September the alarm was given, and mounting my horse, I rode forward with the brigade. On the sand-hills at two leguas from Guinaldo I obtained a clear view of the enemy's movements. Close to me, in the rear of the sand-hills, stood our regiment, brigaded with the 11th Light Dragoons, commanded by General Victor v. Alten. In front of the hills there were a brigade of English infantry and a Portuguese battery. The French cavalry, numbering about 2,700 men, together with some horse artillery, advanced boldly, and stormed the Portuguese artillery. The Portuguese gunners took refuge under their guns, while the French, cutting the traces, attacked the English brigade, which had formed square. At the same time (probably in order to discover whether there were any troops in the rear) the enemy dropped howitzer shells over the sand-hills among our cavalry brigade, which, being short of several squadrons, amounted only to 330 men. This was the signal for our brave fellows. At a

slow trot they advanced through a hollow between two
sand-hills, and then, accelerating their speed, ultimately
seemed to merge with a loud cheer into the black mass
of the French cavalry.   Again they appeared, and after
having formed once more in the hollow, returned to the
charge with a loud cheer.   Incredible as it may seem, it
is nevertheless true that for three-quarters of an hour they
continued these tactics and charged in all eight times
(official reports say ten *), and with such success that,
where they made their thrusts, the French flew asunder,
leaving great gaps in their ranks.

It was in such encounters that the mettle of the English
and Hanoverian cavalry † was proved, and they ought
always to have been employed in this way.   Unfortunately the French were very much superior to us in
numbers.   We were one to five.   But it always was so.
When for once we had the opportunity of practically
annihilating the French cavalry, we did not happen to be
at home.   This was the case now.   The brigade of heavy
cavalry under General Slade (of inglorious memory !),
which had been ordered to join us early that morning,
came too late.   The excuse was that it was not considered
advisable to overheat and fatigue the horses by too fast
a ride.‡   If this brigade had been with us, certainly not
one quarter of the French cavalry would have escaped
unscathed, despite all their numerical strength !

While the French were engaged in this fashion, the
Portuguese artillery (who were crying like madmen for
their commanding officer, Captain Victor v. Arentschildt,
who was in Lisbon) had obtained a little breathing space,
and having joined up their severed traces, had begun to

---

* Beamish (*op. cit.*, Vol. II., p. 15) says Sir Frederick Arentschildt declared that the
Allied squadrons charged forty times on this day.   *Cf.* Napier (*op. cit.*, Book XIV.,
Chap. VIII.), who says that the Allied cavalry charged twenty times.   *Cf.* Fortescue
(*op. cit.*, Vol. VIII. p. 263), who says the cavalry delivered from thirty to forty
separate attacks.—Tr.

† After Waterloo the cavalry of the K.G.L. was incorporated in the Hanoverian
Army, which, when Prussia took possession of Hanover, was absorbed into the Prussian
Army.   It is interesting to note that the Prussian " Husaren-Regiment Königin
Wilhelmina der Niederlande (Hannoversches) Nr. 15 " bore as an honour on their
helmets " El Bodon."—Tr.

‡ For General Slade's qualities as a cavalry leader, see Fortescue (*op. cit.*, Vol.
VIII., pp. 115, 229, 452), who speaks of him as " deplorable," and as " a byword for
inefficiency throughout the army."—Tr.

retreat.   The small square of English infantry followed
slowly, and then our brigade, skirmishing the whole time.
The morning sun was shining in all its splendour.   A
confused mass of troops, concealed beneath a cloud of
dust, and sparkling with the glint of a thousand sabres,
passed like a threatening storm across the plain.   It made
a magnificent battle picture.   The Portuguese artillery
passed me at the gallop and frightened my horse, which
wanted to return with them, and at this moment I saw my
friend Lieutenant Ernst Poten, accompanied by a hussar,
fall out of the crowd and ride quickly to the rear.   He
looked pale, his fur was all cut to pieces, and his sword
dangled from his loosely hanging arm, which had been
shattered by a shell.   I accompanied him to Fuentes
Guinaldo, and as no surgeons happened to be at hand
at the moment, I attended to his first dressing.   This I
did by running like a madman into the house and library
of the Spanish village priest, and seizing the homilies of
St. Chrysostom bound in pigskin, to the horror of the
unfortunate priest, who stood by as if petrified, I proceeded
to eviscerate it.   Flinging the text into a corner, I ran
off with the binding.   In this binding, which I doubled
up to form a sling and splints, Poten laid his arm, and this
gave him great relief.

Meanwhile Captain Bergmann had arrived with his
knee smashed by a shell.   As it was impossible to tell
what might happen in the course of the day, both
men, after they had rested a while, refreshed themselves, and being properly dressed, were laid in an English
hospital wagon on springs, and conveyed to Celrico.
Bergmann told me about the scoundrelly way the French
had behaved.   A French officer of the Chasseurs,
infuriated by the bravery and endurance of our men,
insulted our officers by calling them Hanoverian *coquins*,
etc., and challenged them to come out and fight man to
man.   Bergmann accepted the challenge and sprang
forward immediately.   The French officer also dashed
forward, but brought four chasseurs along with him, and
just at the moment when Bergmann was making a dash
at him, the chasseurs fired their carbines and shattered

his knee.   Laughing with triumph and malice, the French
rascal then returned to his squadron.*   As the French
could make no headway against us either with their
superior numbers or with their swords, they fired their
carbines at us from a distance, and this was how my friend
Poten had his arm shattered.   We of the 1st Hussars
lost three troopers and twenty-three horses killed, and
forty troopers, several officers, and twenty-five horses
wounded.   The 11th Light Dragoons suffered a little
less, but the French had twice or three times as many
casualties as ourselves.†   In order to conceal the extent
of their losses, however, they took care after the
engagement to cut the tails of all their fallen horses
quite short, so that the Spaniards might take them for
English.

In the afternoon the whole of our regiment bivouacked
with the rest of the army in front of Guinaldo, and as Lord
Wellington had fortified this place a little by means of
light entrenchments, he led both the French and ourselves
to conclude that he intended taking post here and offering
battle.   I had established my bivouac in a small field, and
in the evening the quartermasters came to me to draw
rations.   They could tell me nothing new.   After I had
had supper, I wandered about in the dark smoking a cigar,
and got on to a slight eminence from which I could see the
thousands of bivouac fires, which seemed to join our own
and the enemy's elevated positions with the stars.   What
a magnificent sight !   What a wonderful illumination !
I went to bed at ten, and must have been asleep a few hours
when I awoke with nightmare.   Just as I was thinking
of falling asleep again, it seemed to me as if I could hear
the sound of footsteps and the clatter of arms in the
distance.   I raised my head from the pillow, and laying
my ear to the ground, listened.   It must be the brigades
arriving, which are expected for to-morrow's battle, I

---

* Against this we might quote the chivalrous action of the French officer, who in the
same engagement saluted instead of striking Felton Harvey of the 14th Dragoons, the
moment he saw that he had only one arm.   See Napier, *op. cit.*, Book XIV., Chap. VIII.
—Tr.

† According to Fortescue (*op. cit.*, Vol. VIII., p. 262), the loss of the French was
about 200 men ; that of Wellington did not exceed 160.—Tr.

thought ; and again I tried to fall asleep, when it occurred to me that the sound was not like that of troops entering our area, but more like troops departing from it. Thereupon I sprang up, called my stores foreman, the Hussar Becker, and told him what I fancied I had heard. He mounted his horse at once, and galloped through the darkness in the direction from which the sounds came ; a moment later he returned and reported that our whole army was retiring, and that the rearguard, with a few stragglers of which he had spoken, had already been quietly posted. It appeared that orders had been issued at eleven o'clock that night to increase the bivouac fires and then quietly to withdraw.

As I feared that the French would follow on our heels the moment they got wind of our movement, and even expected to see a patrol of the enemy appear at any minute before my tent to take me and the whole of my establishment prisoner (for the ground that separated us was now quite open), I felt that I must extricate myself from my position with great caution. I durst on no account tell the muleteers how critical my situation was, for they would simply have run away with fright, and not taken their loads with them. I therefore woke up my chief, the foreman of the brigade, showed him in the dark a very old letter, which I held in my hand with an innocent air, as if I had only just received it. Thereupon I informed him that orders had just come from the Commissary-General to retreat forthwith, as a great battle was to be fought here on the morrow, and ordered him to summon his muleteers immediately, and after saddling up, assemble them for loading. Hardly had he turned his back when I pulled down my own tent, and had my baggage strapped on the mules and despatched. As soon as I was satisfied that this was safe, I thought to myself, what if I should let the stores go to the deuce, would it matter ? But then, mounting my horse, I hastened the loading of the mules as fast as they arrived, and at about 2 a.m. hurried away from the place with the last of them. A few belated baggage convoys and stragglers showed me the way the army had taken towards the heights of Casillas de Flores.

The sun was just rising as I ascended these heights through a narrow gorge, where I met our General, Sir Stapleton Cotton, who called to me and said : " Look sharp and get your mules up and out of the road, or they will all be done for. Where have you been all this time ? The French are already debouching, and things will look lively here in a moment." Thereupon I travelled *viâ* Alfayates and Aldea da Ponte to Sabugal, where I bivouacked in a wood.

But everybody had not been as lucky as I in escaping capture. Late that night, for instance, after headquarters had left Fuente Guinaldo, a number of stray people belonging to the army (including an English army chaplain) appeared with their baggage on the spot the troops were just vacating, and not suspecting what was happening, were so highly delighted and astonished at finding so many beautiful huts vacant and ready for them that they occupied them and made themselves comfortable. On the following morning they were all surprised in their sleep by the French and taken prisoner ; it was even said that many of them were barbarously slaughtered. In the evening the two wounded fellows, Poten and Bergmann, arrived here in their hospital wagon and were deposited in the same wood with me. I refreshed them with soup and beefsteaks. In the night our army withdrew to Soito, where we remained until the 30th, while the French retreated on Albergaria and then further on to Salamanca and Plasencia. On the 1st October the Light Division again advanced to Aldea da Ponte, and General Cole's 4th Division went to Navo de Aver, where I also was stationed. The weather was very bad, and we had storms and rain.

In order to dry and warm ourselves we endeavoured in my quarters to build a fireplace of stones in a doorway that led into a yard, where my bullocks, exposed to the wind and the rain, stood knee-deep in mud. But hardly was the fireplace finished and the fire burning brightly, when the bullocks knocked it down with their horns from outside, and thrust their heads through the opening in order to get some warmth. In the evening my brother

Edward, who was Commissary to the 4th Heavy Dragoons, and camping with them in the neighbourhood, came to have supper with us and to drink a glass of grog. The bullocks who thrust their heads inquisitively through the doors and windows were the spectators at the feast.

On the 6th October General Craufurd again marched to Guinaldo, while General Cole marched to Gallegos into a position we had formerly held. Headquarters were at Freneda. I marched to the Quinta de Agila again, which I reached in the rain and wind, and found our chief, Colonel v. Arentschildt, already installed at table lunching with Baertling and his Donna Maria. As old Arentschildt was not decent enough to invite me to join them, I had to wait, wet and hungry as I was, until my baggage appeared. On the 14th October General Renaud, the Governor of Ciudad Rodrigo, attempted with a portion of his garrison troops to pursue Don Julian Sanchez' guerillas, who had surprised and driven away 250 bullocks belonging to the French, which were quietly browsing on the glacis of the fortress. But the French ventured out too far, and were not only cut off by the guerillas, but also taken prisoner. This feat, which, in the daring way it was planned and executed, was perhaps unique in the annals of the war, was quite characteristic of the insurgent warfare of the Spaniards.*

On the 21st October we heard that Captain Bergmann had died of his wounds. He was a soldier body and soul, and refused to have his limb amputated, preferring death to being maimed and incapable of service in the field. On the 24th October we were ordered to march to Muisella, Povada and Serdeira, and from here we expected to be allowed to enter our much-coveted haven of rest. For this is how things stood : in view of the fact that our regiment had been engaged on outpost duty for three years without respite, and our uniforms, saddlery and other appointments were showing signs of wear (though we were still magnificently mounted), Lord Wellington

---

* See Oman (*op. cit.*, Vol. IV., p. 587) for a somewhat different account of this.—Tr.

had promised us a few months' rest at Covilhao, so that both our men and horses could recoup, and our equipment be restored and completed.   Thus every day we expected the orders to arrive ; but they did not, and my cousin Gustav used to exclaim : " If Covilhao does not come to us we shall certainly never go to Covilhao ! "

Chapter 23

*Arrival in Covilhao—Our happy Life there—The Ague gets worse—
Mr. Augustus goes to Lisbon on Sick-leave and is ordered to Sicily—Life
in Lisbon—Mr. Augustus leaves the Legion and becomes a proper Deputy
Assistant Commissary-General.*

AT last the hour of deliverance arrived, and on the 7th
November the regiment marched to Covilhao,
a town romantically situated high up on the
rocky slope of the Estrella mountains. The long march
thither was such an effort for me that the moment I
dismounted I was seized with the ague. I was given
quarters on the market-place in the house of a wealthy
cloth merchant. The town, with its steep, hilly and badly
paved streets, was not a small one. It contained about
900 houses, thirteen churches, two convents, and 45,000
inhabitants, engaged in cloth and stocking weaving,
dyeing, the manufacture of military equipment, agriculture,
and the production of wine ; and many of them were
quite well off. A third of their number consisted of Jews,
who were ostensibly members of the Catholic Church,
but it was said that they had secret synagogues where they
worshipped Jehovah after the manner of their fathers.
As regards morals, I must confess that in all my travels I
have never come across such a Sodom and Gomorrah as
that place was. The girls and women of the higher as
well as of the lower classes were practically all disreputable.
Pure virgins were rare ; and that is why some parents
even made use of the mediæval contrivance of the chastity
belt in order to protect their daughters. This was a
strange expedient indeed, but on a certain not unpleasant
occasion I was able to convince myself that it was an
actuality. One of our officers in his quarters lived on
terms of intimacy with the wife, the daughters and the
maidservant.

The life we led here was heavenly, no duties and no
fatigues. We slept until nine o'clock, breakfasted, and
then spent our morning riding, or sitting on a low wall
in the market-place cracking jokes to kill time, until at

four o'clock the trumpeters, mounting some battlements that soared high above the market-place, blew a lively fanfare summoning us to mess. Captain Moritz v. Müller had established the mess in his quarters, and there we ate and drank until eight o'clock. After that we either went out in the street to play all sorts of pranks, or else we had a grog party. We retired to bed between twelve and one. We also frequently made excursions into the surrounding country, visited the farms, and tasted the finest apples that I have ever seen in Portugal.

[TRANSLATOR'S NOTE.—As all their saddlery and equipment had been distributed among the various saddlers and bootmakers of Covilhao to be repaired, Schaumann and his regiment did not expect to be disturbed for some time. On the 24th November, therefore, they conceived the plan of inviting all the ladies of the town to a great ball. Hardly had this been settled when, to their great dismay, they suddenly received orders to march. The whole night was occupied in collecting their equipment together again, and by six o'clock next morning they marched out of the town fully equipped and victualled. The reason of these sudden marching orders, interrupting their promised rest, was a movement by the French on Ciudad Rodrigo. In a week, however, the French retired again, and the regiment returned to Covilhao. On their return Schaumann gave the officers a splendid dinner, and once more the subject of the ball was discussed. With the view of avoiding the risk of further marching orders coming along before the ball was given, it was decided to hold it forthwith. Schaumann was elected grand steward, and was advised and assisted by a committee of six officers. A large room was found in a half-ruined palace which was suitably decorated with foliage, and enormous supplies of fruit, biscuits and sweets of all kinds were procured. Then the officers of the 2nd Light Battalion of the Legion were invited to attend with their band, and finally Schaumann and the committee undertook to call upon and invite the notabilities of the town.]

We were received everywhere with great friendliness, and all the male members of the families we approached accepted with joy. Imagine our dismay, however, when we learned that all the ladies without exception asked leave to be allowed to decline our invitation. This was all the more inexplicable to us seeing that we had got to know them in a very different light, while we were aware that their refusal could not be accounted for by the jealousy of the men. Utterly bewildered, we called upon the most highly esteemed and most wealthy man in the place, on whom General Sir Stapleton Cotton was billeted, and who was the Capitao Mor, or district military officer. He was a foolish person whose clothes were always covered with massive gold buttons—those on his waistcoat even having diamonds in their centre—and who always wore gold spurs and gold chains instead of straps on his overalls, and had silver stirrups on his saddle. At first, when he heard our grievance, he almost died of laughter, but when he had recovered his gravity he explained the matter as follows :

At the time of Junot's first invasion a certain corps had enjoyed many days' rest here, and had given a ball to the whole town. Although the French were cordially loathed by the inhabitants, the men had not liked to refuse to attend the function, though the women had distinctly objected to going. Nevertheless, in order to avoid a scandal, the latter resolved to send their chambermaids and other working-class girls to the ball in their stead, decked in their mistresses' fine clothes and jewels. But some one betrayed the ruse to the French officers, who, in order to avenge the affront, arranged between themselves that the moment the quadrille was over they would, at a given blast from a trumpet, fall upon the women and overpower them—a plan that was actually carried out, amid the most terrifying shrieks. As, therefore, a certain wag had declared, with respect to our own ball, that in all heretical countries such as England, France and Germany, unpleasant as it might be to the fair sex, the barbarous custom nevertheless prevailed at all balls to turn out the lights as soon as supper and the quadrille were over, and to fall upon the women, the ladies of the town, wishing on this occasion to escape any such outrage, had refused our invitation. Our friend, however, assured us that as he knew our better nature, and recognised that, as perfect gentlemen of good education, our morals were superior, he would accompany us to the houses of the said ladies and convince them of their error. This he did, and with such good effect that a few earnest words spoken privately to the various families concerned altered their decision. The ladies, now reassured about a certain point, all accepted with joy.

On the day of the ball all the officers of the 2nd Light Battalion of the Legion were our guests at luncheon, and we all drank pretty heavily.　At six o'clock I went to the ballroom in order to have a last look at the arrangements. Two of our troopers' wives were selected to stand behind a sort of buffet in their best clothes and serve tea, while a number of waiters had also been engaged to hand round refreshments.　A hogshead of wine, a smaller barrel of claret-cup, and about nine gallons of punch, stood on the sideboard.　I had also had shelves erected against the wall, on which there were great pyramids of cakes, apples, melons, and grapes.　Finally, I had lined the street leading up to the door of the ballroom with forty of our men bearing straw torches,* so that they formed a dazzling approach to the place of entertainment ; and in the middle of the ballroom, facing the orchestra, I had arranged a large number of chairs for the use of the ladies.

Gradually crowds of guests began to arrive, and when the great hall itself and the adjoining rooms were thronged with people, the general effect was very brilliant indeed—I might even say, barbarously brilliant.　The great naked walls of the hall, with their faded ornaments and their decorations of flowers and foliage all brilliantly illuminated; the sombre, old-fashioned and slovenly dress of the Portuguese gentlemen, together with their sallow complexions (most of them were not shaved); the tasteful and dazzling uniforms of our English general staff, and a corps of sixty to seventy handsome officers; the display of flowers made by the ladies, with their fiery black eyes and their coloured and white silk gowns, their gold chains and costly, though old-fashioned, diamond ornaments; the troops of servants, who, according to the custom of the country, accompanied their masters and mistresses as part of the family, and stood between the chairs, each behind his or her respective lord and lady (so that the " poor souls " † might also see some of the fun, as everybody said in apologising for them), and confronting the

---

* These torches, which are called *arxotes*, are made of straw dipped in resin, and are to be found in every Portuguese town (Schaumann).

† The Portuguese word is *coitadinhos*, which means poor souls or poor creatures.—Tr.

ladies behind with a fine view of their backs; the crowd
of priests and monks (who, although not invited, managed
to find their way in) in every variety of clerical garb; and,
finally, a number of children, guttersnipes and raga-
muffins, who had managed to creep in at the back of the
building—all these together presented such strange and
comical contrasts that we could hardly believe our eyes.

The band struck up, and tea and cakes were offered
round, both of which were heartily partaken of by the
servants standing behind the chairs.   At last the dancing
began, and I have neither the space, the time, nor the
necessary vocabulary for describing the scenes that then
took place, particularly when once our wine, our punch,
our grog, and the power of love had sufficiently enlivened
the party.   Spanish, English and German dances were
executed amid the most appalling tumult.   The ladies
were beside themselves with joy.   Some of them, in order
to facilitate their movements, had pinned up their dresses
tightly in front of them, so as to outline their figures very
sharply behind, while others had pinned them behind,
producing the reverse effect.   Everybody was extremely
lively.   Even our general, Sir Stapleton Cotton, our
Quartermaster-General, * Colonel Elley, and our old
Lieut.-Colonel v. Arentschildt, laid aside their gravity and
danced *sarabandes* and *fandangoes* with the rest.

While the whole throng were whirling round the ballroom, or looking on in open-mouthed wonder at the
splendid scene, the men who were not dancing, the
servants and the children swarmed like locusts round the
buffet, and, after stuffing themselves with all they could,
actually began filling their pockets. Hardly had an hour
elapsed before one of the trooper's wives, who had been
pouring out tea, assured me that a certain fat monk, whom
she pointed out to me, had had no less than twenty-four
cups of tea and twenty-four biscuits, and that he was
coming back for more.   At eleven o'clock I was told that
my huge supplies were beginning to run short.   I
quickly had all the provisions in the town available at that
late hour collected together, and made a fresh display,

* Schaumann means adjutant-general.—Tʀ.

but at one o'clock I was again warned that refreshments were running short. At this I lost patience. I was, moreover, tired and jaded, and leaving the further direction of affairs to one of the committee, I returned home with my host, his two daughters and my clerk, Mr. Baldy. On the way one of the young ladies hung back a little and seemed engrossed in a conversation with Baldy. This so infuriated her father that, ordering her to come forward, he gave her such a sharp cut across the haunches with his cane that the girl cried out. Thus ended the happy events of this bright carnival day, with a blow and a full stop. *Reflexions faites*—though these were not of a very serious nature—I crept into bed as tired as a dog.

As meanwhile my ague had refused to yield to any sort of treatment, the doctors prescribed a change of air, rest, and sea baths. I accordingly wrote to Mr. Commissary-General Bisset, and begged for leave to go to Lisbon.

Shortly after New Year's Day I received two quite unexpected letters—one from the Commissary-General and the other from Lord FitzRoy Somerset. They informed me that, in pursuance of an order from Lieut-General Calvert, the Adjutant-General,* I was to leave the Commissariat and repair to my regiment, the 7th Battalion of the Legion, in Sicily. As it was impossible to appeal against this decision, I resigned myself to my fate. A further letter, dated the 1st January, from the Commissary-General notified me that another commissary, Mr. Major, would soon appear to take my place with the 1st Hussars. I accordingly arranged my affairs and prepared to take my departure. Finally, on the 2nd January Mr. Major arrived, and I handed over my stores to him on the 4th. As, however, I had some brigades of mules up country, I was not able to hand over to him completely until the 13th January. On the 14th I received from the Juiz de Fora, or mayor, of Covilhao a certificate in which he declared that I had discharged all the regiment's obliga-

* This was Sir Harry Calvert, Adjutant-General of H.M. Forces, and residing in England, not Adjutant-General under Wellington in the Peninsula.—Tr.

tions to the town, and that I left the place with an honourable record. In the afternoon, to my great satisfaction,
our Adjutant-General, Colonel Elley, made a public
speech, in the presence of all the officers assembled in the
market-place, in which he spoke of me in the most
flattering terms. He said that ever since the battle of
Vimiero he had known me and observed me with pleasure.
I was always to the front, had shared all the dangers,
difficulties and fatigues of the light cavalry, and had
always met the demands made upon me and performed
my duties, however arduous, to the satisfaction of my
superiors. I was therefore considered one of the best
cavalry commissaries in the army, the regiment was
parting with me most reluctantly, and he himself regretted
my departure, and wished me the best of luck. " And
as for you," he added, turning to my successor, who was
standing by, " you will be well advised to follow in
Schaumann's footsteps."

Deeply moved, I thanked the colonel for his kind
words, which I felt I hardly deserved, and, greatly embarrassed, withdrew. As my friend Ernst Poten, who had
lost an arm at El Bodon, had left hospital and had come
back to us on his way to England on leave, I hoped to
travel as far as Lisbon in his company. He was, however,
detained by business, and I therefore decided to go to
Castel Branco and to wait for him there.

[TRANSLATOR's NOTE.—Schaumann takes leave of his regiment on the
23rd January, 1812, and travels to Fundao, where he stays the night.
Next day he crosses a lofty ridge of the Estrella mountains and reaches
Castel Branco late in the afternoon. Poten joins him later at Castel
Branco, and they leave the place on the 5th February. Then, travelling
by easy stages, they reach Lisbon on an afternoon early in February.
Both Schaumann and his friend Poten put up at Lahmeyer's Hotel on
the Largo de S. Paulo. Schaumann's reasons for putting up here are
worth reading, and I have translated the passage accordingly.]

As I expected to remain many months in Lisbon, I
thought it would be more economical to be billeted at a
private house, and I therefore went to the town major.
Had I previously been acquainted with General Peacocke,
the Commandant at Lisbon, I would have spared myself
the pains of having to run about for hours in the company

of a Portuguese military policeman while my pack mules and my horse stood starving in the street. First this house had no stable; then we found a stable and no house; anon we came to a place which already had people billeted in it, or to the abode of a conde or marques who was exempted from supplying quarters. This April fool system of organising the billeting was the work of General Peacocke, who, incapable of taking command in the field, had been specially sent here by Lord Wellington, who knew his eccentric and harsh character, in order, by means of every kind of interference, to make the life of English officers in Lisbon as difficult and unhappy as possible. At last it struck me that, as I had a bag containing 1,000 piastres in my chest, I could well afford to live in a hotel, and that I should be a fool any longer to dance to General Peacocke's piping. I therefore turned quickly back, brought along my baggage, and put up at Lahmeyer's, and, as the place was rather full, I shared a room with Poten. On the following morning I reported myself to the Commissaries-General, Mr. Pipon and Mr. Vaux.* The latter, an inspector of accounts, made a place for me in his office, where I could put my papers in order undisturbed. On the way I had already observed that my fever had abated, and the first day of my stay in Lisbon it altogether disappeared. On the other hand, I noticed that I had developed an appetite, better health, and enjoyed a feeling of indescribable well-being.

We arrived in Lisbon in February, 1812—that is to say, at the beginning of the orange harvest. In common with other equally happy parts of the world, the spring here is a season of extraordinary splendour. How pleasant and comforting the sun seemed already ! The flowers and the blossoms on the trees seemed to vie with one another as to which should be the first to bloom, and soft breezes wafted their fragrance right into the heart of the town. I started my life here full of good cheer and in the best of spirits, and if space and time allowed, how

---

* Schaumann is constantly using the expression " Commissary-General " in referring to people who never held that rank. Except, therefore, when he is speaking either of John Murray, Kennedy, or Bisset, he must mean Deputy Commissary-General and not Commissary-General.—Tr.

gladly would I recapitulate all the details of the joyful existence I led.   Let me, however, by way of recording the whole experience, describe one typical day of my life in Lisbon.

After having had my sleep out like a monarch, I would slip on my cloak, and going downstairs, would take a boat to one of the large floating baths on the Tagus, and here I would bathe in the fresh sea-water that had just flowed in with the tide.   After that I would dress, and then, sitting by an open window, from which I enjoyed one of the most lovely views imaginable, my friend and I would eat our English breakfast.   Among the beautiful objects that met our eyes were *pro primo* a number of wonderfully pretty women on the floor below us, who were enjoying the cool air of the morning on their balcony, and whose plump white shoulders and necks served as a target at which we fired rosebuds.   If we struck a bull's-eye, our reward was a tender glance full of mock reproach.   *Pro secundo* we had spread out before us the whole of the fruit, fish and flower market, consisting of row upon row of small booths filled with the riches of Pomona and Ceres, tended by maidens even more exuberant, comely and trimly dressed than the famous Brunswick gingerbread girls of Germany.   Among these girls there were many whom we knew, and from whom we made a point of purchasing our figs, oranges, melons or peaches, with whom we flirted, and to whom we waved a good-morning from our balcony.

All sorts of people strolled round this market : vendors as well as purchasers ; English and Portuguese soldiers ; priests ; idlers ; chefs and cooks ; sailors ; Greek seamen in red caps and short wide trousers ; sullen-looking Algerians and Tunisians in their turbans, embroidered velvet waistcoats, ample short trousers and yellow morocco leather slippers, with their legs and necks all bare, the former being as thick as bullocks' and the latter with calves that would have done credit to Hercules. Then we would see detachments of English soldiers pass through, or a procession, etc.—in short, a motley throng, through which a number of donkeys bearing mountains of salads on their backs, as also a drum and bagpipes, were very laboriously driven. The donkeys were urged on by a couple of priests dressed in red cloaks, one of whom bore a flag on which figured a cross and the Lamb of God, and the other a box, in which he gathered alms from the fruit-sellers for the church of San Paulo. There were also monks to be seen, carrying a small figure of the Holy Child in a cardboard box, the glass front of which they allowed the faithful to kiss in exchange for alms. Finally, a crowd of beggars, ballad-singers, pedlars, etc., filled up the gaps in this indescribable maze and confusion of people. On the Largo de San Paulo, opposite Lahmeyer's Hotel, a number of carts had driven up with white bread for sale.

Pro tertio there was the majestic Tagus, filled with fleets of warships, transports, and merchant vessels, whose bright flags and pennants fluttered in the morning breeze; and thousands of boats, crossing each other at lightning speed in all directions. Now and then the firing of guns on an outward-bound ship would mingle with the melodious chimes of the church bells, calling the whole of Lisbon to mass, and would lend a note of extra liveliness to the magnificent panorama. Finally, beyond the whole scene, shimmering in the mist, there lay the opposite bank of the Tagus, studded all over with tiny villages and towns, spread out beneath a sky and a sun the clearness and lustre of which we can form no conception of in Northern climes.

Mr. Vaux had installed his office in the Convent of Necessidades, and we started work. I and a colleague, my good friend Mr. House, sat in the same room. The work was light; we did not overdo it, and talked a tremendous deal. At one o'clock we laid down our pens and walked home. The heat was terrific. Provided the shutters had been closed on the sunny side, the cement floor sprinkled with water, and gorgeous bunches of flowers placed all about, our room was cool enough. Then we would take off our clothes, lie on the sofa, and read novels. At two o'clock Lahmeyer's maidservant, Jacinthe, would appear, and announce that our meal was

ready.   At the *table d'hôte* there sat officers of the Legion,
business men (chiefly foreigners), and first-class ship
captains.   As, however, among such a motley crew, there
were many amusing wags, whose jokes, conversation,
expressions and arguments were extremely odd, the
temper of the company at that table may well be imagined.
Never have I laughed as much as I did during my stay
at Lahmeyer's Hotel.   Of the thousand and one mad
scenes I witnessed let me just describe one.

One night, after we had drunk heavily both at table and
afterwards, Poten and I were suddenly awakened at one
o'clock by a most appalling uproar, in the midst of which
we could distinctly hear some one cry : " Help ! I am
being murdered ! "   Feeling alarmed, we rose, snatched
up our swords and dashed towards the rooms whence the
sound seemed to come, which turned out to be those of
Captain Dobrowan and Quartermaster Sylvester.   But
we found the doors locked.   As, however, ˙Sylvester
continued to roar " Murder ! Murder ! " and slashed at
the window and the furniture with his sword, we ran to
Lahmeyer's rooms and demanded a light.   By this time
everybody was out of bed, and we all foregathered in the
billiard room in our night-gowns.   The sight of the
various forms of night attire when the lights were brought
was certainly singular.   Presently the door of the bedroom was opened with a master-key, and we found
Sylvester in his nightgown standing in the middle of the
room, rolling his eyes and foaming at the mouth, and
holding his sword in his hand, the perspiration streaming
from him, while all around lay the fragments of the
windows, the brackets, the vases and the furniture he
had shattered.

" In heaven's name, Sylvester, what are you up to ? "

" Dobrowan came to my bed with a drawn sword and
wanted to kill me," he replied, mad with rage.   We
turned to Dobrowan, whose sword, in its scabbard, was
hanging peacefully on the wall ; but he was so hopelessly
drunk that he lay on his bed unable to stand, or even move,
and could not therefore murder any one.   We asked him
whether what Sylvester had told us was true.   But very

soon everything was quite plain ; for Sylvester had only dreamt that Dobrowan wished to murder him !

In the hope of driving away heat by heat we drank heavily. After dinner we used to go to a Greek café to drink coffee, smoke, and watch the crowd. Then we would have a delicious fruit ice,* drink a glass of Noyeaux, and proceed to the San Carlos Opera, where we saw a number of pretty ballet dancers in amazingly short skirts, all of whom were kept by various notabilities in the city. As soon as the ballet was over we would visit certain houses, of which there were plenty in those days, where girls both young and pretty were to be found. We would usually return home about nine o'clock, and taking our seats at the *table d'hôte*, stop there drinking, arguing and laughing until eleven or twelve o'clock, when, feeling a little top-heavy, we would go to bed.

During the day we often made excursions either into the country or on the river, and took provisions with us ; or we would watch the processions on feast and holy days, of which there seemed to be a prodigious number. The most amazing procession I ever witnessed in Lisbon was one which was formed by a number of Christian slaves whose freedom from bondage had been purchased by a certain pious institution. There were about seventy or eighty of them. As I marvelled to see these people looking so well-fed and healthy, a Portuguese at my side informed me that the majority of these slaves are so well looked after by their masters in Algiers that they do not at all like the idea of being liberated. Slave and master, therefore, usually agree between themselves to share the purchase money, by means of which the slave becomes a free man ; the latter then proceeds to Lisbon, takes part in the procession, and finally of his own accord, sails back to Algiers by the first available ship, only to let himself be purchased again by the holy fathers of the mission a few years later, *et sic porro !*

Another equally strange and amusing sight was an auction which was held in a tent erected against

---

* This appears to be a forerunner of the " Dringer " invented by a Harrow boy in the nineteenth century.—Tr.

Lahmeyer's Hotel, the proceeds of which were for the benefit of a certain saint and his church or monastery. The perseverence with which a hired clown in a flaxen wig with huge spectacles on his nose, who played the part of auctioneer, attracted the people and induced them to laugh and outbid one another from morning to night by means of jokes, obscenities, cries, grimaces and tricks of all sorts, was perfectly marvellous, particularly in view of the great heat. The booth was filled with worthless trifles of every description, and any one who by out-bidding his neighbour drove up the price of a dove, for instance, to two dollars, was considered exceptionally pious ! Altogether the means by which the priests here extract money from the people's pockets are too numerous to be told.

But now let me return to my own private affairs. Among these I ought to mention that I had fallen hope-lessly in love with Lahmeyer's daughter, Minchen. She was an interesting girl, sixteen years of age, very pretty, fair, a trifle wild, but also good-natured, jolly and inge-nuous. Although she did not lack admirers, she seemed to show a preference for me. But it was a pity that she should have been spoilt by so much flattery, for it made her a flirt, and caused me such terrible pangs of jealousy that I sometimes thought my heart would break. The little witch, however, did not care a fig for this, and imagined that she would only gain a faster hold of me by tormenting me in this way. She went so far that at last I began to wonder whether my heart were really captured and my future happiness in her hands. When I spoke about the matter to her parents, who seemed very anxious to see us united, and pointed out to them that Minchen would be ruined by the flatteries of the gentle-men staying at the hotel, and of a certain maidservant, a very cunning young negress, who had succeeded in insinuating herself into her little mistress's confidence, they resolved to send her to the house of a relative named Behrens, a merchant in Setubal. When this gentleman came to Lisbon to have his child baptised as a Protestant, he fetched Minchen, and we accompanied her by water as far as Moita. But, as Mrs. Behrens was a bit of a shrew, who was very severe with Minchen and made her work very hard, the girl began to write such unhappy letters that her father and I were obliged to go to her to comfort her. A fortnight later, however, she declared she could stand it no longer, and as her mother had a soft heart, we had to fetch her back.

Meantime, while I had been living quietly in Lisbon, our army had been engaged both in battles and sieges, and whenever I read the reports of these events I regretted that I was not on the spot. On the 8th January, 1812, for instance, Lord Wellington laid siege to Ciudad Rodrigo, and twelve days afterwards, when the enemy had thrown 10,000 bombs and fired as many cannon shots, he stormed the place at nine in the evening, when the breaches were practicable, and carried it at the point of the bayonet. The storming of this fortress cost us in killed alone, two generals (Craufurd and McKinnon), six other officers and 140 men, while our wounded amounted to 60 officers and 500 men.* The German legion distinguished itself particularly in this affair. In the fortress we took 78 officers and 1,700 men prisoner, 109 pieces of ordnance, consisting of rampart guns on carriages, 44 cannon, a siege train, and an enormous amount of material. Despite the fact that it was winter, and the rain had flooded everything, including, of course, our trenches, and that the bridge we had been obliged to throw across the Agueda had once been washed away by the torrent, and that a formidable French army had concentrated in the neighbourhood to relieve the fortress, its investment, siege and capture were undertaken and effected with such unprecedented speed and boldness by Lord Wellington, that by the time General Marmont had at last mustered his army at Salamanca and marched down to the relief of Ciudad Rodrigo, it was already in our hands.

The town was repaired, re-victualled, and handed over to the Spaniards. Only one infantry division and a few

---

* Fortescue (op. cit. Vol. VIII., p. 366) gives our losses as 553, of whom 136 were Portuguese.—Tr.

cavalry pickets remained in the region of the Agueda, in order to mask the movement against Badajoz which Lord Wellington contemplated executing with his customary speed.   General v. Alten, with the 1st German Hussars, had taken up a position near Tenebron, between Ciudad Rodrigo and Salamanca, partly with the view of observing the enemy, and partly with the object of deceiving them concerning our withdrawal—which, considering the small number of troops at his disposal, was no easy task.   At first they were glad to be able to contain the enemy by means of well chosen positions ; when, however, General Marmont came ever closer and closer with the whole of his forces, General v. Alten was obliged to retire on Castel Branco in order to avoid being surrounded.   Not far from this town his vanguard, under Lieutenant G. Schaumann, had a stubborn fight with the enemy's advanced posts, in which the latter, thanks to the daring and good judgment of the said officer, were repulsed with great loss.   The moment Marshal Marmont retreated, General v. Alten quickly followed at his heels.

Among the prisoners that appeared from time to time in Lisbon there was a whole regiment of men from Hesse Darmstadt, who had been forced to lay down their arms in the citadel of Badajoz when this place was stormed. They were confined in the Castle dos Moros, where, as fellow-countrymen, we visited them, and with the permission of the governor, invited them in turn to dine with us. They were good fellows.   On one occasion my guest was a young subaltern who had been so grievously fleeced by our men in Badajoz, that he went about in a ragged uniform, coarse woollen socks, and regulation army boots. I discreetly refrained from asking him his name, and after the meal showed him round Lisbon, and took him to the opera. The following day his regiment was suddenly ordered to embark for England, and when I returned home in the afternoon, I found a farewell card from him, on which I was not a little surprised to read the name, " Franz Graf zu Erbach."

[TRANSLATOR'S NOTE.—Schaumann had applied again and again for an extension of leave, and this had been granted him.   When, however, seven months had elapsed in this way, he thought he could hardly postpone his journey to Sicily any longer, and made preparations to join his battalion there.   Nevertheless he was much exercised by the question whether it would not be better for him to resign from the 7th Battalion and remain in the commissariat.   His friends strongly advised him to do this, particularly as there seemed to be some doubt as to his chance of getting a pension as an officer in the German legion.   Had he known that Parliament was ultimately to grant half-pay to the officers of the German Legion, he would have remained in his regiment.   But he decided to remain in the commissariat, particularly as he had recently been promoted to the rank of Acting Commissary-General on 20s. a day.   Subsequently he learnt, however, that on re-entering the department, he would have to start afresh, in the rank of Deputy-Assistant Commissary-General, but his friends comforted him with the assurance that he would soon receive promotion again.   Meanwhile Commissary-General Sir Robert Hugh Kennedy had returned to Lisbon from England, and as Schaumann had finished his accounts, he accepted his proposal to rejoin the Army under him.   After purchasing a charger for £80, engaging the Lahmeyers' son Fritz as his clerk, and receiving a Mr. Stanley from England as a further assistant, Schaumann was ready to start.   The Lahmeyers had given him their cook, a fellow named Manoel, and on the 1st September, he received orders to rejoin the Army in Madrid, and to travel ahead of Commissary-General Kennedy, as the latter's quartermaster, and make provision for the comfort of himself and his staff at the various points along the road. Attached to Sir Hugh Kennedy's staff were Major Sir Edward Pellew of the 16th Dragoons, Commissary-General Aylmer, and a Mr. Coffin.]

Chapter 24

How Mr. Augustus Travels from Lisbon to Madrid—On the Way he has to Stop at Truxillo and Take Charge of a Large Stores Depôt—However, he Leads a Happy Existence, and is Ultimately Ordered Back to Portugal.

I WAS given the itinerary, and proceeded to pack and to pay my account at Lahmeyer's. The latter amounted to 700 Spanish dollars, or 1,400 gulden, for the whole of my stay from the 1st February to the 31st August, including the hire of carriages and other expenses. I then bade them all farewell, and noticed that Minchen Lahmeyer took my departure so coolly that I felt utterly dejected. At last, on the afternoon of the 2nd September, I boarded a boat which was to take me across the Tagus to Aldea Gallega, and the whole of the Lahmeyer family stood on the quay waving their handkerchiefs to me.

While I was seeing about quarters for Sir Robert and his suite, I must have caught cold, for I had such a violent attack of colic that I thought I should die. But as I had always to be a day's march ahead, I could not stay here ; so, plucking up courage and quaffing a large glassful of mulled wine, I started off at nine in the evening, with my staff, and a guide in the van, through the pine wood that lies behind Gallegas on the left bank of the Tagus. It soon grew so dark that I could scarcely see my hand before my face, and at about eleven o'clock, just as I was beginning to slumber in the saddle, my horse started and made such a sudden plunge to the side of the road that I almost lost my stirrups. What had happened ? A huge wolf, whose broad, powerful and dirty white breast and fiery eyes I was able to discern quite plainly, was lying stretched in the middle of the road. " A wolf ! A wolf ! " shouted my staff in terror ; whereupon the brute, at which I had quickly fired a shot, got up and ran away.

[TRANSLATOR'S NOTE.—Schaumann passes through Badajoz, where he sees the melancholy traces of the late terrible siege. On reaching San Pedro, near Merida, he hears that a convoy of mules had been attacked and plundered by robbers that day. On his arrival Sir Robert Hugh Kennedy advises Schaumann to procure an escort of Spanish militia before continuing the journey, but Schaumann scorns the suggestion. On the way to Truxillo they encounter a number of wounded English soldiers, travelling on donkeys to the hospital at Elvas. On reaching Truxillo, Schaumann finds that the local commissary, Mr. Dankaerts, is lying very ill with fever, and when Sir Robert arrives—for he had ordered a day's rest at Truxillo—he instructs Schaumann to take Dankaert's place, as the stores depôt is an important one. As Major Sir Edward Pellew, who had heard of Schaumann as a good cavalry commissary, had intended asking him to join his regiment, the 16th Dragoons, Schaumann is bitterly disappointed. But he is obliged to remain at Truxillo notwithstanding.]

I did not lack assistance here, for my *personnel* was large. An intelligent, energetic and fiery young Portuguese, called Manoel Antonio Gracio, who wrote a very good hand, and whom I found here, was particularly useful to me. A man like him did more work than three English clerks. Compared with my former heavy work with the light cavalry, my present post, although demanding plenty of energy and judgment, seemed to me like paradise. The current work was usually disposed of between 9 a.m. and 3 p.m., when we had an excellent dinner. After that we mounted our horses, and taking a couple of bullocks from the large herds under my charge, drove them on to the heath and goaded them to fury, whereupon my clerks and I, assisted by a few young Spaniards, proceeded to hunt them. This afforded us much good sport, as well as danger, and there were many somersaults. But we generally succeeded in dodging the animals round the many rocks and bushes about the place, and it was most amusing.

As I invited all officers passing through to dine with me, I had many visitors. One of these, who was on the Quartermaster-General's staff, told me a remarkable story. He had been sent from Seville with despatches from Lord Wellington, and, in the neighbourhood of Truxillo, had been stopped by the same band of robbers to which I referred in San Pedro. They took him prisoner, and conveyed him to their hiding place in the mountains. When he arrived there he found that it was a proper bivouac with huts, and that the band consisted of from sixty to seventy men. When he told them that he was bearing despatches, and that if they ill-treated, robbed or murdered him, Lord Wellington would wreak most drastic and terrible vengeance upon them, the robbers treated him very kindly, and not only gave him a hut, but also a good supper, and fed and attended to his horse into the bargain. On the morrow, after blindfolding him, they led him back to the main road, and wishing him the best of luck, allowed him to trot away.

On the 16th and 17th October General Skerret passed through with his Anglo-Portuguese troops. They had landed in Cadiz, taken the French garrison in Seville by surprise, and driven it out, and were now on the way to join Lord Wellington's army in Madrid. The victualling of this corps, which had a day of rest here, gave me plenty to do, but I was even more put out by the haughty and puffed-up attitude of General Skerret (as a matter of fact, he was only a colonel), who had just arrived from England, had seen very little service, and, unable to forget his heroic feat in Seville, had gone completely off his head.

[TRANSLATOR'S NOTE.—On the 24th October, 1812, Mr. Commissary Jolly arrives to relieve Schaumann of his duties.]

All things considered, I had done very well here, for one of the trifling advantages of a depot of this sort was that, without being able to reproach myself with the smallest suspicion of bribery, dishonesty or corruption, I was nevertheless able at the end of the short time I had spent here,* to remit over £700 to England to be invested in 4½ per cent. stock. Able at last to take a little rest, I stayed a few days in Truxillo and looked about the town. During my stay here I corresponded very diligently with Minchen Lahmeyer, whose epistolary style left a good deal to be desired. Born in Lisbon, she knew only Portuguese well, and, though she spoke German, French and English, she was not able, owing to insufficient study, to write well in these languages. Meanwhile, my passion for the girl cooled ever more and more, particularly in view of the fact that my friend, Captain Kemmester, who was still living at Lahmeyer's, and whom I had requested

---

* A little over a month. Schaumann left Lisbon on the 2nd September.—TR.

to keep a look out for me, wrote to inform me that she was carrying on rather ostentatiously with other men, especially with Lieutenant v. Estorff and a Portuguese purveyor, Senhor Sebatini, who also lived at the hotel. In fact, my informant feared that the latter would cut me out. I questioned very much, therefore, whether I should ever be happy with such a girl. She was too young and her education had been neglected, and I therefore decided, with a very sore heart, not to be in too great a hurry.

While I had been in Truxillo, Lord Wellington had tried to besiege Burgos, which was in command of the French General, Dubreton, but he had had to abandon it owing to lack of heavy guns and ammunition (he had only three heavy guns, five howitzers, and about 100 rounds of ammunition)*, and also because the castle was too well fortified, and, owing to its position, very difficult to attack. After munitions had arrived from Santander a breach was made on the 18th October, the place was stormed, and in spite of determined resistance, the first line was carried. Even the third line was escaladed by a detachment of the German legion, but it was lost again owing to a desperate counter-attack delivered by the garrison at the point of the bayonet. Although, with the help of the heavy siege train which was on its way from Santander, we confidently expected to batter Burgos sufficiently in two days to be able to take it, circumstances had so completely changed since the first days of the siege, that its capture was no longer of any consequence to us.

As soon as Wellington heard on the 21st October of the movements of Joseph and Soult on Madrid, he raised the siege of Burgos, marched his whole army away in the night under the very guns of the citadel, and crossed the bridge over the Arlanzon—a daring feat, performed without any loss, and by means of which he stole a march on the French General Souham, who was only able to catch him up on the 23rd. Then the whole of the French

* That is to say, three eighteen pounders, and five seventy-four-pounder howitzers. —Tr.

cavalry attacked our rearguard, dispersed the Guerilla cavalry, and pressed upon our cavalry, which consisted of only two brigades. The latter, having reached a deep trench, charged the enemy in vain, until the 1st and 2nd battalions of the light infantry brigade of the legion, under General Halkett, advanced and met the enemy with such a terrific salvo that they retired with heavy losses. Rather than take doubtful risks by giving battle to the enemy, who were twice as strong as himself, Lord Wellington preferred to allow his army an opportunity of resting and recovering themselves ; for what with sieges, forced marches, deficient victuals, bad roads and appalling weather, they were thoroughly tired and their shoes were almost worn to shreds.

While retiring across the wilderness of Spain, our army very often had nothing else to eat than pork (without either salt or bread, of course), which was obtained through our men hunting and shooting the pigs on their way as they came across them feeding in the woods on the acorns and chestnuts. Lord Wellington was so much infuriated by the slaughter of these pigs, as also by the many other irregularities inseparable from a retreat, that he afterwards, in an angry general order, administered so severe a reproof to the officers that all of them were most indignant at the injustice and discourtesy of its language. The army had really not deserved such a harsh rebuke.

On the 15th* our army left San Cristobal, near Salamanca, and continued its retreat on Portugal. Owing to the appalling weather that had just set in, and the lack of victuals, its condition became deplorable. The enemy, however, followed so close on its heels that on one occasion their cavalry actually succeeded in piercing their way between two divisions on our line of march, and taking General Sir Edward Paget prisoner. On the 18th headquarters reached Ciudad Rodrigo. The French retired, and our army went into winter quarters between Lamego and the Pass of Bejar. Headquarters were at Villar Formoso.

* This must be November.—Tr.

These events were in progress, when, on the 12th November, Deputy Commissary-General Prouth arrived in Truxillo and ordered the removal of all stores as quickly as possible to Elvas. As he had decided to leave on the following day, and I wished to enjoy both his company and the protection of his escort, I also prepared to march on the morrow. Many Spanish fugitives came through here. Early on the 13th November we started off with a large amount of baggage, and with an escort of twenty-five infantrymen to protect us against the robber bands that hung about between Miajadas and San Pedros. The whole of Truxillo seemed to mourn our departure as we marched away. Our first halt was at Miajadas, where we spent the night. From Miajadas we could plainly see the town of Merida, on the Guadiana, and we left it again on the 17th ; then, travelling *via* Montijo and Arronches, we reached Portalegre on the 22nd.

Just as we were leaving Portalegre on the morning of the 23rd we came across an old woman outside the town, of whom we asked our way, and for a long time we could not understand why it was that to all our questions she repeatedly replied that she had no wine, but that there was an inn up the road where we would find some. At last we discovered that she was stone-deaf, but as she believed that when an Englishman asked a question he was always in search of wine, she had made it a rule to answer all questions in the manner described. At last we reached Malha de Sarde on the 30th November, and decided to stay there, as, with headquarters at Villar Formoso, it would be impossible for us to find any accommodation there. I was shown a general order here which read as follows :

"SALAMANCA, 15*th November*, 1812.

" A. Schaumann, late lieutenant in the King's German Legion, is appointed to act as Deputy Assistant Commissary-General, the appointment to bear date the 1st September last."*

* The G.O. was, as a matter of fact, dated the 12th November, 1812, and ended, " this appointment to bear date from the 15th of Sept. last." He is now called " Schaumann."—TR.

[TRANSLATOR'S NOTE.—Detained until the 5th December at head-quarters by the task of settling his accounts, Schaumann was given his orders on the 7th and went with his staff to Coria. He followed the road along the Sierra de Gata, and travelled in the pouring rain through wonderful scenery to a village occupied by General Hill's infantry division.*]

We were given quarters in a house occupied by a number of officers. Owing to the swollen state of the river and the consequent destruction of the bridges, this infantry division had been cut off from their supplies, and had been living for two days on nothing but meat, acorns, and chestnuts. With my well-stocked kitchen hampers, I was a welcome guest among the officers at my quarters, and I was most respectfully given the place of honour at their table in the evening. While we were all sitting together drinking one night I wanted to leave the room on some errand, but forgot that the soldiers had removed the wooden banisters from the stairs leading to the lofty landing on which our room was situated. The consequence was that, walking along in the dark, I stepped over the side instead of turning to the right down the stairs, and thus fell 20 feet on to a hard stone floor below. At first I thought I had smashed my legs to pieces, but when they came with a light to pick me up, I found that I had only given my back and hips a bad jar. A certain captain, who occupied a small room in the house, gave up his bed to me, on the mattress of which, made of hard maize straw, I had to spend several days and nights in great pain, while being treated with camphor and spirit by the regimental doctor.

At last, losing all patience, I had myself lifted on to my horse and marched away. Fortunately my horse, a great grey beast, trod very softly, and it was only when by accident he jerked me that I gave vent to a loud yell of pain. The worst of it was that we had to ride through a number of rivers swollen by the rain, and the water often reached our saddles.

On arriving at Coria I heard from Mr. Aylmer, the commissary stationed there, that the 9th Dragoons had

---

* This was apparently the British 3rd Division.—TR.

had to move to Portalegre owing to lack of forage. As
there was no other way of crossing the Tagus except by
the bridge at Alcantara, we directed our march thither.
In a small village not far from Alcantara, where we wished
to spend the night, we found a portion of the 5th Dragoon
Guards, and as I knew my brother Edward was commissary to that regiment, I looked him up. Unfortunately,
however, he was away on business. On the following
morning, just as I was preparing to resume my journey,
I heard a shot fired, and shortly afterwards a howl of pain.
On reaching the courtyard I saw two baggage boys, one
of whom belonged to my staff and the other to my brother's,
run away like mad, and in the stable discovered my dapple
grey horse bleeding from one of his hind legs, and standing
with his fore legs in the manger. It turned out that the
little rascals had been playing with a loaded carbine,
which had gone off and shot my horse in the thigh. The
regimental vet. was called immediately, but as, after
careful examination of the wound, he found that no bone
or blood vessel had been injured, and that the bullet had
only pierced the muscle, the place was dressed with oint-
ment and lint, and we went on. The horse had such a
powerful constitution that such trifles did not affect him.
He was not even lame. I never again saw or heard of my
Portuguese boy, but by taking flight he certainly escaped
a sound thrashing.

At midday we reached the rocky banks of the Tagus
and the famous old Roman bridge leading to the town of
Alcantara, on the opposite bank. One of the arches of
this bridge had been blown up, and slung across the breach
by means of chains there was a plank bridge which was
being guarded by a detachment of English pioneers in
a hut. Charmed by the imposing beauty of the bridge,
we halted, and only the stamping and restless fidgeting
of our horses, who scented the stable, recalled us from the
ecstatic reverie into which we had fallen. Then, as we
could not dream that the inhabitants of Alcantara, who
were the descendants of the ancient Romans and the
hospitable Moors, could do anything but welcome us in
a manner befitting our position as Englishmen and their

protectors to boot, we rode cheerfully towards the town. But the Spanish commandant, who was just having his siesta, kept us waiting an eternity, and then not only received us very badly, but also gave us quarters which could not possibly have been worse.

We had been told that Lord Wellington, who was on his way to pay a visit to the Junta at Seville, was expected to pass through here. And, lo and behold, as we were contemplating the bridge, he unexpectedly arrived. The resident English officer on the quartermaster-general's staff met him at the end of the bridge, and handed him a plan, together with a report, while under the triumphal arch on the bridge he was greeted by the magistrate, the Spanish commandant, and a number of Alcantara people, who conducted him into the chapter-house. How simple, and yet how great, Lord Wellington again appeared on this occasion !

[Translator's Note.—Leaving Alcantara on the following morning, Schaumann marches towards Portalegre, which, owing to the accidents which befell him and his horse, he reached only on the 19th December. On the 23rd he left Portalegre and marched to Fronteiras, which he reached on the evening of the same day.]

WE were given quarters in the house of a wealthy
widow living in a narrow street, who gave us
the whole of the upper part of her house.
After reporting myself to General Long I took over the
regiment on the 27th December. My Portuguese
assistant, Senhor Gracio, who had left me at Portalegre,
and repaired to his home in Alter do Chao to fetch his
wife and sister-in-law, Donna Lucia, now arrived and
came to live in the same house with me, so that with
young Lahmeyer and my clerk, Mr. Stanley, my family
consisted of six people. We installed ourselves very
comfortably. I found the regiment very much the worse
for the hardships it had suffered after Madrid, and as a
result of the retreat. The horses in particular were
exceedingly thin. The brigadier, Major-General Long,
a good little man, who lived in Cabeza de Vide,* hardly
ever showed his face. The officers, who were mostly
young men of noble birth, and well versed in all the
dissolute pastimes of London, did not trouble much
about their regimental duties, nor did Major Gore, the
officer commanding the regiment. They would go out
riding, loaf about the market-place, hold races, devise all
kinds of *tours de force*, eat wonderful meals at mess, and
drink barbarously. These were their principal occupa-
tions. While engaged in drinking their favourite form
of entertainment was to tell the most salacious and obscene
stories and anecdotes, and once, when I dined at the mess
and could not refrain from expressing my astonishment
at this kind of amusement, they actually condescended
to offer me proper apologies for their detestable habits.
Nevertheless, I must admit that among the senior officers

* This is surely Cabeco de Vide, north of Fronteiras.—TR.

there were exceptions, who directly after mess spent the evening quite decently with me over wine and tea.

Fronteiras is a small town with cobbled streets. It shows traces of having once been fortified, and lies on a hill surrounded by other wooded hills. A thick olive wood stretched down from the town to a small river below, which was well stocked with fish. The country around was wooded and romantic, but was very unsafe owing to robbers. Nobody dared to go about unarmed. Not a day passed without a murder or robbery being committed. A certain robber chief, a terribly desperate fellow, who had quarrelled with his friends and been shot in the head by them, was found by shepherds in some bushes outside Fronteiras and brought into the town. He died the following day, swearing and grinding his teeth in his death agony. It was quite funny when the town undertook a crusade against this rabble. A few days previously the militia had been summoned; and on a certain morning marched out with drums beating. But the robbers, who were warned of this, naturally took to their heels, and the whole expedition proved futile.

Once, when I was standing in the market-place chatting with an old pensioned officer of the Portuguese army, a boy ran up to him and informed him that the whole of a supply of coffee, biscuits and tea, which he was bringing from Portalegre on donkeys, had been plundered by the robbers. Never shall I forget the poor devil's rage and despair. At first he lashed the air furiously with his Spanish cane ; then, clasping his hands above his head, he ran home, shouting as he went through the streets : " *Oh, minha incommenda ! minha incommenda !* " * The Juiz de Fora, for fear lest he should be shot in the street by one of the robbers in disguise, locked himself up in his own house, and would only take a walk if we went with him. But in spite of all this I used to ride out across the hills on business, and often took pleasure rides into the surrounding romantic country without any escort, though I always had my pistols loaded in my wallets.

We often went down to the river to fish. As a rule,

* " Oh my commission, my commission ! "—Tr.

the fishermen first made a dam, and then, binding two large bundles of reeds together, embarked on these strange craft and went out into the river to draw their nets. A remarkable feature of the river was the extraordinary number of turtles it contained. They were about 1 foot long and 9 inches broad, and were so greedy that they would bite the moment one threw out a line. As they were supposed to be good to eat, we took home a basket full of them. On the following morning, when I was on my way to the stores, I was surprised to see a number of turtles walking about the street. They were ours ! They had escaped from the basket in the night, had descended a long staircase into the yard, and creeping through a stone gutter in the wall of the yard, had reached the street, and were now all hurrying along with their heads turned instinctively in the direction of the river. When they had been well cooked, skinned and made into a fricassée we found the shoulders and legs of these turtles very good, and as white and tender as chicken. We also caught a few large fish, of which the river was full. I had a raft built of small empty rum casks, and then, sprinkling smutted corn over the surface of the water to stupefy the fish and make them rise to the surface and roll about as if they were drunk, we caught them with our hands.

On one of these fishing parties I invited a good many ladies and gentlemen from the town and one or two officers of the regiment, in addition to Senhor Gracio's wife and sister-in-law and the Juiz de Fora and his wife, and we rode down to the river on donkeys. But just as some of the younger members of the party had settled themselves on the raft and begun fishing one or two of the rum casks broke loose, and caused the raft to sink on one side. The whole of the fishing party thereupon very naturally sprang to the other end of the raft, and by overbalancing it caused it to turn turtle, so that they all fell into the river amid the most terrible outcry. Dry clothes were immediately fetched from the town for those who had had the ducking, and after they had changed their attire in a mill close by, tea was served on the grass with pastry, wine,

grog and cigars.   It was quite idyllic, and feeling grateful
to our God, we sat there comfortably regaling ourselves,
while now and again the ladies would sing tender melodies,
accompanied by the Portuguese gentlemen on their
guitars.

Thus the time went by, and when March arrived the
9th Dragoons suddenly received orders to hand over
their horses to the 13th Dragoons and embark for
England.   I was also notified that I should have to
accompany the regiment as far as Lisbon, and there take
over the 18th Hussars, who had meanwhile arrived from
England.

As I had had some experience of troops freshly landed
from home, who were unfamiliar both with the country
itself and with war conditions, and as I was also aware of
the ridiculous pretensions of English cavalry regiments in
general, and cordially detested them, my disgust may well
be imagined.   At first I tried as best I could to get out
of it, and requested to be allowed to join the 13th Light
Dragoons, whose commissary, Mr. Cundell, did not like
service with the cavalry, and wished to be relieved of his
post ; I even reported myself sick, and got my clerk,
Mr. Stanley, to take the 9th Dragoons to Lisbon.   But it
was no good.   I had now acquired the reputation of being
a good and experienced cavalry war commissary, and in
the end I had willy-nilly to swallow the pill.

The 9th Dragoons left Fronteiras on the 29th March ;
but as I had reported myself sick, I remained there until
the 8th April.   Then, putting my affairs in order, I took
leave of all my fair friends, who were in tears, and marched
off with my retinue, not without some qualms regarding
the local robber bands.   The ladies were on mules, and
we travelled to Alter do Chaõ, where I was quartered with
my clerk Senhor Gracio's parents-in-law, who treated me
splendidly.   Gracio's wife and sister-in-law remained
behind here, and we continued our journey *viâ* Abrantes
and Santarem to Cartaxo.   Here we despatched all our
baggage and horses by land to Lisbon, while we ourselves
embarked on a boat from the island of Mugem, and sailed
down the Tagus to the capital.   It was eleven o'clock at

night when we reached our destination and were put down at Lahmeyer's Hotel. My feelings for Minchen Lahmeyer had very much cooled. My rival, Mr. Sabatini, had taken up his abode at Lahmeyer's, and had turned my absence to such good account that Minchen seemed entirely devoted to him. As soon as I saw this I became most reserved, and, what with this and the prospect of my new post, I was not in very good spirits. At last the day for my departure arrived, and after I had sent my baggage and horses ahead to Saccavim I left Lisbon in a mule chaise with young Lahmeyer, who again wished to accompany me. My farewell to Minchen, who affected the most complete indifference, was cold and formal. On the 24th April I reported from Barquinha, where I had found quarters, that I had taken over my duties with the 18th Hussars. Mr. Hodson, a clerk, who until my arrival had discharged the functions of commissary for the regiment, was beside himself with joy when I came to relieve him. The description he gave of the ludicrous pretensions of the officers of the 18th Hussars was not an edifying one, though it was nothing new to me.

On the very morning that I reported myself to the commanding officer, the Right Honourable Lieut.-Colonel Murray, I had a mishap, for a horse that was being groomed by one of the men in front of his door bit me so savagely in the arm that it caused a violent swelling. Whether the tickling of the curry comb had driven it mad or not I do not know, but I was crippled for a week. Not a very good omen, I thought !

We had only been two days in Cea when the trumpets sounded and summoned us to move further afield. Our destination was Alverca. And now the dear old troubles with the forage started afresh. Every day we commissaries were called before Sir Colquhoun Grant* to be reprimanded, and to listen to peremptory orders and threats. Our protests and proposals, based upon the experience of many years, were as good as useless. He imagined that everything would be the same here as in

---

* Not to be confused with the more famous Colquhoun Grant, Wellington's intelligence officer.—Tr.

England, and thought it exceedingly strange that we should dare to contradict so great a man as he thought himself to be. Was he not six feet high, and had he not a huge black moustache and black whiskers ? Had he not in a dashing fancy hussar uniform, carried out the most brilliant cavalry parades on Blackheath ? And was he not in addition, aide-de-camp, equerry and favourite of the Prince Regent ? His whole manner bore the stamp of unbounded pride and the crassest ignorance, and he tried to conceal the latter beneath positive assertions which he did not suffer to be contradicted. We all came away from such interviews swollen with rage and righteous indignation.

We were only comforted by the consciousness of having done our duty to the best of our ability, and the knowledge that Lord Wellington, who was better acquainted with what could be demanded of the commissariat in this country, would be the first to put him in his place if he should venture to complain about us. Every dog his day, we thought to ourselves. I did not get the smallest help from the regiment. The whole crowd were like fledglings ; they only knew how to open their mouths to be fed. If anything was lacking the officers knew no other remedy than to exclaim to one's face in a cold and stately fashion : " I shall report it ! " How different things were in the 1st German Hussars !

As Lord Wellington wanted to inspect our brigade, we marched out on the 18th May. The ground chosen for the parade lay six miles beyond Freixada, on the way to Fresneda. It was a wonderful sight to behold these three regiments manœuvring with their magnificent horses. The 10th, the King's Own, were all mounted on half-blood horses worth from thirty to forty guineas apiece, while the officers' chargers were animals of a nobler breed and all thoroughbred horses worth 100 to 150 guineas, and more. Moreover, the 10th regiment wore scarlet shakos. Lord Wellington appeared with a brilliant staff. During the manœuvres poor Colquhoun Grant had to gallop himself almost to death, racing about *ventre-à-terre* with his brigade adjutant, Lieutenant Charles Jones, who was also adjutant to the 10th King's Hussars. The latter was a small man with fox-red hair, a red moustache and red whiskers, and he also wore a red shako. It was very funny to see him galloping behind the tall black-whiskered general, who wore an enormous three-cornered hat with a long fluttering feather ; and from that day those two were never spoken of in the brigade except as the black giant and his red dwarf.

At this parade proud Sir Colquhoun Grant, who, as the Prince Regent's favourite and equerry, expected to be most highly honoured by Lord Wellington and thanked in the most flattering terms, was to suffer his first humiliation ; for the Commander-in-Chief hated these puffed-up favourites who were sent out to him from England. At the end of the function, therefore, Lord Wellington turned his horse round sharply, and putting a hand to his hat merely galloped past Sir Colquhoun, shouting as he went in sonorous and very precise tones : " Grant ! If you will dine with me, I dine at six o'clock ! "

Never shall I forget Sir Colquhoun's face when he heard this laconic invitation. It was pitiable !—quite crestfallen ! Even the Prince Regent had never dismissed him as haughtily as that ! Out of respect for the Commander-in-Chief he could not decline the invitation, and he was therefore obliged to ride over to headquarters at Villar Formosa and back, a matter of at least four leguas, despite the fatigue occasioned by the parade. A good job, too ! Silently shaking his head, he looked sadly at Lord Wellington's back, and then gesticulating violently, he rode away with his red dwarf. " *Traga la, perro !* " * thought I.

Hardly had we returned home after the parade than marching orders arrived. We therefore broke up the camp and marched two leguas to Torre de Moncorvo, a large town, where we crossed the Douro in boats. As Torre de Moncorvo was very full I bivouacked in a garden, and in the evening bathed in a small waterfall which poured down into the garden from an old Roman wall as from an aqueduct. The Douro has a very strong

* " Swallow that, you dog ! "

current here. The town itself is fine, has good streets, a magnificent church, and an unfinished castle of some beauty, where the Alcade lives.

When we continued our march we met a peasant on a hill just outside Zamora, who showed us the French bivouacs on the other side of the town, and assured us that there were no more Frenchmen there. With our telescopes we could see the French quite plainly moving about like a swarm of bees in their bivouacs situated in a valley on the left of the town. But the sight so completely unnerved my foreman mule driver, Senhor Romero, that in a shaking voice, and trembling all over, he implored me to allow him to remain behind with his men, for he said if they should be caught by the French they would be hanged without mercy as Spaniards assisting the enemy. As none of my arguments made any impression upon this hare-brained individual, the only thing we could do was to order him and his men to remain on the spot to wait for us, while we, accompanied by our clerks and grooms, rode into Zamora. Near a mill situated on a hill in front of the gate of the town there was a crowd of people who welcomed us with cheers. Then we hurried on to the market-place, where the clatter of our horses' hoofs attracted numbers of people, who formed a ring round us. As they seemed to have taken our party for Lord Wellington's general staff, a magistrate's junta soon appeared in their frock coats, tall hats, and white silk stockings, in order to greet the supposed hero ; but these gentlemen soon turned up their noses when they discovered their mistake.

I recognised many old acquaintances in the crowd, among them Mr. Commissary Kearney's former host, in whose office I had done most of my work here, and I was just about to open negociations with him concerning corn, when suddenly a Spanish peasant elbowed his way through the crowd, and to my astonishment began to address me in English, speaking softly, but with great anger. " Schaumann ! " he said, " have you taken leave of your senses in daring to come into Zamora like this ? What do you want in this place ? Don't you know that the

French, whose sentries must have seen you long ago, and must already have despatched patrols after you, can pounce upon you here at any moment ? You are attracting the enemy's attention on the town again after they had left it, and by so doing you are compromising me, who yesterday evening came down the Douro in a boat in disguise, as a spy sent here by Lord Wellington. I beg you, for God's sake, to get out again as soon as possible." So saying he vanished. But I had recognised him. He was a Spanish colonel named Alava, and was on Lord Wellington's general staff. As soon as I had told my colleagues, Riddel and Jolly, what I had heard, we decided to withdraw, but in such a way as not to allow the Spaniards to say that we had run away like cowards from fear of the French. We therefore remained talking for a while, and took some refreshments that were offered us, and then, looking at our watches, and saying we should be back on the morrow, we mounted our horses and rode slowly away. In the crowd my assistant, Senhor Gracio's horse lost a shoe, and he had to remain behind at a blacksmith's close to the gate of the town to have the animal re-shod. But we rode slowly on.

When we reached the hill on which the mill stood, a priest ran out from the staring crowd, and coming up to us cried : " Senhores, save yourselves ! See, there is a strong French cavalry picket coming along to bar your way ! " And the next moment we saw twelve lancers galloping through the high corn and trying to reach the crest of the road before we could do so. As their horses were somewhat exhausted and out of breath from having galloped up a long hill, we rode slowly forward until they were about two yards from the road ; then, putting spurs to our magnificent English horses, and waving our hats, we charged down in front of them, and vanished from their sight like lightning.

On returning to the spot where we had left our mules we could not see them anywhere ; they had disappeared long before. We waited a whole hour for my poor Gracio, and as he did not come along, we gave him up for lost. I was the more distressed at losing him seeing that he had 50 dubloons, or about 150 gulden, of current coin in his valise, with which I wished to purchase some corn. I was so much worried by this terrible business that I was quite unable to sleep that night, and at dawn, hardly had the trumpets sounded the call to water and feed, than I was up and ready to ride to Zamora again, into which town Lord Wellington proposed to enter that day. The first sight that met my eyes as I came on to the market-place was my friend. Gracio, strolling along under the arcades, quietly smoking a cigar. He then informed me that the moment he had realised that he was cut off from us he had galloped back to the market-place, and had immediately been shown a house, where his horse had been concealed behind a stack of timber and he himself hidden in the cellars. The French had afterwards entered the town and enquired who we were and what we wanted, but no one had betrayed him. In the evening he had been fetched from the cellar, given a splendid supper and an excellent bed, in which he certainly slept better than we did in our cold and damp bivouac. In the morning they had given him chocolate and a good breakfast. I also heard that the French had retired in the night, and blown up the bridges of Zamora and Toro.

Our headquarters and the Guards now began to pour into the town, all the bells began to ring, and the guns to roar, and Lord Wellington, in his familiar grey cloak, entered the place amid the cheers of a huge crowd of people. He was received at the gate by the Alcade Major, the Junta and the Church dignitaries, who conducted him into the hall of a large building, where he was welcomed with long speeches and a sumptuous luncheon. General Sir Thomas Graham, afterwards Lord Lynedoch, sat by him. These hollow ceremonies seemed to be boring and painful to Lord Wellington, for he was not over pleased with the Spanish nation, and he had gathered that the French had not been at all unwelcome to the inhabitants of Zamora and Toro. He was very grave, talked only to General Graham, and did not touch any of the delicacies he was offered. The Spaniards, accustomed to their own and the French generals, who affected a sort of oriental pomp in their uniforms covered with gold lace, embroidery and stars, and always appeared surrounded by locust swarms of pretentious, dandified and voracious aides-de-camp, could not understand Lord Wellington's simplicity. " Is that Lord Wellington ? " they exclaimed ; " the man who is sitting there so meekly in a grey coat, has only one officer at his side, and will not eat or drink anything ? Good God ! "

On the morning of the 3rd June I went to Toro, three long leguas from Zamora. Not far from Toro the dress of the inhabitants changes, the red stockings of the girls being particularly noticeable. If they are asked why they wear red stockings here and brown ones in Zamora, all they reply very charmingly is : " Because it is the fashion, sir ! " * Toro is a pretty town. It stands rather high, is surrounded by old walls, and has a large and magnificent tower built in the purest Arabian style.

While I was looking about the place in search of corn, I suddenly heard a great noise, and discovered that a few hundred French cavalrymen, who had been taken prisoner, were being escorted into the town by a detachment from our brigade. Some of the latter told me that the French rearguard had made a stand the day before, not far from Morales, and had accepted battle, but that they had been terribly cut to pieces by our excellent brigade and had also lost a couple of guns.† What surprised me was the fact that the inhabitants of Toro, and especially the women, instead of receiving the French prisoners with curses, greeted them with much sympathy, and even shook hands with some of them, as if they had been old acquaintances, and distributed bread and wine among them. The peasants, however, did not share the townsfolk's love for the French.

I now hastened to rejoin my regiment, and crossing the scene of the combat of Morales that had taken place on the previous day, I made an excursion to Valladolid with one of my colleagues. My portion of the prize-money

* " *Es el stilo, Senhor !* "
† This is the combat described by Oman in Vol. VI., p. 331, of his History. He gives the number of prisoners taken as 208, but does not appear to mention the guns. —Tr.

for the horses and guns taken by our brigade amounted to
£20 sterling.   As, however, the bridge across the Douro,
which leads to this town, was destroyed, and only a ferry
was available, and as I feared that this excursion would
take me too far from the regiment, and lead to trouble,
I left one of my foremen drivers and the mules with my
colleague, who insisted on going into the town in search
of pleasure and also to purchase bread and corn.   Not far
from the town I admired one of the blockhouses, together
with a cavalry bivouac, which had been built by the French.
They had constructed numbers of these places along the
high roads to protect their communications with France.
If, however, a village happened to be conveniently
situated, and to contain a church, the latter was converted
into a fort.   All such posts, lying at a distance of about
three leguas from one another, were occupied by troops,
and constituted a small chain of forts extending right
across Spain to the French frontier.   All couriers, sick
convoys, and consignments of money, were, according to
their destination, escorted by the garrison of one of these
posts to the next, in order to protect them from the
attacks of the guerillas, and the escorts themselves were
relieved at each stage.   Now and again these small
garrisons would combine to form mobile columns, either
with the object of collecting contributions or of punishing
some refactory guerilla village by fire and plunder.

On the morrow I caught up my regiment, and on the
7th June we marched *en parade* through the large town of
Palencia, amid the thundering cheers of the inhabitants,
who, together with the women and the priests standing
on the balconies, waved their handkerchiefs at us.   Our
destination was Villaloban, where we encamped.   The
French, who were very much loved in Palencia—much
more so than in the country round about—had taken
away many pretty girls from the town when they left it.
Only the day before Joseph Bonaparte had concentrated
his army close to this town.   The Spaniards refer to this
monarch by the following names : *El Patrilla*—a dignified
old masher ; *el colosa de Rodas* (the Colossus of Rhodes),
el tio Pepe (Uncle Joseph).   The heavy rain that came

on in the night made our bivouac very wet, cold and uncomfortable. We were close to the rest of the cavalry, and our bivouac covered a range of hills at the back of the town. At midday on the morrow I rode up to the outposts and asked for four men to help me reconnoitre the villages lying between ourselves and the enemy for corn, bread and wine. In some of the first and largest we entered we were received in a friendly way by the inhabitants, but as the French had taken everything only that morning, and had warned the people that they would return in the afternoon and set fire to their homes if they heard that we had been given the slightest assistance, there was nothing to be done.

Then we rode on to a small village that was entirely deserted except for one deaf old woman who was washing clothes in a stream. Continuing our way we reached a mill on a height. From this eminence we perceived a French bivouac lying in a valley not very far away, and the French sentries were just in front of us. Hardly had the latter caught sight of us when they gave the alarm, and a picket of twelve chasseurs trotted out towards us. We waited until they reached the foot of the hill, and then retired slowly. The Frenchmen halted on the hill, and watched us as we rode away. On returning to our outposts I met General Sir Colquhoun Grant, who for the first time spoke to me in a friendly and affable way, and congratulated me on my courage. I reported the position of the enemy to him.

Very early in the morning of the 13th June we heard two terrible explosions, like claps of thunder, and very soon discovered that the French had blown up the castle of Burgos, and in their haste and imprudence had lost 400 men in the operation. When we reached our outposts we were able with our telescopes to see Burgos covered by a cloud of smoke, and shortly afterwards we saw the shattered ramparts collapse.

[Translator's Note.—Schaumann follows his regiment *viâ* Bivar, Ona and St. Martin to Puente Arenas.]

While our brigade remained stationed here our army

was concentrated on the 20th June, on ground lying
almost to the right of the enemy's flank, and separated
from the plain in which Vittoria lies only by a somewhat
lofty, but not very long range of hills.   Meanwhile, we
had fought a small engagement near St. Millan and Osma
and close to the River Bayas, with one or two French
detachments, who were on their way to join the main
army.   That same evening, after Lord Wellington had
reconnoitred the position, he began to make preparations
for the battle.   At dawn on the 21st June, just as I had
got up and crept outside my tent, Lord Wellington, with
a large staff, suddenly passed down the road which led
straight from the town to my tent.   I was still so drunk
with sleep that I was taken completely unawares by this
cavalcade, which I had not seen coming along, and my
attire and occupation at the moment they rode by was so
négligé that I saw many smiles among the grave and
fateful faces of Lord Wellington's party.   One of the
latter, the Spanish Colonel Alava, whom I knew particularly
well, rode up to me and said : " Schaumann, hurry up and
get mounted, there will be interesting things to see to-day.
This morning Lord Wellington is thinking of making a
heavy attack upon King Joseph, who is said to have taken
up a strong position with his whole army in front of
Vittoria.   If he makes a stand there will be a great
battle."

I dressed quickly, and after issuing the necessary
orders to my staff, had breakfast.   The whole bivouac
was busy preparing to move, but no one knew whither.
I rode in the direction that Lord Wellington had taken,
and soon found myself on the slope of some rocky
heights.   Below I could see a long and narrow valley
covered with cornfields, and broken by plantations, clefts,
ravines and villages, but the town of Vittoria was not
visible, as it lay concealed behind another range of hills.
In the clefts of the rocky slope on which I was standing
I noticed a number of red patches, the odd appearance of
which struck me as rather curious.   But when I looked
through my field glasses I recognised them as a brigade
of our infantry, who were quietly sitting on their knap-

sacks under cover, waiting for orders. Soon I also perceived the enemy, who were disposed in order of battle opposite to us. They had taken up a strong position. Their centre extended along the small River Zadorra, which runs in a southerly direction on the west of Vittoria. Their right wing rested on some hills above the village of Abechuco on the right bank of the river. Their left wing was thrown back far away to the other side of the river, and rested on the village of Subijana de Alava. In front of the latter, however, a weak corps had taken up a strong position on the lofty Puebla heights, in order to act as a support to the centre, which, as it formed a pivoting point, was comparatively feeble. In this way the enemy covered all the three main roads which converge on Vittoria. On a dominating height on the right of the French centre, there fluttered a large white flag. It marked the spot where French headquarters, and consequently, King Joseph, were posted. It is an imposing sight to behold a strong enemy army in order of battle. Lines and columns are in process of formation. Generals and aides-de-camp gallop busily up and down the dark lines, and here and there a gun is fired as a signal. On our side, the infantry are striking their flints, or getting their cartridge boxes ready. Guns, followed by their ammunition carts, rattle into position, aides-de-camp gallop in all directions carrying their general's orders to the heads of the columns that are forming. The moment which is likely to bring ruin, death or victory, draws steadily nigh. Calmly and coldly stood our lines. Every heart seemed to be cheered by the thought that to-day for the first time we should be equal in numbers to the French ; we should be able to measure ourselves against them man for man, put our physical strength in the balance, and consequently gain a victory. On the march here we were joined by Generals Giron, Longa and Morillo, with about 14,000 inferior troops.* With these our army numbered about 74,000 men, and the French only 60,000.† If, therefore,

* Napier (*op. cit.*, Vol. V., Book XX., Chap. VIII.) estimates the Spanish auxiliaries at over 20,000.—Tr.

† *Cf.* Oman (*op. cit.*, Vol. VI., p. 388), who gives Wellington's force as 75,000 and the French 57,000.—Tr.

we regarded the Spanish host as mere ciphers, we were
equal in number to the French.   But the French were
superior to us in artillery, while they also had this advantage, that they were drawing ever closer and closer to the
supplies and depots of their base, whereas we were getting
ever further away from ours.   It was a heavenly morning,
bright and sunny, when, at about eight o'clock, we heard
the rattle of musketry fire behind the lofty heights on our
right.   It ultimately spread to the very ridge of the hills,
and was slowly extended towards the left.   The bright
morning sunshine, the gloomy wooded hills, the flash of
the muskets, the rolling thunder of the fire, and the
wonderful shapes formed by the smoke in and out the
groups of trees covering the hills, lent a picturesque
grandeur to the scene, which it is difficult to describe.   In
order to get a better view of the whole, I rode out to the
left, on to a convenient open height.   Our army was now
marching down from the hills in three columns towards
points at which it was to attack.

The Battle of Vittoria

THE battle opened with a cavalry skirmish. In the course of the fight the divisions composing our left wing crossed the Zadorra in rapid succession, and seizing the high road to Bayonne, threw back the enemy's right, centre and left towards Vittoria, so that, apart from the road to Pampeluna, no other means of retreat remained open to them. All these manœuvres were accompanied by such heavy artillery fire from both sides that the earth shook, and every time the guns abated a little the French could be seen gradually abandoning every village, every height and every position, and falling back in confusion on Vittoria. In all directions there was nothing but fire, smoke, moving columns, troops forming square or occupying conquered heights, dead and wounded men and horses, and shelled houses and trees ; while weapons of all kinds, forage caps, strips of uniform, cartridge boxes, paper cases, buttons and shoes covered the ground. The standing corn was trodden under, and the broad paths across it marked the passage of the troops.

As Vittoria was surrounded on both sides by gardens, vineyards and trenches, the French had only one road open to them, and that was the one through the town. The streets of Vittoria, however, had become so badly blocked by retreating guns, whose horses had dropped, either wounded or exhausted, as they galloped to the rear, that, in order to reach the gate on the far side of the town, the retreating infantry had either to climb over these obstacles or else work their way with the cavalry through narrow side streets, or reach the high road by breaking down the garden walls round the place, and thus force their way out. Owing to the mad raging throng that soon collected, the French were not only prevented from saving their remaining large guns, but also lost their baggage and the whole of King Joseph's household goods, which lay

outside the town.   All the officers in charge of transport
had packed up, but, in their light-hearted belief in victory,
in which they had been encouraged by King Joseph
himself, instead of retreating, they had all remained close
to the town; aye, and in the town itself a great banquet
had been ordered, at which the French expected to
celebrate their victory over the English.

While the French were retreating through Vittoria our
army tried to force its way through the town on the north
and south by tearing down the garden walls.   A detachment of the 10th Hussars (The King's Own) of our
brigade were the first to get round the north side of
Vittoria, and reach the main road leading to Pampeluna.
There they were just about to bar the road to a fine
travelling coach drawn by eight horses, when they were
held up by a broad trench.   Nevertheless, their sudden
approach caused the coach to stop, and as it did so a
number of officers descended from it, sprang on to some
horses that were being led behind, and galloped away.
Among these officers who escaped from our hussars
was King Joseph.   As our army had been fighting all day
without anything to eat or drink, and was very much
exhausted, it bivouacked partly north and partly in front
of the town (except the Guards, who remained in Vittoria),
and leaving the French to their retreat, plundered their
baggage, which was lying about everywhere.

I marched to within about a legua of the town, where
I let my staff bivouac in a field on the right of the wood
while I repaired to Vittoria.   In two villages through
which I passed it was heartrending to hear the cries of the
wounded, who were being collected.   Everywhere we
could see French guns, the blackened muzzles of which
showed that they had been diligently used.   On each of
them there was a name, as for instance, *Egalité*, *Liberté*,
or *Fortune*.

It was already dark when I reached the gate of the town
and found it guarded by a strong detachment of horse-
guards, who forbade admittance to all.   But when I
declared that I belonged to the general staff, they allowed
me through.   English headquarters and the Foot Guards

were in the town. After wandering about for a long while, a Spaniard at last conducted me to a hotel crammed with English officers. With great difficulty I found room for my horse, and left him in the care of a Spanish servant belonging to the hotel, who, in exchange for a handsome sum, undertook to feed and look after him. Then, in a large room I found two long tables spread for a meal (tables at which French officers had arranged to feast after their victory), and seated at them about 150 English officers of all ranks and regiments. Famished as we were, we devoured everything that was placed before us. The dishes consisted chiefly of roast mutton and various birds, and were very well cooked. But what was most welcome to our parched lips was the wine—Médoc, Burgundy and Champagne—all of which the hotel waiters evidently thought must come from Bordeaux, for they called it all by the same name, that is to say, *Vino de Bordeaux*, and they pronounced the latter word *Borde-auchs !* I had neither seen nor tasted these wines since the year 1803 ; for in England, owing to the high import duty, old Hock and Claret cost 21*s.* a bottle. Accustomed as we had been for years to the hot and heavy wines of Spain and Portugal, and thirsty as we were, we could not stop partaking of these wines, which the landlord had stocked with the view of pleasing the French, and which we now quaffed out of huge Spanish tumblers. Everybody was shouting : " Taste this one, taste that one ! " And we tasted so often that not one of us remained sober. At last, overcome by sleep, we ached for beds, and the land-lord and his men were obliged to bring every available mattress, cushion and blanket down into the dining-room, where they spread them all along the walls. Upon these extempore couches we dropped pell-mell, with our spurs and everything on. A few officers who were completely drunk remained lolling on their chairs, or fell under the table, while others who could find no beds lay on the table itself. At five o'clock everybody got up hurriedly and hastened away.

I, too, mounted my horse, partly with the view of looking for my staff, and partly in order to inspect the town, in which the most horrible confusion seemed to prevail. Carts laden with English, Spanish and French wounded bore their melancholy loads to the various convents which had been selected for hospitals. Wounded officers, with their uniforms covered with blood and dirt, could be seen proceeding on horses, mules or donkeys, led by their men, to the quarters allotted to them. Some of them were already half dead, and the others looked exhausted, weak and suffering. Columns of French prisoners were brought in and locked up in the churches. Spanish troops, headed by their bands, entered the town to occupy it. Large convoys of laden mules, carts and baggage, belonging to our army, passed along the streets. Detachments of English soldiers could be seen about the town, while the inhabitants, who had long been groaning under the yoke of the French, seemed to be astonished at their sudden release.

The ground all round the town was littered with broken wagons of all kinds, boxes, cases, trunks and baggage, while masses of papers, maps, account books, and letters lay about as thick as snow. In their lust of plunder the soldiers had not only torn the cushions and seats of vehicles, and the enemy's palliasses, and strewn their contents abroad, but they had also pilfered all the wagons and boxes belonging to the civil and military accountancy departments of the army, and scattered the lists, letters and documents that had been accumulated for years. I saw huge and beautifully kept ledgers belonging to the Royal Treasury, wonderful maps, and expensively bound books from the Royal Field Library, trodden under foot, and sodden with the rain that had fallen during the night. Surely never before in the history of the world can such losses in artillery of all kinds, and in baggage, have resulted from a single battle, not to mention the indescribable confusion in which one after the other of the enemy's corps was repulsed. Our rapid advance left them no time to clear obstacles out of their way. Transformed into a riotous mob, and only scantily covered by their cavalry, they rushed through Vittoria like a torrent. The nature of the ground, together with the walls and trenches round the town, made it impossible for them to save their artillery, their baggage and their transport. And so little had they anticipated the disaster that befell them that even the most prominent people of the Court had to escape with their wives as best they could, and many of them, fleeing across the fields with their children, were obliged to follow the army on foot. Even rich Spaniards of high rank were obliged to turn their backs on their own property, and cross the frontier like beggars, barefooted and hungry. Numbers of ladies and gentlemen of the Court, and the wives and mistresses of officers, who had come upon the scene as if to witness a review, and eagerly expected to behold the flight of the English, fell into our hands with all their fine equipages.

Our losses in dead and wounded amounted to about 5,000.* Many of our men, and particularly those who found diamonds, became rich people that day ; but many others who only found Spanish dollars and silver ingots among the royal treasure and plate which they plundered, were unable to carry their spoil with them, and had to throw it away. Again and again I was offered a whole shako full of Spanish dollars in exchange for a guinea, a napoleon, or any gold piece, but I was obliged to decline the offer, not only because I had no gold pieces with me, but also because I could not carry such a load of Spanish dollars about with me. The unmarried ladies belonging to the French army, most of whom were young and good-looking Spanish women, dressed in fancy hussar uniforms and mounted on pretty ponies, or else conveyed in carriages, were first robbed of their mounts, their carriages and their jewels, and then most ungallantly allowed to go. But, as all they wanted was protection and a new lover, both of which they soon obtained, they were to be had for the asking.† In some cases, particularly over the plundering of the wagons carrying the war treasure, our

---

* Cf. Oman (op. cit., Vol. VI., p. 446) : " The allied casualties were just over 5,000, of whom 3,672 were British, 921 Portuguese, and 552 Spaniards."—Tr.

† In his " Notes of Conversations with the Duke of Wellington " (third edition, p. 144) Stanhope reports the following words spoken by the Duke about Vittoria : " One of their prisoners said to me after the battle, ' Le fait est Monseigneur que vous avez une armee, mais nous sommes un bordel ambulant.' "—Tr.

men fought to the death.* No officer dared to interfere. In short, more thorough and more scandalous plundering has never been known, and I heard later that Lord Wellington was most indignant and angry about it ; for what the men could not take with them they broke up, tore up, and scattered in all directions.

Meanwhile English officers in charge of detachments were left behind in Vittoria, to collect all the French guns and take them into the town in safety. The French had only been able to save one howitzer and one cannon, and even these were recovered from them the following day. I saw a number of Spaniards on the battlefield (many of whom were smoking cigars) busily engaged plundering the French ammunition wagons and stealing the gun cartridges. I heard afterwards that, owing to carelessness, one of these wagons blew up and killed a number of men.

* Napier (*op. cit.*, Book XX., Chap. VIII.), says that out of 5,500,000 dollars in the money chests of the French, not one dollar came to the public. *Cf.* Oman (*op. cit.*, Vol. VI., p. 448) : " Wellington had hoped to secure the 5,000,000 francs of the French subsidy, which had just arrived at Vittoria before the battle. His expectations were deceived ; only one-twentieth of the sum was recovered."—Tr.

Chapter 27

March to Pampeluna—Fight in the Pyrenees—Life in Olite and Oscotz*
during the Blockade of Pampeluna—St. Sebastian is taken by Storm—
Pampeluna Capitulates.

AS the army started off early in pursuit of the enemy, I had to hurry up and find my regiment. A few marches brought us on the 24th June, 1813, to Aizurain,† where we bivouacked partly alongside of the high road, and partly in houses in full view of the town and fortress of Pampeluna. In the country beyond Vittoria the people speak Basque, and as this language bears no resemblance to any other tongue either living or dead, it was utterly incomprehensible to us. It is said to be the language that was spoken by Tubal, Noah's nephew, who came to Spain 143 years after the flood. But as the inhabitants also spoke Spanish we were able to make ourselves understood. The Biscayans boast that there is neither any Moorish nor any Jewish blood in their veins, that their language existed long before the Romans subjugated Spain, and that they still speak it as purely as they did then. The Spanish monarch does not rule as a king over the Basque provinces, which possess their own ancient rights, but only as a Senhor.

The country through which we marched between Vittoria and Pampeluna is very picturesque and romantic. Unfortunately, owing to the incessant rain, we had a good deal to put up with, particularly during the first two stages.

Our regiment had been ordered at the battle of Vittoria to hurry through the town, but being held up by the crowd and treated to wine by the inhabitants, it had got drunk and become dispersed. This had given it time to plunder the royal baggage, and our men were therefore loaded with spoil. When we halted and bivouacked in the evening, a great jumble sale was held, which afforded us much amusement. The royal kitchen wagon had been rifled and a number of delicacies taken. Every officer, for

---

* This appears to be meant for Ostiz.—Tr.
† Schaumann probably means Irurzun.—Tr.

instance, got a hermetically-sealed tin which when opened disclosed a wonderful roast joint or fowl in aspic, perfectly fresh and delicious to the taste. Some of these tins contained preserved fruit or jam. Every evening some of these tins were opened, and we enjoyed them immensely.

The French, in full flight after Vittoria, had reached Pampeluna in the utmost confusion ; and when they had reinforced the garrison there, and devastated the plains all round in order to supply the fortress with provisions, they continued to retreat at top speed into the Pyrenees, at the foot of which Pampeluna lies. Meanwhile, we kept so close on their heels that their rearguard had hardly left Pampeluna before the guns from the ramparts of that fortress began to fire upon the left wing and centre of our pursuing troops. On the 26th June we marched to Noain, three leguas beyond Pampeluna. In the afternoon the enemy attacked so suddenly that in our haste we hardly knew what to catch hold of first. In the confusion I lost, among other things, a silver mounted buffalo's horn, which I was in the habit of filling with wine and hanging from my saddle on the march. On the 28th June we marched from Olite viâ Caparozo to Tudela, and bivouacked close to the other divisions in fields and woods near Caseda. Another jumble sale of Vittoria plunder was held in this camp. I purchased a whole sackful of candlesticks, teapots, silver ingots bearing the treasury mark, plates, knives and forks for half their proper value ; also a chamberlain's coat of blue velvet and gold lace. Some infantry officers showed me some priceless sporting guns inlaid with gold which had belonged to King Joseph, and a good deal of personal underclothing consisting of superfine shirts and silk stockings. The latter had " J " embroidered on them in red silk, surmounted by a crown, which proved that they were the property of the King. What astonished us most, however, was the vast number of military and court uniforms, belonging either to the King, his marshals, or to other dignitaries and officials of his entourage, made either of fine cloth, or brown, blue and scarlet velvet, and covered with gold lace. We had jackets and forage caps made out of them.

Nearly every officer in our brigade had one of them. Watches, crosses of the Legion of Honour, and gold stripes were to be had by scores. The crosses of the Legion of Honour were bought up at any price by our vindictive Spanish muleteers, and slung on their mules' tails with the view of casting scorn and mockery on the French.

On the 30th June we returned to Olite. On arriving at our quarters I felt thoroughly exhausted by the exertions we had made. For, in addition to my duties as commissary, the constant long marches; which were trying even to the brigade, made my life quite intolerable. Every morning at three o'clock the trumpets called us to water and feed, at four o'clock to saddle and bridle, and at 4.30 to march. As a rule it was still dark when we left our night quarters. The cavalry soldier, however, as everybody knows, has got to go out into the fields to cut corn and forage not long after he has turned into bivouac. Now we hardly ever halted to bivouac until late in the afternoon, and frequently had to ride a distance of two or three miles to water. Then we had to draw our rations, divide them up with our fellows and cook them. So by the time we had seen to our saddles and appointments, and cleaned them, it was frequently ten or eleven o'clock before we got any rest, and even then some disturbance in the horse lines would wake us up during the night. So that when the trumpet blew again at three in the morning we were necessarily very tired, and being drunk with sleep it was not unnatural that many of us were difficult to rouse. Thus it happened that first this and then that regiment of our brigade would turn up a few minutes late on parade, and when this occurred, our commanding officer, Sir Colquhoun Grant, who had had no experience of war, and seemed quite ignorant of the circumstances I have just described, would curse and swear and rave like a madman. Waited on as he was by a team of servants in some comfortable house, and given an excellent dinner, he was able to retire early to a good feather bed, and sleep his sleep out, and could naturally reach the parade ground first and in comfort. His favourite procedure on these occasions was to order the regiment that appeared first on parade to march off and form the head of the column for that day, and to ride over the regiments that were not ready. But the regiment thus selected for the lead was too shrewd to do this ; for had they done so it would have led to a fight to the death.

Opposite one of the gates of Olite there stood a castle which had recently been destroyed by General Mina ; opposite the other gate was a large convent. The plain in which the town lay was dusty, the heat was terrific, and the inhabitants gloomy and ill-natured. This was particularly true of the agricultural labourers, who used to walk through the streets at night in gangs, and carried carbines under their cloaks. They were so jealous that no hussar was safe whom they saw joking with a girl. They actually killed two men of the 10th Hussars close to the gate of the town, and tore their eyes out. The eyes were found afterwards about twenty feet away from the bodies. They used to shoot from the street at the window of my chief muleteer, when he was quietly lying in his room at night, and the bullets almost grazed his ears. When our adjutant, Duperrier, and the officers of the brigade were returning home at night, after a grog party at my house or elsewhere, they frequently had to fight their way through this mob with their swords and compel their respect. One evening they even wounded one of my Portuguese mule boys, who was quietly sitting on my doorstep, and they would have killed him if my man Manoel, who was as strong as a giant, had not gone to his assistance.

And they would have killed me, too, but their attempt to do so only ended in their wounding my poor Manoel, who got a small bullet through his neck. The plot to kill me (either owing to my foraging parties, or to the fact that I was on intimate terms with many pretty women and girls) only failed because the brutes fired too soon and in too great a hurry. Directly after the shot was fired, a troop of them passed by with guitars and castanets, playing a sort of serenade through the streets ; but probably, all they wished to do was to ascertain as they went by what effect the shot had had. When I complained to the mayor about this and other similar incidents, very drastic inquiries were instituted, but they led to nothing. Incidentally, Manoel recovered.

In Olite I had plenty of love affairs. In the first place there were the Donnas Francisca and Stephania from Seville, the daughters of a wealthy landowner, who were very responsive. Then in Lieutenant Bäcker's house there was a handsome beauty who was the wife of a Spanish colonel, and who took no pains to conceal her attachment to me. I also had a pretty girl who paid me many visits ; and finally the legitimate spouse of an organist, who always availed herself of her husband's duties in the church in order to come to me. I therefore had plenty of variety.

While we were here the liberation of Spain from the French yoke, and the proclamation of the acceptance of the constitution by the Cortes in the name of Ferdinand VII., was publicly celebrated. A throne was erected in the market-place, on which a portrait of the King was placed, and in front of this the Alcalde read the constitution aloud.

One day the famous General Francisco Espozy-Mina passed through the town. He was in command of a guerilla of about 5,000 men in our neighbourhood, and did endless damage to the French cause. He ruled and lorded it to such an extent in this part of Spain, and was so independent and powerful, that he was jokingly called the King of Navarre. The whole town went out to meet him when he came through, and the people kissed his hands, the hem of his garment, and his sword. Very much inflated with pride at all these attentions, his behaviour all too frequently betrayed his lowly origin and his total ignorance of decent manners and decorum. Once I sent one of my convoy leaders to him with a respectful and courteous letter begging him to send one of his commissaries to see me. This man had overrun the whole country, and had been guilty of many acts of violence, even in our cavalry district, and I wished to come to an understanding with him concerning the boundaries of the districts in which we should have the right to

forage—such boundaries to depend upon the particular
position of our respective troops.   In this way I hoped to
put an end to all strife.   Not only, however, did the
general not answer this letter, but he dismissed my convoy
leader, a Spaniard, with the threat that if ever he dared to
come again with such a letter, even if it were written by
Lord Wellington himself, he would lay him across a
bundle of straw and have him soundly thrashed by two
corporals.

While we were here Lord Wellington's wrath at last
descended upon the officers of the 18th Hussars, who had
lingered in Vittoria in order to plunder.   They had been
expecting it long enough, and as the result of a report
despatched to England, their promotion was suspended
for twelve months.   As, moreover, the officers of the 10th
Hussars had hatched all kinds of plots against their chief,
Colonel Quentin, whom, as a foreigner and a favourite
equerry of the King, they heartily loathed, and the whole
brigade accused Sir Colquhoun Grant, our commander,
of untruthfulness, and of having maligned them to
Lord Wellington, the result was that Sir Colquhoun in the
first place received a sharp rebuke from the Marshal for
all these irregularities, and then fell into disgrace.   And
this so deeply humbled his pride that he went about like
a whipped dog.   "*Traga la perro!*"   I thought.   In
order to complete his misery the officers of the 10th made
a caricature of him, in which he was ludicrously repre-
sented on horseback with his adjutant, Captain Jones,
galloping along behind him, and under the drawing they
wrote the inscription "The Black Giant and his Red
Dwarf."   Then they stuck this up on the public notice
board of the town on which the mayor exhibited his
official orders.

Meanwhile, during our peaceful sojourn here, General
Graham had besieged St. Sebastian with 10,000 men, the
Count of Bispal had blockaded Pampeluna with 10,000
Spanish troops, and the French had again made a stand,
this time beyond the Pyrenees, which led to the "Battle
of the Pyrenees."

On the 14th September we suddenly received marching

orders, with the result that, with much rejoicing we left the inhospitable and gloomy assassins' nest known as Olite.   As far as I was concerned, the change was opportune, for what with the heat and my lovemaking with the ladies of the place, I was feeling very low, and my ague showed signs of returning.

[Translator's Note.—Schaumann marches with the brigade, and reaches Oscoz* on the 20th September.   He instals himself comfortably, and, as usual, entertains the officers of his brigade very hospitably in his quarters, providing them with grog parties and a warm fire every evening.]

Oscoz was a fairly large and flourishing village, with houses built in a style which was reminiscent of Switzerland.   Owing to the high altitude, the maize had not yet been harvested.   The inhabitants spoke only Basque. The girls were pretty, and wore their hair in two long plaits, the tails of which were bound with pale blue silk ribbon.   We were not so lucky with these Basque girls as we had been with the Spanish women ; for they were shy, and we did not understand their language.   But we consoled ourselves with the beauties among the soldiers' wives, whom we courted in the fragrant woods and with whom we dallied on the grass and among the flowers.

The people cultivated flax on a large scale, and also span, though not with the spinning-wheel, but in the old style, with the distaff in one hand and the spool turned on a wheel by the other.   Bullock-carts were used for transport by the farmers, but as the roads were rocky and bad, the bullocks were shod.   For this purpose a special stall stood at the door of every blacksmith, by means of which the bullock was hoisted into the air and his hoofs stretched back and secured.   The process of shoeing the brute is rather comical, for, while it is taking place, the bullock looks extremely abject and has a most pitiful expression on his face.

Not far from Oscoz, in the environs of which there is a great deal of picturesque and magnificent mountain scenery there was the great Etchicharte Pass, through which, not far from Letassa and Irurzun, the road to Tolosa runs.

* This again is meant for Ostiz.—Tr.

Meanwhile the siege of St. Sebastian had been continued with the utmost vigour. On the 31st August, after the breaches had been made, the place was stormed for two hours. At last we succeeded in entering the town through the breaches, and in driving the French into the citadel, which was situated on a lofty height. As, however, the inhabitants had made common cause with the French in defending the town, our men showed them no mercy, and accounted for them all with their bayonets. The whole of Spain re-echoed with the tale of the barbarity shown to the Spanish by the English troops on this occasion, but no word was said about the treachery of the Spaniards in the town.*

Pampeluna capitulated on the 31st October, after a blockade lasting four months. The garrison, which from all accounts had held out so long that all provisions— aye, even to the last rats, cats and dogs in the place—had been consumed, became prisoners of war. Early on the morning of the 31st young Lahmeyer and Mr. Stanley rode over to Pampeluna to have a look at the town, while I was obliged to remain at my post, as marching orders were expected at any moment. The orders arrived so suddenly on the 1st November at midday that our food, which was cooking on the fire, had to be thrown away half raw. Our road led from beyond the village of Oscoz upwards across some lofty wooded heights. Never shall I forget it. The roar of the mountain streams, mingled with the cry of the eagles, the sound of our horses' hoofs and the singing of the hussars, made a curious melody. Now and again we would meet a Biscay peasant, looking blooming and robust, with his blue baretta on the side of his head, and his cloak carried on his mountaineer's stick ; and as he leapt lightly and boldly past us across the rocks in his sandals, he would greet us affably. Higher up we

* St. Sebastian fell on the 8th September, and, according to Napier (*op. cit.*, Book XXII., Chap. II.), the villainies perpetrated by the storming troops " would have shamed the most ferocious barbarians of antiquity." Napier continues : " At Ciudad Rodrigo intoxication and plunder had been the principal object ; at Badajos lust and murder were joined to rapine and drunkenness ; but at San Sebastian the direst, the most revolting cruelty was added to the catalogue of crimes. One atrocity, of which a girl of seventeen was the victim, staggers the mind by its enormous, incredible, indescribable barbarity." —TR.

came upon a number of peasants employed and paid by Lord Wellington's general staff, who were levelling some of the more dangerous portions of the road with bundles of wood and logs and making them practicable for artillery. Very often the road ran alongside a precipice, down which, if a horse slipped or shied, both horse and rider plunged and perished. Here and there we came across some snow. When we came to a sudden sharp turning on the ridge of the mountains, a magnificent panorama presented itself to our view, reaching as far as the Bay of Biscay, and we even fancied we could discern the fields of France.

After a march of four leguas we reached Donna Maria, a straggling sort of village lying in a valley high up in the mountains. Having business with the mayor, I found myself in the village hall, which consisted of only one room on the level of the ground, and I was surprised to see that it was being used as a barber's shop; for there were a number of peasants waiting to have their chins shaved, and some of them seemed to have a rather plentiful growth of beard. The shaving was performed without soap or water. Every stroke of the razor made it ring as if it were being used to mow dry thistles, and the peasants who were being shaved sat there with the tears coursing down their cheeks and the skin of their faces flaming red.

The weather, which had been fairly good for some time, now became intolerable. Every day we had storms, rain, hail and snow, and the roads became impassable. On the 10th November we reached Sare.* This was because Lord Wellington was taking the offensive again, and was about to carry out a big manœuvre. Our army was divided into three corps. The corps on the right, under General Hill, consisted of the divisions of Stuart, Clinton and Hamilton, a Spanish division under Morillo, and our cavalry brigade under Sir Colquhoun Grant. The corps on the left, under Sir John Hope, was made up of Howard's and Oswald's divisions, two Portuguese brigades under Wilson and Bradford, and an English brigade under Lord Aylmer; while the centre corps,

* Schaumann probably means Sarre.—Tr.

under Marshal Beresford, had the divisions of Colville, Cole, and the Portuguese General Le Cor. Our flanks were covered by the light division under General Carl v. Alten, the Spanish army under General Giron and Don Manoel Freyre, and Victor v. Alten's cavalry brigade. Our whole force amounted to 85,000 men.*

The French had thrown up formidable entrenchments on uneven rocks and hilly ground alongside of the River Nivelle, and we were to drive them from their position. These fieldworks, redoubts and bridgeheads began at St. Jean de Luz, which was fortified, and ran all the way to the heights of the village of Ainhoa, and thence to the lofty mountains where the Nivelle has its source. They had fortified the high range behind the village of Sare, as also the lofty hill known as La Rhune, particularly strongly. The plan of battle was as follows : General Hill was to attack and take the village of Ainhoa ; Beresford, covered by General Giron, the centre, and v. Alten and Longa the hill known as La Petite Rhune. General Freyre, with a corps of Spaniards, and Sir John Hope's corps, were to threaten the remaining portion of the enemy's position as far as the sea, and thus prevent him from detaching troops as reinforcements. General Cole's division opened the dance by a heavy bombardment of the principal redoubt in front of Sare, and after surrounding it, carried it with storming ladders. The French then sprang over the breastworks, and some of them were caught in the ditches, and when Le Cor's division, together with the horse artillery, attacked the neighbouring trenches in the rear, firing upon and threatening them, the enemy left them and bolted. General Cole then took Sare. General Carl v. Alten, who had led his division close up to the fieldworks of the Petite Rhune before daybreak, was equally lucky ; and as soon as it was light he stormed and took one line after the other. At last he reached the redoubt ; but the enemy, not waiting to be stormed, fled in confusion, and v. Alten took possession of the height.

* Napier (*op. cit.*, Book XXIII., Chap. I.) seems to reckon this host at over 90,000 men.—Tr.

Then the whole army advanced against the trenches occupied on the hills behind Sare. Colville's and Le Cor's divisions bravely stormed the heights. Once more, however, the French did not wait for the attack, and proceeded to evacuate not only these trenches, but also those lying on their left wing, which were not quite finished ; whereupon both divisions, having suffered only slightly from the artillery fire, established themselves on the ridge of hills. The French retired down the hills in great confusion, and made towards the bridge leading across the Nivelle. Only one French battalion remained standing behind a strong redoubt, but they, too, were dispersed by a Portuguese battalion and by General v. Alten's troops, who were advancing from La Petite Rhune. General v. Alten was at this moment about to attack all the remaining trenches which lay before him ; but it seemed probable that they were covered by impenetrable gorges, and the only access to them was by means of a small ridge of hills which was swept by the cross fire of two redoubts and other works. At last an eminence was found, which afforded cover to the troops attacking and wishing to enter the position, and the 52nd, under Colonel Colborne, quickly advanced in file under a very fierce fire. As soon as they had taken post behind the hill, the bugles gave the signal for a general advance ; whereupon our troops stormed up the hill, cheering as they went. The French did not wait to be stormed, and, except for one redoubt whose fire cost us 200 lives, they left their trenches. Contenting ourselves with blockading them, we left them alone until at last they surrendered with 560 men.

Meanwhile, Hill, having forded the Nivelle, the banks of which were steep and rocky, advanced without firing a shot against the heights of Ainhoa, and attacked the enemy who were posted in front of five redoubts. Appalled by the calm and energy with which this manœuvre was carried out, they preferred to retire rather than wait to be stormed. A few trenches lying on some heights to the rear, which nevertheless belonged to the same ridge as those of Ainhoa, were taken in the same way

by General Stuart. Two divisions then marched immediately towards Espelette, and this movement forced some
French troops, who were still holding their ground in
works around Ainhoa, to evacuate their trenches and to
retire by a circuitous route the moment Morillo attacked
their front. Repulsed at all points, the French concentrated upon the heights behind St. Pé ; but once again
they were beaten by Colville's and Le Cor's divisions,
which had crossed the river near St. Pé without meeting
with any resistance. The increasing darkness ended the
operations for that day, and we had lost only 500 men.
The French retired on Bayonne, and fifty pieces of
artillery, 1,500 prisoners, and quantities of ammunition
and provisions fell into our hands.*

The country between St. Jean de Luz and Ainhoa,
which is broken by innumerable hills, and, particularly
in the neighbourhood of the Nivelle, by rocky heights and
ravines, bore a strange and terrible aspect. At the cost
of considerable pains and much treasure the French had
fortified every height, and blocked every gorge with
felled timber. The number of redoubts, trenches and
earthworks was incalculable, not to mention the isolated
peasant farms that had been surrounded by moats and
supplied with drawbridges. For miles around every
copse and every tree had been cut down to form barricades.
Behind these chains of miniature fortresses, arranged in
two or three tiers, Soult had posted his army of 70,000
men, parcelled out in small detachments; and it was here
that his great error lay. For the moment our army,
divided into three strong and compact columns, opened
the attack at three specific points, we only had to take one
or two of his rocky redoubts in order to imperil the whole
of the troops occupying the same line ; and these forces,
fearing lest they might be caught in the rear or cut off,
lost courage and retired. By their retreat, however, they
spread panic among the rest, and increased the confusion.

* Napier (*op. cit.*, Book XXIII., Chap. I.) gives the losses of both sides as follows:
" The Allies had two generals, Kemp and Byng, wounded, and they lost 2,694 men and
officers. The French lost 4,265 men and officers, including 1,200 or 1,400 prisoners,
and one general was killed. His field magazines at St. Jean de Luz and Espelette fell
into the hands of the victors, and fifty-one pieces of artillery were taken."—Tr.

And what was the good of placing a handful of men consisting of about one battalion in front of a redoubt, to add
to the strength of the garrison occupying it ? Our columns
could hardly be held up by such a force ! This explains
how it was that we made such incredible progress with
such small losses in a single day. Certainly the French
no longer fought as bravely as they had done hitherto.
Their courage seemed to have been broken by the battles
of Vittoria and the Pyrenees. Even Soult himself seemed
to be muddled. That evening our regiment bivouacked
near Sare, three leguas from Etchalar, and we spent the
night in mud and rain and suffered pitiably from the cold.
Owing to the nature of the ground, we had not been able
to play much of a part in the events of the day ; but from
the top of La Petite Rhune I obtained a view of the battle
which I shall never forget.

[TRANSLATOR'S NOTE.—On the 11th November Schaumann again
marches forward through wooded country, and losing touch with his
regiment and his baggage, he spends the night with some Portuguese
officers in a goat-shed, where he and his horse suffer miserably from
hunger. In the morning he finds his servant Manoel installed with the
baggage in a house only 20 yards away from his resting-place, and hears
that the man had prepared his bed and cooked him a dinner on the previous
evening all in vain. After shaving and washing himself, and changing
his clothes, he mounts his horse and goes in search of his regiment.]

We had now entered France, and it amused me to hear
all the peasant children whom we met on our way
speaking French together. The. fact that we were on
French soil, however, was also made plain by other signs,
particularly by the national hatred that began to be felt
here. The Spanish and Portuguese troops seemed
verily to have pledged themselves to wreak vengeance
on France, and to repay her for all she had done to them.
Their eyes were aflame. Every Frenchman who fell
into their hands was ill-treated or secretly murdered.
Before leaving a village they always plundered it and set
it on fire. All the inhabitants were taking flight. Even
the men of our legion, remembering the ill-treatment
Hanover had been forced to suffer, fancied themselves
called upon to make reprisals on the French. But Lord

Wellington, who was clever enough to see whither such behaviour would lead, issued one or two furious general orders, and constituting his brother-in-law, General Pakenham, head of the military police, gave him the most stringent and solemn instructions to hang without trial or mercy any one who was caught red-handed in *actu flagrante*. Pakenham, supported by a powerful guard and the provost marshal, then began to ride up and down our columns like a raving lion seeking whom he might devour. His command, " Let that scoundrel be hanged instantly ! " was executed in a twinkling. Over 200 men, chiefly Spaniards and Portuguese, were put to death in this way, before the plundering and incendiarism were stopped. I saw the body of one Spanish muleteer, who had entered a house to steal apples, hanging from the window of that house as a warning to all marauders. In his mouth, which had fallen open in the process of strangulation, they had stuck an apple, to show what he had coveted ! On the other hand, Lord Wellington frequently showed himself merciful towards regiments of which he was fond. On one occasion, for instance, during this period he came upon the 1st German Hussars, who were just about to enter bivouac, and as he was standing talking to Lieut.-Colonel Arentschildt and the other officers, one of the men of the regiment came riding up with a bleating sheep which he had stolen. The moment Lord Wellington saw the man, however, he only smiled, and turning his back on him, pretended not to have noticed anything, although the officers at his side were shuddering with fear.

[TRANSLATOR'S NOTE.—On the 15th November Schaumann marched with his regiment in appalling weather to St. Pé. His stores depôts were situated at St. Jean de Luz and Passages. The roads thither from St. Pé consisted of seas of mud, and it was a common occurrence to find a mule suddenly disappearing in the mire, with nothing but a bubble to indicate its grave. Lord Wellington's headquarters were established in St. Jean de Luz, where the severest discipline was observed, and everything was done to ingratiate the inhabitants.]

On one of my excursions to Passages I rode, in the company of several officers, over to the fortress of St. Sebastian, which had capitulated, after a bloody defence,

on the 9th September, 1813.   The traces of General Sir
Thomas Graham's siege were visible everywhere.   All
the roofs were off the convents, summer-houses and other
buildings.   The doors, windows, staircases and floors of
the houses had been used as fuel, the walls were perforated
by the cannon-balls from the castle, the gardens were
devastated, and the whole place was deserted.   A stillness
as of death reigned everywhere.   From the distance the
fortifications did not seem to have suffered much.   But
when we reached the gate of the town things looked
different.   The drawbridge had fallen into the moat,
and it was not safe to cross it.   The massive gates of the
fortress had been torn from their supports, and one half
lay flat on the ground, while the other stood leaning
against the wall.   In the town itself, nothing but the
débris right and left showed where the high street had
been ; while of the fine houses, five stories high, both
stately and massive in style, only the walls and fronts
remained, and they were all blackened by dust and smoke.
The roads were blocked by *débris*, broken furniture, heaps
of rags, crushed shakos, bandoleers, cartridge boxes,
broken weapons, shells, fragments of bombs, and corpses
already in an advanced state of decomposition ; and a
pestilential stench hung about the ruins.   Apart from a
few survivors among the inhabitants who, with faces
grown wild and haggard from hunger, anxiety and
sorrow, were groping about among the ruins of their
former homes, there was nobody to be seen.   At the
breaches the sight was even worse, for they were literally
covered with decomposed carcasses, the smell of which
poisoned the air.   We stood on a breach where a French
mine which had been fired prematurely killed 300 of their
grenadiers of the Imperial Guard.   It was this explosion
that had given access to our storming column, which,
attacking in bright weather at midday on the 31st August,
1813, suffered heavy losses from the enemy's cross fire
as it attempted to ford the river.   When at last other
storming columns entered at other points, every street
of the town, stubbornly defended by the inhabitants as
well as the military, had to be taken by storm.   It was in

the street fighting that many houses were set on fire. The carnage is said to have been terrible. At last the French retired, and shut themselves up in the castle. As soon as our men had taken the town, they broke open the wine cellars, made themselves drunk, defied their officers, plundered and murdered all the inhabitants, and when night fell camped among the smoking ruins to sleep off their liquor. The following morning they got drunk again, started plundering afresh, and finally set fire to the whole town, and converted it into a heap of ruins. An enormous amount of spoil is said to have been taken, but as the men in quarrelling and fighting over it, threw money and valuables about, a good deal fell among the ruins and the *débris* and was lost. In any case, this much is certain, that the horrors perpetrated in Magdeburg by the egregious Tilly during the Thirty Years' War were mere child's play compared with what occurred after the fall of St. Sebastian.*

The Spanish army had been ordered to occupy the town and fortress of St. Sebastian after its fall, to bury the dead, and to clear away the *débris* ; but, in keeping with its excellent traditions, it had done nothing of the sort. There was not a Spanish soldier in the place. After we had satisfied our curiosity we rode out of the town, and halting upon a height from which we could have another good view of the picturesque country round St. Sebastian, we had lunch and rode back to Passages.

On these excursions I used to pass through the various infantry cantonments, where it was most interesting to see the way in which our officers installed themselves and made themselves comfortable. They were quartered chiefly in deserted villages and buildings. They spent their day either hunting or fishing, and as there were heaps of trout in the rivers, the latter sport was most productive. In the evening, after changing their clothes, they would feast in the mess, and then drink grog and smoke cigars by the side of a comfortable fire. Even Lord Wellington amused himself by hunting, and I often used to meet him with his entourage and a magnificent pack of English

* See p. 389, *ante.*—TR.

hounds, riding out to a fox hunt.   On these occasions he is said to have been in the best of spirits, genial, and *sans cérémonie ;* in fact, just like a genuine country squire and fox-hunter.   No one would have suspected at such moments that he was the Field-Marshal of three nations. How different was his demeanour on a day of battle! Then he seemed like an angry god under whose threatening glance every one trembled.   This life lasted for a period of twenty days, unbroken by any other duty than an occasional early parade, the relief of outposts, the changing of quarters, a slight alarm, the digging of trenches, and the building of other works to safeguard the position.   The weather was bright and frosty.

The town of Irun, where I often had to transact business, is an exceedingly gloomy, dirty and melancholy-looking place.   Verily, he who first enters Spain through Irun must have a fright !   It was full of Spanish troops. Once, in order to get under cover during a sudden downpour of rain, I tried to get my horse and myself under the sheltered entrance to a large house in which a Spanish general was quartered.   The sentry, however, drove me away at the point of his bayonet, and the general himself, who was standing at his window, seemed to be looking on with approval at the behaviour of his guard.   I shook my fist at him threateningly, and pointing to my pistols, implied that, had he not been a general, I would have responded very differently to the insult I had received ; whereupon I rode proudly away.   The reason why this general treated us English so shabbily was because he wished to have his miserable revenge.   He was writhing with hopeless and impotent rage, because having with his division acted in a cowardly and careless manner during the advance on St. Jean de Luz, and having preferred to fight, ill-treat, plunder and murder the defenceless inhabitants and set fire to villages rather than to press forward, Lord Wellington had severely reprimanded him, and had banished him and his division from the English fighting line, and ordered him to remain in Irun, in Spanish territory, until he was summoned !   *Hinc illæ lacrimæ !*

ON the 12th November we suddenly received
marching orders, and marched *viâ* Espelette
and Cambo, where a bridge leads across the
River Nive. In front of Cambo the French had cut
down a beautiful wood of oak trees to build a barricade. There were earthworks, trenches, and barricades in all directions, which did not help the enemy
in the least. The weather and the roads were equally
appalling ; one downpour followed another. After
several days of marching, the regiment camped out,
partly on the main road, which was knee-deep in mud,
and partly in hill clefts, valleys, rocks and deep ravines.
If one of us happened to be invited to a dinner or
grog-party of an evening, it was a work of art of
extreme peril to find one's way back in the dark. The
weather continued to be very dreary. Rain, sleet or hail
was the order of the day. Our boots, even if we had
several pairs in use, were never dry. We always had
cold and wet feet. The very sight of the stone floors in
the house here made one shiver ; while the smoking
chimneys drove one to desperation. In the evening
we used to console ourselves with grog and cigars
by the kitchen fire ; but alas, cigars began to run
short—none were to be had for miles ! Then we
began to feel really miserable. At last we were rescued
from our wretched plight. On the 22nd December,
accompanied by sleet and hail, we marched to
Urcuray, a pretty little town. I celebrated Christmas
here, and invited many of the officers of the 1st
German Hussars to dinner. The Spanish guerilla here
was very strong and well organised, well armed and
equipped. It had grenadiers on its strength. The
French were quite close to us, and often reconnoitred
with strong detachments. On one occasion this led to

a serious fight, in which Captain Balton* of the 18th Hussars was killed.

On the 30th December we marched to Hasparen, a pretty little French town. The country around was delightful, and my quarters not bad. Major Aly of the 1st German Hussars had the honour of being specially selected by Lord Wellington for the duty of organising the whole chain of mounted guards, and of posting pickets. This meant that among the whole of the four English Hussar regiments which, with ourselves, discharged these duties, there was no officer that Lord Wellington could have used in this capacity. As for myself, my duties were, as usual, very onerous. A rustic of the district pointed out to me that if I chopped up the prickly thistles that flourished on the heaths about here into chaff, and mixed them with corn and hay, they made very good fodder for the horses, and that the horses would like them. The matter was immediately reported to the general, and having tried it, it was approved ; but owing to the prickles the thistles had first of all to be crushed, otherwise the horses would not touch them. The crushing process was performed as follows : our men would lift a barn door off its hinges, lay it on the ground, and then beat the thistles upon it with clubs until they were flattened out. And the sound of this curious threshing operation could soon be heard in all directions. But it was a laborious job ! It was only long afterwards that I heard that this method was known to the old Romans ; for Fabricius and Quintilius Varus, cavalry generals, received the thanks of the Roman Senate for having, at a time when forage was scarce, discovered this means of overcoming the difficulty, whereby discipline was maintained.

We conducted foraging parties almost daily in front of our line. My road led through Hasparen, past our remotest hussar picket, and then along sunken roads to various farms scattered about in the small villages below. We went in search of maize. As, however, the French, who were opposite us, did the same, these expeditions

* This should be Captain Bolton.—Tr.

were very dangerous, for in the thousand and one ramifications of these hill-clefts it was an easy matter to be cut off, attacked, or surprised. Very often I would find on reaching a certain farm that a French commissary and his escort had only just left it. The town of Hasparen is tastefully built, clean, and breezy. Monsieur le Maire was a friendly, obliging man, an anti-Bonapartist who had fled and had now returned, and did everything to further our interests. The girls, of Basque blood, were fresh, pretty, and strongly built.

On the 15th [January ?] we again received marching orders, and continued our advance. But I ought to mention that before we left Hasparen I was not at all well. I was suffering so acutely from costiveness, inflammation of the eyes, hæmorrhoids, and slow fever, that every day my condition grew more and more serious. Dr. Fiorillo, of the 1st German Hussars, in whom I felt more confidence than in the doctor of the 18th Hussars, advised me to report myself sick and to stay behind in order to consult the French doctors. And this I did the moment we reached Bardos. Fortunately, in the local doctor, M. Harristay, who lived in a country house not far from my quarters, I happened to light upon a very clever man. He complained only of one thing, and that was the scarcity of drugs ; for Bayonne was besieged and his apothecary had been plundered by the doctors of the retreating French Army. I was suffering from four or five different ailments. Leeches were recommended, but they were difficult to find at this season of the year. Nevertheless, my landlord had the kindness to paddle about for me in an icy-cold swamp, and succeeded in getting a few. Another part of my cure consisted in drinking a preparation of warm whey every morning in bed. But it was only after I was cured that I understood why my cook Manoel always made such a wry face when he brought me this concoction every day. The doctor had discovered that the usual separation of the curds from the whey, which, I believe, is brought about by means of some acid, was pernicious, because the whey thus produced was deleterious to the human system. He therefore, separated the milk by means of snails, and thus produced whey which was much more wholesome. The snails were torn from their shells and first thrown into cold water, so that all their slime came from them. One snail thrown into a saucepan of boiling milk was enough to turn the whole instantly into the most beautiful curds and whey. And this is why Manoel was so very much disgusted ; but he had been told to keep the secret of the process from me. My cure was a slow business, and the month of March was almost over before my fever and the inflammation of my eyes abated. The weather was raw and stormy. I used to sit all alone in my secluded dwelling, by the side of my only window, which afforded me a magnificent view of the Pyrenees, just in front of my house. Romantic, peaceful, and sublime as my view was from one side of the house, however, it was sufficiently warlike on the other ; for the siege of the fortress of Bayonne, which lay close by, had begun on the 27th February, and we could hear the roar of the guns quite plainly. Owing to the intervening heights, we could not actually see the town and fortress, but one evening, from the ground floor of the house, we were able to observe very distinctly beyond the horizon the fiery flight of the Congreve rockets that set alight a French frigate lying on the far side of the Adour.

The fortifications round Bayonne are about four and a half miles in circumference, and Sir John Hope had only 15,000 reliable troops with which to surround it, for the 34,000 Spaniards with him were not much good. The fortress capitulated on the 7th April.

My hosts and the whole neighbourhood could not cease from singing the praises of our army, and of its good behaviour and discipline ; for the French, with the object of getting the people to rise against us, had spread the report that we were murderers, robbers, and incendiaries, that we were particularly fond of the flesh of children, and that in order to procure it we seized all the children we could lay hands upon, killed them, and then roasted them over the fire with our ramrods.

Romantically beautiful as was the country round

Bardos, it was rendered very dangerous from time to time by the wolves which came down from the Pyrenees to visit the battlefields and also to devour the bullocks that had travelled right across Spain from Portugal, and had collapsed and perished of hunger and fatigue both on this and on the Spanish side of the Pyrenees. Many thousands of bullocks perished in this way, and one was to be seen almost every four or five yards. The wolves had grown so daring that, when my doctor left me one morning and took a short cut home through the garden and out at the back door, he was just issuing from the latter and entering a gorge which formed a portion of his road when an enormous wolf advanced towards him. He retired at once, slammed the door quickly behind him, and burst into my room looking deathly pale. It was only when I had given him some arms and an escort of my servants that he dared to return to his house.

Although large armies were in the district, there was no lack of the kind of provisions I most required. Chickens, capons, pigeons, fresh eggs, good milk, rice, butter, and particularly good dried plums were to be had in abundance. To crown all, however, the district rejoiced in a special kind of water-cress which, for its aromatic flavour and delicious taste, beat any water-cress —or, for that matter, any fresh salad—that I had ever eaten in my life. I could actually feel it refreshing my blood and promoting my cure.

Nor did I lack entertainment. The notabilities of the town of Bardos, the priest, and my doctor paid me constant visits, and used to gape with astonishment at my worldly wisdom. For, owing to deficiencies in their education, and other well-known causes, provincial French people, even of the cultured classes, are incredibly backward. For instance, it is tremendously amusing to examine a Frenchman in geography. With the priest I used to discuss religion, and he used to get so angry over my heresies that he always ran away ; but my coffee, my snuff, and my Château Margot drew him back to me again. Sometimes pretty girls from the neighbourhood would come in and sing their Basque songs to me. When

the spring began to advance, and the weather grew warm
and mild, I was well enough to go out into the open.
Then the young men and the girls would gather upon a
grass plot in front of my house and dance their national
dances, to the accompaniment of a shawm and the Basque
tambourine. Wrapped in my cloak, with a cigar in my
mouth, and a table with glasses and bottles set beside me,
so that I might from time to time give refreshment to the
dancers, I would sit, surrounded by the old as well as the
young people of the village, under the burgeoning green
of an old elm, in front of the door of my quarters, stared
at, admired, extolled, and belauded by everybody. They
frequently called me " *un homme estimable, homme rare,
homme de bon cœur,*" or " *ange,*" and wished that I might
always live among them. But this was not all ; for their
veneration and confidence was such that one morning
they surprised me—aye, even frightened me (for the party
consisted chiefly of men armed with pitch-forks)—by
sending me a deputation, which was led by a white-haired
old patriarch, urgently imploring me to assume the post
of the local justice of the peace. The prefect and the
mayor—both Bonapartists—had fled ; the tribunal in
Bayonne was closed owing to the siege, and the whole of
the legal business of the commune had got into such a
state of stagnation and confusion that it had become intolerable. I was to judge them according to English law,
and they would see that my judgments were fulfilled. At
these words a dozen of the party dropped their pitch-
forks and flails with such violence upon the ground that
I was easily convinced that they would see my judgments
fulfilled with emphasis. Utterly confounded and surprised by this request, I tried to explain to the dear
people that it would ill become me to assume such a *rôle*,
and that I would incur Lord·Wellington's very righteous
anger if ever he discovered that I had ventured to settle
legal questions or to usurp the functions of a mayor or
a prefect ; and I concluded by begging them to spare me
the ordeal, well meant as I knew their request to be. As,
however, their pleadings, prayers, and protestations did
not cease, and they swore that they would shoulder all the

responsibility for the step, I told them at last that I acquiesced, but on one condition, which was that I might be allowed solemnly to protest there and then against the fulfilment of my judgments. " Aye ! Aye ! " cried the party, " we take the whole responsibility." After I had settled myself in my arm-chair, therefore, and assumed what I imagined to be the demeanour becoming to a judge, the court opened.

While I had been indisposed, my cook Manoel had also been ill, and my muleteer, who at the blacksmith's one day had wished to give the French a display of Spanish agility by trying to vault on to my mule from behind, had had his skull fractured by the animal. Four men carried him, seemingly lifeless, on a door into my quarters. Fortunately, the doctor happened to be with me at the time, and although he had not got his instruments with him, he gave us a demonstration of how skilful French surgeons are ; for, without deliberating an instant, he took my landlord's finest chisel and, prising up the depressed bone in a way that made it actually creak, he proceeded to bleed the man, and treated him so cleverly that by the time I left the place he had completely recovered. All that remained of the accident was a bright red scar on his forehead in the form of a hoof.

At night, when everybody was in bed and I was unable to sleep, I used to sit by my fire and allow my thoughts to run riot, and on these occasions I formulated various plans which, if only I had abided by them, would have saved me from many a sorrow, many a burden, and many a cloud in the future. Among other things, I thought of marriage, but as often as I compared the pleasant with the unpleasant side of this estate, and weighed the troubles, the anxiety, and the heavy responsibilities which it involves, and all the suspense and risk that are inseparable from it, I always arrived at a result from which I could not help shrinking. The plans I made for my future establishment and career were brighter and more attractive. I was sick of war ; I longed to lead a peaceful life. Possessed of a decent income, and certain of my half-pay on retirement, I thought of buying a small property and of living in rural retirement, among my books, my pictures, and my flowers, and ending my days in simple comfort and homeliness, indulging in hunting, fishing, and other country pastimes, and doing just as I pleased. The only companions I wanted were a devoted servant, who would also act as a gardener, a good horse, and a faithful dog. But man proposes and God disposes. Meanwhile I longed for the day when the doctor would tell me, " *Vous êtes guéri !* " During my illness I had kept a sort of journal on the margin of a large wood-cut repre-senting Our Lord on the Cross, which hung from a nail over my mantelpiece. This journal, written in German, which I kept from the 23rd February to the 2nd May, 1814, and which was full of remarks about my condition, the weather, and complaints about the tediousness of my days, may still be hanging in its place, and Monsieur le Curé will have tried in vain to decipher its meaning. At last the doctor declared that I could move ; and as my friend and colleague Mr. Major had already been with me several days, I packed. The whole commune was gathered together to wish me good-bye. The tumult and distress were terrible. All the girls were in tears ; my hosts also wept, and M. Harristay, who could not recover from his astonishment at my generosity—I had given him ten napoleons in gold—proclaimed me aloud as the best of men, the like of whom he had never seen before and never expected to see again. I, too, was moved. Reluc-tantly I bade farewell to my little room, the garden, and the Pyrenees ; for although I had endured a good deal of physical anguish at this place, there was much that bound me to it, and I shall always remember the time I spent there as among the brightest and most peaceful moments of my life.

How Mr. Augustus travels through a Portion of the South of France, finds the 18th Hussars at Mezin, continues his Journey and is stationed at Mont de Marsan—Peace is Declared—The Army embarks—Departure from Bordeaux.

ALL along the road which I had followed from Hasparen I was much interested in the number of ruined châteaux which I passed. They were not, however, the ruins of bygone centuries, but the ancestral estates of the oldest and noblest families of France, who up to the time of the Revolution had lived here in happiness and peace. The scions of these families had seen them set on fire and left to the mercy of the popular fury, while they themselves had had to take refuge abroad, where, suffering from the most terrible privations, many had died of hunger. Regarding the fate of the unhappy owners of these châteaux, all I could hear was that Monsieur le Marquis had gone abroad, or that he had been murdered ; while the estate itself, which was probably parcelled out, was being sold in part for the tenth time.

A touching incident occurred when our cavalry passed by Gramont and the château of that name, which, although in ruins, still looked wonderfully attractive, with all its ancient glory. During the Revolution soldiers had been quartered in it, and through some piece of carelessness they had set fire to the place. Now in the 10th Hussars there was a Captain Gramont, son of the Duc de Guiche, who was the present lawful heir to the property as well as to the marquisate, and fate decreed that he should be quartered in Gramont itself. As a child he had left France with his father, and the latter had died in England. When, therefore, Captain Gramont made himself known, and discovered a few old people who remembered having seen him as a child, there were great rejoicings in the neighbourhood. Everybody tried to get at him, and while some clasped his knees and others implored him to take possession of his heritage, others stood around weeping with joy. At last a former servant of the family turned up who had carried Captain Gramont in his arms as a child. Shortly after this Captain Gramont was reinstated in his title as Duc de Guiche by Louis XVIII.; but whether he ever recovered his ancestral estates I do not know.

[TRANSLATOR'S NOTE.—Schaumann continued his journey *via* Orthes, Pau, Tarbes and Agen, and reached Mezin on the 10th May, where he found the 18th Hussars quartered. He was given a good billet with Mr. Buckham, the commissary of the regiment, and, as all his attempts to resume the commissaryship of the regiment ultimately failed, he proceeded to get his papers in order, and to settle his accounts with the regiment.]

On the 7th June, 1813, I received orders from the Commissary-General to proceed to Vic, and thence to Condom. A convoy of money which was expected to arrive in Vic I was to direct to Bordeaux ; in Condom I was to receive 9,000 francs and take them to Auch ; there I was to assist the local commissary in his work, if required, and then proceed to Bordeaux *via* Mont de Marsan. As the Mayor was away and the convoy had not yet arrived, I spent a few days there in a pleasant inn, *cum otio et dignitate*; then went to Condom, and on to Auch. In Auch there was an English stores depôt, under the direction of Mr. Commissary Hodson, to whom I handed the 9,000 francs and offered my services.

Meanwhile my friend Brigadier Baertling had arrived with his little Donna Maria, and as Mr. Hodson explained to me that the procession of troops through Auch had almost ceased, and that he would soon break up the depôt and no longer require my services, Baertling and I decided to travel to Mont de Marsan together. On the 18th June, therefore, we started off. Donna Maria behaved in the most charming way between us two rivals ; all jealousy was at an end. On our way we passed several Spanish regiments which were being sent back home. They made a dreadful tumult as they marched along. Their hatred of the English, and particularly of Lord Wellington, who had them hanged whenever they robbed or were guilty of disobedience, manifested itself even towards me as I turned aside and halted to let them march by. They used insolent language, made threatening gestures with their bayonets, insulting my men, and seemed quite disposed to plunder my baggage. This behaviour, which, with my pistols clasped in my hands, I could only encounter with the most contemptuous of looks, was allowed to continue without the smallest reproof from the Spanish officers, who did not dare to open their mouths, but, looking a little shamefast, slunk by in a state of complete apathy. One of these regiments had a drum-major who was wearing the complete ceremonial uniform of Marshal Soult, which had been taken at Vittoria.

On reaching Mont de Marsan, I was given good quarters. My work was not heavy. Among the people who supplied me with provisions, my neighbour, the baker woman, was the most interesting. She was a widow and really so beautiful that the whole of Mont de Marsan looked upon her as something wonderful. I did not, therefore, trouble to write her name on my requisition slips, but simply wrote à la belle boulangère. Thanks to this trifling compliment, she regarded me with special favour, and we spent many a happy hour together. Like all Frenchwomen, she was wonderfully refined and cultured. She received many offers of marriage from officers passing through, but refused them all for the sake, apparently, of her little boy, who was six years old.

The general feeling of the inhabitants was altogether against the Bourbons, who were openly cursed in the streets, while Bonaparte was extolled. The girls were eager to marry. Many of them eloped with our officers, while others married in continenti. Among others, there were two of our officers in the place, Irishmen by birth, who, having been wounded, were passing through as convalescents. They courted two sisters, belonging to a respectable family, for no longer than twenty-four hours, and then married them and took them away.

I had spent about four very pleasant weeks in Mont de Marsan when all Portuguese troops, together with innumerable brigades of mules that had been released, and a vast gang of contractors, servants, head drivers, sporting dogs, mistresses, canteen men and women—in fact, the whole body composing the camp followers whom Lord Wellington,* in his own sketch of the plan of the Battle of Lützen, so aptly described as " *la canaille*," and placed in the rear of the army—passed through this place from Bordeaux on their way home.   I also heard that the English Army was beginning to embark ; and on the 13th April a messenger arrived in Toulouse with the news that the Allies had entered Paris on the 13th March, 1814, that Bonaparte had abdicated, and that according to a proclamation of Louis XVIII. of May 2nd, 1814, the Bourbons had resumed the reins of government.

I too, therefore, longed to leave Mont de Marsan, and as my duties were no longer very heavy, Mr. Wright, the old Commissary-General whom I assisted, agreed to let me go.   Before leaving I sold all my silver plate to a gold-smith, although I might have obtained a good price for it in England, and I also disposed of my famous old grey horse for fifty pounds sterling to Commissary-General Aylmer.   The latter, being entrusted with the liquidation of all English stores, expected to remain in Passages for some time.   It was not without regret that I parted from the beast that had borne me so safely and comfortably all the way from Lisbon and across the Pyrenees, and had shared all my exertions, hunger and thirst, and all my nights in bivouac.   Then I heard from my brother Edward, who was on his way to Bordeaux, that he would pass through here and pick me up.

As soon as he arrived our baggage was sent ahead, a vehicle was hired, and I and three others—that is to say, Edward, young Lahmeyer, and an English officer—left Mont de Marsan on the 3rd July, and reached Bordeaux three days later.   Our coachman drove us to the Hotel au Lion d'Or on the Boulevard du Théâtre.

Suddenly orders came along commanding all officers and men of the English Army quartered in Bordeaux to leave the place immediately, and I was obliged to go.   It was exceedingly difficult to sell either horses or mules in the town, for the whole of the army passing through for

* Schaumann must mean Napoleon.—Tr.

embarkation, especially the infantry, had got rid of all
their riding horses, mules and donkeys at any price they
could get for them. Thus every stable in Bordeaux was
packed full, and nobody wanted to buy. In vain did I
offer my steed for a mere song ; I found no one who
would bid. I was at last able to dispose of a horse and
a couple of mules, but the rest I gave to my servants for
their journey home. Many officers are said to have been
forced to abandon their horses at the harbour. I be-
queathed my camp bed, my cooking utensils, and a
portion of my wardrobe to my faithful valet and cook,
the good Manoel. Fritz Lahmeyer boarded a cargo
vessel that was sailing to Lisbon. It pained me to part
from all these dear people; and Manoel shrieked and wept
like a child.

At last, having got rid of all my impedimenta, I boarded
a boat with my brother Edward and Lieutenant Wallis, of
the 18th Hussars, and sailed down the Garonne to
Pouillac.* I had spent a week in Pouillac, which was full
of tiresome military people of all kinds, when I made the
acquaintance of the agents of a cargo ship, the *Elizabeth*
(Captain Petersen), flying the Swedish flag, which was
bound for London. As my stay in Pouillac became more
and more distasteful to me every day, I got permission
from Mr. Wright to avail myself of this opportunity, and
on the afternoon of the 4th July, 1814, my brother
Edward and I got into a boat with our luggage in order
to find our ship, which was lying in the roads.

When we were taken on board, we were surprised to
find the deck was so completely occupied by passengers,
wrapped in blankets, who had already retired for the
night, and the cabin, the berths, and the whole ship so
hopelessly crowded with officers, servants, invalids,
women, children and luggage (even Lord Wellington's
pack of hounds and a number of horses were on board),
that for a while we could find no room whatever. As the
agents in Pouillac had not mentioned that the ship was
overcrowded when we had paid them our passage, but,
on the contrary, had assured us that we would be able to

* This appears to be meant for Pauillac.—Tr.

make ourselves comfortable in the cabin, we lodged a complaint with the captain. But he denied all responsibility, laid the whole of the blame on the agents, and cursed and swore about them so bitterly that we soon understood that he had had no share in the swindle. What was to be done? Our boat had gone, and the night was stormy. We had to remain on board and manage as best we could.

On the 25th July, owing to unfavourable winds, we remained at anchor. On the 26th, however, the wind, though blustery, was at least favourable, and in the early morning we weighed anchor and sailed out of the Gironde. The wind was strong, the sky was overcast, and the sea was rough. Very soon we found ourselves in the terrible Bay of Biscay. The waves rose high, and the ship tossed dreadfully. Food and drink on board were detestable ; disorder and confusion reigned everywhere. My bed was installed in a narrow groove, among a heap of trunks and baggage of all kinds. Many of the passengers were sick ; women and children wailed, the hounds set up a howl, and the horses stamped and tore themselves free. Among the passengers there were brawls, quarrels and feuds of all kinds, and much cursing and lamentation. On the 28th July the weather improved a little, and as the sun began to shine in the afternoon, the captain hastened to take his bearings. But he did not seem to understand much about it. Fortunately, among the passengers there was a ship's captain, who had lost his ship on the French coast. He helped with the business. There was also an English midshipman—probably a fellow who had been dismissed from a man-o'-war owing to incompetence—a powerful, coarse and useless-looking lout, who assisted the captain. Very soon, however, he began an argument with the captain who had volunteered his services, and challenged him to a fight. The deck was cleared, both men removed their coats, and a terrible boxing match began. At first the old captain had the advantage, but soon his strength gave out, and he fell ; whereupon, contrary to all rules, the midshipman caught him by the hair and with his fist almost hammered one of his eyes out.

At this the whole boatload of passengers and crew were roused and, falling in a body upon the midshipman, called him a dastardly coward and a blackguard ; and had he not prayed for mercy, would have flung him overboard.

After this interlude we adjourned to our meal, which was served on deck ; but the food was so bad and the portions so exiguous, that we complained to the captain about it.   He again laid all the blame on the agents in Bordeaux, who had given him insufficient supplies and too many passengers.   After making a rough estimate, we arrived at the pleasant conclusion that, in view of all the passengers, horses, and dogs on board, our supplies could last only two days longer, and that if we suddenly encountered bad weather and were driven out to sea— that is to say, if we were unable to reach the English coast in two or, at the most, three days—we should all die of hunger !   We therefore compiled a memorandum, signed by all the passengers on board, and addressed to the Swedish Consul in Portsmouth, in which we exposed the reprehensible conduct of the ship-owners and the captain.

On the 31st July we passed the Isle of Wight, and at last cast anchor in the harbour of Portsmouth at midday. The harbour was so full of men-o'-war and transport ships and merchantmen, that our vessel had literally to press its way in, and could hardly find room.   The confusion, too, was so great that, although the captain had announced our arrival, and we had waited for several hours for the Customs officials, who were to inspect our luggage, no-body arrived ; and, losing patience at last, we hired a boat, threw our luggage into it, and were rowed ashore. Nobody paid us the slightest heed.   If only we could have foreseen this, what a splendid supply of Bordeaux wines and lace we might have smuggled in !

We rested on the 1st August, but as on the 2nd I happened to hear that a great victory festival was to be held in London on the 3rd, and I was anxious to witness it, I booked a seat in a mail coach which was starting in the evening.   My brother Edward, who did not wish to travel by night, remained behind.

On reaching London in the early morning, I hired a

hackney coach with the object of finding a lodging ; but the festival had attracted such enormous crowds from the provinces that I tried at a dozen hotels in vain. Everywhere they were full up ! At last I found a room in a small coffee house on the Strand, and was given a clean bedroom and a very good luncheon. At about three o'clock I went to St. James's Park and Kensington Gardens to look at all the splendid things with which, by the King's command, the Peace Festival was to be celebrated. The preparations were on a grand scale. Everywhere I saw artillery detachments standing ready with large supplies of rockets and other fireworks. There were pagodas, Chinese towers (one of which, on the canal bridge in St. James's Park, was exceedingly high), triumphal arches, stars, rosettes, globes, illuminated names, and suitable devices formed with coloured Chinese lanterns, such as " Peace and Plenty," " Rule Britannia," etc. All trees and avenues were hung with coloured-paper Chinese lanterns. On a small lake, either in Kensington Gardens or the Green Park, there were two fleets of miniature men-o'-war, one English and the other French, properly manned and mounted with guns, which were to fight a naval battle ; and on the water in St. James's Park there was a regatta of beautiful boats, rowed by sailors in bright-coloured silk jerseys and caps, who were going to have a boat race. To the north of St. James's Park there stood a huge Temple of Peace, which was still concealed from view by a large screen of grey canvas ; in front of it there was a battery of fifty guns, and close by an enormous pavilion with boxes and benches, all covered with red cloth, for the King and the nobility, the ambassadors and foreign princes. Row upon row of huts and booths— some offering refreshments, others sheltering brass bands —covered the ground. It was interesting to see the people of London streaming in at all the park gates ; 500,000 people are said to have been present. And in all this crowd I felt that I stood alone, known to nobody, heeded by nobody—a feeling the pathos of which defies description !

The moment the naval battle began in the Green Park

and the roar of the guns was heard, everybody rushed to the spot ; then the regatta started, followed by the fireworks, which lasted a long time. The finest sight of all was to see the so-called Congreve rockets ; they were immediately followed by the fifty guns, which fired as rapidly as possible. They fired 500 rounds, making an uproar that almost deafened me, and while they were thus engaged the screen of grey canvas was suddenly lifted and the Temple of Peace was revealed, all glittering with its beautiful illumination of lamps. Water flowed from the jaws of lions into golden basins, and on the roof of the temple there stood a detachment of the Foot Guards with the Royal Standard, who gave three loud hurrahs. Then the people began to wander among the tents and booths, and the eating and drinking began. A noteworthy feature of the celebrations was the fact that there was no disorder, no fighting, no pickpockets, and no importunate fast women. The news that Bonaparte had been banished to Elba, the prospect of peace and of happy relations with France, and the hopes expressed by the Prince Regent (subsequently King George IV.), in his speech from the throne at the opening of Parliament, that, after all the nation's afflictions, they were now to experience a period of plenty, of reduced expenditure, of cheaper commodities, and of a revival of trade, had evidently made a good impression upon the people. Meanwhile, John Bull, who had never yet witnessed such a national festival, did not seem to know very well how he ought to behave. Looking somewhat abashed, he contemplated the splendid display open-mouthed until, having been sufficiently stimulated by grog, he began to express his delight by shouting and openly capering about.

At two o'clock in the morning I went home, and the stream of people that poured down the Strand with me was so great that every time I stopped to try to find the number of the house where I had put up it dragged me along with it.

As soon as Edward arrived, we settled our accounts and handed them to the chief commissary at the Treasury. We had spent a fortnight settling our business and seeing the sights of London, when I received a letter from my brother William in Hanover, in which he said that, if I wished to see him and his wife before he left for Brabant to join the army of observation there, I ought to come to Germany pretty soon. Being, moreover, anxious to see my parents, my relations, and the place of my birth after having been absent such a long time, the moment the Treasury had accepted my application to retire on half-pay I quickly packed my things and, climbing on to a dazzling mail coach, travelled to Harwich. When we had spent two days in this place, we went on board a packet-boat called the *Nelson* (Captain May), which was bound for Cuxhaven, and sailed from Harwich in high spirits in the afternoon.

On arriving in Cuxhaven we were taken in a barge to Hamburg, where we put up at the Römischen Kaiser, in the finest and busiest part of the town, and spent a very happy time there. At last the hour of departure arrived and, continuing our journey through Hamburg, we ultimately came in sight of the market tower of Hanover, which we greeted with joy.

THE END

THE NAPOLEONIC LIBRARY
New editions of classic works
on the Napoleonic Wars
Published by Greenhill Books

JOURNAL OF THE WATERLOO CAMPAIGN
by General Cavalié Mercer
ISBN 0-947898-04-2.
Napoleonic Library 1

THE NOTE-BOOKS OF CAPTAIN COIGNET
Soldier of the Empire, 1799–1816
by Captain Jean-Roch Coignet
ISBN 0-947898-13-1.
Napoleonic Library 2

A BRITISH RIFLEMAN
Journals and Correspondence during the Peninsular W
and the Campaign of Wellington
by Major George Simmons
ISBN 0-947898-33-6.
Napoleonic Library 3

WELLINGTON'S ARMY, 1808–1814
by Sir Charles Oman
ISBN 0-947898-41-7.
Napoleonic Library 4

THE CAMPAIGN OF WATERLOO
by the Hon. Sir John Fortescue
ISBN 0-947898-49-2.
Napoleonic Library 5

STUDIES IN THE NAPOLEONIC WARS
by Sir Charles Oman
ISBN 0-947898-63-8.
Napoleonic Library 6

WATERLOO LETTERS
by Major-General H. T. Siborne
ISBN 1-85367-156-8.
Napoleonic Library 25

NAPOLEON AT BAY, 1814
by F. Loraine Petre
ISBN 1-85367-163-0.
Napoleonic Library 26

NAPOLEON AND IBERIA
The Twin Sieges of Ciudad Rodrigo and Almeida, 1810
by Donald D. Horward
ISBN 1-85367-183-5.
Napoleonic Library 27

LIFE IN NAPOLEON'S ARMY
by Captain Elzéar Blaze
ISBN 1-85367-196-7.
Napoleonic Library 28

NAPOLEON AND WATERLOO
The Emperor's Campaign with the
Armée du Nord, 1815
by A. F. Becke
ISBN 1-85367-206-8.
Napoleonic Library 29

TWENTY-FIVE YEARS IN THE RIFLE BRIGADE
by William Surtees
ISBN 1-85367-230-0.
Napoleonic Library 30

MEMOIRS OF BARON VON MÜFFLING
A Prussian Officer in the Napoleonic Wars
by Baron von Müffling
ISBN 1-85367-273-4.
Napoleonic Library 31

WATERLOO LECTURES
by Colonel C. Chesney
ISBN 1-85367-288-2.
Napoleonic Library 32

THE JENA CAMPAIGN, 1806
by Colonel F. N. Maude
ISBN 1-85367-310-2.
Napoleonic Library 33